Contents

PREFACE
PAGE 8

INTRODUCTION
PAGE 10

2 The star, the emblem of the Sun King, shows Apollo, the god of peace, the arts, medicine and light. All the decorations that Louis XIV wanted in Versailles palace mixed images of the god and the king in a form of identification that came to symbolise the French monarchy.

7 Registan square in Samarkand is the site of three Koranic schools. The photograph shows a detail of one of the three, the Shirdor, that means 'the building with lions'. It was built in the seventeenth century.

One-hundred art treasures

The Americas

1 UNITED STATES - NEW YORK
2 UNITED STATES - TAOS
3 MEXICO - GUANAJUATO
4 MEXICO - OAXACA
5 CUBA - HAVANA
6 CUBA - TRINIDAD
7 GUATEMALA - ANTIGUA
8 COLOMBIA - CARTAGENA
9 PERU - AREQUIPA
10 BRAZIL - SALVADOR DE BAHIA
11 BRAZIL - BRASILIA
12 BOLIVIA - SUCRE
13 ARGENTINA - CÓRDOBA

Europe

14 PORTUGAL - TOMAR
15 PORTUGAL - SINTRA
16 SPAIN - BARCELONA
17 SPAIN - ALCALÁ
18 SPAIN - GRANADA
19 SPAIN - CÓRDOBA
20 SPAIN - SIVIGLIA
21 FRANCE - REIMS
22 FRANCE - PARIS
23 FRANCE - VERSAILLES
24 FRANCE - MONT-SAINT-MICHEL
25 FRANCE - CHARTRES
26 FRANCE - LOIRE VALLEY
27 FRANCE - ARC-ET-SENANS
28 FRANCE - AVIGNON
29 GREAT BRITAIN - IRONBRIDGE GORGE
30 GREAT BRITAIN - WESTMINSTER
31 GREAT BRITAIN - CANTERBURY

32 BELGIUM - BRUGGE
33 BELGIUM - BRUSSELS
34 NETHERLANDS - KINDERDIJK-ELLSHOUT
35 GERMANY - POTSDAM
36 GERMANY - AACHEN
37 GERMANY - WÜRZBURG
38 GERMANY - VÖLKLINGEN
39 GERMANY - MAULBRONN
40 DENMARK - KRONBORG
41 SWEDEN - DROTTNINGHOLM
42 NORWAY - URNES
43 NORWAY - BERGEN
44 FINLAND - VERLA
45 ESTONIA - TALLINN
46 LATVIA - RIGA
47 RUSSIAN FEDERATION - KIZHI POGOST
48 RUSSIAN FEDERATION - SAINT PETERSBURG
49 RUSSIAN FEDERATION - MOSCOW
50 POLAND - KRAKOW
51 CZECK REPUBLIC - PRAGUE
52 CZECK REPUBLIC - LEDNICE-VALTICE
53 AUSTRIA - SHÖNBRUNN
54 ITALY - MILAN
55 ITALY - VICENZA
56 ITALY - VENICE
57 ITALY - RAVENNA
58 ITALY - PISA
59 ITALY - FLORENCE
60 ITALY - ASSISI
61 ITALY - VATICAN CITY
62 ITALY - CASERTA
63 CROATIA - DUBROVNIK
64 HUNGARY - BUDAPEST
65 BULGARIA - IVANOVO
66 GREECE - MOUNT ATHOS
67 GREECE - METEORA
68 TURKEY - ISTANBUL
69 TURKEY - SAFRANBOLU
70 CYPRUS - TROODOS

Africa

71 MOROCCO - FEZ
72 MAURITANIA - OUADANE, CHINGUETTI, TICHITT, OUALATA
73 MALI - BANDIAGARA
74 MALI - DJIENNÉ
75 LIBYA - GHADAMES
76 EGYPT - CAIRO
77 ETHIOPIA - GONDAR
78 TANZANIA - ZANZIBAR

Asia

79 SYRIA - DAMASCUS
80 ISRAEL - JERUSALEM
81 YEMEN - SANA'A
82 IRAN - ISFAHAN
83 UZBEKISTAN - KHIVA
84 UZBEKISTAN - SAMARKAND
85 PAKISTAN - LAHORE
86 INDIA - DELHI
87 INDIA - AGRA
88 SRI LANKA - GALLE
89 NEPAL - KATHMANDU
90 CHINA - THE GREAT WALL
91 CHINA - BEIJING
92 CHINA - BEIJING
93 CHINA - TAISHAN
94 CHINA - LHASA
95 LAOS - LUANG PRABANG
96 VIETNAM - HUÉ
97 REPUBLIC OF KOREA - HAEINSA
98 JAPAN - KYOTO
99 JAPAN - HIMEJI-JO
100 JAPAN - ITSUKUSHIMA

Asia

83

84

91 92

90 93

94

85
86 87

89

88

97

98
100 99

95

96

Indian Ocean

Oceania

preface

The Earth and its inhabitants have left the modern world a veritable treasure trove of natural and cultural heritage, from the tropical rainforests of Brazil, the delicate coral reefs of Australia, the volcanic mountains of Russia, and the wildlife sanctuaries of Africa to the Buddhist Monuments of Asia, the pyramids of Egypt, the historic city centers of Italy, and the cathedrals of France.

Thirty years ago, UNESCO's General Conference called the world's attention to the importance of safeguarding this invaluable heritage by adopting the resolutions of the 1972 *Convention concerning the protection of the world's cultural and natural heritage*. Since then, 167 nations have ratified the Convention, pledging their allegiance to conserving not only the World Heritage Sites situated within their borders, but also to protect their national heritage in general, thus forming a World Heritage community. An international community whose underlying belief is that there are some places on Earth which are of such "outstanding universal value" for their natural features, historical significance, or spiritual meaning that their protection is not just the responsibility of a single nation but of all of humanity.

The Convention's focus on both cultural and natural heritage makes it the pre-eminent international legal tool for conservation. It establishes the criteria for the kinds of natural or cultural sites that can be considered for inscription in the World Heritage List, and sets the standards for sustainable management and measures for protection.

Today, there are 721 cultural, natural, and mixed properties from every corner of the world inscribed on the World Heritage List. Despite the due prestige this awards, many of these sites are inherently fragile and vulnerable. Ensuring that sites do not lose the very values for which they were designated as "World Heritage" eligible has become an increasingly complex challenge. Thirty-one World Heritage sites have been formally declared as World Heritage in Danger, while many others face a variety

of threats to their long-term integrity and survival. The effects of urban development, tourism, deterioration, and unfortunately, vandalism and destruction increasingly threaten cultural sites, while natural sites are endangered by the impact of infrastructure construction, improper use, the expansion of tourism, pollution, and the long-term effects of climate change. World Heritage sites belong to all of us, no matter where they are located, and it is our shared responsibility to look after them. We must remember the French proverb, "*on connaît la valeur d'une chose lorsqu'on l'a perdue,*" which points out that "we only recognize the value of something once we have lost it," and not wait until it is too late to repair a situation.

With limited resources, the World Heritage Fund is a small step in the right direction. An important part of the World Heritage Convention, the Fund offers preparatory assistance for nominations of new sites, help in projects aimed at safeguarding properties already inscribed on the List, emergency assistance, technical support, and training courses. It also enables awareness-building about the World Heritage Convention and its aims, and supports UNESCO's Special Project "Young People's Participation in World Heritage Preservation and Promotion," which was launched in 1994 to encourage youth to become involved in World Heritage protection.

I hope you will enjoy learning more about World Heritage as you read through this beautiful and informative book, and I encourage you to consult our web site at http://www.unesco.org/whc for more information about how to become involved in protecting our shared World Heritage.

Francesco Bandarin
Director
UNESCO World Heritage Center

introduction

On November 23, 1972 in Paris, the General Conference of UNESCO drew up the institutive Convention of the World Heritage List that became active on December 17, 1975. The ambitious aim of the United Nations Educational, Scientific, and Cultural Organization was to identify, study, and safeguard monuments, complexes, and sites – whether natural or manmade – that have "outstanding universal value" from a historical, artistic, scientific, naturalistic, archaeological, or anthropological standpoint.

Thirty years later, the list of World Heritage Sites is an extraordinary inventory of places and works that simultaneously embrace the histories of Man and the Earth, providing a tool for understanding nature, culture, and above all, the ties that bind them together. The list of World Heritage Sites is a summary of the planet's historical development. The aim of this book is to present a cross-section of the priceless legacy under the aegis of UNESCO.

To be able to deal with such a vast assortment, the subject matter has been divided into three volumes, dedicated respectively to treasures of art and architecture, natural sites, and ancient civilizations. The distinction between cultural and natural properties is explicitly defined in the Convention, but the demarcation line between architectural monuments and sites of archaeological interest was more difficult to define. A purely temporal criterion would probably have misrepresented historical understanding, therefore, it has been considered opportune to include in this volume all the sites that have been continuously inhabited, even though some of these, for chronological reasons, could just as easily have been included under the heading of archaeological heritage.

To merit inscription in the World Heritage List as a cultural property, a monument, a complex, or a site, at least one of the following criteria must be met:

i) represent a masterpiece of human creative genius; or

ii) exhibit an important interchange of human values, over a span of time or within a cultural area of the world, involving developments in architecture or technology, monumental arts, town planning, or landscape design; or

iii) bear a unique or at least exceptional testimony to a cultural tradition or to a civilization which is living or has disappeared; or

iv) be an outstanding example of a type of building, or an architectural or technological ensemble, or a landscape which illustrates (a) significant stage(s) in human history; or

v) be an outstanding example of a traditional human settlement or land-use which is representative of a culture (or cultures), especially when it has become vulnerable or is under the effects of irreversible change; or

vi) be directly or tangibly associated with events or living traditions, with ideas or beliefs, or with artistic and literary works of outstanding universal significance (a criterion applied only in exceptional circumstances, and together with other criteria).

Using these criteria as a starting point, 100 of the 400 sites that represent Man's artistic and architectural heritage have been selected for this collection. The uniqueness of the cultural value of each has made it hard, and in many cases painful, to exclude one in favor of another. For that reason, we have attempted to provide a sample, however partial, that does not discriminate against any country or culture so that the overall representation remains as comprehensive as possible.

As for the subject matter dealt with in the pages that follow, it would have been reductive and, to some extent, narrow-minded to consider the large works produced by civilizations purely for what they are. Hence, the text does not overly dwell on the works' stylistic quality as an end in itself, but attempts to show how Man's creations are the products of the history that has shaped them and the culture that surrounds them.

List of the Sites

Europe

It is almost inevitable that in a round-up of cultural sites Europe would have the foremost role. Of the approximately 400 sites inscribed in UNESCO's World Heritage List for architectural importance, over half of them are located in the Old World. During the almost two millennia encompassed by this book, Europe experienced an extraordinary flourishing of civilizations that stimulated the development of transnational cultural currents and the growth of local artistic movements of great originality.

A summary of Europe's cultural evolution – and consequently also of its architectural development – revolves around three dominant factors. The first factor, for chronological reasons, was the advent and spread of Christianity. Religion represented, particularly during the late Middle Ages, a source of inspiration for generations of artists. Ecclesiastic power also provided the patronage that fostered the production of artistic works of inestimable value and the development of styles – Gothic, with its many regional variations, is one example – that had repercussions on the structures of European cities and the history of architecture itself. The religious motif permeated all areas; it was the thread that joins the wooden church of Urnes Stavkirke, in the extreme north of Norway, to the painted churches of Troodos in Cyprus, close to the Holy Land. It was the inspiration for the architecture of the Monasterio de los Hieronimos in Lisbon and also for the cathedral of Bagrati in Georgia.

The second factor was the political organization of the states, whether they were small dukedoms like that of the Medici in Florence, large empires like that of the Hapsburgs, long established kingdoms such as those of France, England, and czarist Russia, or fledgling monarchies like that of the Savoys in Italy. While the history of European civilization has been seared by fierce conflicts for political and territorial domination, it has contemporaneously undergone continuous cultural exchange, and ruling dynasties and the families of the aristocracies have competed with one another in a quest for cultural prestige. This rivalry was inevitably expressed in the size of residences and the artistic taste that characterized them. Such celebration of power produced masterpieces like the palaces of Versailles, Caserta, Schönbrunn, and Würzburg, and an entire city in the case of St Petersburg.

The third factor was economic development. The list of World Heritage sites includes several historic centers of European cities that had in common long periods of commercial prosperity. This was the case for Venice, which dominated the Mediterranean for centuries, Lubeck and Bergen, which were ports in the Hanseatic League, and Bruges, the main port in the region of Flanders. In the eighteenth century the Industrial Revolution began in England, and this development also created a place for itself in the history of culture, resulting in profound changes in working activities and the customs of everyday life.

These three factors, however, are not sufficient to express the amazing variety of Europe's cultural legacy. Spain, for example, which shares first place with Italy for the largest number of architectural sites, can boast the extraordinary stimulus provided by Islamic architecture as well as, more recently, the marvelous creations of the unique genius of Gaudì. Moreover, throughout the continent the twentieth century marked the breaking away from tradition: first with the sinuous and refined lines of Art Nouveau, and then with the extreme rationalism of the Bauhaus, bringing new vitality to European architecture.

Urnes Stavkirke

NORWAY

Luster, Sognefjord
Registration: 1979
Criteria: C (i) (ii) (iii)

URNES

OSLO

The Norwegian 50 cent coin has the picture of a dragon on one side. It is the mythological animal also shown on the north doorway of Urnes Stavkirke, the oldest wooden church in the country, which stands at the end of a wide bend in the Sogne, which, measuring 126 miles in length, is the longest fjord in the world.

Stavkirke literally means "church of staves," and it is estimated that there were at least 800 similar churches in medieval Norway, which have since been lost, demolished during the eighteenth century to make way for stone constructions. The name is derived from the construction technique of driving staves into the ground to act as load-bearing supports. The first churches of this type were short-lived because the wood quickly deteriorated in the damp earth. To avoid this, in the twelfth century a wooden base was built to which the staves were fixed, thus giving greater solidity to the structure.

They were called the "cathedrals of the poor" because of the simplicity of their external appearance, and the church at Urnes was no different than the others. However, its internal decorations are brought to life by the warm color of the pinewood (now hundreds of years old) and gave rise to a new style, known as Urnes, which is the most explicit form of the religious life of the Norwegian people. The style mixes the character of Asatru – the pagan cult of Germanic origin practiced by the Vikings that mainly worshipped Odin and Thor – with medieval Christianity and Lutheranism.

Sea expeditions during the tenth century brought the Vikings in contact with other European peoples and many of their military leaders embraced the Christian religion, having themselves baptized and encouraging their troops to follow their example. This is what happened to Olav Trygvason, who converted to Christianity in 991 during an invasion of England. When he returned home, he was proclaimed king of northeastern Norway and made efforts to have his subjects converted. It was his successor, Olav Haraldsson, who brought about the definitive conversion of Norway to Christianity in 1015. Killed in battle in 1030, King Olav was canonized just a year later and became the patron saint of Norway.

Over the following centuries, the sacred architecture, in the present day represented by Urnes, was developed. Built roughly between 1100 and 1150 using pinewood from a previous place of worship built on the same site, the church has three naves supported by 16 columns adorned with finely historiated capitals. The bishop's throne in the choir, the iron candlestick, and the sculpted figures of Christ, the Virgin, and Saint John date from the twelfth and thirteenth centuries and are clearly inspired by Christianity. The benches added at the time of the Reformation (which arrived in Norway in 1537) and the altar and the pulpit, both built at the end of the seventeenth century, are the result of the same religious inspiration.

On the other hand, Christianity merges with paganism in the runic inscriptions discovered below the floor and in historiated images on the doorway. According to one interpretation, these exquisite incisions represent lions and snakes engrossed in a struggle. Other sources consider them to be the dragons that existed in the *Edda*, the ancient Scandinavian sagas. Vine shoots, a recurring symbol in Christian iconography, are wrapped around the coils of these fantastic creatures with the head of a lion and the body of a snake. In the artist's imagination, this would represent the triumph of good over evil and of the true faith over the false beliefs of the Norwegian people's forefathers.

16 Early Viking cults exhibit a mixture of iconography altered by medieval Christianity in the botanical and zoomorphic decorations carved in the pinewood walls of Urnes Stavkirke.

17 top Built around 1150, the church at Urnes Stave is the oldest, largest, and best conserved of the 40 or so wooden churches that still exist in Norway.

17 bottom Modest in size, the altar was embellished at the end of the seventeenth century with a shrine that frames the medieval wooden figures of Christ, the Virgin, and Saint John. Besides being one of Norway's most visited places, the church is used for marriages, funerals, and Sunday services.

Bergen
NORWAY

BERGEN
REGISTRATION: 1979
CRITERIA: C (III)

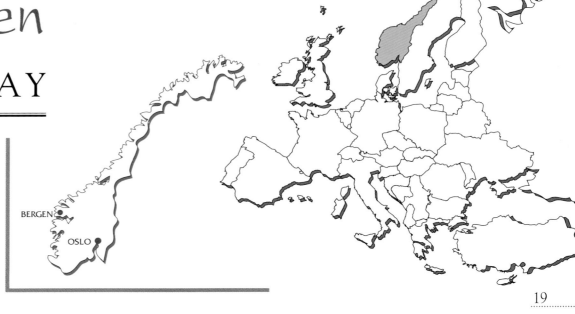

It is in Bergen that, in a certain sense, the story of haddock is written. Here the fish arrived from the ports of northern Norway to be smoked – there were 23 different types with just as many prices and customers – and stored in large warehouses before being loaded onto ships headed throughout Europe. Stockfish was for at least four centuries almost the only Norwegian export.

The roots of Bergen – the ancient wharf of Bergen built on the east shore of the Vågen (bay) – are closely connected to the medieval origins of the town founded by King Olav Kyrre around 1070. By the thirteenth century, the wharf was the crowded commercial and economic center of the town, where 30 or so warehouses stood to hold the goods that arrived from the British Far Øer (Faroe Islands) and the Baltic coast.

In 1360, the economic life of Bergen's port reached a turning point when it was chosen to be a *Kontor*, or a trading office of the Hanseatic League, along with Novgorod, Brugge (or Bruges), and London. From that moment and for the next four centuries, German traders held a monopoly over the port, the name of which is in fact a contraction of a Norwegian word, *tyskerbryggen* (wharf of

the Germans). In exchange for the stockfish, for which there was great demand, particularly in Catholic countries, the Norwegians received cereals, as very little grew in those latitudes, and precious goods like fabrics, pottery, glass, and wine from the Rhine valley.

Bergen *Kontor* was an exclusively male community whose members were strictly forbidden the company of the local women. Wives, fiancées, and female company of various types were only allowed on the site between spring and autumn each year and had to return home for the remaining months.

The community eventually reached

18 Many of Bergen's wooden buildings have been destroyed by fires over the centuries. Those that remain were built at the start of the twentieth century yet faithful to the original style.

19 top Now crowded with pleasure boats, Bergen Wharf (the name is a contraction of Tyskerbryggen, meaning "wharf of the Germans") was one of the main centers of the Hanseatic League, the powerful trading network that for nearly 400 years linked northern Europe's major ports in an economic alliance.

19 center A view of the top of Vågen fjord. Bergen Port formed the nucleus of the city of Bergen and is still located on the eastern shore.

19 bottom Painted bright colors, Bergen's port warehouses now accommodate artists' studios, restaurants, and the Hanseatic League Museum.

1000 resident Germans and was governed by its own rules, among which the most important was the ban on lighting fires. The houses in Bergen, often containing shops, were two- or three-story buildings called *lofts* made entirely from wood, with residential rooms on the upper floors and plank roofs covered with tiles. Even the narrow passageways between buildings were paved with planks. At the rear of each *loft* were the *schøtstuer*, communal rooms where the traders met at the end of the working day. Despite the severity of the regulations, Bergen was repeatedly ravaged by fire, but on each occasion the buildings were rebuilt according to the same criteria. The need to restart trading quickly prevented any evolution in the constructions' design, thus the layout of the port area remained unaltered over time.

At the start of the seventeenth century, the trading network of the Hanseatic League began to weaken as many European nations took back control of the trade of their own goods. In 1630 Norwegian merchants began to buy the first warehouses, and a century later the Germans owned only nine. On October 17, 1754, the *Kontor* of Bergen passed permanently into the hands of the Norwegians, but they maintained the

existing regulations and even kept German as the common trading language.

After 1850, however, the Industrial Revolution made its effects felt on the coasts of Scandinavia, and the traditional stockfish industry suffered at the hands of other types of business. The port area soon proved to be inadequate, and on December 31, 1899 the *Kontor* was shut down.

Since then, Bergen has suffered a series of misfortunes. In 1910 the buildings in the south of the site were demolished to make room for brick warehouses. In 1944, an explosion destroyed many of the roofs, and in 1955 a fire burned down half the remaining buildings. Today only 58 constructions remain in the world's oldest trading center, which have been partly rebuilt in accordance with the original criteria and painted bright red. They house restaurants and art galleries, and one of them, to commemorate their past, contains the Museum of the Hanseatic League.

20 top This photo shows some of the old houses behind the port. The community in Bergen was exclusively male, and women were only allowed to visit during the summer.

20 bottom left A corner of a merchant's house in the Hanseatic League Museum. The paintings and other precious objects are indicative of the merchant's wealth.

20 bottom right A picture of the kitchens where people would gather after the working day. For safety reasons, fires were forbidden in all other rooms of the buildings.

20-21 Opened in 1976, the Hanseatic League Museum is one of the most beautifully laid out in Europe. It has been carefully reconstructed with original furnishings and fittings. Of particular interest is the store where the salted cod was stored and the Fiskeskrue, the press used to extract cod liver oil.

21 bottom This photo features another room in the museum. In addition to pieces from Bergen's golden period, the display includes one of the most important collections of runic stones in the world plus archaeological finds from the Bergen area.

22 top left and 22-23 The panorama of the Baroque park at Drottningholm provides a view of its perfect symmetry. This section stretches for about 2,300 feet from the entrance to the palace and was embellished with fountains and bronze statues by the Flemish sculptor Adrian de Vries. The figure below is of Hercules.

The Royal Domain of Drottningholm

SWEDEN

22 top right Rebuilt in 1763, the pavilion is composed of a main body and four lateral buildings. It holds a large number of Chinese and Japanese works of art which were very much in vogue with the aristocracy of the period.

23 top The most outstanding feature of the park is the Chinese pavilion built by King Adolf Frederik for his wife Lovisa Ulrika for her thirty-third birthday.

In 1981, Karl Gustaf XVI of Sweden and his family moved their permanent residence to an island on Lake Mälar, a few miles from the capital. This may have been because a change in the country's constitution during the previous year had limited the monarch to only representative power. With the need for the king to always be at the center of the political life of the country eliminated, the country estate of Drottningholm appeared the ideal solution.

The name Drottningholm, literally "Queen's Island," had its roots in the sixteenth century when King John III built a palace there for his consort Katherine Jagellonica. The building did not last long, having burned to the ground on December 30, 1661, a few months after coming into the possession of Edvige Eleonora, the regent of the young Karl XI. Its reconstruction by Nicodemus Tessin the Elder and, later, his son was supposed to pay tribute to the greatness of Sweden, which had emerged from the Peace of Westphalia in 1648 as one of Europe's leading powers.

The palace marked the triumph of Nordic Baroque. The central part of the building is dominated by a monumental stairway faced onto by magnificent rooms adorned with statues, stuccoes, and frescoes. During the same period, the landscaping of the surrounding land was begun. A Baroque garden was created in the style of Versailles, a place of delights beautified by statues by the famous Flemish sculptor Adrian de Vries.

Drottningholm remained the residence of the women at court until 1744 when it was given to Princess Lovisa Ulrika of Prussia to celebrate her marriage to the heir

24-25 Designed by K.F. Adelcrantz and completed in 1766, the Slottsteater is the oldest theater in the world to have retained its original structure. In 1920, it was equipped with electricity, the ropes for quick scenery changes were replaced, and the nineteenth-century sound system was renovated.

to the Swedish throne, Adolf Fredrik. A golden age began during which the most famous artists and scientists in the kingdom were gathered together at court, one of whom, Carl von Linné, catalogued the royal collection of "natural objects." On Lovisa Ulrika's wishes, some of the rooms were redecorated in Rococo style.

These were the most glorious years of the East India Company and the royal courts of Europe were shot through by an attraction for anything that came from the Orient. To mark the thirty-third birthday of Lovisa Ulrika in 1753, her husband gave her a Chinese pavilion built in Stockholm and – to increase the scenic effect – had it assembled during the night in front of her window. However, within only ten years the wood began to rot and the pavilion was replaced by the Kina Slott, the extravagant blue and gold building that can still be seen today, thanks to the careful restoration work carried out based on the building's original plans.

During the same period, Karl Fredrik Adelcrantz was commissioned to design what today is the best conserved Baroque theatre in Europe. Completed in 1766, the Slottsteater is built from simple materials but to impressive effect. The stage is 66 feet deep, and the sophisticated and perfectly preserved theatrical machinery, built by the Italian Donato Stopani, allowed rapid scenery changes to be made. The stage was equipped with mobile panels able to recreate moving clouds and waves and special effects like thunder, wind, and lightning.

At the end of the eighteenth century, Swedish interest in the theater declined, and little by little the Slottsteater was forgotten. Rediscovered in 1920 by Agne Bejier, a historian of the theater and literature, it was restored to its original glory. The scenery machines were repaired and the ancient backcloths were mended. On August 19, 1922, the curtain was raised once again and the theater began to win back its international reputation for its festivals of works by Haydn, Handel, Gluck, and Mozart. Today, besides being used by the Royal Opera of Stockholm, the theater is a study center for eighteenth-century music and ballet.

24 bottom A cultured and sophisticated queen, Lovisa Ulrika commissioned artist Jean Eric Rehn to decorate the library.

25 top The bedchamber designed by Nicodemus Tessin the Elder for Queen Edvige Eleonora is a perfect example of Swedish Baroque. Finished in 1683, it took a number of Scandinavia's most famous decorators 15 years to complete.

25 bottom The superb stairway that faces onto the Trapphallen is the centerpiece of the royal palace. Its balustrades feature marble statues of Apollo and the Muses by the Italian sculptors Giovanni and Carlo Carove.

Verla

FINLAND

By the middle of the twentieth century, modern wood-processing techniques had pretty much taken the upper hand in an industry that had developed rapidly around the end of the nineteenth century. Consequently, the Verla groundwood and board mill, situated halfway between the two small Finnish towns of Jaala and Valkeala, was forced to shut down in July 1964. During its heyday it had employed up to 140 people and produced 2,200 tons of boards per year.

The industrial revolution reached the valley of the Kymi torrent, where the Verla factory and its attendant village stand, around 1870. In just a few years the valley was invaded by sawmills, carpenters' workshops, and paper mills founded above all by rich foreigners, mostly German or Norwegian. The young engineer Hugo Neuman, on the other hand, was Swiss. In 1872 he was the first to build a company for the production of the wood paste used in paper manufacture, but his ambitious project was destined to fail. Neuman did not have sufficient capital to expand the factory and had problems transporting the products. Furthermore, due to a drop in prices on the Russian market, the largest wood paste importer, and a fire in 1876, the young company was finally destroyed.

In 1882 the Austrian Gottlieb Kreidl and

26-27 An attractive winter view of the Verla Groundwood Factory and Board Mill shows the brick building around the old wood factory that stands on the right of the massive, four-floor plant used for drying the wood paste. It was built in 1892 after the original drying area was destroyed in a fire.

PROVINCE OF KYMI,
MUNICIPALITY OF JAALA AND VALKEALA
REGISTRATION: 1996
CRITERIA: C (IV)

27 center This view features the canal on which the dam was built in the 1920's that provided power to a small hydro-electric station from 1954 on.

27 bottom Raised above a canal, the owner's residence was designed in 1895 by Friedrich Wilhelm Dippell. He was the principal shareholder in the factory until 1906.

VERLA

HELSINKI

the Germans Louis Haenel and Friedrich Wilhelm Dippell built a new, larger, and better equipped factory. Dippell, who in the meantime had become the largest shareholder in the project, died in 1906, but the company continued production even during the Finnish civil war in 1918. It was then purchased by another groundwood company that was based on the same river, but the new owners did not renew the machinery and production gradually began to diminish. The only alterations made to the company were, over the decades, a new dam in the 1920s and a hydroelectricity production plant in 1954.

When the last worker reached retirement age, the parent company UPM-Kimmele closed the factory but decided to preserve this extraordinary relic of the industrial revolution. Originally, the entire complex (factory, owner's residence, and workers' living quarters, which were completed in 1886) was built from wood. Most of the workers lived in modest huts on the other side of the torrent. Because of their gardens they blended harmoniously with the surrounding vegetation.

Destroyed by a fire in 1892, the paste-drying section was replaced by an imposing four-story building designed by Carl Eduard Dippell and made from red brick to prevent a repetition of the incident. In 1895 the other building was constructed, this time of two stories, which enclosed the old wooden factory. The last of the constructions designed by Dippell, who had adopted modern construction techniques even though his buildings were neo-Gothic in appearance, was the warehouse, whose walls were made from light feldspar bricks in 1902.

The machines with which the wood was processed by hand merit a word apart. First of all, they cut the trunks into blocks five feet long using a hand-powered circular saw. Then they stripped the bark off the blocks and passed the pieces through the two grinding machines, inside which was a rock weighing three tons. From here the wood paste was sent to the mixers which in practice were torsion presses able to extract the greater part of the excess humidity from the paste. The boards were then hung to dry at a temperature of about 158°F. After three days they were measured to separate them into the required thicknesses, then packed in bundles, each weighing 440 pounds.

In 1972 the Verla factory was turned into a museum. Since then, its machines for processing wood and producing cardboard have remained in their place to record the pioneering epoch of an industry in which Finland is still one of the leaders.

28-29 Built in several stages between 1870 and 1918 on the banks of the Kymi, Verla Groundwood Factory became the property of UOM-Kymmene Corporation in 1922, which later turned it into a museum.

29 bottom The torsion presses that extracted the moisture from wood paste are perfectly preserved. The equipment at Verla is all original.

30 top Consecrated in 1582, the chapel in Kronborg Castle still has its multicolored wooden decorations from the Renaissance era. What we see today is the result of a nineteenth-century restoration made necessary after soldiers, who occupied the castle in 1785, used the chapel as a powder magazine.

30-31 A view of Kronborg Castle. Despite a series of modifications, its current appearance still reflects the design by Jan van Pæschen, commissioned by Frederik II to enlarge the ancient fort in 1574.

31 top left One of the upper decorations in the chapel gallery; they are based on the coats of arms of the families of Frederik II and Queen Sophie.

31 top right The castle, which is surrounded by a double ring of walls, looks onto the Øresund at the eastern tip of Helsingør.

Kronborg Castle

DENMARK

HELSINGØR
REGISTRATION: 2000
CRITERIA: C (IV)

Abas-relief portrait of William Shakespeare stands above the entrance to Kronborg Castle though the mystery that surrounds the life of the great English playwright means that no one knows if he ever visited the castle. What is certain, however, is that by setting the tragedy of Hamlet here, he became the site's greatest benefactor. A tormented prince by the name of Amleth appears in a Danish legend recounted by the Danish historian Saxo Grammaticus around 800 years ago, but at that time the castle did not exist.

It was only around 1420 that Erik of Pomerania, the king of Denmark, demanded payment of a toll by all the ferries that crossed the Øresund, the strip of water that separates Denmark from Sweden, and which at Helsingør is hardly nine miles wide. As a sign of intimidation, construction began of a large fort which was named Krogen. It was only in the second half of the sixteenth century, during the reign of Fredrik II, that the complex of buildings surrounded by walls was rebuilt and turned into the most magnificent Renaissance-style palace in northern Europe, adorned with towers, colonnades, and statues. To underline the change, a royal edict was issued on January 24, 1577 changing the name to Kronborg, and a hard and fast law threatened anyone referring to it by the original name of Krogen with the punishment of a fine.

Kronborg was the residence of the royal family of Denmark for a century and a half, during which time it experienced many different events, including the fire of 1629 and the Swedish occupation of 1688. Fifty years later it was turned into a prison and later a barracks. In 1816, on the two hundredth anniversary of the death of Shakespeare, the Danish soldiers put on a production of *Hamlet* for the first time, and thus began a tradition that continues even today. In 1866, under pressure from some of the most important figures in the kingdom, restoration lasting some 30 years was undertaken of the enclosure walls. During World War II, occupying German troops were stationed in Kronborg because of its strategic position.

Much of the castle can be visited,

including the royal apartments on the first floor, and the chapel and the magnificent ballroom on the second floor. The ballroom fills the entire length of the south wing, and its measurements of 36 by 203 feet make it the largest reception room in northern Europe. The original decorations were destroyed in the 1629 fire, and the castle has never since recovered its early splendor. Fortunately, 14 of the 40 extraordinary sixteenth-century wall-hangings portraying the Danish royal families were saved (seven

the role of the castle as Denmark's defensive bulwark says that the statue of Holger Danske will reawaken if the security of the nation is threatened.

In the meantime, the organization that looks after Kronborg has begun an ambitious project to restore and modernize the display areas, which will be completed in 2010.

32 top left The guest apartments fitted out by Frederik II for his mother-in-law, the Duchess of Mecklenburg. Note the Renaissance-style sculpted chimney.

32 top right The "King's Study" was decorated in the seventeenth century, during the reign of Christian IV, with round and clover-shaped allegorical paintings on the ceiling.

32 bottom Most of the Flemish tapestries ordered by Christian IV were destroyed in a fire in 1629. Of those that remain, seven are on display in the royal apartments in Kronborg and seven more in the National Museum in Copenhagen.

are still kept in the castle while the others are exhibited in the National Museum in Copenhagen).

Kronborg's military past is evident when one visits the casemates; the warren of underground corridors, storerooms, and secret chambers could accommodate up to 1000 soldiers for six weeks in the event of a siege. This is where the statue of Holger Danske is kept, a legendary king and general who became the symbol of the Danish people. His myth is in fact derived from the *Chanson de Roland*, a masterpiece of French medieval literature, which was adapted in 1534 by Christian Pedersen and given a Nordic slant. Pedersen was originally from Helsingør, and for this reason the figure of Holger Danske was immediately associated with Kronborg. A popular belief linked to

33 top Manufactured in Flanders around 1550, this tapestry based on an engraving by Albrecht Dürer shows a rhinoceros and other small animals. The first known example of a rhinoceros in Europe arrived in Lisbon from Goa in 1515.

33 bottom "Orpheus Enchanting the Animals" is the title of this tapestry, woven at the start of the seventeenth century in the workshop of the Flemish artist Frans Spierings.

Kizhi Pogost

RUSSIAN FEDERATION

Lake Onega, Province of Olonets, Karelia
Registration: 1990
Criteria: C (i) (iv) (v)

34 top The typical onion-shaped domes of the Church of the Transfiguration are symbolic: the five highest domes represent Christ and the Evangelists, and the others saints and prophets.

34 bottom One hundred and three icons painted in the sixteenth and seventeenth centuries remain in the Church of the Transfiguration. This one portrays the Virgin and Child.

To visit the island of Kizhi, 40 miles north of Petrozavorsk, the capital of Karelia, it is a good idea to leave the shore of Lake Onega before dawn, for as the rays of a weak sun begin to pierce the haze, the domes of the Kizhi can be seen emerging from a finger of tundra.

Consisting of two churches, one of the Transfiguration and one of the Intercession, and a bell tower, Kizhi Pogost is a jewel in a complex of roughly 70 buildings and represents the apex of the region's traditional wooden architecture. The island has been inhabited since the first millennium A.D. when a large Lap community performed pagan rituals there in honor of the sun and rain gods. Some scholars even believe that the place name is derived from the Karelian word *kizhat*, meaning "ritual." When the Russian people invaded the area and assimilated the local ethnic groups, the island did not lose its religious character; a church was built there with a *pogost* (graveyard). Since then, the term has taken on the meaning of "administrative unit" because the meetings of the members of the community were held in front of the church. In the sixteenth century, the area of Kizhi Pogost covered 130 villages and was one of the largest administrative units in northwestern Russia.

The early eighteenth century, when Russia underwent the reforms of Peter the Great, was a golden period for the country. To celebrate his victories, the people of Karelia began to construct a number of buildings. The most important was the Church of the Transfiguration (1713-1714)

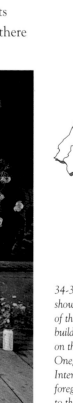

34-35 The aerial view shows the entire enclosure of the three main wooden buildings at Kizhi Pogost on the shores of Lake Onega. The Church of the Intercession is in the foreground, the bell tower to the left, and the Church of the Transfiguration to the right.

35 right Built between 1713 and 1714, the Church of the Transfiguration was the first monument in Karelia to celebrate the victories of Peter the Great.

KIZHI POGOST

MOSCOW

which was built on the foundations of the previous temple that had been destroyed by a fire. A legend has it that the craftsman who built it hurled his axe into the lake when it was completed, crying, "This church has been built by Master Nestor; there has never been one like it and never will be again."

Standing 121 feet tall and made completely of pine, fir, and poplar, it has a single octagonal nave with an apse at each of the four points of the compass (the altar stands on the east side, the refectory on the west). It is composed of three buttresses (also octagonal) placed on top of one another that decrease in size. The highest points of the first two octagons terminate in a *bochka* (an onion-shaped pediment) which supports a cylinder adorned with a *lukovista*

(an onion-shaped dome). In the same way, each apse terminates in two domes of the same shape for a total of 22 domes: eight on the apses and lower octagon, four on the middle octagon, one above the altar, and one on the apex of the entire structure. As in many religious buildings in Russia, the five highest domes represent Christ and the Evangelists, whereas the others celebrate Moses, Elijah, and the Saints in paintings on the iconostasis inside.

Many of the original icons are now exhibited in Moscow museums, however there are still 103 from the sixteenth and seventeenth centuries, hung in rows divided by finely painted panels called *tyabla*. The icons on the ceiling, though, have been lost following work at the end of the nineteenth century when the structure was

strengthened with pieces of iron. The church was deconsecrated in 1937.

The next-door Church of the Intercession, built in 1764, suffered the same fate but was reconsecrated in 1955 to celebrate services on the most important Orthodox festivals. Standing 86 feet tall and also made from wood, it is in the shape of an octahedron topped by a quadrilateral and crowned by ten domes. The bell tower was built during the same period.

The three religious buildings and others have been part of the Museum of History, Architecture, and Ethnography of Kizhi since 1966. The administration is responsible for the conservation of the culture of the island and has a collection of over 30,000 artifacts and a library of some 30,000 books.

The Historic Center of St. Petersburg

RUSSIAN FEDERATION

REGISTRATION: 1990
CRITERIA: C (I) (II) (IV) (VI)

For more than half a century the cruiser Aurora, the historical ship belonging to the Russian navy that is also used as a school, has been anchored in the river Neva in front of the Nachimov Naval Academy in the center of St. Petersburg. As it lay there on the morning of November 7, 1917, it was its own cadets that fired the ship's cannons signaling the start of the assault on the Winter Palace, thus setting in motion the October Revolution. A year later, Lenin moved the country's capital to Moscow and deprived St. Petersburg of the role it had played since the times of Peter the Great.

When he ascended to the throne of Russia at the age of ten, Peter the Great had already witnessed the palace intrigues by which members of his family were gradually removed. By the time he became free of his unwelcome tutors, he also began to dislike the conservative atmosphere of Moscow. A passionate sailor (he had traveled a great deal and worked in a Dutch shipyard), he dreamed of turning Russia into one of the great European powers. He therefore planned to build a new capital on the

islands in the Neva, a river that flows from Lake Ladoga to the Baltic Sea at the eastern end of the Gulf of Finland.

In the summer of 1703 he ordered his army carpenters to build a hut from which he could watch construction progress on Petrogradskaia Storona (Petrograd Island). For six years he lived in two modest rooms with his most precious belongings: a frock coat, a compass, and a rowing boat. Later, the Czarina, Catherine II, had this hut

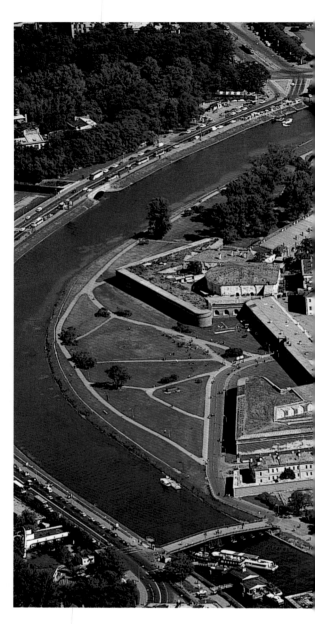

enclosed in brick walls to honor the memory of the city's founder.

Construction of St. Petersburg began with a large defensive building, the SS. Peter-Paul Fort, on the small Hare Island (Zayachy Island). Initially the walls were made from wood, but later Peter asked Domenico Trezzini to build solid bastions, and the Italian architect placed the two-headed eagle, the emblem of the Romanov dynasty, with Saint George and the dragon on the entrance to the fort. Trezzini was also responsible for the design of the SS. Peter-Paul Cathedral, begun in 1712 and completed in 1733. Massive and finely decorated marble columns, huge

chandeliers, and a polychrome vault surrounded the carved wooden and gilded iconostasis built by Ivan Zarudnyi. In 1725, before construction was complete, Peter the Great was buried in the cathedral, initiating the tradition of the Baroque church being the final resting place of the Romanovs.

1712 was also the year in which St. Petersburg was proclaimed the capital of Russia. Soldiers and manual laborers dug the canals that were supposed to turn the city into the Amsterdam of Russia, and they built the Summer Palace, the czar's first official residence in the city. Trezzini adjusted his creativity to suit the plain Dutch taste of the emperor, designing a two-story palace decorated with bas-reliefs that celebrated the naval triumphs of the czar. Following Peter's early death, the court was returned to the luxury of Moscow during the short reigns of Catherine I and Peter II, but in 1730, Czarina Anna opted for St. Petersburg once more, where she recreated a court inherited from Elizabeth, the daughter of Peter the Great, in 1740.

During her reign, St. Petersburg entered the history of architecture thanks to the contribution of Bartolomeo Rastrelli, who arrived in Russia with his father in the service of Peter the Great.

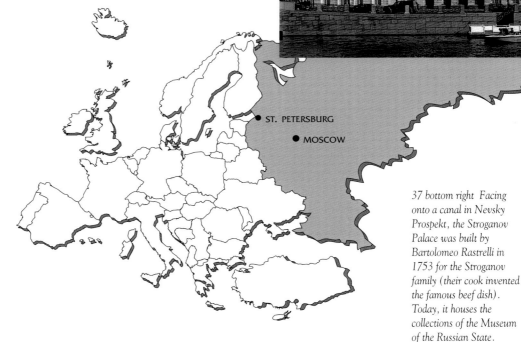

37 top right The czars in the Romanov dynasty, apart from Peter II and Ivan IV, were all buried in Sts. Peter-Paul Cathedral. Pink and green Corinthian columns, arched vaults, and lovely crystal chandeliers surround the sarcophaguses, made largely from Carrara marble.

36 top right Smolny Cathedral is part of the convent founded by Czarina Elizabeth II. Rastrelli designed the cathedral in 1748 using an admirable fusion of Russian and Italian Baroque.

36 bottom left The elegant gilded spire of the bell tower of Sts. Peter-Paul Cathedral. The commission for this religious building in the Peter-Paul Fort was awarded to the Italian, Domenico Trezzini, in 1712.

36-37 A view of Hare Island (Zayachy Island), the original nucleus of the city founded by Peter the Great. In 1703, the czar had a wooden fort built here that was later replaced, section by section, with a stone fort by Trezzini. An exquisitely elegant Baroque masterpiece, Sts. Peter-Paul Cathedral stands in the center of the island.

• ST. PETERSBURG
• MOSCOW

37 bottom right Facing onto a canal in Nevsky Prospekt, the Stroganov Palace was built by Bartolomeo Rastrelli in 1753 for the Stroganov family (their cook invented the famous beef dish). Today, it houses the collections of the Museum of the Russian State.

Rastrelli designed buildings in pure Baroque style, including the Stroganov Palace (the residence of Count Sergei), the Vorontsov Palace (long an exclusive military school), and Smolny Convent, which combines Russian architectural tradition with Western taste. However, the masterpiece of this particular blend was the Winter Palace, built between 1754 and 1762. Whereas the interiors have undergone repeated modification, the exterior has retained its original appearance and is a superb example of Russian Baroque.

The Winter Palace was immediately used by Peter III for trysts with his lover, Princess Vorontsova, and this is perhaps one of the reasons why his wife, the German Sophie von Anhalt-Zerbst, instigated a palace plot that ended, after just six months of his reign, in his deposition by the Imperial Guard and assassination. Having usurped the throne and crowning herself as Catherine II, Sophie subjected Russia to tyranny for over 30 years, but during that time gave St. Petersburg some of its most magnificent treasures.

An insatiable art-lover, she bought a huge number of works of art. In the ten years between 1764 and 1774, 2,500 paintings, 10,000 sculpted gems, 10,000 drawings, objects in porcelain and silver, and statues arrived in St. Petersburg. In 1771, having already built the Small Hermitage close to the Winter Palace, she began construction of the Great Hermitage, designed by Yuri Velten, to house her collections. Between 1785 and 1787 she commissioned the Hermitage Theater from Giacomo Quarenghi, and in the mid-nineteenth century the complex was further enriched with the New Hermitage. In 1851, Nicholas I opened the Great and the New Hermitage as public museums; today, with three million objects on display, including some of the most famous works by Impressionist painters, the Hermitage is the largest museum in the world and has the most exceptional collection of paintings, with the possible exception of the Louvre.

39 top One of the Hermitage galleries. Opened as a public museum in 1851 by Nicholas I, it boasts an encyclopedic collection of art works with almost three million objects on display.

39 center left A masterpiece of the genius of Bartolomeo Rastrelli, the broad Jordan Staircase embellishes the Winter Palace. Its name comes from the fact that the royal family watched the

ceremony of the Baptism of the Neva from this point, in commemoration of the Baptism of Christ in the Jordan.

39 center right One of the rooms that hold Catherine II's silver collection. An insatiable collector of art, between 1764 and 1774 the czarina purchased 2,500 paintings, 10,000 carved gems, 10,000 drawings, and thousands of statues and works of porcelain and silver.

39 bottom left The immense section dedicated to painting is one of the most visited in the Hermitage. The collection of European art from the Renaissance to the late eighteenth century testifies to the personal and often unconventional taste of the royal family. Nineteenth- and twentieth-century works mainly came from private collections.

39 bottom right The Hermitage Theater was commissioned from Giacomo Quarenghi by Catherine II.

38-39 This photo captures the south face of the Winter Palace, which looks onto Palace Square. The magnificent building is part of the Hermitage complex and is one of the most famous museums in the world. It was built by Bartolomeo Rastrelli between 1754 and 1762. The exterior is embellished with 400 columns and 16 different types of window.

On Catherine's death, the Russian throne passed to her son, Paul I, who had always had a tempestuous relationship with his mother. He detested both her lifestyle and her reign. In constant fear of a plot on his life, he thought he would be safe from his enemies by building the Engineers' Castle, a solid brick building surrounded by a dike, equipped with secret passages and escape routes. In 1801 he finally moved in but it did not prove impenetrable after all and, three days later, he was assassinated in his bed.

His successor, Alexander I, completed construction of the cathedral of Kazan, one of the city's most magnificent churches. Inspired by St. Peter's in Rome, Andrei Voronikhin designed a curved colonnade 364 feet long to hide the direction of the building, which was laid out parallel to St. Petersburg's main street, the Nevsky Prospekt. Supported by red granite columns adorned with capitals and decorated with an elegant mosaic floor, the church contains the tomb of Mikhail Kutuzov, the Russian hero from the Patriotic War against Napoleon. To celebrate his victory over the French emperor, in 1818 Alexander commissioned the enormous St. Isaac's Cathedral from Auguste de Montferrand. Its construction took 40 years. The Neo-Classical dome, lined with 220 pounds of gold, is visible from the Gulf of Finland, and in order for the marshy land to be able to support the 330,000 tons of the building, the ground was consolidated with thousands of wooden piles.

The city inherited by Nicholas I in 1825 was already shaken by the initial rebellious tremors that were to explode in the October Revolution a century later. The reforms demanded by the people and army were either ignored by the absolutist policies of the czars or answered by bloody repressions, which resulted in pages of passionate literature such as the cutting satire of Gogol and the dramatic novels of Dostoyevsky. But the court of the Romanovs was more involved in extricating itself from the shackles imposed by the palace than solving the problems of the populace. The architectural wonders along the Nevsky Prospekt, the residences of the nobles and court officers, formed a barrier between the poor section of St. Petersburg and the magnificence of the court. The revolts became more frequent and more violent until they began to result in the loss of important lives. On March 1, 1881, just a few steps from the Field of Mars and Engineers' Castle, Czar Alexander II was killed by a group of insurgents.

His successor, Alexander III, began a period of ferocious repression and had the Church of the Resurrection (better known as the Church of Spilt Blood) built on the assassination spot. With an imaginative juxtaposition of architectural elements, it falls within the tradition of the onion-shaped dome architecture. Inside, the iconostasis, the canopy, and the floors are adorned with innumerable types of material, including Italian marbles, porphyry, Norwegian granite, and jasper. As the last great work in a city created out of nothing that became a triumph of European architecture, including styles from the Baroque to the Neo-Classical, the name of the church was sinisterly prophetic. As soon as it was completed, Nicholas II was forced to abdicate. The new Russia did not spare the Romanovs.

40 top One of the most majestic churches in St. Petersburg is Kazan Cathedral. It features an arch overlooking Nevsky Prospekt formed by 96 Corinthian columns arranged in four rows. Voronikhin's design was inspired by Bernini's colonnade at St. Peter's in Rome.

40 bottom left Designed by Auguste de Montferrand in 1818, the magnificent St. Isaac's Cathedral was built over a period of 40 years. Its gilded dome weighs 33,000 tons and can be seen from the Gulf of Finland.

40 bottom right Decorations in the cathedral include extraordinary ceiling and wall frescoes, many by Karl Bryullov, 14 different types of marble, and 43 types of precious and semi-precious stones. The interior of the church has a surface area of 43,000 square feet.

41 The Church of Spilt Blood is decorated with gold, marble, mosaics, and enameled ceramic tiles. It was built in 1883 for Alexander III on the spot where his predecessor, Alexander II, was assassinated.

The Kremlin and Red Square

RUSSIAN FEDERATION

MOSCOW
REGISTRATION: 1990
CRITERIA: C (I) (II) (IV) (VI)

With the collapse of the Soviet Union at the start of the 1990's, the President of the Russian Federation, Boris Yeltsin, launched a daring plan to restore the Great Palace to its original splendor. Built between 1838 and 1849 inside the Kremlin (from *kreml*, "fort") by architect Konstantin Thon for Nicholas I, the Great Palace – which cost the huge sum of 12 million rubles – was the former Imperial Palace of the czars and Russian princes until the Russian Revolution in October 1917.

Unable to bear the glorification of czarist Russia, Stalin had some of the most representative rooms of the era demolished between 1932 and 1934, including the rooms of St. Andrew and St. Alexander. In their place, the Supreme Soviet and representatives of the Russian Federation were installed in an area measuring 260 x 65 feet able to seat 3000. Thanks to photographs of the original design found in the royal archive in Windsor Castle in Great Britain, financing of 300 million dollars, and the work of 2500 people, the rooms were completed in 2000 with elaborate stucco decorations and gilded friezes. The Palace once more blazoned the magnificence of the Romanov dynasty.

Leaving aside the Napoleonic ambitions of the czars, it must be said that the Kremlin was for centuries the center of Russia's political and religious life. It was here that the czars, princes, and patriarchs of the Orthodox Church resided, and it was here that the czars continued to be crowned even after the capital was transferred to St. Petersburg by Peter the Great at the start of the eighteenth century. The majestic Red Square that lies in front of the Kremlin was the setting for the military parades that commemorated the October Revolution. And, it was in the Great Palace – despite Stalin's aversion – that Nikita Khrushchev honored Yuri Gagarin on his return from

42 top The red walls around the Kremlin are fortified by large towers. The side seen in the photograph, which faces Moscow, was the first to be built, with construction beginning in the fifteenth century.

42 center The Great Palace and the cathedral are seen here with the walls in the background. Built between 1838 and 1849, the majestic residence of the czars is the largest building in the Kremlin and has a surface area of 484,000 square feet.

MOSCOW

42 bottom The gilded domes of the Cathedral of the Annunciation and the façade of the Great Palace stand out against the background of modern Moscow.

42-43 There are four cathedrals in Sobornaya Square, the spiritual heart of the Kremlin. The origins of the Muscovite fort date from the eleventh century, but it was only at the end of the fifteenth, during the reign of Ivan III the Great, that the Kremlin began to take on its present appearance with the construction of the religious buildings and crenellated walls.

43 top The magnificent interior of the small Cathedral of the Archangel Michael, designed by the Italian architect Alvise il Nuovo, features columns and walls entirely covered with frescoes. The remains of Moscow's princes and czars are buried here.

space in 1961, following the first orbit of the Earth by man.

The oldest archaeological finds in the Moscow area date from the Bronze Age, but the first traces of a Slav settlement are no older than the eleventh century. This was the period during which construction of a fortified village was begun on an area that covered no more than 12 acres on Borovickaya hill, a promontory above the confluence of the Neglinnaya and Moskva rivers. In 1147 under the rule of Yuri Dolgoruky, the prince of Kiev, this first village expanded beyond the cramped enclosure, and it was during this period that the city of Moscow was officially founded. It was only in the fourteenth century, during the reign of Ivan Kalita, that the fort began to be considered a separate zone, an administrative nucleus of the town. In 1367-1368, Prince Dimitri Donskoy built a large fortress with white walls and tall towers, and as a result Moscow became known as "the white-walled city."

Between 1485 and 1495, when it was completely rebuilt by Ivan III the Great, Czar of all the Russias, the Kremlin began to take on its current appearance. The white walls were replaced by crenellated fortifications over a mile long along which 20 towers stand at the corners and the various entrances. The civil and religious buildings in the enclosed area (measuring 68 acres) date from different eras and were designed by architects of different nationalities. Some of the works were commissioned from Italian architects such as Marco Friazin, Pietro Antonio Solari, and Aristotele Fioravanti in the fifteenth and sixteenth centuries.

Entering the Kremlin by the Troickaya Tower, the second-most important, which faces onto Alexandrovsky Garden, the Arsenal, which is home to the Kremlin's military garrison, appears on the left. In front of the building, which was supposed to become a museum of the 1812 Patriotic War during the mid-nineteenth century, there are over 800 cannons captured from the Napoleonic army during that year. Next door there is the Senate, built between 1776 and 1787, which today is the residence of the President of the Russian Federation. The Palace of Congresses stands opposite these two buildings. Built in 1961 during the Soviet era, it is the only architectural complex in the Kremlin that seems out of place, but fortunately Khrushchev had it built 50 feet below ground level so as not to spoil the view of the other buildings.

Further on, a bell tower, completed in 1600 and, at 266 feet high, the tallest building in Russia at the time, dominates Ivanovskaya Square. At its base stands the "Czar Bell," a masterful bronze work by the founders of Moscow that, at 20 feet tall and

44

44 top left The large salon on the first floor of the Palace of Facets – the oldest civil building in the Kremlin – has a single square central column, and from this point all the frescoes on the vaults seem to come to life.

44 bottom left A room in Terem Palace decorated with floral motifs. Located next to the Palace of Facets, this building contains the ceremonial thrones and was the property of the reigning family.

weighing 220 tons, is the largest bell in the world. Following a fire in 1737, it fell from its support and broke in two. A century later, it was placed on a pedestal to commemorate the sad event. The nearby "Czar Cannon" also suffered an unfortunate fate: the largest cannon in the world with a 900-millimeter caliber and weighing 44 tons, it was withdrawn from service without ever having fired a shot.

In Sobornaya Square where Moscow's first church once stood, the spiritual and architectural heart of the Kremlin can be found. Constructed by Fioravanti between 1475 and 1479 for Ivan the Great, the Cathedral of the Assumption is the oldest and most imposing temple in the square. This is where the czars were crowned, the most important decrees read, and the metropolitans and patriarchs of Moscow buried. Behind the cathedral stands the small church of the Deposition of the Gown and, to its right, the church of the Twelve Apostles and the Patriarchal Palace. On the other sides of the square can be seen the Cathedral of the Annunciation and the Cathedral of the Archangel Michael, both with onion-shaped domes. Each one contains treasures of Russian iconic art and frescoes by masters such as Andrei Rublev.

Further on appear other palaces such as the Palace of Facets by M. Ruffo and Pietro Antonio Solari. This is the oldest civil building in the Kremlin and is named after the unusual white prismatic facets on its façade. Then, there is the Terem Palace, rebuilt in the seventeenth century by the early rulers of the Romanov dynasty, where a collection of ceremonial thrones is kept, and the Armory Museum, where the treasures of the czars are held and the Russian diamond collection.

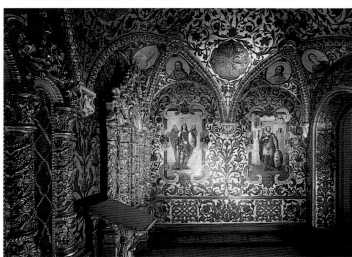

44-45 The czars used to receive their guests and advisors in the Gold Room in Terem Palace. Citizens could leave requests for their sovereign in a box in the petition window situated next to the throne.

45 top right The Boyar Room in Terem Palace was named after Russia's feudal lords. Boyars enjoyed great privileges and met in this room to settle disputes, discuss State administration, and, it is said, to hatch plots against the czar.

45 bottom right A view of the nineteenth-century frescoes on the east wall of the oratory in Terem Palace.

46-47 The nine domes of St. Basil's Cathedral represent the main Orthodox festivals.

46 bottom left Construction of the most famous of Moscow's monuments, St. Basil's Cathedral, was begun by Ivan the Terrible in 1552 to celebrate his victory over the Tatars.

46 bottom right Built completely in brick in accordance with Russian tradition, St. Basil's Cathedral also contains examples of wooden architecture. Inside, outstanding frescoes from the sixteenth century can also be found.

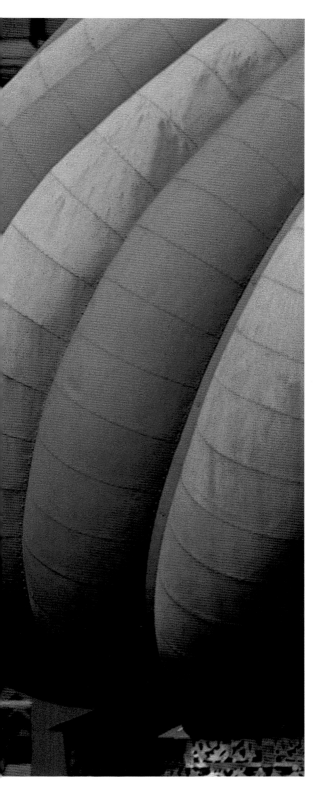

The section of the Kremlin that overlooks Red Square is dominated by Spasskaya Tower (Savior's Tower), built in 1491 by Pietro Antonio Solari for Ivan the Great and named for an icon on one of the walls. In the past, anyone entering the door had to take off their hat in a show of respect for the grandeur of the place.

Just in front of the tower stands the Church of the Intercession (or the Cathedral of St. Basil the Blessed), perhaps the most famous monument in Red Square. The square is not named after the Soviet power but from the term *krasnij*, Russian for "beautiful" and now used to mean "red." It was Ivan the Terrible who began construction of the cathedral to commemorate the taking of Kazan, the capital of the kingdom of the Tatars who had long raided and plundered Moscow. The basilica was designed by the Russian architects, Barma and Postnik, who built it on a plan of eight cylindrical chapels surrounding the ninth and largest, covered by a sloping roof. Each chapel is dedicated to one of the Orthodox festivals.

Completing the perimeter of the square are Neoclassical buildings like the one that has housed Moscow's first large shop, Gum, since 1893. With the collapse of the Soviet Union, traces of the Soviet regime have slowly disappeared. Though Lenin's Tomb is still located in the Senate Tower, recently Red Square has also seen two "old novelties" reappear which had been removed in the 1920's. These are the Church of the Madonna of Kazan and the doors of the Resurrection, wh ich, until 1995, had been moved to allow the tanks to pass during the large military procession held each November seventh.

47 top Outlined against St. Basil's, we see a night view of Spasskaya (Savior's) Tower, which stands opposite Red Square at the most important of the 20 entrances to the Kremlin. The clock bells were heard for the first time in 1625.

47 bottom Red Square (the name comes from the Russian word krasnij, meaning "beautiful") was the main trading area in Moscow. It used to be separated from the Kremlin by a deep ditch. To enter the fort, there were two bridges where Spasskaya and Nikolskaya Towers stand.

The Historic Center of Tallinn

ESTONIA

PROVINCE OF HARJUMAA
REGISTRATION: 1997
CRITERIA: C (II) (IV)

48 top The origins of Tallinn are uncertain, but a city was probably founded here during the Middle Ages. The first-known record of the Estonian capital was written by the Arab geographer, al-Ibrisi.

48 bottom The outline of the Alexander Nevsky Cathedral stands out against the old city and the bell towers of the churches of St. Mary and St. Nicholas.

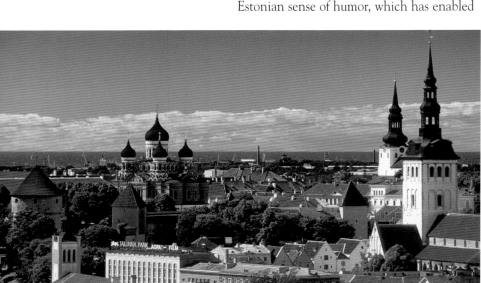

48-49 The historic center of Tallinn features walls built in the twelfth and thirteenth centuries that stand 49 to 52 feet high and stretch for one and a half miles. Despite their age, they are still in excellent condition.

At 151 feet high, the Kiek in de Kök is the highest tower in Tallinn's defensive wall. Its name literally means "a peek in the kitchen" because it is said that from the slits in the walls it was possible to spy on the feeding habits of the inhabitants. The northern entrance to the city is protected by a squat tower known as Paks Margareeta, or "Fat Margaret."

To climb to the Toompea, the upper city, one can follow the Pikk Jalg (long leg), which is a road that rises gradually as it follows the line of the walls. Alternatively, it is possible to take the more strenuous Lühike Jalg (short leg). These names exemplify the Estonian sense of humor, which has enabled them to survive the various invasions that have marked their history.

The first documentation of the existence of Tallinn was written by the Arab geographer, al-Ibrisi, who, in 1154, marked on a map a place called Qualeveni that corresponds to the present location of the city. The name Qualeveni is derived from that of Kalev, the legendary hero that the Estonians identify as their forefather. In 1219, the ships of King Waldemar II of Denmark arrived bearing the troops who subjugated the Estonians and made Qualeveni a military and commercial port. A fort was built, a bishopric was created, and the city was renamed Tallinn, from *taani linn*, meaning "city of the Danes."

In 1227 the Teutonic Knights arrived, but in 1238 Tallinn was again occupied by the Danes, and in 1258 it joined the Hanseatic League, becoming one of the main trading centers in northern Europe. As the wealth of the city's dominators increased, the discontent of the Estonians grew. In 1343 following one of innumerable popular revolts, the Danes ceded Tallinn to the Teutonic Knights once more, this time in exchange for 19,000 silver marks. The new rulers reigned unchallenged until the time of the Reformation, which heralded tensions that found their outlet in 1577 with the arrival of the Muscovites. The Swedes came to help oppose the Muscovites and defeated the army of Ivan the Terrible.

Under the Scandinavian monarchy, the fortunes of Tallinn began to wane. In 1710, the Russian czar Peter the Great took possession of the city, which was to remain almost isolated until the end of the nineteenth century when the railway was built that connected it with St. Petersburg and Moscow. This period also saw a strengthening of the patriotic spirit of the Estonians who took advantage of the October Revolution in 1917 to declare, the following February, the birth of the free Republic of Estonia. The dream came to an end in 1941 with the Nazi invasion, which was followed by dreadful bombardments and Soviet occupation.

In the decades that followed, the country was affected strongly by Russian influence

49 top Alexander Nevsky Cathedral was built between 1894 and 1901. It represents the center of the Estonian Orthodox Church and dominates Toompea, the "upper city."

49 bottom The cathedral is decorated with fine mosaics on the outside walls and ancient icons and paintings inside, including excellent altar pictures.

on the industrial development of the port. Although native Estonians only represented 47 percent of the population when the Soviet Union collapsed, independence was finally theirs.

The changing fortunes of Tallinn have had a very limited effect on the quality of the architecture in the historic center inside the city walls. The castle, on Toompea Hill, was built by the Teutonic Knights in 1229 on the foundations of the Danish fort and reorganized by the Russians in the eighteenth century. Opposite the castle stands the Orthodox cathedral of Alexander Nevsky, which, in spite of its lovely design, onion-shaped domes, mosaics on the façade, and many icons inside, has always represented the hated Russian dominion. This connection was so strongly felt that, in 1930, the Estonians devised a plan to move the building outside the city. A short distance away stands Toomkirik (St. Mary's

Church), built by the Danes in 1240 and rebuilt in the sixteenth century in Late Gothic style.

In the Old City – the lower section of Tallinn – the Church of St. Nicholas can be found, built in 1315 and rebuilt a century later, thanks to the donations of merchants belonging to the Hanseatic League, after a fire. The items of the greatest artistic value inside are the altar with a dual altarpiece by the master of Lubeck, Herman Rode, and *Danse Macabre* by the painter Bernt Notcke.

In the nearby square, Raekoja Plats, stands the only intact Gothic city hall in northern Europe. This is where the Pikk Jalg starts, the main pedestrian street in old Tallinn, lined with buildings with Gothic façades that housed the guilds of the Hanseatic League. The most impressive is number 17, the Great Guildhall, now the seat of The Historical Museum. The Guild of the Brotherhood of Black Knights stands at number 20, a late sixteenth-century palace built in Renaissance style. This congregation had the difficult task of defending the city and – perhaps not by chance – was the last guild to be suppressed, in 1940.

50 top left and right Many historic buildings face onto the Municipal Square (left) and the old city (right). The most important are the Gothic buildings where the Guilds of the Hanseatic League were based.

50-51 Towers along the ancient city walls dominate the approaches to the historic center. Eighteen of the original 60 that protected Tallinn in the sixteenth century have survived to the present day.

51 top left The architecture of this palace that dominates the Raekoja Plats resembles a religious building. In fact, it is Tallinn City Hall, the only Gothic building of this type to have been conserved in northern Europe.

51 top right Built in 1315 by German merchants who had settled in Tallinn, St. Nicholas's Church was heavily damaged in the sixteenth century during the iconoclastic period. After suffering from bomb damage in World War II, it was rebuilt and then turned into a museum and concert hall.

The Historic Center of Riga

LATVIA

REGISTRATION: 1997
CRITERIA: C (I) (II)

In 1970 Leonid Brezhnev conferred the Soviet Union's highest honor, the Order of Lenin, on Riga for the city's contribution to economic growth. Leaving rhetoric aside, the nomenclature of the Communist Party had made the Latvian capital a model of progress and considered it a credit to the country.

Since its foundation, the nearby states had fought over the important port on the river Daugava. Officially, Riga was founded in 1201 by Bishop Albert of Brema. In just a few years, the *Fratres militiae* Christi of the

evident from the outside, but the interior has been retouched over the centuries in Gothic, Renaissance, Baroque, and Neoclassical styles. In 1884, it was enhanced by what, at the time, was the largest organ in the world, with 6718 pipes made from wood and metal. Three other churches built under the Holy Roman Empire still remain in Riga: St. Peter's (1209), St. Jacob's (1226) and St. John's (1234).

The advent of the Reformation marked the end of German domination over the

enterprising prelate conquered all of Livonia (this territory covered modern Latvia and southern Estonia) and turned it into a German feud. During the thirteenth century, the city flourished thanks to the trading of skins, wheat, fish, wood, and the highly-valued amber, and in 1282 it entered the Hanseatic League, the powerful confederation of merchant cities that dominated the Baltic and North Seas.

During this period of prosperity, the cathedral was built, between 1211 and 1271. The original Romanesque style is still

city, and it was conquered in 1582 by the king of Poland, Stefan Bathory; forty years later it passed into Swedish hands. The enlightened Scandinavian monarchy fostered substantial economic, social, and cultural development but this too was short-lived. In 1710, the troops of Peter the Great of Russia entered Riga to initiate a reign that was to last until 1918, when independence was gained. This breathing space was lost at the start of World War II when the country was again occupied by the Germans.

52 left An aerial view of the city. In the foreground we see the bell tower of St. Jacob's Cathedral, which was founded in 1226 and consecrated to the Catholic faith. Behind it is the bell tower of St. Peter's Church that, at 236 feet high, is Riga's lookout tower.

52 right Surrounded by a park and excellent Jugendstil buildings, the elaborate palace houses the

Planetarium. Its domes and decorations imitate the style of czarist Russia.

52-53 The historic center from the Daugava River. The city boasts eleven parks and many elegant bell towers. The largest tower is that of the cathedral, the biggest religious building in the Baltic countries. Despite its many renovations, its exterior retains a Romanesque quality.

53 bottom left One of the nearly 1,000 buildings from the early twentieth century in the city center. With Latvia's independence, many of these were purchased by foreign companies who have returned them to their original splendor.

53 bottom right The large brick building housing the Latvian Academy of Arts. Opened in 1905, it has a museum with a fine collection of paintings by Latvian and Russian artists.

54 top Riga underwent notable expansion at the start of the twentieth century. The new city plan included wide boulevards lined with opulent mansions, like those in the photograph. The most imaginative were the work of Michail Eisenstein.

54-55 Typical houses in Skarnu Jela (Butchers' Street) in the city center. Note the small church dedicated to St. John, founded in 1234. Its pediment is the only example of Gothic architecture in Riga.

55 top An aerial view of the historic center with its pastel-colored house façades. In the seventeenth century, Riga was a flourishing trading city and its merchants, associated in guilds, built lovely homes that were also used as stores.

55 bottom left Built in 1330 by the Knights of the Order of Livonia, the castle is now home to the Museum of Latvian History, the Museum of the History of Literature, and the Museum of Foreign Art. Its tower affords a good view of the riverbank.

Riga continually assumed the character of a city of international standing. With a population of half a million, it boasted an intellectual class linked prevalently to the world of music, and was chosen by Richard Wagner as a refuge between 1837 and 1839 when he fled his homeland to avoid debts he had contracted.

In the mid-nineteenth century, Czar Alexander II decided to change the face of the city; he demolished the walls and launched the architectural revolution that was to give Riga its uniqueness and

55 bottom right The splendid buildings and towers of the Small and Large Guilds. The original structure was built in the fourteenth century, but in the mid-nineteenth century the complex was restored in an inventive English Neo-Gothic style.

culminate a few decades later in the triumph of Jugendstil, or Art Nouveau. This style merged architecture, painting, and sculpture to form a combination of decoration and functionality. The buildings in Riga's historic center have geometrical and curved façades, floral and animal motifs, and masks and figures sculpted at the street corners.

All this symbolized the spirit of the age, with its emotional intensity shot through with modernity.

Riga has a thousand or so Jugendstil buildings designed by different architects:

the most representative are to be seen in Alberta, Elizabetes, Antonijas, and Tallinas streets. These include the masterpiece by Michail Eisenstein, father of Sergei, the film director of *The Battleship Potemkin*, which is a residential building that stands at 13, Alberta Jela. It was built in 1904 for a Chancellor of State named Lebedinsky. Like the other façades designed by Eisenstein, it alternates iron and wood volutes in bow windows with statues and majolica bas-reliefs on several floors to create a theatrical and dramatic effect.

Given to the Soviet Union after the end of the war, Riga was subjected to a strong process of Russianization. People from the other republics in the Soviet Union emigrated there and monumental buildings were built in Stalinist style, though they did not spoil the architectural heritage of the historic center. With independence in 1990 and the introduction of a market economy, at least one third of the Art Nouveau buildings have been sold to western companies who have indulged in restoration work, though not always conservative in nature.

Ironbridge Gorge

GREAT BRITAIN

RIVER SEVERN, SHROPSHIRE,
ENGLAND
REGISTRATION: 1986
CRITERIA: C (I) (II) (IV) (VI)

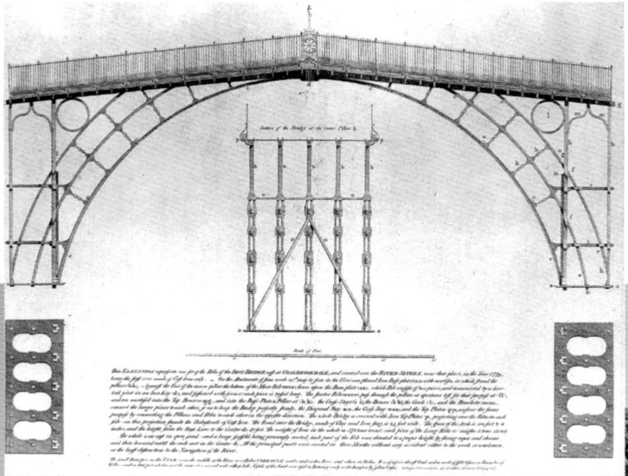

"Arriving in Coalbrookdale is like entering a circle of Hell. A dense column of smoke rises from the entrails of the earth; the machines spew clouds of steam; a black cloud rises from the smokestack of the foundry. In the middle of this darkness I descended towards the banks of the Severn, which flows placidly between two tall hills, and I found myself before a bridge built entirely of iron. Night was falling and the view seemed like a door that opened onto mystery." This was the description of Ironbridge Gorge by an anonymous Italian traveler in 1787. The gorges of the Severn, Great Britain's longest river which runs for almost 210 miles through the heart of England, are rich in coal and iron. At the start of the eighteenth century, they were the setting for the dawn of the Industrial Revolution. It was here that Abraham Darby I, a Quaker and the owner of an ironworks, found a method to lower the costs of production while improving the quality of the iron by combining it with carbon coke creating an alloy – cast iron – which he patented in 1707. As a result of this invention, the region of Coalbrookdale, named after Darby's company, was transformed into one of the most heavily industrialized areas in the world. In the space of a few years, the Severn became the second most congested river in Europe in terms of river traffic, and the factories that had been built there began to turn out machinery of every description. John Wilkinson built the first boat with a metal hull, and James Watt cast the cylinders for his steam-powered engines. The fortunes of the iron industry ensured that the region attracted engineers and workers. Houses, schools, churches, and banks were built for

56 top left *The architect Thomas Farnolls Pritchard (1723-1777) – portrayed here – suggested building a bridge over the river Severn to facilitate transportation of industrial products to Shropshire.*

the new inhabitants, thus creating the new village of Coalport. After the mid-eighteenth century, however, the generous banks of the Severn became an obstacle to development, and the architect Thomas Pritchard suggested building a bridge to facilitate access to the factories and to avoid the caprices of the climate that often prevented river crossings. In the year 1773, Abraham Darby III, the grandson of the inventor of cast iron, presented a plan that had taken him two

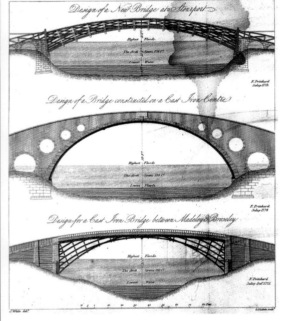

impressive structure had immediately aroused the interest of engineers and travelers from all over the world and the area had become a place of "pilgrimage" for gentlemen of the era. Abraham Darby III received a flood of orders for bridges like Ironbridge, from Wales to Jamaica. However, the marvel of progress soon seemed to be in danger. Already by 1782 the bridge began to suffer structural problems, although, surprisingly, it was the only bridge to withstand the flooding of the River Severn in 1795. Only seven years later, a long series of rebuilding work began. In 1926, the idea to demolition it was first proposed, partly because in the meantime industrial production had ceased. In 1930, the Ironbridge was closed to traffic.

Miraculously, salvation arrived in 1967 with the setting up of the Ironbridge Gorge Trust, a foundation whose purpose is to safeguard the historical heritage of the Industrial Revolution. Two years later, one of the largest open air museums in Great Britain was opened in the offices of the Coalbrookdale Company and some of the houses of Coalport, in which people dressed in period costume re-evoking the days of the area's prosperity.

56-57 *To recover the costs of construction, a toll was required to transport goods across the bridge since it was first opened. Soon, however, the Ironbridge began to suffer structural damage due to the frequent floodwaters of the river Severn. Since 1930, it has only been open to foot traffic.*

57 center *The fame of the Ironbridge resulted in the factories in Coalbrookdale receiving a great many orders for the production of bridges at the end of the eighteenth century. This picture shows three different projects for structures in iron.*

57 bottom *A general view of the houses in Coalport, the village that grew up in the area around Coalbrookdale to house the factory's workers and their families. By the first half of the nineteenth century, the factory had over 2,000 workers.*

56 top right *A rare engraving of the bridge by William Ellis held in the Ironbridge Gorge Trust archives. The first in the world to be built from iron, the bridge over the Severn spans 102 feet and therefore did not prevent boats from passing on the river below.*

years of study, and which was to require a further two years before the work was finally undertaken. In 1779, the Ironbridge was eventually completed, the first cast-iron bridge in the world. It had a single span, was about 100 feet long, and weighed 423 tons overall. The production and building costs amounted to 6,000 pounds of that time, including 15 pounds to cover the beer offered free on the day it was inaugurated. No trace remains of the plans for the construction of the bridge in the Coalbrookdale archives, though curiously one has recently been discovered in Sweden, perhaps because the

Westminster Palace, Westminster Abbey, and St. Margaret's Church

GREAT BRITAIN

LONDON
REGISTRATION: 1987
CRITERIA: C (I) (II) (IV)

58 top The entrance to Westminster Hall. Built in the eleventh century at the time of Richard II for court entertainments, this room is the only part of Westminster Palace to have survived the disastrous fires of 1512 and 1854. Today Westminster Hall – which over the centuries has been a pivot of events in the kingdom – is used for important ceremonies.

58 bottom The Neo-Gothic spires on Westminster Palace. The building contains the Chambers of the Lords and the Commons and was designed by Sir Charles Barry in the early nineteenth century.

Each year, on the official opening of the British Parliament, a deputation of footmen in seventeenth-century costume performs a scrupulous search of the cellars of the Palace of Westminster. This ceremony commemorates the danger faced during the Gunpowder Plot in 1605 in which the Catholic Guy Fawkes and a group of followers attempted to blow up the seat of the Protestant British power.

For British citizens, the religious aspect of the story is an unending one. The history of the Palace of Westminster is 900 years long. Today the building is enormous, with 1200 rooms, 100 staircases, and nearly two miles of corridors, but little remains of the original building that was the principal residence of the English royal family from the middle of the eleventh century, under William I, to 1512, under Henry VIII. In 1512, a fire destroyed most of the original palace, with the exception of the medieval Westminster Hall, St. Stephen's Chapel, and the Jewel Tower, the latter built in 1366 to hold the monarch's private possessions. With reconstruction, the building became the House of Lords, whereas St. Stephen's Chapel was converted to the House of Commons.

The palace was once again reduced to ashes in 1834, but on this occasion, too, Westminster Hall was spared. The design for a new home for the Parliament was the work of Sir Charles Barry who, in tribute to the nearby Westminster Abbey, produced a Neo-Gothic construction. Seriously damaged by German bombing raids in World War II, the palace was restored in 1948-50 following Sir Charles' designs to the letter.

The focus of the complex is the huge octagonal room entered through the principal entrance, St. Stephen's, a masterpiece of Victorian architecture. From here two corridors depart: the north corridor leads to the House of Lords and the south corridor to the House of Commons. The House of Lords was built in 1847. It is an ornate chamber measuring 79 by 46 feet that contains an imposing Neo-Gothic throne on which the Queen sits when she makes her speech at the opening of Parliament each November. The House of Commons, on the other hand, measures 69 by 46 feet and reflects the style of St. Stephen's Chapel. The members sit in rows, the majority party on one side of the hall and the opposing minority party on the other. The center of the room is occupied by the table on which the symbol of royal power, the mace, is placed during parliamentary sessions. Beneath the table, there is a carpet on which two red lines are

58-59 Westminster Palace seen from Westminster Bridge over the Thames. The world's most famous clock tower, Big Ben, stands to the north of the building. The name Big Ben was originally given to the 14-ton bell that has struck the hour uninterruptedly since it was installed in 1859.

marked at a distance of two sword-lengths. The members of the House are not allowed to cross these lines in order to prevent the debate from degenerating into disorder.

Westminster Hall was built in 1097 but its magnificent beamed roof is from the fourteenth century. The Hall covers roughly 16,000 square feet and was used originally for coronation banquets. Over the centuries it has been used for State trials – for example, those of Sir Thomas More and the Gunpowder Plot

the name commonly given to the clock tower that has become the symbol of London. Built in Neo-Gothic style and inaugurated in 1859, it is named after its 14-ton bell that strikes the hour. The four clocks, one on each side, each have a diameter of 26 feet. To reach the top, 322 feet high, there is a flight of 334 steps. From the tower, the view takes in the enormous Westminster Abbey, an architectural masterpiece with Gothic spires, whose construction spans the thirteenth to sixteenth centuries.

59 top right This equestrian statue of Richard I, who was killed in battle in 1199, was raised in front of the east face of Westminster Palace in 1860.

59 center right Niches holding elegant statues and other Neo-Gothic decorations adorn the façade of Westminster Palace. It was built in this style in tribute to nearby Westminster Abbey.

conspirators – and, on those occasions, filled with peddlers and goods, it became a center of London social life. Today it is used for the most important public ceremonies such as the Silver Jubilee of Her Majesty, Queen Elizabeth II, in 1977, then for the fiftieth anniversary of the United Nations in 1995, and a year later for the meeting of the South African President, Nelson Mandela, with the two Chambers of Parliament.

At the extreme north stands Big Ben,

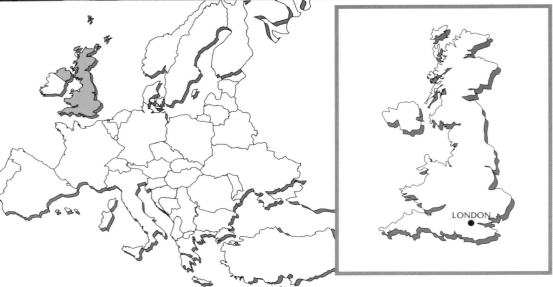

LONDON

Originally a Benedictine monastery, the Abbey was incorporated into the Westminster Palace complex by King Edward the Confessor in 1065. A year later, William the Conqueror was crowned there upon reaching London after winning the Battle of Hastings, but that building burned to the ground in 1298.

Soon after, Henry III had a new building designed by Henry de Reyns. This was the golden period of French Gothic and the architect was sent across the Channel to learn the secrets of the masters of Chartres and Amiens Cathedrals. On his return, de Reyns produced an extraordinary

building with large windows, but these, unfortunately, have been destroyed.

The nave, which measures 505 feet in length and 112 feet in both width and height, is the largest in Great Britain. It leads to the High Altar, under which Edward the Confessor is buried. The south aisle leads to the large cloister in front of the Chapter House, the octagonal room with a vault supported by a single pillar where the English Parliament first used to sit.

Since the thirteenth century, the building has undergone many renovations and additional building work; the more important interventions were the vaulted ceiling added in 1506 and the Neo-Gothic façade from the eighteenth century that includes two slender bell towers 223 feet tall. Restoration work on the exterior (lasting 25 years and concluded in 1998) included the addition to the niches above the main entrance of statues that represent

the modern martyrs of Christianity, the victims of oppression and persecution in the twentieth century.

The most important events in English and British history are celebrated within the walls of Westminster Abbey. Since William the Conqueror – with the exceptions only of Edward V and Edward VII, neither of whom were crowned – the British monarchs have always been crowned in the Abbey. During the last coronation, that of Elizabeth II on 2 June 1953, the Abbey held 8200 people.

The coronation throne was made from oak in 1307 during the reign of Edward I. Representations of the king are included in its decorations, portraying him standing on a lion and surrounded by motifs of plants and birds. The throne was built to fit over the Stone of Scone, a stone associated with the crowning of Scottish monarchs, which was taken from the Scots in 1296 and remained at Westminster for 700 years before it was

restored in a solemn ceremony to its legitimate owners by Prime Minister John Major on November 13, 1996.

The political and religious importance of the Abbey meant that Elizabeth I, daughter of Henry VIII – the king responsible for the break with the Catholic Church – reformed its statute by conferring upon it a "royal peculiarity." This brought the Abbey under the jurisdiction of the monarchy and, in consequence, its political role grew. The same status was granted to the adjacent St. Margaret's church, built in the eleventh century and rebuilt in Perpendicular Gothic style 300 years later.

Even today, St. Margaret's is the "parish church of the House of Commons," and its role is to represent the union of Church and Parliament.

Westminster Abbey was also, until the end of the eighteenth century, a place of royal burial. In the center of the Lady Chapel, a masterpiece of Tudor style dating from the start of the sixteenth century and built for the burial of Henry VII, there is the splendid marble tomb of Elizabeth I, carved in 1605 by sculptor Maximilian Colt. Next to Elizabeth lies her half-sister Mary I, imprisoned in the Tower of London and beheaded by Elizabeth in 1558, and Bloody

Mary, also known as Mary of Scotland.

In addition to the many monarchs, Westminster Abbey is the resting place of many of the most famous individuals in British history, 3300 in total. In Poets' Corner there are the funerary monuments of Geoffrey Chaucer, William Shakespeare, Charles Dickens, Rudyard Kipling, and George Byron, just to mention the most famous. Elsewhere there are politicians, scientists like Charles Darwin and Isaac Newton, actors like Lawrence Olivier, and national heroes. St. George's Chapel is dedicated to the RAF pilots who died in World War I.

The only "common citizen" to be honored with a tomb in the most important church in Great Britain is Thomas Parr. In 1653, King Charles I wished to honor the memory of one of his subjects who, it is said, lived to the age of 153 years and 9 months, a lifetime that spanned the reigns of ten monarchs.

60 left Poets' Corner in the south transept, where the most important writers in British history are buried, is one of the most visited sections of the Abbey. The first writer interred was Geoffrey Chaucer, while the body of William Shakespeare, who died in 1616 in Stratford-upon-Avon, was transferred here in 1740. The scandalous life led by Lord George Byron meant that he was only admitted to the Abbey in 1969, over 100 years after his death.

60 center The choir was designed by Edward Blore in the mid-nineteenth century in Victorian Gothic. It stands in the nave of Westminster Abbey, which at 111 feet tall is the highest in England.

60 right The oak coronation throne in St. Edward's Chapel was made in 1300 by Edward I. It is decorated with leaves, birds, and animal motifs, and the back shows the monarch reposing on lions.

61 top The austere Gothic façade of Westminster Abbey. Its towers are 223 feet tall and the whole building covers an area of 31,980 square feet. William the Conqueror was the first ruler crowned here on Christmas Day 1066. The Abbey held 8,300 people on the day of Elizabeth II's coronation in 1953.

61 bottom A detail of one of the many lovely windows in Westminster Abbey, many of which were made over the last two centuries. The set of buildings holds many works of art. The Abbey Museum contains an extraordinary collection of royal effigies.

Canterbury Cathedral

SAINT AUGUSTINE'S ABBEY AND SAINT MARTIN'S CHURCH

GREAT BRITAIN

COUNTY OF KENT, ENGLAND
REGISTRATION: 1988
CRITERIA: C (I) (II) (VI)

62-63 *The façade of Canterbury Cathedral. Construction was begun in 1077 by the Norman archbishop Lanfranc, but it has since been enlarged and rebuilt several times so that the architecture is a sort of compendium of medieval styles.*

From his pulpit in Canterbury Cathedral on Christmas Day 1170, the Archbishop of Canterbury, Thomas Becket, issued the order of excommunication against the Archbishop of York and the bishops who had taken part in the crowning of Henry II's young heir. With this act, supported and followed by Pope Alexander III, Becket reacted to the offence perpetrated by the king who had flagrantly breached the

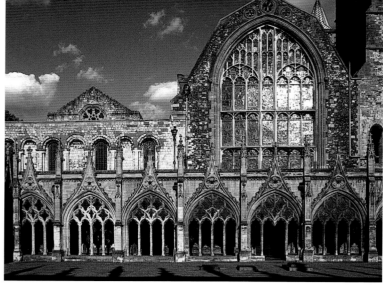

62 bottom The north side of the cathedral where the Great Cloister stands. This was the center of monastic life during the period when Canterbury hosted a Benedictine community. Next to it stands the Chapter House, which owes its name to the fact that each morning the monks gathered there to read the Chapter of the Rule of St. Benedict.

63 top left The Great Cloister. Although its construction dates from the time of Archbishop Lanfranc, its current appearance is the result of remodeling in elegant Gothic style in the thirteenth and fourteenth centuries.

63 center right The pointed arch structure of the gallery in the Great Cloister is Gothic. The Benedictine community in Canterbury was active until the mid-sixteenth century when Henry VIII broke with Rome and ordered the suppression of all monastic orders.

63 bottom right The statue of Jesus on Christ Church Gate, the main entrance to the cathedral.

63

immemorial right of Canterbury to hold the coronation ceremonies. This was neither the first nor the last of the episodes in the struggle between the monarch and the Church. Four days later, the conflict between Henry II and Becket reached its tragic end in the cathedral when four knights, hoping to win glory in the eyes of the king, killed the archbishop.

The deed, however, did not bring royal satisfaction but instead made Canterbury Cathedral famous, immediately becoming one of the most important places of pilgrimage in medieval Europe. In remorse, Henry II himself made the utmost effort to communicate and preserve the memory of his bitter opponent throughout every corner of Christendom. Thomas Becket's fame reached its pinnacle with the publication of *The Canterbury Tales* written by Geoffrey Chaucer in 1387.

The history of Canterbury began in 597 when Pope Gregory the Great sent the Benedictine monk, Augustine, across the Channel to convert the Angles. The mission became successful when King Ethelbert of Kent allowed himself to be baptized, quickly followed by many of his subjects. In Canterbury, Augustine founded a monastery in the center of which he built a church. The cathedral was later built on the foundations of this original house of worship. The monastery was enlarged and continued to be active until the middle of the sixteenth century when Henry VIII, having broken off relations with Rome, decided to suppress the monastic orders.

The small church dedicated to St. Martin also probably dates from the time of Augustine. It stands on a hill to the east of the cathedral and is considered to be the Mother Church by the Anglican community.

Lanfranc, the first Norman Archbishop of Canterbury, initiated the construction of the cathedral in 1077, but the work continued until the end of the Middle Ages. Of that first construction, only the crypt in late Romanesque style has survived to the modern day, adorned with carved colonettes and rare wall-paintings dated around 1160.

Following the devastating fire of 1174, the remaining Romanesque architecture was altered by the addition of what are considered masterpieces of English Gothic. These include the eastern side and the immense choir, the longest in England, which culminates in the Trinity Chapel built to hold the shrine of Thomas Becket.

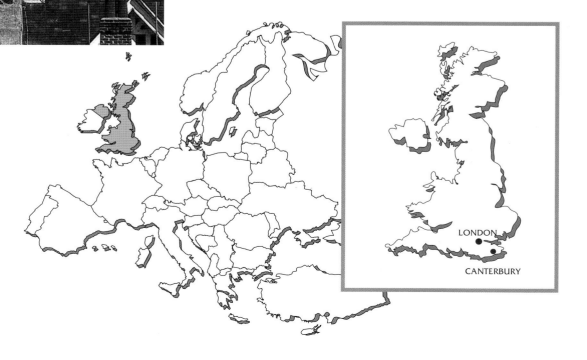

LONDON

CANTERBURY

Later, Canterbury was to accommodate other tombs, in particular, that of Edward III, the Prince of Wales, known as the Black Prince.

The stained glass windows are also from the end of the twelfth century and rival those of Chartres and Bourges for beauty. They illustrate episodes from the Old and New Testaments in such a way as to show how the events of the former were preparations for those in the latter, with an inspiration based on the *Biblia pauperum*, the most popular of the medieval religious texts.

The nave, 558 feet long, and the western part of the cathedral escaped the destruction of the fire but were rebuilt at the end of the fourteenth century in accordance with the canons of the Perpendicular style, developed in response to the extreme forms of Flamboyant Gothic. Examples are the pointed vaults to be seen in the interior and most particularly in the towers including Canterbury's unique pride, the magnificent Bell Harry Tower built in 1496.

Canterbury played a political and religious role of major importance during the Anglican Reformation, thanks to a succession of archbishops of great personality. In 1642, during the Civil War, the cathedral was plundered by Puritans and the Chapter was dissolved, but the return of the monarchy restored the cathedral's prestige. The building's true rebirth, however, occurred thanks to restoration work in the twentieth century. As a result, the popularity of pilgrimage to the city increased and interest in religious music was renewed, of which Canterbury is one of the liveliest centers.

64 left St. Michael's Chapel, also known as Warriors' Chapel, contains tombs of military commanders and the colors of the Queen's Regiment.

64-65 Trinity Chapel was built four years after the murder of Thomas Becket (1170) to hold his tomb, but the tomb was destroyed in 1538 on the orders of Henry VIII. Since then, in commemoration of the archbishop, the Altar of Sword Point was established in which there is a single, perpetually burning candle.

65 top left The late-Romanesque crypt is adorned with finely carved capitals and rare wall paintings. It is the only part of Lanfranc's cathedral to have survived the devastating fire of 1174.

65 top right A detail of the splendid tomb of Edward, Prince of Wales (1330-1376), the son of Edward III and known as the Black Prince. The tomb is one of the cathedral's sculptural masterpieces.

65 bottom right The windows are one of the cathedral's greatest treasures. Many of the original thirteenth-century windows made by English and French craftsmen (thanks to donations by pilgrims) have been destroyed. Those remaining in Trinity Chapel represent images of the life and miracles of Thomas Becket. Those on the walls of the choir contain an extraordinary Bibli Pauperum.

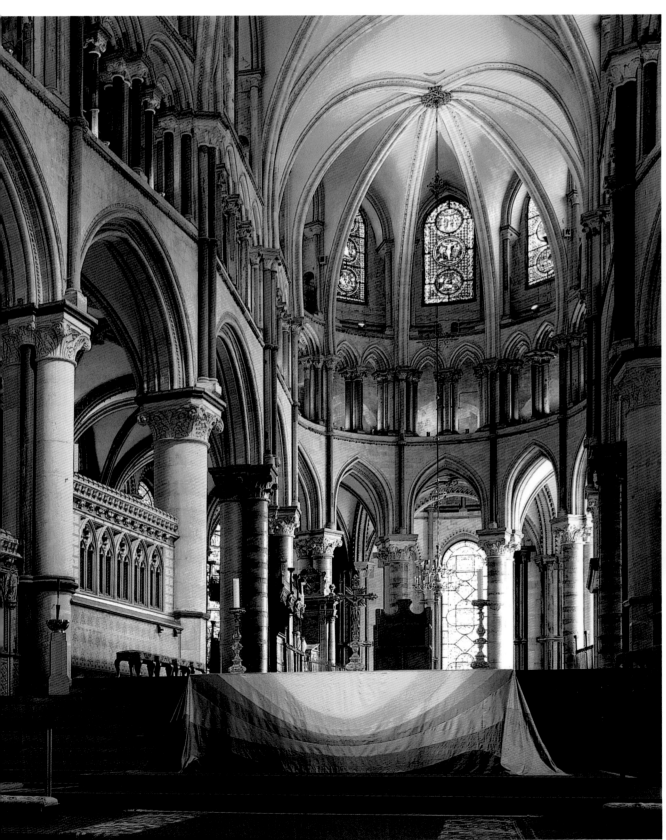

The Mill Network at Kinderdijk-Ellshout

ALBLASSERWAARD, NEAR DODRECHT
REGISTRATION: 1997
CRITERIA: C (I) (II) (IV)

THE NETHERLANDS

"God created the world but the Dutch created Holland," said Descartes, the French philosopher who lived for a certain amount of time in the Netherlands. But, his love for the country had deceived him: evidence now shows that many areas subsequently invaded by the sea had been inhabited 5000 years ago. Nonetheless, the battle fought by the Dutch against the sea has spanned many centuries.

The first drainage canals were built along the Alblasserwaard polder in the eleventh century, and just 100 years later a dike surrounded the entire area, including the basin of the Alblass and the Giessen, the two rivers that cross this region of the southern Netherlands. Thus, the districts of Nederwaard (lower land) and Overwaard (upper land) were created, and in 1277 Count Floris V set up the Water and Polder Administration to maintain the dikes.

Yet, despite the efforts made, the area suffered a number of floods. The most tragic was referred to as "Elizabeth's flood," which occurred on the night of November 18, 1421; a violent storm caused a sudden

66-67 *The first eight brick mills were built in 1738 on the Nederwaard, which lies along the final stretch of the river Lek. The zone is enclosed by the Kinderdijk and measures 174 square miles.*

67 top *One of the eight octagonal wooden mills built on the Overwaard in 1740. Made obsolete by more modern water-pumping technologies, the Kinderdijk mills are operated every Saturday during the summer months to demonstrate their efficiency to visitors.*

rise in the level of the sea and as a result the banks overflowed and 60 villages were buried. The story goes that a cat miraculously saved a newborn baby by pushing its cradle to the highest point of a dike, which from then on has been known as Kinderdijk, or "child's dike." Kinderdijk became the final station of the waters in Alberblasserwaard, which covers an area of

174 square miles along the final stretch of the river Lek.

After at least thirty catastrophes, the last of which occurred in 1726, the authorities had to accept the insufficiency of their defenses and decided to build drainage mills. In 1738, the first series of eight brick mills was built in Nederwaard and followed two years later by eight more in Overwaard, but built this time in wood and on an octagonal plan. Over time, they were enlarged by the addition of new mills, barrages, and pumping stations.

Life in a windmill was very hard. They were inhabited by poor families with often at least ten children. Their livelihood was based on fishing and growing vegetables for their own subsistence. The prohibitive conditions of life were reflected in the architecture of the mills. The lower wheel and a large multi-purpose room (including the kitchen and beds of the parents and younger children) formed the ground floor. The beds of the other members of the family were located on the first floor, and the fish-smoking room occupied the second. The top floor was known as the "fat room" and housed most of the equipment for the mill's operation: the brake, the upper wheel, the main shaft, and the sliding blocks on which the dome turned.

The mill itself consisted of four vanes attached to a hub that was fixed to the dome and connected to the upper wheel. The long wooden shaft (up to 33 feet long) was rotated by the upper wheel, thereby turning the lower wheel and, through a series of gears, the wheel for draining the water. The dome rotated 360 degrees, allowing the

vanes to face any wind head-on. When the vanes began to turn, the draining wheel forced the water to flow towards a metal gate that separated the upper basin from the lower one. If the pressure on the gate exceeded the pressure of the water on the other side, the water in the lower basin would be forced through, thus draining the land. When the mill was in operation, the vanes were covered with canvas like a ship's sail that would tauten or slacken depending on the speed of the wind.

Of the 10,000 windmills built in the Netherlands to win back land from the sea, only about 900 remain, 19 of which are in Kinderdijk. Although their work has been supported by a steam-powered (and then diesel-powered) water scoop since 1869, they still function perfectly, as was demonstrated during World War II when a lack of fuel meant their services were required. Every Saturday during the summer months, the windmills of Kinderdijk are put into operation to rekindle the memory of the heroic age of the battle against the waters.

The Historic Town of

BELGIUM

REGION OF FLANDERS
REGISTRATION: 2000
CRITERIA: (II) (IV) (VI)

At 26 Walplein, in the heart of Brugge (known by the French-speaking Belgians as Bruges), you can taste the specialty of De Halve Maan, or "The Half Moon" brewery: Straffe Hendrik, a fermented beer made mainly of malt, hops, and special yeasts. During a guided tour, you'll discover that the brewery was listed in the city archives as early as 1564. In 1856, the Maes family took over the brewery, introducing modern production methods but also preserving the origins of this historic place. The entire town of Brugge, the leading

trade center of northern Europe from the fourteenth to sixteenth centuries, has preserved the features of its age-old tradition.

The history of the city dates from the early Christian era when a Gallic-Roman settlement was founded. Around the year 27, Germanic populations attacked the cities on the Flemish coast, but the Romans managed to keep a fort there until the fourth century. The city continued to grow, and by 650 it was one of the most important cities along the Flemish coast. It soon began to trade with Scandinavia. In the ninth century, Brugge – whose name is derived from the Old Norse word Bryggia, or "landing place" – started to

coin its own money and boasted a well-established center, the Burg.

Starting in the eleventh century, the city also began to develop in the areas now known as Steenstraat and Oude Burg outside the original district. These two areas are where Brugge's oldest parish churches are located. The Onze Lieve Vrouwekerk, or the Church of Our Lady, was started in 1220 and took two centuries to complete. It has white walls and bare columns, following the medieval style, whereas the side chapels, which were added later, are richly decorated in the Baroque style. The church is home to a sculpture of the *Madonna and Child*, carved by Michelangelo in the early sixteenth century. Purchased by a Flemish merchant, it was the only work by Michelangelo to leave Italy during the artist's lifetime. The Sint-Salvator Kathedraal, the Cathedral of the Holy Savior, was built as a church during the same period and was made a cathedral in 1788. This simple yellow-brick building has an enormous interior that is bare except for precious tapestries from Brussels and a valuable seventeenth-century organ.

In the thirteenth century, Flanders became one of the most densely populated regions in Europe, thanks also to the importance of Brugge, which attracted merchants from across all of Europe. The city exported valuable wools, crafts' shops were soon established, and the Flemish and Italians founded the city's first banks. Business burgeoned, but during the fourteenth century Brugge was shaken by the violent revolts of the lower classes. It prospered again in the fifteenth century, and culture and the arts also flourished with the creation of the Flemish school of

painting. The death of Queen Mary of Burgundy in 1482 and the ascent of her husband, Maximilian of Austria, to the throne triggered revolts that once again led the city to chaos. In 1600, Brugge surrendered its important position to Antwerp. Trade continued for many years, but slowly weakened. Bypassed completely by the industrial revolution, Brugge was the poorest city in Belgium by the middle of the nineteenth century.

The medieval city winds its way around the Burg, the political and religious center and the location of *Heilig Bloed Basiliek*, the Chapel of the Holy Blood, which hosts one of the most important reliquaries in Europe. It is divided into two sections. The Chapel of St. Basil on the lower floor has an arched nave and an entrance with stone pillars,

68 top right The spires of the Church of Our Lady (Onze Lieve Vrouwekerk) are the highest in Belgium. Built over a period of two hundred years beginning in 1220, this is the city's oldest parish church.

68 center left Detail of the façade of the basilica of the Holy Blood. It contains one of the most important reliquaries in Europe, the result of votive offerings made by merchants returning from trips to the Mediterranean.

68 bottom right The majestic Gothic vaults in St. Savior's Church. Other features are splendid wall hangings from Brussels, a Baroque organ decorated with angels, and many paintings from the Flemish school.

69 The Burg has retained its medieval character. It was the political and religious center of Brugge and the heart of the European trading network from the fourteenth to the sixteenth centuries.

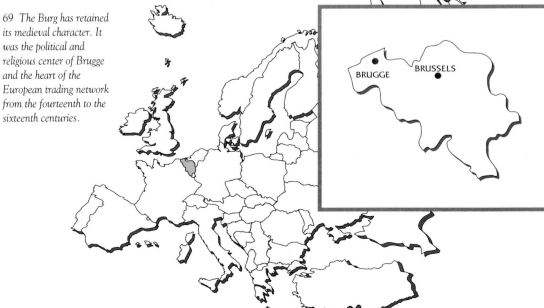

while the upper chapel houses a vase that is said to contain drops of blood and water from the body of Christ. Located near the church are the ancient Registry Hall, the Provost's House, built in the seventeenth century at the height of the Baroque movement, and the Town Hall, which was built between 1376 and 1420 and is one of the city's oldest Gothic public buildings. Brugge's most important square has always been the Markt, which is lined by the luxurious town houses of merchants from the city's golden age.

The old Hospital of St. John stands on Mariastraat outside the Burg. Built in the thirteenth century, it remained open for six hundred years. Six masterpieces by the painter Hans Memling are exhibited in its church and in the adjacent chapel. Other paintings can be seen in the wards and, naturally, at the Groeninge Museum, together with works by Rogier van der Weyden, Jan van Eyck, Hieronymus Bosch, and Pieter Bruegel the Younger, proof that Brugge was also a major center of European art.

70 top Quai du Rosaire is one of Brugge's loveliest streets. Untouched by bombardments during either World War, the city has adopted a hard line in conservation. The traffic in the city center is strictly limited and billboards are prohibited.

70 bottom The medieval buildings in Quai du Rosaire are reflected in the Dijver, one of the city's waterways. Brugge's layout has not undergone substantial modification since the fifteenth century when the Dukes of Burgundy ruled the city.

70-71 A view from the bell tower. The medieval houses of the richer merchants face the Markt (market square). Most of these residences date from the fourteenth and fifteenth centuries.

71 bottom left Built on Mariastraat in the thirteenth century, St. Jans Hospital remained the city hospital until 1976.

71 bottom right A night view of the Markt overlooked by the Beffroi (Belfort in French), the octagonal bell tower built in the thirteenth century.

The Major Town Houses of the Architect Victor Horta

BELGIUM

BRUSSELS
REGISTRATION: 2000
CRITERIA: C (I) (II) (IV)

72 left A triumph of Art Nouveau, Maison van Eetvelde was built in avenue Palmerston in 1895. Although the façade does not betray the daring lines of the interior, Horta established his new architectural style with the construction of this building.

72 bottom right Maison Tassel in Rue Paul Emile Janson was the first house in which Victor Horta broke with architectural tradition and began his journey that led to Art Nouveau.

The old shoe-repairer Pierre Horta must have had a nasty surprise when his favorite son, twelve year-old Victor, was expelled from the vocal instruction course at Ghent Conservatory. It was 1873 and the boy had only just entered the prestigious college. Already all hopes for the future had been dashed.

Like so many other rejections, Victor Horta's was providential, as he was led to begin a course of architecture at the Académie des Beaux Arts where he remained until 1877. Brilliant and restless, after a short stay in Paris he returned to Belgium where he settled in Brussels and found work in the studio of Alphonse Balat, the architect to King Leopold II, and where he remained until 1892. It was with Balat that Horta became interested in the new architectural materials. From his mentor he learned the Neo-Classical forms of the nineteenth century and how to manipulate them. The results were quickly forthcoming for, at the age of just 23, he won the Godecharle Prize for a plan he had presented for the Belgian Parliament.

Horta soon began to receive commissions to design private homes: first at Ghent,

then, in 1893, in Brussels, where he began to gather converts from among friends in intellectual circles. One of these was Émile Tassel, an influential collaborator of the industrialist Ernest Solvay. Tassel asked Horta to design a modest house that reconciled the frivolous requirements of his drawing room with the discretion of a grandmother who was almost one hundred years old. In rue Paul Emile Janson, Horta built Tassel the first of his manifesto houses in which he broke with the traditional symmetries of the plan to organize the spaces along a single axis that cut through the whole ground floor of the building. The Neo-Mannerist façade, which reflected the Italian taste of the sixteenth century, relinquished masonry materials in favor of a skeleton made of iron and glass to give the appearance of lightness; it was also given an Egyptian-style entrance topped by a bow-window and flanked by massive brackets on either side. In the spacious reception room, from which stretched a suite of rooms in strict Italian Renaissance tradition, the classical and exotic were harmonized through iron columns built to resemble palm trees in a tropical garden.

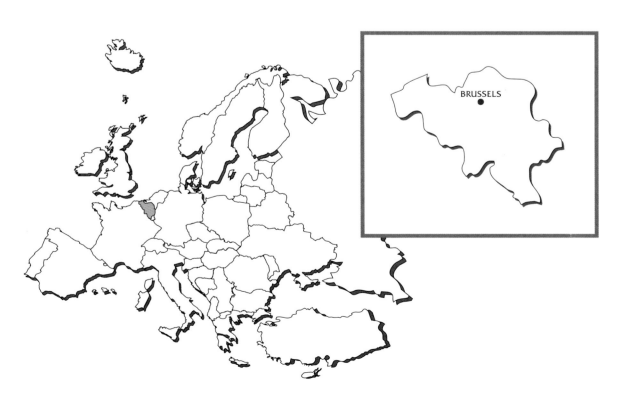

BRUSSELS

References to Nature inside the rooms were rendered even more explicit a year later in the Hôtel Solvay, where Horta took advantage of the large garden to bring air in from the outside through a series of pipes. It was in 1895 that the break with classicism took place when Horta produced his first Art Nouveau design. Edmond van Eetvelde, a baron and diplomat recently appointed Secretary of State in the independent Congo, was looking for an architect who combined talent with courage. For him, Horta built a house in avenue Palmerston based on a plan that closely followed the

constructed in iron, which was bent to comply with the decorated windows. Because the lines of the city plan were incorporated into the project, the diagonal corridor that leads to the winter garden is an alleyway that opens out into a square.

Horta's most revolutionary design was perhaps the one he kept for himself when, in 1898, he built his own house at 23-25 rue Américaine. In this building, Horta's stylized decoration reached its peak with his setting of natural forms as though in a theater wing, and the use of transparent materials to better exploit natural light.

modernism for his early works because he broke with nineteenth century styles to introduce Art Nouveau into architecture. On the other hand, his mature works reflected an about-face in his style and a revisionism that led Horta to align himself with conservatism and plunge into futile academism.

In 1944, three years before his death, Horta drew up his will, including in it a spiritual recognition of his master, writing, "What I owe, I owe to the purest (and most personal) of the classical architects, Alphonse Balat."

winter garden in the royal greenhouses designed by Balat. The main section of the house – the reception room – opened onto an entrance in the form of an octagon which stretched for the entire length of the building and was flooded with natural light from the roof. Load-bearing columns, balustrades, and ornamentation were

Maison Horta was perhaps the last of the architect's more innovative projects. In 1902, he suffered a creative crisis that led him to return to more conventional designs and a simplification of lines.

Victor Horta has a double reputation in the history of modern architecture. On the one hand, he is considered the founder of

73 For Maison van Eetvelde, Horta stood glass domes on iron columns, while balustrades and decorations resemble objects from nature. Like other creations by the architect from Ghent, the house was designed to suit the personality and role of its owner.

Palaces and Parks of Potsdam and Berlin

GERMANY

BRANDENBURG, SOUTH-WEST OF BERLIN
REGISTRATION: 1990, 1992, 1999
CRITERIA: C (I) (II) (IV)

74 top A view of the Baroque garden in Sans Souci Palace. Though Frederick II commissioned the work from Georg Wenzeslaus von Knobelsdorff in the mid-eighteenth century, it was the sovereign himself who determined the design of what was to be his maison de plaisir.

74-75 A birds-eye view of Weinberg Hill on which Sans Souci and its six parabolic terraces were built. The Baroque garden and the fountain in the center lie at the foot of the hill.

75 left A lover of music, Frederick II enjoyed entertaining his guests by playing the pianola in the Concert Hall. Superb paintings and furniture decorate this superlative Rococo room.

75 top right Sans Souci's magnificent library is decorated with beautiful stuccoes, gilded bronzes, and a Rococo fireplace. Voltaire himself, the leader of the Enlightenment, filled the library with books.

The son of Frederick William of Prussia, Frederick of Hohenzollern was born in Berlin in 1712. Besides being a strict reorganizer and restorer of the war-ravaged electorate following the Thirty Years War, his father was a devout Lutheran and wanted to educate his son in accordance with the restrained practices he was preparing to impose on his court in order to deal with the huge debts he had inherited from Frederick I. But the century of the Enlightenment was approaching, and the cultured but rebellious Frederick of Hohenzollern was to leave his mark on eighteenth century Europe, partly as a result of his political and military skills, but above all for his progressive views and the intellectual and artistic impetus he gave to his kingdom.

The iron discipline of the palace prompted the young prince to try to escape to the court in Great Britain, but the inflexible authoritarianism of his father cost him two years close confinement at Küstrin where he wrote two works of political philosophy: the *Antimachiavelli and Instruction for the Education of the Hereditary Prince*. In these works, he

countered the reasons of State set out by the Italian writer with his own criteria for creating good government, a moral conception of justice, and the intellectual emancipation of the people.

He came to the throne in 1740, and between 1742 and 1745 Frederick II took advantage of the impressive military resources built up by his father, taking possession of Silesia, the richest of the Hapsburg provinces, thereby winning himself

the nickname Frederick the Great. During this period he also launched his cultural program, commissioning Georg Wenzeslaus von Knobelsdorff to design a summer residence to be built in Potsdam in an area of countryside between Lakes Havel and Glienicke. The first stone was laid on the brow of a hill on April 14, 1745, and the Sans Souci Palace was completed within two years. This came as a surprise because Frederick had held animated discussions with the architect about his idea. Moreover, it was Frederick himself who drew up the plans of the building that was to become a symbol of German Rococo. The king did not want a luxurious or ostentatious palace but a place where he could relax and dedicate himself to art and literary salons.

The north entrance to the single-story palace opens with a hemicycle colonnade onto the Weinbergterrasse, a cascade of six terraces featuring niches and vines, at the bottom of which lies a Baroque garden with a pool and a fountain at its center. The south entrance is decorated by 36 sandstone sculptures that alternate with large windows. Inside, covered by a domed roof, there is the large, oval Marble Room that was used for receptions.

75 bottom right The Marmorsaal (Marble Room) is the largest room in Sans Souci. Used for court receptions, it is elliptical and crowned by an airy dome.

76-77 *Filled with statues, grottoes, and artificial ruins, Sans Souci park was the perfect architectural and landscape representation of* *Frederick II's intellectual interests. In the background we see the Orangerie inspired by Italian Renaissance villas.*

76 bottom *Another view of Sans Souci park and one of the ruins. The purpose of these anachronistic* *constructions was not merely to be evocative; they were used to hide the water tanks that fed the fountains.*

The wings on either side of this room each contain no more than four rooms.

Frederick liked to stay in this intimate and peaceful building from April to October each year, taking long walks and entertaining such guests as the elderly Johann Sebastian Bach and Voltaire. Invited to organize the marvelous cedarwood library decorated with gilded bronze, the French leader of the Enlightenment accepted the hospitality offered him by Frederick II and stayed at Sans Souci from 1750 to 1753. During this period he filled the library with 2200 volumes either

written in or translated into French, but in doing so he endorsed what was increasingly becoming an absolute and intolerant monarchy.

New buildings, grottoes, ruins, the gazebo, and the Chinese tea-house were all built on the grounds. In 1763, the Bildgalerie was built, first under the direction of Knobelsdorff and, later, Johann Gottfried Büring to house 124 paintings by Flemish, Italia,n and Dutch masters such as Van Dyck, Rubens, and Caravaggio.

Clearly satisfied, Frederick charged Büring with the construction of a new and more official royal residence. By 1769, Sans Souci park (which had now been extended to cover 74 acres) also contained the Neuen Palais, the impressive and last symbol of German Baroque. The monumental three-story building is 722 feet long, crowned by an enormous drum dome, and decorated with 428 large sculptures. It contains more than 200 large rooms, an imposing colonnaded court, and official reception rooms decorated with marble and other stones to save what the king called "pointless" transfers to the hated "paternal" city of Berlin. Two buildings facing the Neuen Palais were built to accommodate the staff, the kitchens, and other service rooms.

Frederick the Great died at Sans Souci on August 17, 1786 after reigning for 46 years. The legacy of Great Prussia remained in safe hands even if the architectural taste of his successors was less certain. His nephew, Frederick William II, also wished to put a personal stamp on the site of Potsdam so he had the superb Neuen Garten with the modest Marble Palace laid out between 1787 and

1797 on the banks of the Heiliger See. Inspired by the romantic taste of his wife, he also built a decadent palace on the Pfaueninsel (Peacock Island), which was later transformed into an English garden by his successor Frederick William III.

The road that led backwards to the architectural past was by now clearly laid out and the buildings constructed in nineteenth-century Prussia were obviously influenced by this trend. In 1824, Prince Charles purchased Glienicke Castle, the ancient residence of the Counts von Hardenberg, and had it transformed into Italian Neo-Classical style using fragments from antiquity set in its walls. Two years later, Frederick William III built an entirely new district in the city of Potsdam – the Russian colony named Alexandrovska – for the members of the choir that Czar Alexander I had sent to the court in Berlin.

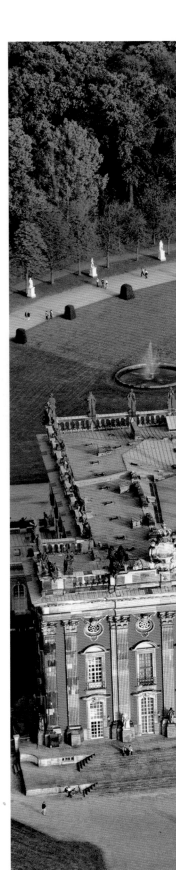

78 top left The Grotto Room in the Neuen Palais is decorated in a fantastic manner, making use of minerals, shells, and branches of coral.

78 top right Of the 200 rooms in the Neuen Palais, the Marble Room is perhaps the most dramatic. The walls are set with precious panels painted by artists of the French school in the eighteenth century.

78 center Built between 1787 and 1797 by Frederick William II, the Marble Palace is an elegant building of modest size that looks over the Heiliger See.

78-79 A masterpiece of German Baroque, the monumental Neuen Palais is 722 feet long, three stories high, and culminates in an enormous drum and dome. Ostentation was the principal feature of the architectural style.

After coming to the throne in 1840, it was Frederick William IV who made the greatest changes to the garden of delights that Potsdam had by now become. The "romantic king" planned to unite the estate of Charlottenhof, which had been a rural area until 1825, with Sans-Souci Park. With contributions from architects like Schinkel, Persius, and Lenné, he transformed the main building into a small palace in Biedermeyer style with interiors inspired by mosaics from the town of Pompeii. He rebuilt the *orangerie*, turning it into a monumental Classical-Romantic building. But above all, he dramatically changed the farming landscape, turning it

into an English garden with vast terraces covered with lawns, small pools, and copses, and he built highly elegant Roman baths, with statues, mosaics, and frescoes.

Under the rule of Frederick William IV, Potsdam was endowed with religious buildings. First came the Friedenskirche (Church of Peace), which is a basilica with a bell tower in early Christian style. In a similar vein is the Church of the Redeemer of Sacrov, which stands on the shore of Lake Havel between the Neuen Garten and the Pfaueninsel.

In the mid-1830's, even Prince William, the younger son of Frederick William III and future Emperor William I, made his contribution. After much hesitation, his father had given him the property of Babelsberg near Potsdam. At the suggestion of his wife, Augusta of Saxe-Weimar, in 1833 William began construction of a Neo-Gothic residence in Tudor style unwillingly designed by Schinkel, who was not in favor of medievalism. The compromise between the architect and the demanding princess resulted in a simply decorated building with clear lines that looked out over the countryside. Once again designed by Lenné in typically Romantic style, the park has twisting paths that lead into openings where unusual buildings stand. One such example is the Matrosenhaus, where the man in charge of the royal boats lived, and another the Gerichtslaube, a tea room built from stone taken from the ancient City Hall in Berlin.

With the exception of the Kaiserbahnhof, the imperial train station built between 1905 and 1908 near the Neuen Palais, the only alteration made to Potsdam during the twentieth century was the Cecilienhof. Built in the Neuen Garten to satisfy the wishes of Emperor William II, it is an unpretentious building resembling an English country house. It was finished in 1916, shortly before the abdication of the emperor, so that it was never inhabited by the imperial family. However, it entered history as the site of the Potsdam Conference of August 2, 1945, when Churchill, Truman, and Stalin decided the sanctions to be placed on the defeated Germany and put an end to the powerful and solid Reich that, two centuries before, had evolved out of the skillful political and military maneuvers of Frederick William I.

Aachen Cathedral

GERMANY

RHINELAND-WESTPHALIA
[NORDRHEIN-WESTFALEN]
REGISTRATION: 1978
CRITERIA: C (I) (II) (IV) (VI)

A t the sides of the entrance of Aachen Cathedral are a bronze wolf and pine-cone. The first is an obvious reference to the foundation of Rome, and the second – a symbol of spiritual power – alludes to the *Roma secunda* that Charlemagne wished to appoint capital of the Holy Roman Empire. In truth, the cathedral was designed so that every stone and decoration would be laden with symbolic meaning. For this reason, in 786 Charlemagne did not give the most inspired architect of the period, Odo of Metz, complete control of the project, but paired him with his own learned biographer, Eginhard.

The conceptual "inheritance" from Rome began with the chosen site of a pagan temple built in honor of Grannus, the Celtic god of health (from which came the Latin name of the city, Acquae Granni), on which an early Christian church was built and, later, a Palatine

Holy Roman Empire, solid on the earth and inspired by Heaven. The number 12 recurs in its measurements and ratios, for 12 was the number of Apostles and the tribes of Israel. In the symbolism of numbers, the product of 12 multiplied by 12, 144, was considered the perfect number, and the circumference of the first chapel measured 144 feet (a Carolingian foot was equal to 13 inches).

In 805, the cathedral was consecrated by Pope Leo III, who, five years earlier, had crowned Charlemagne "Emperor of

80-81 The south side of Aachen cathedral faces the Münsterplatz. The core of this extraordinary monument, dedicated to the Virgin, was designed in the late eighth century by Odo of Metz with help from Charlemagne himself.

chapel dedicated to St. Mary by Pepin the Short. The original structure of the cathedral was inspired by the Basilica of San Vitale in Ravenna and the Hagia Sophia in Byzantium. It had an octagonal base with two floors of galleries above, and was covered by a dome. The octagon represents the meeting point between the circle, the form of the divine, having no beginning or end, and the square, which signifies the world with its four cardinal points. The cathedral, therefore, was supposed to symbolize the idea itself of the

the Romans" in St. Peter's in Rome, thus investing him as the protector of Christendom. Despite many modifications made in later centuries, the place still preserves all the power of Carolingian art. Among its many masterpieces, there is the white marble throne on which 32 kings of Germany (and Holy Roman Emperors) were crowned from 932 to 1531. Charlemagne died in Aachen in 814 at the age of 72, and his body was buried in the cathedral in a spot that is still unknown today.

81 bottom The historic center of Aachen overlooked by the cathedral. The octagonal structure of the original building can no longer be seen from the outside because numerous chapels have been added to it over the centuries. The most recent is the Baroque-style Hungarian Chapel designed by Giuseppe Moretti in 1767.

On December 29, 1165, Charlemagne was canonized in a solemn ceremony attended by Frederick I Barbarossa, who had made every effort to win this distinction for his predecessor, for, if the founder of the empire was a saint, the power of his successors would be consolidated. On that occasion, Frederick donated to the cathedral an immense chandelier symbolizing the Heavenly Jerusalem that measures 14 feet in diameter and is made from gilded copper in the shape of a crown with 16 towers, each bearing 48 candles.

Wanting to emphasize the uniqueness of his church in 799, Charlemagne had important reliquaries brought there: from Jerusalem he imported the bands that wrapped Christ, the dress that the Virgin wore on the day of Christ's birth, and the garment John the Baptist was wearing on the day he was beheaded. Over time, these important reliquaries ensured that Aachen became one of Europe's most important places of pilgrimage. The number of pilgrims increased progressively, and in 1355 it was decided to enlarge the cathedral. Consequently, the most famous architects of the period were invited to build Aachen's "glass reliquary." The height of Late Gothic technical perfection, the extraordinary Choir, inspired by Sainte Chapelle in Paris, is formed by over 10,000 square feet of glass separated by 14 slender columns that rise to the ceiling. The glass windows, all

destroyed in 1729, were only replaced after World War II.

Today the octagonal plan of the Carolingian building is no longer recognizable from the outside. Over the centuries, mainly during the Gothic era, a crown of chapels was added to the main section of the building, many of them decorated in Baroque style. Aachen has also accumulated a collection of bronze and marble sculptures and works of gold which can be seen in the cathedral and nearby buildings.

82-83 A view from below of the Gothic Choir Room. Construction of this extraordinary room began in 1355 and took 60 years to complete. The room is delimited by 10,700 square feet of glass divided by 14 columns. Destroyed in the early eighteenth century, the panes were replaced after World War II.

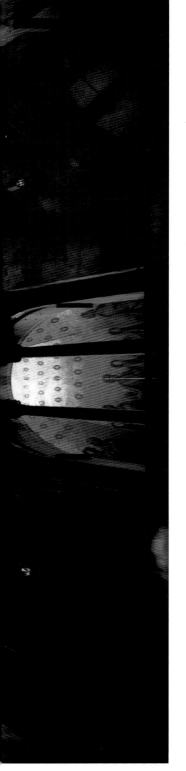

83 top One of the many fine bronze decorations on the vestibule wall where Charlemagne's tomb lay in the Middle Ages. The emperor is now buried inside the cathedral but the exact location is unknown.

83 center left The interior of the Carolingian Palatine Chapel. Its octagonal plan was based on the Holy Sepulcher in Jerusalem and was built between 796 and 805 AD.

83 center right The bust of Charlemagne, which has since become a reliquary, is studded with precious stones and is a masterpiece of the goldsmith's art of the fourteenth century. The high point of the devotion shown to the emperor-saint was reached in the twelfth and thirteenth centuries. Chronicles of the period indicate that up to 145,000 pilgrims used to arrive in Aachen on St. Charles' Day.

83 bottom Thirty rulers were crowned in Aachen between 936 (Otto I) and 1531 (Ferdinand I) on the marble imperial throne featured in the photograph. The throne stands on a platform with six steps, the number of stories in the Tower of Babylon.

The Würzburg Residence

GERMANY

LOWER FRANCONIA, BAVARIA
REGISTRATION: 1981
CRITERIA: C (I) (IV)

Throughout Germany the seventeenth century was grim and marked by bloodshed. The Thirty Years War had brought hunger and devastation, and the Peace of Westphalia had reduced the Holy Roman Empire to a mere symbol of the power that had since migrated elsewhere. However, the dawn of the new century brought with it the wind of optimism; Prussia grew to dominate the entire region, and the religious conflicts that, since Luther, had created feuds and particularisms found a peaceful solution.

Bavaria was an example of this new era. The Grand Dukes of Munich, the abbeys, and the prince-bishops sealed an agreement that allowed each to return to their former glory. Tangible evidence of this achievement are the many civil and religious buildings that were commissioned at the start of the eighteenth century, the period during which the Baroque was in full flower. The German version of this architectural style was the perfect manifestation of the enthusiasm that was linked to the optimistic mood of the time.

In Würzburg, the prince-bishop Johann Philipp Franz von Schönborn invited Johann Balthasar Neumann, Germany's most celebrated architect, to design a magnificent new residence for him. It seemed that no person of rank could afford to not live in a building unless it had been designed by Neumann. The architect accepted the task and began to work on the job that would take 20 years. He allied his genius to that of Lucas von Hildebrandt, the court architect in Vienna, Robert de Cotte from Paris, and Maximilian von Welsch, the architect of the Elector of Mainz.

The result was a building considered the masterpiece of German Baroque, a style that was to lead into the even more exuberant and joyful Rococo. Facing onto a wide square, the Residence in Würzburg is composed of three sections that enclose a main courtyard, and the two wings, in turn, enclose internal courtyards. The back of the building faces onto an immense garden in which superb statues decorate the flowerbeds. Neumann designed the structure to feature the alternation of straight lines and curves; monotony is avoided by the continuous movement of filled and empty spaces, balustrades, and statues. However, it was the interior that the architect's imagination struck with greatest force.

84 left The rear of the Würzburg residence faces onto the immense park. Twenty years were required to build this German masterpiece of Baroque. The design and direction of the works were assigned to Johann Balthasar Neumann, the most famous German architect of the eighteenth century.

84-85 This façade looks onto the main court. Neumann based his design of the residence on alternating straight lines and curves, and he managed to avoid monotony – despite the building's huge size – by employing a continuous series of filled and empty spaces and by inserting balustrades and statues.

85 top A detail of one of the many beautiful statues in the park's flowerbeds.

85 bottom A view of the park and the side section of the residence. This was the only part to escape the disastrous fires that damaged the building during World War II.

85 center right Some of the rooms were frescoed by Giambattista Tiepolo. This fresco depicts the Marriage of Barbarossa.

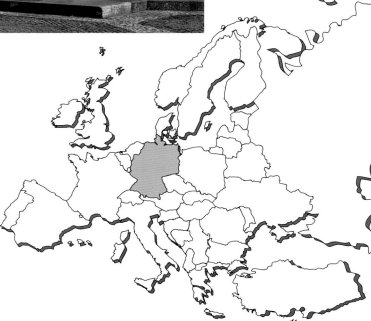

86 top The main staircase lies just inside the entrance. It is a mammoth work in which imagination and engineering techniques have been perfectly blended. The immense vault of the staircase is only supported by the sidewalls. The ceiling frescoes by Giambattista Tiepolo represent the four continents visited by the Würzburg family throughout its history.

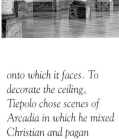

86 bottom left The exuberant Baroque decorations, which eventually evolved into the Rococo style, in the chapel of the Würzburg princes-bishops were designed by the Swiss artist Antonio Bossi, a master of stucco work.

86 bottom right The spectacular beauty of the Gartensaal. Its high, luminous lateral colonnade extends its size and mediates the park onto which it faces. To decorate the ceiling, Tiepolo chose scenes of Arcadia in which he mixed Christian and pagan scenes.

86-87 The Kaisersaal, the most magnificent room in the residence, was used for official receptions. The ceiling was also painted by Tiepolo and is an allegory of the marriage of Frederick Barbarossa to Beatrice of Burgundy, which took place at Würzburg in 1156.

The rather dark entrance with a low ceiling is a sort of joke that Neumann contrived so that the visitor would be even more amazed at the sight of the main stairway, a cyclopean work in which creativity and engineering skills are perfectly combined.

During the final construction stage, Neumann needed a decorator to complete the sense of marvel the architectural features had created. He chose the Swiss artist Antonio Bossi, who was considered a virtuoso of stucco work. In 1746 the building was ready, although it was necessary to wait another four years for the arrival of the Venetian artist who was to make Würzburg the most envied residence in Germany. Accompanied by his sons, Giandomenico and Lorenzo, Giovan

Battista Tiepolo worked for three consecutive winters to fresco the ceilings with magnificent illustrations of episodes from the city's history, which told of its rulers' greatness.

In the vault over the main stairway, Tiepolo orchestrated an allegory populated by hundreds of mythological figures, angels, and animals as a tribute to the four continents that the prince-bishops of Schönborn had visited during the glorious history of the family. In the central medallion of the ceiling in the Kaisersaal (the reception room), the artist celebrated the wedding of the emperor Frederick I Barbarossa to Beatrice of Burgundy, which had taken place in 1156 in Würzburg, elevated to a bishopric for the occasion. In the fresco, Apollo leads the bride to

the side of the sovereign, while sunlight forces its way through the clouds and lights up the blue of the sky.

On the ceiling in the Gartensaal, supported by a colonnade that helps to broaden the space and thus create a dialogue with the garden onto which it faces, Tiepolo painted an Arcadian scene of satyrs, naiads, hunters, and shepherds.

An air raid on March 16, 1945 utterly destroyed 80 percent of the city. The fire caused by the bombs reached the royal Residence, but prompt action saved the frescoes and the main stairway. Over the following years, careful reconstruction has restored the building to the splendor it enjoyed during the happy age of the Baroque.

The Völklingen Ironworks

GERMANY

SAARLAND, NINE MILES WEST OF SAARBRÜCKEN
REGISTRATION: 1994
CRITERIA: C (II) (IV)

88 top The gigantic turbines in the Völklingen plant came into operation during the early twentieth century. Covering a surface area of 64,500 square feet, they produced energy by exploiting gas generated in the blast furnaces.

On the night of March 17, 1945, the Allied troops crossed the Siegfried Line, the river Saar, and took several towns in the German mining region. One of these, Völklingen, was famous for its iron and steelworks and had never, not even in the most crucial moments of the war, ceased producing materials for the Reich. The plants resumed production the following May, and the Saar was only reintegrated with Federal Germany on January 1, 1957 after a referendum.

In 1873, the engineer Julius Boch

88 bottom Founded by the Röchling brothers in 1881, the Völklingen plant was a state-of-the-art technological center in the iron and steel industry for over half a century. Only after World War II did the machinery start to become obsolete and production to fall.

founded an iron production plant at Völklingen, but he soon found that orders were not numerous enough and he was forced to close down. On August 27, 1881, the factory was bought by the Röchling brothers who established the Völklinger Eisenwerk Gebrüder Röchling O.H.G. Imperial Germany was experiencing rapid industrial growth and there was an exceptional demand for metals. In 1883, the number of employees jumped from 450 to 1150, and profits allowed the

construction of a blast furnace, the first in the region.

Growth was dizzying. In 1890, the Völklingen plants were the largest iron producers in the country, smelting 77,000 tons. In 1891, a Thomas plant was started up, which exploited the principle that allowed steel to be produced directly from minette, an iron mineral rich in phosphorus. In 1893, four more blast furnaces were installed, and production was diversified to include semi-finished products. Four years later, a carbon coke plant was installed. As the principal reducing agent for the production of cast iron from mineral iron, the production of coke required a complex treatment of coal, but the proximity of the blast furnaces allowed the cycle to be completed on-site.

The start of the twentieth century brought new technologies: in 1900, construction began of the first gas vent for the blast furnaces. Until that time the energy had been provided by steam engines, but exploitation of the gas generated in the blast furnace made the process more economic. In just 14 years six turbines were installed in an area over 64,000 square feet. Between 1907 and 1908, the first electric Röchling-Rodenhauser furnace was implemented for the production of steel.

When World War I broke out, the plants were converted to produce arms. Völklingen produced shells, grenades, barbed wire, and armored plating to protect both people and vehicles. At the end of the war, the industrial buildings were placed under the supervision of the League of Nation,s but the occupying French troops were not withdrawn until 1935.

Despite the war debts, expansion of the

88-89 Until the end of the nineteenth century, the energy for the blast furnaces was produced by steam-engines, but these were replaced by large internal combustion technology.

steelworks did not stop. In 1927, a concrete production plant was set up that used production waste. Strong postwar competition led to the search for new ideas, and in 1928 the first sintering plant was installed. This process produced worked items by compressing and reheating metal powder at a temperature much lower than its melting point.

In March 1935, the Saar was returned to German jurisdiction, but Hitler's self-governing policy created supply problems, and new techniques were developed to deal

the 1970's, the crisis in the metal and steel industries hit all of the Saar, and the Völklingen plants inexorably became obsolete, supplanted by newer, more efficient production techniques.

On July 4, 1986, the blast furnaces and coke plants were permanently closed, but the iron and steelworks in Völklingen are a unique monument of industrial history. In no other place in the world is the production process that transforms coke to steel so well illustrated nor the activities allied to heavy industry so clearly preserved.

89 bottom A view of the Völklingen metal works in the Saar, which were at the center of the German steel industry. Closed in 1986, the steelworks were declared a national monument by the German authorities in 1992.

with poor quality iron minerals. However, with World War II about to break out, the population was evacuated on September 1, 1939, and the plant had to close down. In December it was reopened specifically for war duties. The war ended with defeat for Germany, but the plants at Völklingen – unlike other industries in the Saar – did not suffer heavily. Production in the region, governed by a joint French and German administration, fell under the control of the European Community of Coal and Steel. In

The Maulbronn Monastery Complex

GERMANY

90

90 top Overall view of the Klausur at Maulbronn. Considered the best-preserved medieval monastic complex north of the Alps, it is one of the earliest and best examples of German Gothic.

90 center The nave of the basilica was built in simple Romanesque and then embellished with agile Gothic vaults and wall frescoes. Note the massive stone cross on the transept.

90 bottom A fountain inside the complex. The Cistercian monks at Maulbronn displayed exceptional engineering skills. In the fifteenth century, they provided the monastery and farms with an irrigation system and water tanks.

In 1137, a small group of Cistercian monks from Alsatia was sent to spread the sacred rules of the Order in Germany. After ten years of wandering, they reached Salzach valley where they were able to found a basilica with three naves in simple Romanesque style and a *Klausur* (enclosure) thanks to a substantial donation by the bishop, Günther von Speyer. The monks worked quickly, and in 1156 they were the owners of eleven *Grangien* (farms). Their efficiency caught the notice of the emperor, Frederick Barbarossa, who placed the monastery under his direct protection.

As the farms ensured the monks' subsistence, the Cistercians were ready to give the monastery a solid and long-lasting structure that would replace the wooden houses in which they were temporarily lodged. Thus began a task that was to last 390 years and which was to see Maulbronn surrounded with walls and enhanced with buildings, the style of which was a prelude to German Gothic. During the first half of the thirteenth century, an architect from Burgundy (whose name has not survived the journey through time to the present day) was commissioned to enlarge the basilica with a portico, known as the *Paradies*. The load-bearing structures of the original Romanesque construction were replaced by lines of columns from which hexapartite vaults fan out. The capitals are sculpted with motifs of trees and fronds.

During the same period, *Lesegang* (the wing built for reading in the lee of the southern part of the church), the *Laienrefektorium* (the dining room for the lay brothers who helped with tasks and construction), and the *Herrenrefektorium* (the monks' dining room) were constructed. The last of the three was considered the most important section of the monastery and was composed of two

naves. To its right stands the hypocaust (the ingenious under-floor heating system), and to its left, the kitchen.

For two centuries Maulbronn prospered, expanding its territory into neighboring areas. Religious architecture in Europe had by that time embraced Gothic, and the Cistercians of Salzbach conferred the complex with the form and appearance that has lasted to the modern era.

The interior of the church was augmented with Gothic vaults over the central and right-hand naves, and the walls were painted with ornamental frescoes.

In 1440, Maulbronn had 130 monks and lay brothers, but in 1504 decline set in when Duke Ulrich of Württemberg conquered the area and the monastery was removed from the protection of the emperor. By 1535 the Reformation had reached the Dukedom, and the monks were forced to abandon their property.

Twenty years later, the Württemberg family – pioneers of the tradition that was to lead to obligatory education in Germany – transformed the monastery into a Protestant seminary and set up scholarships for needy students. This

90-91 The Chapter Room that faces onto the portico known as "Paradies." Probably built at the start of the thirteenth century by an unknown architect from Burgundy, the Paradies has a load-bearing structure made from rows of columns that open onto hexapartite vaults.

A large stone crucifix was placed in the partition and the Choir was historiated with a Madonna and richly decorated stalls. The enclosure walls were expanded to include the new cloisters and a series of trellised buildings. The monks also showed that they had exceptional engineering skills as, during the fourteenth century, they designed and built a network of irrigation channels and water tanks that had no equal throughout medieval Europe.

began a new and flourishing period for Maulbronn, which turned out students who were to become important artists and scientists. The astronomer Johannes Kepler, who frequented the seminary from 1586 to 1589, was one of the first students to enjoy great success. At the end of the eighteenth century, the halls of Maulbronn accommodated the poet and writer Friedrich Hölderlin and, one hundred years later, Hermann Hesse studied there;

however, the future Nobel prize winner experienced his first existential torments in the monastery and was forced to leave the school prematurely.

Today Maulbronn is the best conserved medieval monastic complex north of the Alps to the extent that it was chosen to be the setting for some of the scenes in the film *The Name of the Rose,* based on the novel by Umberto Eco.

The Historic Center of Krakow

POLAND

REGISTRATION: 1978
CRITERIA: C (IV)

At the top of each hour, a trumpeter climbs to the top of the tower of the church of Kosciol Mariacki (St. Mary) in the market square and plays the Marian anthem. The melody, which at one time was played as the gates of the city were opened or closed, is suddenly interrupted, always on the same note, to commemorate the Tatar invasion of 1240 and the moment when the city trumpeter was the first to spot the enemy troops. He was also the first to suffer from their arrival, being shot by an arrow as he blew his instrument to warn the city's inhabitants of the imminent danger.

This unusual tradition is indicative of Krakow's links to its past. The first written evidence of the existence of the city was recorded by a Jewish merchant from Cordoba, Ibrahim ibn Jakub, who in 965 described it as an important trading center that stood below Vavel hill. In the year 1000 the city became an archbishopric, and a castle, cathedral, and various churches in Romanesque style were built on the hill.

The city, which was the capital of the small kingdom of Poland under the Piast Dynasty from the eleventh century, continued to prosper until it was sacked and destroyed by the Tatars. In 1257, reconstruction began and the city was laid out on a new plan that has remained unchanged to the present day. The market square (Rynek), the largest in Europe, was laid out and the city given a new system of fortifications, towers, and gates that was enlarged in later eras.

92 top A view of the impressive Gothic cathedral with its three towers, one of which contains the Dzwon Zymut (Sigismund Bell) cast in 1520.

92-93 This is the view from the Vistula of the Wawel, the hill where Krakow's first medieval settlement was established.

Around the year 1000, the cathedral and a fortified palace were built here. From 1038 on, the palace became the residence of the Polish kings.

93 top left Kosciol Mariacki (St. Mary's Church) in the Market Square is a masterpiece of late Gothic architecture.

WARSAW

KRAKOW

93 top right Kosciol Mariacki holds priceless art works, including the wooden sculpture of the Death of the Virgin (1477-1489) by the German woodcarver Veit Stoss.

93 center The focal point of the royal palace on Wawel Hill is the large cloister onto which most of the official rooms face.

93 bottom right The royal palace is now a museum that holds the Crown jewels and one of the world's most important collections of Flemish tapestries.

94-95 An aerial view of the Rynek, Europe's largest market square. It is dominated by the Renaissance-style Cloth Palace, which contains shops on the ground floor and the section of the National Museum dedicated to Polish painting.

94 bottom The Barbican is Europe's largest fortified rampart. The defensive walls were built in 1498 when the city was at the height of its splendor and capital of Poland. The city was a meeting place for famous humanists and scientists.

and Lithuania and founded northern Europe's most important royal dynasty, which lasted roughly 200 years.

From the mid-sixteenth century on, Krakow enjoyed a period of great splendor. Under the enlightened rule of the Jagellonic kings, the city was made even more secure with the construction of the Barbican, the largest fortified rampart in Europe, and the city attracted famous humanists, artists, and scientists. Nicholas Copernicus studied there before going to Italy, and Veit Stoss, a master woodcarver, arrived in the city from Nuremberg in 1477 and spent 12 years

carving the immense decorative work, *Death of the Virgin*, from limewood for the altar in St. Mary's church. Three years later, having moved from wood to marble, Stoss sculpted the tomb of Casimir IV Jagellone inside the cathedral and thus began the tradition of the great royal tombs in Krakow.

When Stoss returned to his homeland, the Tuscan sculptors Francesco Fiorentino and Bartolomeo Berrecci were called to the city where, in the cathedral, they created some of the most dazzling examples of Renaissance sculpture outside Italy. In those years, the castle on Vavel hill was also rebuilt and decorated with a collection of wall-hangings ordered from Flanders. However, these were the last years of glory for Krakow: at the end of the sixteenth century the capital was transferred to Warsaw, and Krakow, though retaining its

busy intellectual life, had to adapt itself to the role of a supporting city with the characteristics of a small commercial center.

Another jewel, however, was added to its beauty. At the end of the eighteenth century, Prince Czartorysky returned from a trip to Italy with a unique purchase, Leonardo da Vinci's painting *Woman with an ermine*, which can today be admired in the museum that bears the name of its original owner. This masterpiece, miraculously spared from World War II, has found in Krakow a setting to match its own beauty.

95

95 *left The cloister of the Collegium Maius, one of the oldest buildings in Krakow Academy. The Academy was founded in 1364 by Casimir the Great, the last king of the Piast Dynasty, and was later turned into the Jagellonic University.*

95 *center right This hall in the Collegium Maius contains old furnishings and paintings.*

95 *bottom right Another view of the Rynek. In 1899, a monument was raised to Adam Mickiewicz, Poland's best-loved poet, in front of the Cloth Palace.*

Krakow's history reached a turning point during the reign of the last of the Piasts, Casimir the Great (1333-1370). As a patron of the arts and sciences, Casimir founded the Cloth Palace, in the center of the Rynek, the church of St. Mary, and two new centers, Kazimierz and Kleparz, which today are two districts of the city. But above all, he established the Krakow Academy, which was later to be known as the Jagellonica University and became Poland's most renowned center of learning. Twenty years later, Casimir gave his daughter in marriage to the Lithuanian Grand Duke, Ladislau Jagellone, who later became king of Poland

The Historic Center of Prague
CZECH REPUBLIC

REGISTRATION: 1992
CRITERIA: C (II) (IV) (VI)

Havel na Hrad, "Havel at the Castle," the citizens of Prague shouted in the exciting days after the fall of the Berlin Wall in 1989 that represented the return to freedom. Vaclav Havel became the first president of independent Czechoslovakia – which became the Czech Republic after its peaceful split with Slovakia in 1993 – and

the tenant of a luxurious apartment in the Hradcany. The site measures 2,800,000 square feet and contains a cathedral, a basilica, a monastery, a royal palace, and a variety towers and courts. It is a city within a city and for more than a thousand years has been the symbol of Prague. It was also, with its labyrinthine layout, a literary inspiration for Franz Kafka, the best-known citizen of Prague throughout the world.

Since Prince Borivoi built a wooden fort on a hill on the left bank of the Moldava in the eleventh century – next to the hill where another, slightly older fort stood, the

Vysehrad – the Hradcany has seen 40 owners come and go and 30 raids and fires. The Hapsburg emperor and king, Rudolf II, lived here, and in 1583 made Prague the capital of his empire. He was known as the "alchemist king" and believed in the philosopher's stone. He built a laboratory in the towers of the castle, where he welcomed guests like the exuberant Milanese artist Giovanni Arcimboldi to turn lead into gold. Then, in 1618, during the period when Jan Hus had been haranguing his fellow-citizens for more than a decade to rebel against the Church of Rome, three Catholic ambassadors were thrown out of the castle windows. This episode has gone down in history as the Defenestration of Prague and marked the

96 top One of the rooms in the Strahov Monastic Library, which contains one million volumes. The rarest and most precious of these are the first 16 books printed in the Czech language, of which seven are unique. The oldest volume is the ninth-century Strahov Gospel written on parchment with gold uncial characters.

96 center left This is the royal mausoleum in the cathedral of St. Vitus, where several of the most important figures in the history of Bohemia are

buried: Charles IV, Ferdinand I, Rudolf II, and St. Giovanni Nepomuceno.

96 bottom right The large Art Nouveau window by Alfons Mucha in St. Vitus' Cathedral.

97 top A view of the Hradcany (Castle Hill). Still the center of national power, the complex – which covers 2,800,000 square feet – is a city within a city. Its main buildings are St. Vitus' Cathedral, St. George's Basilica, and the Royal Palace.

start of the Thirty Years War.

As it appears today, the Hradcany is the result of Baroque restoration undertaken by Empress Maria Theresa of Austria, which was followed, at the start of the twentieth century, by the rebuilding of many of the interiors by Slovakian architect Josip Plecnik, including the lovely Gold Room. The most attractive sections of the complex, however, are much older in origin such as the immense late-Gothic room in the palace, 207 feet long and 43 feet high, which was built between 1493 and 1502, and the Cathedral of St. Vitus. Construction of the cathedral was begun in 1344 by Matthieu d'Arras on the site of a Roman basilica and was not completed until 1929 when the Neo-Gothic west façade was added with two spires 262 feet tall. The overlaying of styles inside also reflects the long span of construction. Next to the splendid Gothic chapel decorated with precious and semi-precious stones and dedicated to St. Wenceslas, one can admire a charming Art Nouveau window by Alfons Mucha.

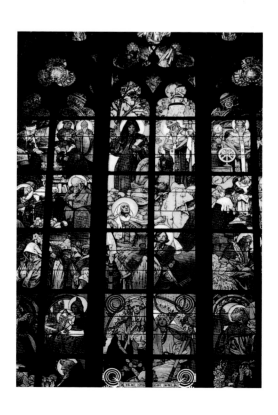

97 bottom The Vladeslas Room (207 feet long and 43 feet high) inside the Royal Palace. Built *between 1493 and 1502, it is considered the masterpiece of Benedikt Ried. Horse tournaments were held here.*

PRAGUE

As a consequence of commercial expansion, starting in the eleventh century a new community, including many Jewish families, arose on the right bank of the Moldava near the original Prague of the Vysehrad and Hradcany. Called Staré Mesto (Old City), this area achieved the status of a district after 1170 when the Judith Bridge was built (the first stone bridge in Prague), and this gave it the right to build walls and defensive ramparts. The heart of the old city is Strarometske Namesti, the central square dominated by the City Hall and its tower, built in 1364. Half-hidden by the houses to the right of the building, the fourteenth-century church of Teyn contains the grave of the Danish astronomer Tycho Brahe. On the opposite side of the square

stands St. Nicholas' Church, a Baroque masterpiece by Kilian Ignaz Dientzenhofer. Until World War II, Staré Mesto was home to a Jewish community of 12,000 people and still contains several synagogues and the oldest Jewish cemetery in Europe.

In 1257, a new district called Malá Strana ('small part') began to grow below the Hradcany. Heavily damaged by a fire in 1503, today the zone is architecturally harmonious with Gothic and Renaissance churches and civil buildings "bound" together by houses with porticoes built in ornate Baroque. In addition, its tiny alleys, romantic gardens hidden behind the facades, and ancient beer-houses make this the most attractive district in the city and the favorite of the city's bohemians for the

past 100 years. One of the loveliest streets in Malá Strana is the paved Nerudova Ulice lined by richly decorated buildings. Wolfgang Amadeus Mozart lived in one of them for a long time.

When it became part of the Holy Roman Empire, Prague continued to prosper. The Bohemian emperor Charles IV governed it from 1346 to 1378 and planned further physical and cultural development. In 1348, he founded the first university in central Europe and began construction of Nové Mesto (New City), St. Vitus' Cathedral, and the Charles Bridge, which was named after him. Constructed in 1357 to replace the Judith Bridge that was washed away by a flood, it is 1,706 feet long, 33 feet wide, and is

98-99 *A view from above of the elegant façades of the palaces in Starometske Namesti. This attractive square in the heart of the old city contains several of Prague's best-known monuments, which represent 500 years of history.*

99 top *The magnificent astrological clock was placed on the City Hall tower at the end of the fourteenth century. The tower is the most impressive building in the central Starometske Namesti.*

99 center left *The pointed towers of Teyn Church face onto Starometske Namesti. Begun in 1380 in the workshop of Peter Parler, it was completed in the mid-sixteenth century. It contains Prague's oldest baptismal font (1414), the tomb of the astronomer Tycho Brahe, and a series of Baroque paintings by Karel Skreta.*

supported by 16 sandstone arcades. It is said that to protect it from bad weather, the emperor ordered that thousands of grapes should be mixed into the mortar.

The bridge was the place from where Giovanni Nepomuceno, a monk, was thrown into the river in 1393 after being tortured. He was canonized in 1729 and became the most worshipped saint in Bohemia. The cause of his death was the anger of King Wenceslas, successor to Charles IV, to whom the priest refused to reveal the confessional secrets of the king's wife. Before his canonization, a statue of Giovanni Nepomuceno by Jan Brokof was added to the Charles Bridge in 1683. This was the cue for the prominent citizens of Prague, as well as the Jesuits who strongly

99 center right *On the other side of the square stands the church of St. Nicholas. Built in 1732 in Baroque style by Kilian Ignaz Dientzenhofer, it was one of the bastions of the Counter-Reformation.*

99 bottom *A view of the Nerudova Ulice, the street dedicated to the Prague writer Jan Neruda, the author of the Tales of Malá Strana. The street is home to some of the city's oldest beer houses.*

supported the university, to compete in funding other statues of martyrs on the bridge, notably Czechs, Italians, and Spaniards, taking as their model the Ponte Sant'Angelo in Rome.

The center of Nové Mesto and of all modern Prague is St. Wenceslas' Square. Built to be the site of a horse market, it resembles a wide street more than a square (in fact it is 2,460 feet long but only 200 wide) and slopes slightly. Most of the buildings that overlook it were built at the

later in protest against the invasion of the city by the Warsaw Pact troops.

The University is centered on the Carolinum, a building rebuilt in Baroque style with a superb Gothic bow-window. This important cultural institution was joined at the end of the sixteenth century by the Klementinum, the third largest Jesuit college in the world and the second largest monument in Prague after the Hradcany. To build it, it was necessary to demolish 32 houses, St. Clement's Church,

and 160 manuscripts given by Charles to the nearby university, an imperial library was built in 1777. Today the Klementinum contains almost six million volumes, 1,200 papyruses, 6,000 medieval manuscripts, and 3,000 incunabula. In addition to this library, there is the seventeenth-century Strahov monastic library with book rooms described as the most spectacular in the world.

Prague has always been a city of culture. It was here that Mozart composed

start of the twentieth century when Prague was overwhelmed by the wave of Art Nouveau. Of special interest are Casa Peterka at number 12, which now contains the National Museum, and the Hotel Europa, at number 25. This was the square where the revolt in 1968 against Soviet rule began – known as the Prague Spring – and where Jan Palach committed suicide a year

two gardens, and seven farms with all their land. Design and construction of the Baroque masterpiece was the work of Giovanni Domenico Orsi. The chronicles of the era state that in 1696 the Klementinum had 1500 students of which one seventh, coming from poor homes, were provided with free education, board, and lodging. To hold the volumes, books,

his two most famous symphonies, and many citizens of Prague have made a huge contribution to the world of culture. Bedrich Smetana and Antonin Dvorak were important contributors to the musical world, and three outstanding names in the literary world are those of Franz Kafka, Rainer Maria Rilke, and the irreverent Bohumil Hrabal.

101 bottom left An evening view of St. Wenceslas Square with the National Museum in the background. It covers the same area as the old horse market, and consequently looks like a wide, slightly sloping avenue.

101 bottom right The façade of the Grand Hotel Europa in St. Wenceslas Square. Early twentieth-century buildings in Art Nouveau or Functionalist architecture line the whole square.

102 top left and right
The 77 square miles of the cultural landscape of Lednice-Valtice form an extensive architectural panorama. On the left, there is the large Romantic Corinthian colonnade where Greek vases are displayed; on the right, the Roman triumphal arch. The park of the duchy of Liechtenstein is filled with dozens of buildings.

The Cultural Landscape of Lednice-Valtice

CZECH REPUBLIC

DISTRICT OF BRECLAV,
SOUTHERN MORAVIA
REGISTRATION: 1996
CRITERIA: C (I) (II) (IV)

Thirty miles south of Brno, in the hilly countryside of Moravia, stands a minaret, a Neo-Classical building with a semi-circular arcade, a Roman triumphal arch, and a colonnade with Corinthian capitals and niches containing Greek vases. Apparently devoid of any logic, these and other buildings are the "follies" of Lednice-Valtice, which, measuring 77 square miles, is the largest landscaped area in Europe.

The transformation of the region began in the mid-eighteenth century when the Liechtenstein family came into possession of the lands around the village of Lednice and built a fortress there. At the time, the terrain was marshy and flooded regularly due to its proximity to the river Dyje. Seven hundred years later, at the end of World War II, the Liechtensteins were obliged to retire to a tiny principality on the borders of Austria and Switzerland, leaving behind an extraordinary park sprinkled with architectural gems and a mosaic of lakes, rivers, and canals. This area had won for itself the name "Garden of Paradise."

A noble family of Austrian origin, the Liechtensteins increased their landholdings thanks to their diplomatic skills. This was particularly apparent in 1654, following the end of the Thirty Years War, when they confiscated nearby territories in Valtice (where there was a castle) and Breclav from the Protestant aristocracy.

In the sixteenth century, the medieval fortress of Lednice was transformed into a Renaissance castle surrounded by a garden, and a century later the family's possessions reached their greatest splendor under Carlo Eusebio Liechtenstein, an enthusiastic patron of the arts. A traveler and author of *A Treatise on Architecture*, Carlo Eusebio commissioned Johann Bernhard Fischer von Erlach to build a Baroque residence in Lednice, surrounded by a park that, in accordance with the aesthetic canons of the day, consisted of six parts adorned with terraces and fountains.

102-103 The Baroque residence of Lednice was a whim of Carlo Eusebio Liechtenstein. Built in the seventeenth century by Johann Bernhard Fischer von Erlach, it is surrounded by a park featuring sculptures and fountains.

103 top left One of the two Baroque statues at the entrance to Valtice Castle.

103 top right The Three Graces is the name of the sculpture that stands in the center of the unusual colonnaded complex in Lednice-Valtice park. Niches along all of the semi-circle contain statues in Neoclassical style.

103 bottom right In the late eighteenth century, Lednice-Valtice was further embellished by what is still the tallest minaret outside the Islamic world.

104 top Also in Neoclassical style, the hunting lodge was built on the shore of a large lake at the start of the nineteenth century.

104 bottom Valtice castle is a fine example of Baroque architecture. Built for Duke Carlo Eusebio, it was begun in the first half of the seventeenth century but only completed at the start of the eighteenth, with an emphasis on the Baroque style of the upper floors.

104

For the reconstruction of Valtice, he appointed the Tuscan architect, Domenico Martinelli, to collaborate with Fischer, but the project was never completed.

In 1715, a wide, tree-lined, four-mile-long avenue was built to join the two properties. Generation after generation, the Liechtensteins continued to embellish the surrounding countryside. At the end of the eighteenth century, they added a minaret

Diana, and Novy Dvur, a farm that produced forage for the horses. The interest of the area was further enhanced by the creation of a park in Romantic style that circled a manmade lake containing 15 islands inhabited by rare birds. The botanist Van Der Scott added 36,000 exotic plants to the 118 endemic species of conifers and 465 species of deciduous trees. Shortly afterwards, the Orangerie was built – the only one in the

decorated in Turkish style, which, at nearly 200 feet tall, was the highest minaret outside the Islamic world. They also built an obelisk in commemorate of the 1797 peace between Napoleon and Archduke Charles Hapsburg, and a copy of a ruined medieval castle that they named Januv Hrad.

During the nineteenth century, the purpose of Lednice-Valtice as a place of leisure was stressed with the construction of a Neo-Classical hunting pavilion, a chapel in the woods dedicated to St. Hubert (the patron saint of hunting), the temples of Apollo and

Czech Republic – and the greenhouse, and the interiors of Lednice castle were decorated in Neo-Gothic style.

The last structural work carried out was completed in 1926 when Moravia's first biological station was established in a building on the shore of one of the lakes.

Today in Lednice-Valtice – an area with a population of 2,400 – work is continuing to ensure the conservation of the buildings and the environment, which, because of its beauty, is one of the Czech Republic's most popular attractions.

104-105 A front view of Lednice castle, the property of the Liechtenstein family for roughly 700 years. It reveals the many modifications and additions made to the original Baroque design.

105 top left The chapel dedicated to St. Hubert, the patron of hunting, stands apart in the woods.

105 top right The artificial ruined medieval castle of Januv Hrad was built in the nineteenth century to add an exotic touch to the property of Lednice-Valtice.

The Palace and Gardens of Schönbrunn

AUSTRIA

VIENNA
REGISTRATION: 1996
CRITERIA: C (I) (IV)

The last important guests to be received in the imperial residence of Schönbrunn were, in 1961, John Fitzgerald Kennedy and Nikita Khrushchev, who met in the Great Gallery of the Hapsburg residence to attempt to put some warmth into the relationship between the West and the Soviet block. Over the centuries the palace had seen other events that had made a deep impression on history, for example, the Congress of Vienna in 1815, when the powers that had defeated Napoleon met to redraw the boundaries of Europe.

Hapsburg property from 1560 on, the Katterburg estate was originally used for farming and consisted of only a small residence with a farm attached. It received its current name when the Emperor Matthias paused to rest during a hunt and named the place where he drank *Schönen Brunnen* (lovely spring). However, the first court summer residence was built there for Eleonora Gonzaga, the wife of Ferdinand II.

It was not until the end of the seventeenth century that Schönbrunn became the epitome of Hapsburg power when, to celebrate the defeat of the Turks after the siege of Vienna, the emperor, Leopold I, invited Johann Bernhard Fischer von Erlach to design a palace that would exceed even Versailles in splendor. Inspired by the villas designed by Palladio, the architect presented his project to the emperor, but the high costs obliged him to be less ambitious. Leopold wanted Schönbrunn to have the character of a family home and to be a mixture between a center of power and a luxurious, but not self-important, residence. The grounds were designed by Jean Trehet in French Baroque style.

The moving spirit of Schönbrunn was, however, Empress Maria Theresa, who raised her 16 children there without neglecting her political duties. Her maternal nature often led her to dispense with court formalities such as the time she took the six-year-old Mozart in her arms in the Mirror Room after his first royal performance.

106 top left The exterior of the Schönbrunn palace and gardens in French Baroque style. The landscape artists Nicolaus Jadot and Adrian van Steckhofen were invited to redesign the park during the reign of Maria Theresa (1740-1780).

106 bottom left The palace seen from the air. It stands in the valley of the river Wien between the Viennese districts of Meidling to the east and Hietzing to the west. The area was

originally a hunting reserve but passed into the hands of the Hapsburgs in 1540.

106-107 The magnificent palace was designed by Johann Bernhard Fischer in line with Palladian architecture. The main court (shown here) has a large fountain and pool in the center. Water is a dominant element at Schönbrunn, as testified to by its name, which is derived from Schönen Brunnen (lovely spring).

107 bottom left The superb Neptune fountain with, in the background, the hill with the Gloriette. The Gloriette was designed by Ferdinand Hetzendorf von Hohenberg as the architectural crown of Schönbrunn Park. Built in 1775, its central section and two galleries are formed by eleven arches on Doric columns, and the whole construction is topped by the symbol of the Hapsburgs: an eagle standing on a globe.

107 bottom right The flower gardens at Schönbrunn. The Hapsburgs were fond of nature and wildlife and loved to collect exotic plants. In 1752, the world's first zoological garden was laid out inside the park. In 1881, a greenhouse – the Palmenhaus – was constructed to hold the palms.

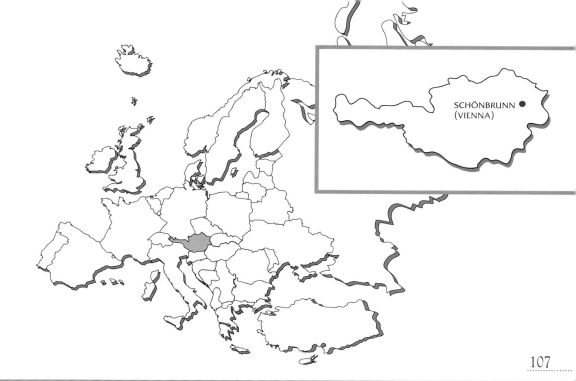

SCHÖNBRUNN
(VIENNA)

Decorated between 1769 and 1777 with motifs taken from nature by Johann Bergl, this room is on the ground floor of the palace. The gilded ceramic stove in the form of a tree trunk is a work of art.

108 bottom A room with sumptuous furniture made from carved and painted wood. Unfortunately, Maria Theresa gave away much of the eighteenth-century furniture to her staff because she liked to replace her furnishings frequently.

108-109 Over 130 feet long and 33 feet wide, the Great Gallery was where the court receptions were held. A superb example of Rococo, it has large windows, mirrors, and stuccoes painted white and gold. The ceiling frescoes were created by Gregorio Guglielmi. Maria Theresa and her consort, Francis of Lorraine, are portrayed in the center surrounded by personifications of their virtues.

Under the guidance of the Italian architect, Nicolaus Pacassi, Maria Theresa had the interiors redecorated in sumptuous Rococo styl, with a profusion of mirrors, gilding, frescoes, and boiserie. Nicolaus Jadot and Adrian van Steckhofen laid out the gardens anew and built the Gloriette, the colonnaded building that is the architectural highlight of the park and from whose terrace the whole of Vienna can be seen. Maria Theresa was also responsible for the Neptune fountain and the attractive copy of a Roman ruin adorned with Neo-

Classical statues. Here, her consort, the future Francis I of Lorraine, founded the first zoological garden in the world called the Früstückspavillon (the breakfast pavilion) around which the cages were arranged.

As Maria Theresa was in the habit of auctioning or giving away her used furniture to her staff at court, few rooms have retained their eighteenth century furnishings, but one of them, the splendid Yellow Room, has Rococo features and paintings of bourgeois children by the young Swiss painter Liotard.

Also original is the Spartan folding bed that was used for decades by Franz Josef and in which he died in 1916, at the age of 88. The emperor was very stern in character. He would rise at half past four each morning, wash himself in cold water, and then pray like the fervent Catholic that he was. He could have slept next to his beautiful wife, Elizabeth of Bavaria, in the sumptuous blue and white wedding chamber furnished in rosewood, but he preferred to leave luxury to her. Elizabeth was better known as the semi-mythical

Princess Sissi, and so many of her *objets d'art* have survived such as her over-elaborate boudoir where she underwent beauty treatments.

Perhaps Franz Josef was aware of the decline of his empire, but it was his successor, Karl I, who, in the blue Chinese Room on November 11, 1918, was obliged to sign the document renouncing affairs of State. The following day the Republic of Austria was proclaimed and the chapter of Schönbrunn's history as an imperial residence was brought to an end.

109 bottom Some of the rooms in the palace are decorated with enormous wall-paintings of bucolic and hunting scenes commissioned by Maria Theresa. In the Ceremonial Room, the empress wanted scenes that realistically represented important moments in the history of the Hapsburgs.

Nôtre-Dame Cathedral, the former Abbey of Saint-Rémi, and Tau Palace in Reims

REIMS, DEPARTMENT OF THE MARNE
REGISTRATION: 1991
CRITERIA: C (I) (II) (VI)

FRANCE

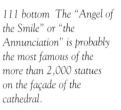

In summer 1429, northern France was occupied by the English troops of Henry IV who was contesting the French throne with the legitimate heir, the dauphin Charles. Inspired by divine will, Joan of Arc convinced Charles to put her at the head of the army which she then led to overturn the English. In her advance, she did not aim straight for Paris but, on July 16, passed through Reims, a city of symbolic importance to the monarchs of France. The next day, Charles was named King Charles VII in the cathedral, thereby perpetuating the tradition that all kings of France – with the exceptions of Henry IV and Napoleon – were crowned at Reims.

The first cathedral was dedicated to the Virgin and built, by order of Bishop Nicasius, on the site of the public baths during the early fifth century. In 496, Bishop Remigius baptized Clovis, king of the Franks, with an act that marked the foundation of the kingdom of France. Officially, however, it was in 816, under the Carolingian King Louis I, that the long tradition of French coronation began in Reims, during the century in which the cathedral – as a tribute to its pivotal role between the church and monarchy – was rebuilt and enlarged. In 1210, a fire provided Archbishop Aubry de Humbert the opportunity to build a new, Gothic cathedral on the ashes of the old basilica and in the image of the existing cathedrals in Paris and Chartres. The project was handed to master mason Jean d'Orbais, and in 1211 the foundation stone was laid. D'Orbais worked on the construction of the choir until 1228, when he was succeeded by Jean le Loup, who built the nave and the façade. Gaucher de Reims

110 The west façade of the cathedral of Nôtre-Dame. Though various master masons were in charge of the construction throughout the thirteenth century, the complex enjoys extraordinary architectural unity. The two 266-foot towers were added in the fifteenth century.

111 top The interior of the cathedral is characterized by an exceptional sense of the vertical. The nave is 125 feet high with pointed arches and a forest of columns and half-columns whose capitals are decorated with naturalistic motifs.

111 bottom The "Angel of the Smile" or "the Annunciation" is probably the most famous of the more than 2,000 statues on the façade of the cathedral.

oversaw the carving of the statues and the inside of the portals, and Bernard de Soissons designed the great rose window that shows the Virgin surrounded by the Apostles and music-playing angels, and completed the construction of the vaults in the nave. By 1285, the interior of the cathedral of Nôtre-Dame had just about been finished, and despite having been directed by several master masons, it was marked by remarkable architectural unity.

The exterior of the immense building – 453 feet long and 125 feet high at the summit of the vaults – features more than 2,300 statues. The elevation of the façade, with its two fourteenth century towers, is

similar to that of Nôtre-Dame in Paris, but the elegance of the lines and the vertical thrust of the tympani make it unique. The nave and two aisles each have a portal; the portal on the left features, among others, the famous statue of the Smiling Angel, an image of solemn serenity in an age in which holy images were often stern. The interior is striking for its stateliness and luminosity. The impression of verticality is accentuated by the dimensions of the nave, which is rather narrow for its length. The cylindrical columns are each surrounded by four half-columns and topped by capitals featuring naturalistic motifs such as acanthus leaves and grapes, in the earliest versions; ivy, berries, and local flora in the more recent examples. The choir only covers the width of two spans of the nave, but the section reserved for worship stretches for three more in the nave. The coronation ceremony and the importance of the chapter required a suitably sized area.

Damaged by the ravages of the weather and by German bombardments that deliberately struck the cathedral

during World War I, several of the statues were transferred to the adjacent Palais de Tau, once the archbishop's palace but now a museum of royal objects, including important sculptures and wall-hangings. The name of the palace comes from the Greek letter 'tau' (the Roman letter "T"), which is the same shape as the first Episcopal crosses. Built in 1690 by Mansart and Robert de Cotte, the palace contains a Gothic chapel and the Tau salon in which the banquet that used to follow the coronation was held. The Benedictine abbey of Saint-Rémi was built during the Carolingian era to hold the remains of the saint who had baptized Clovis, and thus begun the tradition of coronations in Reims. It features a harmonious mix of styles, with a Romanesque façade, a Gothic choir, a dash of Flamboyant Gothic in certain elements, and finally, some finishing touches in Renaissance style. The tomb of St. Rémi (Remigius) is a place of pilgrimage for the faithful from all over France, and it still contains the holy ampoule with which the kings were consecrated.

The Banks of the Seine in Paris

FRANCE

PARIS
REGISTRATION: 1991
CRITERIA: C (I) (II) (IV)

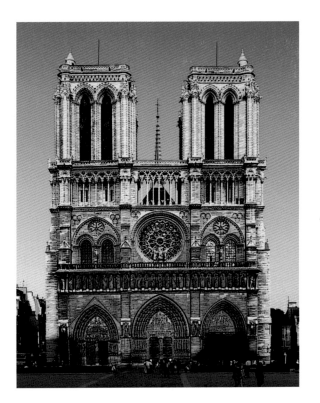

115 top The west face of Nôtre-Dame with its three sculpturally decorated portals, the central rose window dedicated to the Virgin, and the two towers. The tower on the right contains the famous bell, Emmanuel.

115 bottom The starred ceiling of the larger chapel in Sainte-Chappelle. Originally reserved for the royal family, the chapel has walls with 15 marvelous windows – separated by slender columns 49 feet high – that illustrate approximately 1,000 religious scenes and subjects.

When you come to Paris for the very first time, you get the feeling that you are looking at a single, monumental town-planning scheme: it seems as if the Île de la Cité, the esplanade leading from the Arc de Triomphe to the Louvre via the Champs Elysées and the Tuileries, and even the banks of the Seine to the Eiffel Tower, were created by a single, eclectic mind. In reality, Paris is the outcome of seven centuries of renovation, expansion, and restructuring. Nevertheless, there was indeed one person behind this idea of "cultural" unity: Georges Haussmann. Born in 1809 in a modest home on Rue Faubourg de la Roule, Haussmann was to become the city planner for Napoleon III. As prefect of the Seine département, between 1853 and 1870 he transformed the French capital into the famous Ville Lumière, or City of Light.

During the first centuries B.C., the Celtic tribe of the Parisii settled along the banks of the Seine, but a city was not built there until after 52 B.C., when Caesar founded the Roman city of Lutetia. When Julian II (The Apostate) was proclaimed emperor in A.D. 360, the city was renamed "Paris" after its early inhabitants. However, after the fall of the Roman Empire it met with the Viking and barbarian invasions, and it was decimated by epidemics and destroyed by sacking. The Roman buildings were demolished in order to build a walled rampart around the Île de la Cité, where the inhabitants could seek refuge.

Prosperity arrived in the twelfth century with the reign of Philip Augustus. The Île de la Cité, the small island in the heart of Paris set between the banks of the Seine, contains two extraordinary signs of that era, the cathedral of Nôtre-Dame and the Sainte-Chapelle, both masterpieces of Gothic art. In 1163, Pope Alexander III laid the foundation stone of Nôtre-Dame, starting the work that would take 170 years to complete. The cathedral is 427 feet long and supported by flying buttresses, while the pediment is flanked by two towers that are nearly 230 feet tall. Behind the wide transept – topped by the 295-foot-tall spire – there is a carved wooden choir from the eighteenth century that is enclosed by a stone transenna commissioned from Jean Ravy 400 years earlier to shield the services from the noise of the faithful. The interior, with a nave and two aisles, is decorated with paintings and sculptures from different periods. The side chapels hold paintings that the Paris corporations commissioned in the seventeenth and eighteenth centuries from masters like Charles Le Brun. The statue of the Virgin and Child, to whom Nôtre-Dame is dedicated, is next to the transept.

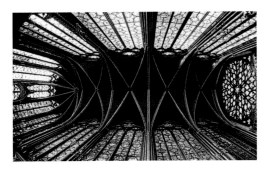

114 top The nave of the cathedral of Nôtre-Dame was completed at the end of the twelfth century. Despite many later alterations, the original style of the nave has been maintained, in particular the hexapartite vault and the massive cylindrical columns of the arches.

114 bottom The smaller chapel in Sainte-Chappelle. The church is one of the greatest works of Western architecture. It was built by Louis IX in 1248 to hold Christ's crown of thorns, a fragment of the Cross, and other precious relics.

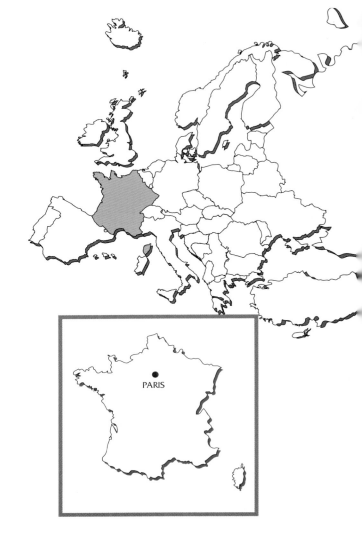

PARIS

In 1248, Louis IX built the Sainte-Chapelle, located near Nôtre-Dame, to hold the relics of Christ, including the crown of thorns the king had purchased from the emperor of Byzantium. The cathedral's lines that stretch up to the sky, the 15 magnificent stained-glass windows of the upper chapel illustrating scenes from the Bible and the Gospels, the enormous rose window, and the carved wooden figures of the apostle earned it the sobriquet of "Gate to Paradise."

Paris was neglected by the French monarchs until Francis I decided that it needed a palace befitting a capital city. As a result, in 1546 construction of the Louvre began, an undertaking that was to span more than three centuries and involve seven different sovereigns. After Francis I, who entrusted to the work to Pierre Lescot, came Queen Catherine de' Medici who had the Tuileries Palace built. Subsequently, Henry IV, Louis XII, Louis XIV (who moved the royal residence to Versailles), Napoleon I, and Napoleon III also left their mark. Despite his love for Versailles, Louis XIV probably had the greatest influence on the construction of the Louvre. Recognizing the stylistic inconsistency of the palace, he asked Gian Lorenzo Bernini, whose fame as an innovator had spread from Italy, to come to Paris to make major changes to the palace. The architect decided to reconstruct the façade but presented plans that were unconvincing. Following the ceremony to lay the foundation stone, Bernini was taken back to Rome and his plans were changed radically. The work was then entrusted to Claude Perrault, who designed the Colonnade enclosing

the existing buildings to give the Louvre its magnificent sense of unity.

The seventeenth century was the city's golden age. Between 1671 and 1676, Louis XIV had the Hôtel des Invalides built on the other bank of the Seine to house aged and invalid veterans. Shortly before this, Cardinal Mazarin built the Collège des Quatre-Nations, now the home of the Institut de France and the headquarters of the national academies. Rue Dauphine and Place Dauphine also date from this period, and about 1650 work was

116 top left One of the majestic galleries on the second floor of the Louvre, dedicated to European painting between 1400 and 1900. Naturally, French artists represent almost half of the immense and priceless collection.

116 top right The halls of the Louvre dedicated to objets d'art, furniture, jewelry, clocks, wall hangings, weapons, armor, porcelain, and much else hold a total of 8,000 items. The picture shows a room filled with eighteenth-century French furniture.

116-117 *The Cour Napoléon, the main court in the Louvre, is lined by buildings from the reign of Louis XIII (1610-1654). Restoration work begun in 1981 under François Mitterand was completed in 1989. The famous glass pyramid over the new entrance was designed by the Chinese-American architect, I.M. Pei.*

117 top *A view of the Roman section of the Louvre shows busts and sculptural groups of extraordinary quality.*

117 bottom left *The Dôme des Invalides is a superb church built in 1676 by the Sun King, Louis XIV. The church was intended to hold the remains of the royal family, but after his death, the project was set aside and the building became a monument to the glory of the Bourbons.*

117 bottom right *The interior of the dome in the Dôme des Invalides. Below it lies the crypt where, in 1861, Napoleon's tomb was placed. The dictator's body was brought back from St. Helena to France at the request of Louis Philippe.*

118 top The Seine from the Eiffel Tower. The bridge in the center of the picture was named after Czar Alexander III, who laid the first stone in 1896. The elaborate Art Nouveau decorations have led it to be considered Paris's most elegant bridge.

completed to transform the Île de Saint-Louis, southeast of Île de la Cité, into a residential area.

In the middle of the eighteenth century, Louis XV commissioned Jacques-Ange Gabriel to create the Place de la Concorde and build the Military School. Across from this, a broad esplanade, the Champs de Mars, stretched to the Seine and was to be the site of France's most important political celebrations. The French Revolution marked an abrupt pause in Paris' development plans, but Napoleon immediately continued the legacy left by his predecessors. At the time, the *quais* (the banks of the Seine) were dotted with a picturesque jungle of boats, warehouses, and windmills. The emperor regulated river traffic and built stone wharfs, but this was just the beginning of his plans for the city. He built the Madeleine, which was to face an

identical church on the other bank. He had the Place de la Concorde redesigned and laid out the Rue de Rivoli so that it would follow the Seine from the Bastille, the symbol of the Revolution, to Place de l'Etoile. Here, in 1805, following the victorious Battle of Austerlitz, work began on the Arc de Triomphe, one of Paris's most famous landmarks. The great bridges over the Seine, the Pont d'Austerlitz, and the Pont d'Iena, were also built alongside the Pont Neuf in order to better link the two banks of the river.

Napoleon stamped his mark on what was already a large metropolis with a population of five hundred thousands. Nevertheless, it was Napoleon III who, during the middle of the century, ordered the town-planning revolution that would give Paris its immortal charm. One of the reasons behind his decision was his fear that the population, with its penchant for

118 bottom Another view of Place de la Concorde. One of the eight statues that symbolize France's most important cities stands in the foreground. In the nineteenth century, the 3,200-year-old Luxor Obelisk was placed in the center of the square. The Eiffel Tower can be seen in the background.

119 top The Champs-Elysées with the Arc de Triomphe in the background. This is the most famous of the 12 avenues that radiate from the monument constructed in 1806 by Napoleon to celebrate his victory at the battle of Austerlitz the year before.

mass uprisings, could again revolt against its leaders. A city with large squares and broad boulevards would allow him to amass an army to defend the monarchy. Haussmann, who conceived and supervised this new layout, created the route leading from Boulevard Saint-Michel to Boulevard de Sébastopol, reorganized the buildings of the Île de la Cité, transformed the Place du Châtelet, and tore down entire city districts to make room for the main thoroughfares that cross the city.

Following Haussmann's glorious makeover, by the end of the nineteenth century Paris was large and splendid enough to come forward as a world capital. Trade flourished, and European culture chose Paris as its haven. The World Exposition of 1889 was held to commemorate the centennial of the French Revolution as well as the resurrection of the city. For the occasion, a monument was planned in order to celebrate the engineering skills of republican France. Maurice Koechline and Emile Nougier from the Gustave Eiffel Construction Company drew up plans for a nearly 1,000-foot-tall tower to be built at the end of the Champs de Mars – strictly for the duration of the Expo. Nevertheless, people were enraged by the plans. A large group of intellectuals signed a petition in an attempt to stop its construction, but

the Eiffel Tower, with the powerful backing of Gustave himself, was built nonetheless and was inaugurated on Sunday, March 31, 1889. And, there it remained, the emblem of modernity with its 11,000 tons of iron and its intriguing tangle of girders and latticework originally invented simply to stabilize the massive structure.

In more recent years, new and colossal works have been built in Paris, particularly under François Mitterrand, with the buildings housing the National Library, the glass pyramid at the entrance to the Louvre, and the extension of the line of sight from the Louvre to the Arc de Triomphe and on to the enormous Arc de la Défense. These projects have continued the thousand-year tradition of Paris and renewed the grandeur of the City of Light.

120 bottom The Eiffel Tower is probably the most famous monument in the French capital. Opened on March 31, 1889 to celebrate the Exposition Universale in Paris, it was the world's tallest building until 1931 when the Empire State Building was completed in New York.

120-121 From the base of the Eiffel Tower, the view takes in the Champ-de-Mars, which are the gardens that stretch as far as the École Militaire. Originally, they were used for the parades of the school's cadets. This is where the large anniversary celebrations to mark the French revolution are held every July fourteenth.

121 bottom left *121 bottom left A section of the Rue de Rivoli. This wide street lined with elegant Neoclassical buildings was laid down for Napoleon in commemoration of his victory at Rivoli in 1797. It connects the Champs Elysées with the Louvre.*

121 top right The tensile structure made of glass and steel in the Grande Arche de la Défense was designed in 1989 by the Danish architect Otto von Spreckelsen.

121 bottom right A view of la Défense. Covering nearly 200 acres, it is the largest office area in Europe. Its careful planning also made it an open-air museum of art and contemporary architecture. The Grande Arche was built as a continuation of the axis on which the Arc de Triomphe and pyramid of the Louvre stand.

The Palace and Parks of Versailles

FRANCE

DÉPARTEMENT OF YVELINES
REGISTRATION: 1979
CRITERIA: C (I) (II) (VI)

122 top left Detail of the statue of Neptune in one of the water parterres in Versailles Park.

122 bottom left The Grand Trianon, built in 1687, was Louis XIV's "resting" palace. Its peaceful atmosphere was also appreciated by Marie-Antoinette, the wife of Louis XVI, who designed its gardens.

Thanks to a secret passage that joined the Queen's apartments to those of the King, on October 6, 1789 Marie-Antoinette managed to evade the angry mob, but her salvation was short-lived. The next morning, Louis XVI and his wife were arrested, and four years later, they were both executed.

The palace at Versailles was thus the setting for the tragic, though temporary, end of the French monarchy, overwhelmed by the debts that Louis XV had left to a son who was too young and unprepared to govern. In truth, Louis XVI was already 20 when he took the throne, whereas his most famous predecessor, Louis XIV, who had built the magnificent palace, was only five when he became king. Furthermore, the Sun King was only 23 when the able diplomat Cardinal Mazarin died, and the king decided to reign France only with the help of his trusted advisor, Jean-Baptiste Colbert.

The history of Versailles began at the start of the seventeenth century when the young heir to the throne, Louis XIII, spent long days hunting in the woods and fields around the village of Versailles. As soon as he became king, he took refuge there to avoid the boredom of court ceremony, and he eventually bought the entire Versailles seigniory on April 8, 1623 where he built a small hunting lodge. This stone, brick, and slate building is now enclosed within the majestic body of the Palace and known as the Old Castle.

Louis XIII, however, did not enjoy the peace of Versailles for long. In 1632, he died prematurely and left the throne to his young son Louis, the future Sun King. Having shored up his kingdom by marrying Maria-Teresa, the Spanish Infanta, in 1660, the young king began expanding his father's palace. Under the guidance of the architect Louis Le Vau, two parallel buildings were constructed in front of the existing palace, the interiors were decorated, and the garden laid out. Yet these improvements were not enough to satisfy the ambitious designs of the king, so in 1668, he decided on a second enlargement. Once again he commissioned Le Vau, who wanted to demolish the older building, but the king opposed this and requested that the new palace be built around it like an "*Enveloppe*." It was within this enlargement that the State apartments were created. With the death of Le Vau in 1670, the design of the terrace that overlooks the garden, which was inspired by the architecture of Italian Baroque villas, fell to François d'Orbay.

In 1678, the Sun King decided to make Versailles the symbol of the French crown. He called on a new architect, Jules Ardouin-Mansart, who, in 6 years, built the gigantic wings to the north and south of

PARIS

VERSAILLES

122-123 Versailles palace replaced the Louvre as the official residence of the kings of France on May 6, 1682. With its 700 rooms and wonderful park, it is one of the most famous buildings in the world.

123 top The Apollo Pool is one of the largest bodies of water in the gardens at Versailles. Lying on the main avenue to the palace, it is a huge octagonal basin adorned with a sculpture of the sun god on his chariot by Jean-Baptiste Tuby.

123 bottom Latona's Pool is another of the extraordinary fountains at Versailles, accessible by a large flight of steps. Fountains and running water were one of Louis XIV's favorite amusements.

the palace, the orangerie, the stables, and the large staff buildings. However, his most important contribution was the transformation of the terrace into the famous Hall of Mirrors, which was to become the emblem of the monarchy's absolute power. This marvelous hall is 240 feet long, 34-and-a-half feet wide, and 39 feet high. At one end there is the Salon de la Paix and at the other the Salon de la Guèrre. Seventeen enormous windows looking out onto the garden are faced by an equal number of mirrors made in a Paris workshop, purposefully fitted out by Colbert to rival those in Venice. The arches rest on marble pillars with bronze capitals decorated with roosters and fleurs-de-lis, the symbols of France. Charles Le

Brun was in charge of the Palace decorations and he painted the ceilings personally: 30 pictures framed by stuccoes emphasize the greatness of the Sun King by means of mythological allusions and references to his military and diplomatic triumphs.

On May 6, 1682, Versailles became the official residence of the French court, replacing the Louvre and Saint-Germain-en-Laye. The project to adapt the site required 36,000 workers, but when the Palace was complete, it could host 5,000 guests. A further 14,000 guards and service staff lived in lodgings annexed to the Palace. The gardens were laid out by the landscape gardener André Le Nôtre. Under his direction, 2,000 acres of land

125

124-125 At 240 feet long and with ceiling frescoes that celebrate the greatness of Louis XIV, the Hall of Mirrors is the symbol of the French monarchy's absolute power. On one side of the hall there are 17 huge mirrors, and on the other, 17 large windows that overlook the park.

124 bottom left In the Salon de la Guèrre, the large medallion carved by Antoine Coysevox celebrates the Sun King's military triumphs.

124 bottom right The Salon de la Paix is named after the painting of Louis XIV. The king asked François Lemoyne to portray him as a bringer of peace to Europe.

125 right Marie-Antoinette was in the queen's bedchamber when revolutionaries broke into the palace on October 6, 1789. Perfectly restored, this room is a perfect example of the splendor with which the royal family surrounded themselves.

were leveled to allow the installation of terraces, avenues, plants, 1,400 fountains, and 400 sculptures.

The extraordinary beauty of the park that lies beyond the Hall of Mirrors cannot be described simply by numbers. Within the grounds, Le Nôtre created dozens of different natural settings joined by avenues that led towards the Étoile Royale. Just behind the Palace lies the Parterre d'Eau, two parallel pools that lead into Latona's Pool and its own Parterre. On the right, to the north, lies the enormous Pièce d'Eau des Suisses, and as

126-127 Two parterres
d'eau *decorated with
superb bronze statues lie
right in front of the
central section of the
palace. The pools are*

*principally ornamental
but they create a highly
dramatic effect by
reflecting the lines of the
building and extending its
architecture.*

one heads away from the Palace, there is
Apollo's Pool and after that the Grand
Canal; the latter is a body of water that
covers 57 acres and has a perimeter of over
three miles, and was the site for water
festivals celebrated during Louis XIV's
reign.

The park contains smaller buildings like
the circular marble peristyle designed by
Mansart in 1685, the spectacular Neptune
fountain by Le Nôtre and Mansart, and the
Petit and Grand Trianons. The Petit
Trianon was built in 1762 as a refuge for

Louis XV's frequent trysts and was later
used for privacy by Marie-Antoinette. The
Grand Trianon was built by Louis XIV in
1687 for his not-so-secret meetings with his
favorite, Madame de Maintenon.

The Sun King's day began precisely at
8:30 with his first appointment held in the
Hall of Mirrors at 10:00 a.m. Here he met
commoners who wished to present him
with petitions. Then, at 11:00, he
transferred to the Chapelle Royale,
construction of which was completed by
Robert de Cotte in 1710. Dedicated to

Saint Louis, it has a raised gallery where
the king sat. The nave was occupied by
courtiers and the women distributed
themselves around the side galleries. Built
in both Gothic and Baroque styles, the
Chapelle has white marble interiors with
gilded stuccoes and fine windows. Its
sculpted pillars, frescoed vaults, and mosaic
floor are typical of the early eighteenth
century. After mass, the king returned to
his private quarters where he held the
daily meeting of the Council of State.
After a short lunch in the company of a

the return to the monarchy, the last great innovation was made by Louis Philippe in 1837. The south wing of the Palace was transformed into the Museum of French History, and 194,000 square feet of space were dedicated to celebrating the *"les gloires de la France."* To complete this immense project, the king commissioned over 3,000 paintings from the greatest painters of the age such as artists of the caliber of Eugène Delacroix. As one wanders through the rooms, the whole of French history unrolls, from the era of the Capetian Dynasty to the mid-nineteenth century.

Versailles is today a symbol of France's

127 top Designed by Jules Hardouin-Mansart with a blend of Gothic and Baroque architectural features, the Chapelle Royale was completed in 1710 by Robert de Cotte.

127 bottom L'Opéra, the court theatre, was built by Jacques-Ange Gabriel during the reign of Louis XV. A complicated mechanical system that raises the auditorium to the height of the stage allowed the theatre to also be used as a reception room.

clutch of courtiers, the king took a long walk in the park and returned at 6:00 p.m. on the dot. This was the time for salon conversation and meetings before dinner and bed.

After the death of Louis XIV in 1715, Versailles was no longer subjected to large scale alterations. Towards the end of the reign of Louis XV, Jacques-Ange Gabriel built the majestic court theater, the Opéra, at the north end of the north wing. Able to hold 700 spectators, the all-wood auditorium provided perfect acoustics. Its

gilded decorations blend harmoniously with the green and pink painted marble. A complicated mechanical device meant that the auditorium could be raised to the height of the stage to allow sumptuous court *fêtes* (parties) to be held. The astounding cost of running the building (10,000 candles would be used on a single gala night) meant that the theater was only rarely used. One of the occasions was the wedding of Louis XVI and Marie-Antoinette in 1770.

Following the French Revolution and

past grandeur, but it still requires a numerous court: eleven curators and three architects to look after the 700 rooms, 67 staircases, and 2,153 windows; 48 gardeners to maintain the park, plant 210,000 new flowers each year, and look after the 200,000 trees; five people to care for the fountains; 18 restorers for the 6,000 paintings, 1,500 drawings, 15,000 etchings, 2,100 sculptures, and 5,000 items of furniture; and, 363 guards to protect this immense artistic heritage that welcomes six million visitors each year.

Mont-Saint-Michel and its Bay

FRANCE

Département of Manche, Ille-et-Vilaine,
Lower Normandy and Brittany
Registration : 1979
Criteria: C (i) (iii) (vi)

Atenth-century manuscript tells how the cult of Saint Michael came to the bay that marks the boundary between Brittany and Normandy. According to the *Revelatio ecclesiae sancti Michaelis*, in the year 708 the Archangel Michael appeared in a dream to Aubert, the bishop of Avranches, touched his forehead with a finger, and ordered him to build a church on the hill known as Mont-Tombe, which stood in the forest of Scissy. This was the period in which the geological phenomenon occurred that caused the subsidence of the land and consequent flooding by the sea, thereby creating the two islands of Mont-Saint-Michel and Tombelaine.

Two centuries later, Duke Richard I of Normandy charged 12 Benedictine monks from Saint-Wandrille with the founding of a monastery where Aubert had built his church of Nôtre-Dame-sous-Terre. In 1023, construction of the abbey's nave was begun with the transept located on the top of the island, and the Benedictines created a community of exceptional spiritual distinction. The mount does not belong to either the land or the sea and is simultaneously threatened and defended by the forces of nature, therefore, it was a perfect refuge for anyone who could reach it. The peace that reigned on the island was propitious for contemplation of the mysteries of the divine.

A part of the abbey was destroyed by fire in 1204 and was replaced by the famous building known as "La Merveille" (The Wonder). It has three floors, is divided into two adjoining sections, and faces the sea to the north of the church. The humblest of the three floors, the ground floor, was where the pantry and refectory reserved for pilgrims were located. The first floor accommodated the dining room used by guests of good standing and the Scriptorium, later called the Knights' Room, in which the monks produced their illuminated codices. On the top floor, the monks' refectory connected with the cloister, which comprised a hanging garden surrounded by arcades supported by columns decorated with floral motifs. The symbolism of the architectural schema is unambiguous. The three floors correspond to the three levels of man: the lowest refers to material drives, the intermediate to erudition and the rational sciences, and the highest signifies communion with God.

Believed to be the earthly representation of the Heavenly Jerusalem, during the late Middle Ages Mont-Saint-Michel became a place of pilgrimage, often inspired by the devotion of the sovereigns, and later became the emblem of French national unity. In 1346, during the Hundred Years War, the English occupied the nearby island of Tombelaine. A brief truce brought peace, but in 1417, they returned to threaten mainland France. In 1426, they tightened their siege of the monastery, which was defended by only 119 knights under the leadership of Louis d'Estouteville. With the help of the monks, the stronghold held out until 1450 when the English abandoned Tombelaine and Normandy was liberated. At the end of the Hundred Years War, the French king, Louis XI, established the Order of the Knights of Saint-Michel and the Archangel Michael was taken to be the patron saint of France. During the long siege, the choir of the church collapsed, and when peace returned, it was rebuilt in the style of Flamboyant

Gothic. With this addition, the abbey became a splendid catalogue of all medieval architectural styles.

In 1790, the monks left Mont-Saint-Michel, which, for the whole of the eighteenth century, had been used by the kings as a political prison. Twenty years later, the mount was officially placed under the

administration of the prisons' authority and was used as a jail for common criminals. The fate of the abbey seemed a sad one, but its existence was vehemently defended by important intellectuals such as Victor Hugo. However, the mount had to wait until 1863 for a decree by Napoleon III that eliminated the prison.

In 1874, Mont-Saint-Michel was registered as a French historic monument and extensive restoration was undertaken that also involved the framework houses in the medieval village that had grown up at the abbey's feet. Three years later a causeway was built to join the island to the mainland so that, for over a century, the tourists who have replaced the pilgrims are no longer required to risk the dangers of the tides.

128 The island has other buildings in addition to the large Benedictine monastery. On the left is Tour Gabriel, the most majestic fortification to be built to withstand the attacks of the English during the Hundred Years War. At the foot of the monastic complex stands the hamlet of framework houses built during the early thirteenth century, the period of Mont's greatest prosperity, when the island was a place of pilgrimage for Christians from all over Europe.

129 top Lit by tall windows, the austere monks' refectory lies to the right of the church and opens into the cloister.

129

129 center The splendid cloister of the Merveille, with elegant pink granite columns, is considered a masterpiece of thirteenth-century Anglo-Norman Gothic.

129 bottom Now connected to the mainland by a raised road, the island of Mont Tombe (on which

the abbey of Mont-Saint-Michel stands) was inaccessible for millennia because of the tides. This extraordinary place lies at the outlet of the Couesnon, the river that marks the boundary between Brittany and Normandy. From afar, it appears suspended between the earth and the sky.

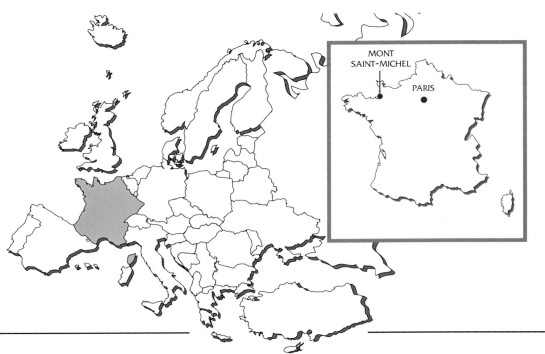

MONT SAINT-MICHEL

PARIS

Notre-Dame Cathedral in Chartres

FRANCE

DÉPARTEMENT OF EURE-ET-LOIR
REGISTRATION: 1979
CRITERIA: C (I) (II) (IV)

130 The cathedral of Nôtre-Dame in Chartres. Built over a period of 25 years thanks to the donations of hundreds of people, it stands on the site of an earlier Romanesque church destroyed by a fire in 1194. Its architecture, which opened the extraordinary Gothic period, has remained almost unaltered since 1260 and has earned it the nickname "the stone Bible."

130-131 The Kings' Portal on the west face shows Christ in Majesty, surrounded by slender statues of figures from the Old Testament. These are the most extraordinary of the roughly 4,000 sculptures on the cathedral.

131 bottom Another view of the west face with the two spires. The taller of the two, on the left, is in pure flamboyant Gothic in contrast to the plainer Romanesque features of the other. The central rose window shows the Last Judgment with Christ seated in the center.

The sculptor Auguste Rodin called it "the Acropolis of France," and, after a pilgrimage there in 1912, the poet Charles Péguy composed a poem that was to rekindle fondness in the hearts of his compatriots for the cathedral that had slipped their memories since the French revolution. Chartres cathedral has remained one of the most important religious buildings in medieval Europe, and its history has spanned a period of 17 centuries.

The origin of the cathedral is shrouded in legend. It is thought that a church was built at the beginning of the fourth century A.D., during the reign of the Roman emperor Constantine, on the site of a miraculous spring worshipped by the Druids and known as the "well of Saints-Forts." What is certain is that, during the Carolingian era, a severe Romanesque cathedral was built here, but it was soon devastated by a series of fires.

In 1020, the famous theologian and court advisor, Bishop Fulbert, initiated reconstruction of the cathedral, which was completed 17 years later. The new building contained a huge crypt (the largest in France), two towers, and a transeptless nave 345 feet long and 112

feet wide. With the advent of the Crusades, the building became one of the main places of pilgrimage in Christendom; this fact may have been due to the presence of a valuable relic, now conserved in the chapel of Saint-Cœur de Marie. It is the veil of the Virgin, which was sent to Charlemagne from Byzantium and, in 876, donated to the cathedral by his successor, Charles II the Bald.

But this ambitious project was also short-lived as, on June 10, 1194, the town of Chartres was struck by another disastrous fire, which spared only the west

part of the cathedral. This new calamity aroused the support of all France: funds and valuables were gathered as well as food to feed the laborers who went straight to work – without compensation – to rebuild the cathedral.

In the record time of 25 years, a new, even more impressive cathedral rose from the ashes of the Romanesque cathedral.

Beautification of the interior was to continue for another 40 years until October 17, 1260 when Pope Louis IX – later to be canonized as Saint Louis – traveled to the cathedral on foot to celebrate the inaugural mass.

The name of the architect is unknown, but this anonymous genius was responsible for the development of a new

architectural style: Gothic. The solidity of the walls of Romanesque cathedrals gave way to a lithe form of architecture that reached towards the sky. Framing the west façade, two tall towers reach upwards, the "clocher Vieux" and "clocher Neuf," both built in the twelfth century and later completed with a ridged roof in a style that heralded Flamboyant Gothic. The "royal gateway" on the same façade owes its name to the crowned statues that decorate it and that are the most admired of the roughly 4,000 figures carved at Chartres.

The dark interiors in earlier places of worship were traversed by mystical rays of light from small windows, but at Chartres the decoration of the interior became part of the architecture itself, for the first time.

The "forest" of round, square, and polygonal columns that rise to spread into the vaults creates a harmonious "naturalistic" effect, accentuated by the play of shadows and light that alter throughout the day.

The triumph of light, however, is signaled by the more than 1,200 windows – the most spectacular in France – that were created between 1205 and 1240. The stained glass illustrates episodes from the lives of the saints, the Bible, and everyday medieval life. Carpenters,

millers, blacksmiths, tradesmen, musicians, nobles parading in their finery, priests, and pilgrims form a backdrop of incomparable artistic value that provides valuable information on society in the Middle Ages. Furthermore, these scenes are even realistic due to the fact that the figures portrayed were those same builders who had devoted themselves to the reconstruction of the cathedral.

132-133 The central nave in the cathedral of Nôtre-Dame is 121 feet high. Here, for the first time in history, the decoration of the interior is architecture in itself. The innumerable columns that blend into the vaults create a "naturalistic" effect accentuated by the light entering through the 150 multicolored windows.

133 top A detail of the wall of the choir decorated with statues showing scenes from the lives of Christ and the Virgin.

133 bottom Situated in the nave, this window shows the Virgin Enthroned. All together, the windows in Nôtre-Dame cover 21,500 square feet.

The Loire Valley between Sully-sur-Loire and Chalonnes

FRANCE

DÉPARTEMENTS OF LOIRET, LOIR-ET-CHER, INDRE-ET-LOIRE,
AND MAINE-ET-LOIR,
RÉGION DU CENTRE AND PAYS DE LA LOIRE
REGISTRATION: 2000 (INCLUDES THE CHATEAU OF CHAMBORD,
REGISTERED IN 1981)
CRITERIA: C (I) (II) (IV)

Leonardo da Vinci, the incomparable Renaissance genius in the fields of art and science, died at the age of 67 in the small residence of Cloux on June 2, 1519. Leonardo had arrived in Amboise – the site of the royal chateau – two years earlier at the invitation of Francis I of Valois, the king of France. In doing so, Leonardo escaped from an Italy being pulled apart by rivalries and intrigues between the feudal territories to find peace in a country that was enjoying the height of prosperity.

His stay in France was spent in the heart of the country, the Loire Valley, which was the cultural, political, and economic center of that period of French history.

Over 620 miles long, the Loire is France's longest river. Its valley contains evidence of Neolithic settlements dating from as far back as the third millennium B.C. With the conquest of Gaul by Julius Caesar, the region passed to Roman control, and with the advent of Christianity, the main cities in the region (Angers, Bourges,

Chartres, Orléans, and Tours) developed into important religious centers.

The Loire has always been fought over. Upon the death of Charlemagne in 814, the dukedoms of Anjou and Blois were created according to the emperor's wishes. The early Middle Ages came to an end with the start, in 1154, of the interminable war with England in which Henry Plantagenet, the Count of Anjou, and Duke of Normandy and Aquitaine, inherited the English crown. In the thirteenth century, Louis IX

134 and 135 top left The 1519 design for the magnificent chateau of Chambord is attributed to Leonardo da Vinci. It took 18 years to complete the chateau, the largest of the manors along the Loire, undergoing several modifications over the centuries to attain its definitive form in 1685. The spires, towers, and domes on the roof make its silhouette unmistakable.

135 top center Louis XIV's bed-chamber is one of the loveliest of Chambord's 440 rooms. The apartments of the Sun King are the largest in the castle.

135 top right A view of the donjon. The interior of the marvelous royal residence is decorated with superb stuccoes and Italian marble.

135 bottom The abbey of St-Benoît-sur-Loire was built between 1067 and 1108 and is one of the best examples of a Romanesque church in France. The nave was later rebuilt in Gothic style.

succeeded in bringing Anjou back under his control, but the war continued on and off until 1453. In 1428, the English had captured the city of Orléans, but Joan of Arc led the French troops to victory, freed the Dauphin, Charles VII, from his hideout in Chinon, and took him to Reims to be crowned king of France. Despite being the setting of the cruel religious wars between Catholics and the Huguenots, the Loire remained the center of French affairs for another two centuries. Although Louis XIV had moved the French court to Paris in the mid-seventeenth century, the turbulent region was still important during the civil war caused by the Wars of the Vendée in 1793.

The Loire runs through a wide, fertile valley between lovely hills dotted with vineyards, sunflower fields, and woods. Following the river and its tributaries from Sully-sur-Loire (the start of the World Heritage Site), the first important example of architecture and history is the Abbey of St-Benoît-sur-Loire, one of the most interesting Romanesque churches in France. It was built between 1067 and 1108 with a plain façade and, inside, a closely packed series of columns that separates the nave from the aisles. The remains of Saint Benedict were buried in

the crypt after being purloined from the monastery of Monte Cassino in Italy, where the monk had established the Order that bears his name.

Proceeding along the river, one comes to Orléans, the medieval capital of France, where there is the rather stark cathedral of Ste.-Croix and a reconstruction of the house that Joan of Arc lived in. The easternmost and largest of the chateaux of the Loire stands in Chambord. This magnificent country house was originally built to be a hunting lodge for Francis I at the start of the sixteenth century. The king organized long hunts in the company of French and Italian nobles, but when he succeeded in persuading Leonardo to join his court, it seems he asked the Italian to design him a new palace.

Chambord was built between 1519 and 1537 by 1,800 workers on the banks of the Cloisson, a tributary of the Loire. The central body of the chateau has a round tower at each corner, but this section was expanded upon by Francis himself and his successors, before achieving its final plan under Louis XIV in 1685. The size of the 440 rooms and the width of the corridors at Chambord make for a truly impressive sight. From the outside, the silhouette of the chateau is composed of a mass of spires, windows, pinnacles, and open galleries that indicate the many different building phases. The building's *pièce de resistance* is the great central spiral staircase made from Italian marble that joins the ground floor with the royal apartments; its innovative design (attributed to Leonardo) is based on the fact that it has two flights of steps that do not meet, one for going up and the other for going down. Of the original furnishings in the chateau, only those provided by Francis I and Louis XIV survived the plundering of the revolution in 1789, along with a room used to store toys.

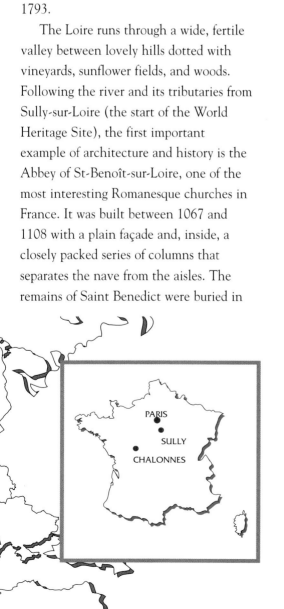

At Blois, a feudal stronghold since the twelfth century, one enters the most beautiful part of the valley. Here, Louis XII established his court in 1498, adding new wings to the home of the Counts of Blois and rebuilding the Chapelle de St.-Calais. Francis I's central staircase, from which the royal family watched court performances, stands in the center of the court.

Further down the Loire, there is a series of extraordinary residences such as the chateau of Chaumont-sur-Loire, situated in a fairy-tale setting on the top of a hill. It was the home of Charles II of Amboise at the end of the sixteenth century. Then, there is the chateau of Amboise, still owned today by the Count of Paris, who is a direct descendant of the last royal family of France. Rebuilt at the time of Charles VIII and Francis I, its most unusual feature is the Chapelle de St.-Hubert, built in enchanting late Gothic style with richly decorated spires, purported to be the place Leonardo was buried.

The valley widens towards Tours, where there is the cathedral dedicated to St.-Gatien. Construction was begun at the start of the thirteenth century but it was only completed 350 years later. In order to see the most splendid of the Loire chateaux, a short side trip must be taken to the river Cher where Chenonceaux stands. In 1512, Thomas Bohier, a royal chamberlain,

bought a medieval manor and entrusted its reconstruction to his wife, Catherine Briçonnet. Since that moment, the history of Chenonceaux has been a history of women. Diane de Poitiers was given it by her lover, Henry II, in 1547; she created a garden there and had a bridge built over the river but upon the king's death, his lawful wife, Catherine de' Medici, reclaimed it for herself. She had the bridge covered to form the broad and romantic Grande Galerie with a checkerboard-patterned floor. Thanks to Louise Dupin, who instituted an intellectual circle there that had a good reputation among the insurgents, Chenonceaux was saved from the plundering that took place during the Revolution. It was restored in the nineteenth century before being acquired by the Menier family. Among its richly decorated rooms, the study belonging to Catherine de' Medici stands out for its simplicity: it is no more than a garret with green velvet walls that looks out onto the river. Completely different in atmosphere is the luminous chapel featuring a vaulted ceiling and pillars carved with acanthus leaves and shells.

Beyond Tours, the Renaissance chateau of Villandry belonging to the Carvallo family is worthy of mention for the perfection of its enormous gardens, in which eight gardeners take care of the

136 top right The General Staff room at Blois was used for assemblies and royal receptions. The room was part of the original thirteenth-century residence, when Blois was an independent feudal stronghold outside the authority of the French crown.

136 center Chenonceaux lies between the banks of the river Cher. Rebuilt in 1512 by the royal chamberlain Thomas Bohier and his wife Catherine Briçonnet, it later became the property of the royal family.

136 bottom The great covered gallery at Chenonceaux makes it the most attractive chateau in the Loire valley. It was built for Catherine de' Medici, wife of Henri II.

136-137 Wrapped in the mist, the chateau of Chaumont seems to come from a fairy-tale. Built in the twelfth century, it was inherited in 1481 by Charles II d'Amboise, who turned it into the one of the first French Renaissance residences.

137 bottom An aerial
view of the town of
Amboise with the enclosed
chateau standing in an
elevated position. The
castle is still the property of
the Count of Paris, a direct
descendant of the royal
family.

139 top Built on a cliff over the river Vienne, the three distinct citadels of Chinon are enclosed by a defensive wall. It was here that Joan of Arc freed Charles VII before taking him to Reims to be crowned king of France.

138-139 From the late Renaissance, the chateau of Villandry comprises three main sections, a donjon, and a main court. Its fame is derived from the spectacular Renaissance garden that the Spanish Carvallo family recreated from original sixteenth-century designs when they purchased the property at the start of the twentieth century.

60,000 vegetables and 45,000 bedded plants. Further on, one comes to the chateau of Azay-le-Rideau, which Honoré de Balzac called "a precious diamond set upon the Indre." Built in 1518 by Gilles Bertholet, it was requisitioned ten years later by Francis I. Then, there is Langeais Chateau with architectural elements from the sixteenth century, and Chinon, which is a fort built above a steep drop over the river Vienne. Here, at the end of the trip through the World Heritage site, it is almost like going back further in time: from the triumphs of Renaissance architecture, the Abbey of Fontevraud (also written Fontevrault),

founded in 1101 by the hermit Robert d'Arbrissel, is a return to medieval religious architecture, and the walls of the fort of Angers, built on the river Maine between 1220 and 1240, are typical medieval defenses reinforced with 17 round towers.

With its marvelous chateaux, churches, and ordered countryside, the Loire valley is a strong reminder of the grandeur of the princes and kings that once lived there. It is a fairy-tale world in which the countless soaring turrets of Ussé Chateau were able to inspire Charles Perrault to write *The Sleeping Beauty* in the seventeenth century.

139 center Begun by Jean de Bueil in 1462 on the foundations of a medieval fort, the chateau of Ussé was later embellished with Renaissance features by the Espinay family, who purchased it in 1485. The pointed towers adorned with imaginative battlements inspired Charles Perrault to write the story of The Sleeping Beauty.

139 bottom The ballroom in Azay-le-Rideau features a huge fireplace and superb Flemish wall hangings.

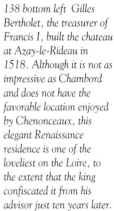

138 bottom left Gilles Bertholet, the treasurer of Francis I, built the chateau at Azay-le-Rideau in 1518. Although it is not as impressive as Chambord and does not have the favorable location enjoyed by Chenonceaux, this elegant Renaissance residence is one of the loveliest on the Loire, to the extent that the king confiscated it from his advisor just ten years later.

138 bottom right The severe lines of Langeais Castle resemble the forts of the feudal period. Built between 1465 and 1490 for Louis XI, unlike many other castles in the region it has conserved its period furniture and furnishings.

Royal Saltworks of Arc-et-Senans
FRANCE

DÉPARTEMENT OF DOUBS, FRANCHE-COMTÉ
REGISTRATION: 1982
CRITERIA: C (I) (II) (IV)

140 top A decorative detail on the workshop wall: the small oblong window is in the shape of the mouth of a jar from which petrified water, symbolizing brine, gushes.

140 bottom The bulky residence of the director sits in front of the center of the saltworks' semicircle of buildings. It has a peristyle courtyard lined with columns topped by alternating cylindrical and cubic drums.

140-141 An overall view of the royal saltworks at Arc-et-Senans, designed by Nicolas Ledoux between 1775-1778 for Louis XVI. The complex comprises eleven buildings, five of which stand in a semicircle. The brine was transported to the treatment plant via a 12-mile-long canal. For this reason, Arc-et-Senans is considered the first integrated industrial site in history.

As a result of his acquaintances at the court of Louis XVI, in 1771 Claude Nicolas Ledoux was appointed officer of the saltworks of Franche-Comté, Lorraine, and Trois-Evêchés. The responsibility of this post was not negligible, for the mining of salt fed the coffers of the State and was a most unpopular duty during the Ancien Régime.

Ledoux was born in Dormans in 1736 and studied architecture in the renowned private school belonging Jacques François Blondel in Paris. His teachers stressed the tradition of the French Baroque yet did not neglect the dictates of English architecture. On completion of his studies, Ledoux had already worked for the Crown as a designer of bridges.

His first act in his role as salt officer was to visit Salins-les-Bains, a village in the Jura known as the "cité de l'or blanc" (city of white gold) as its sole reason for existence was the mining of rock-salt. He found the place rather unpleasant, uncomfortable, and even worse, partially deforested. The refinement of salt required a great deal of wood for burning, so Ledoux proposed transferring the refinement plants to the forest of Chaux following his logic that it was easier to transport saltwater to a forest than vice versa. The forest of Chaux covered 49,400 acres and was one of the largest wooded areas in all of France.

Construction of the royal saltworks in Arc-et-Senans began in 1775. In less than four years, the brine was being conveyed down a sloping channel made from tree-trunks and a further 12 miles to the first integrated industrial site in history. Visionary and totalitarian at the same time, Ledoux's project was formed by a complex of eleven buildings. Five pavilions were arranged in a semi-circle in front of the management's lodgings, and these were flanked by two large structures that contained the ovens for refining the salt. In the center of the arc, the entrance pavilion opened onto a Doric colonnade leading to a grotesque door that seemed the entrance to a cave; stalactites hung from the ceiling and false blocks of white rock represented salt. Even the workshops were punctuated by small holes from which petrified water flowed in a representation of brine.

Inspired by Neo-Palladian architecture from the other side of the Channel and by Roman art as it appeared in the engravings by Piranesi, Ledoux developed a practical and functional style that made use of elements that seemed to anticipate post-modern Classicism. For the residence of the works' director, he designed a massive building featuring a peristyle with six columns that alternated cylindrical and cubic drums.

The royal saltworks factory existed in a society that was not yet industrial, but was also a tribute to the pre-determined social order. It was a reflection of the century of the Enlightenment in its attempt to return all the life of the community to a single space. The village of Arc-et-Senans was home to 400 or so workers and their families. The director's task was to watch over not only production, but also the morality of his employees and their free time. The administrative section was where

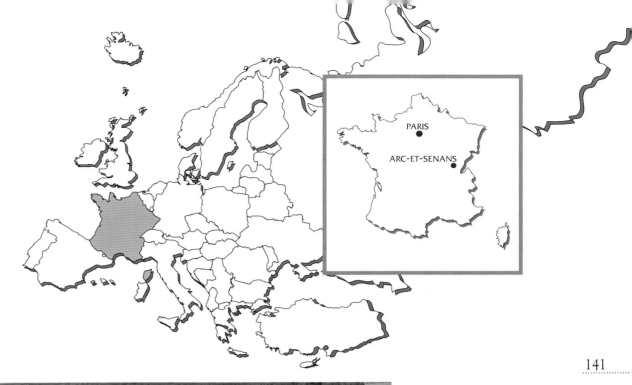

141 right The royal saltwork's entrance pavilion opposite the residence of the director-of-works. Inspired by Palladian architecture, it has a Doric colonnade in front of a door that seems to lead into a cave.

justice was meted out and Mass was celebrated. The only areas not under the director's gaze were the gardens between the buildings and the enclosure walls, and it was here that the workers tended their allotments and enjoyed their few free moments of freedom.

During the Terror, Ledoux was arrested and accused of being an aristocrat. In the two years he spent in prison, he completed his plans for Chaux,

enlarging and turning the saltworks into an ideal city of concentric circles for which he designed every detail. Nevertheless, his Utopian vision of the eternal and perfect city was never to see the light. The saltworks, however, continued operating until 1895, when the use of coal allowed the rock-salt to be processed where it was mined.

After years of abandonment, Arc-et-Senans has today been completely

restored. Even the vegetable patches have today been turned into unusual gardens. Next to the *potagers paresseux*, meaning "the lazy gardens," in which the plants in the beds grow as tall as a man, and the *potager apéro*, which smells fragrantly of aniseed, there lies a potager mesclun fleuri where the flowers peep out between tufts of salad. Overall, it is a sort of ideal kitchen garden in tribute to a city that should also have been ideal.

The Historic Center of Avignon

FRANCE

DÉPARTEMENT OF VAUCLUSE,
PROVENCE
REGISTRATION: 1995
CRITERIA: C (I) (II) (IV)

142 top right The façade of the thirteenth-century Petit Palais. Once the residence of the archbishop of Avignon, it is now home to a museum of Romanesque and Gothic sculptures and of a remarkable collection of paintings of the French and Italian schools, including some by Botticelli and Caravaggio.

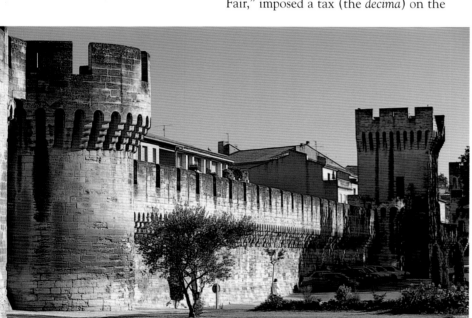

142 bottom left Avignon's solid city walls. The city was built to be a military stronghold rather than a religious center due to the violent nature of the political and religious climate in fourteenth-century Europe.

142-143 The city of Avignon is dominated by the monumental Palais des Papes. Enclosed by ten towers and built to be unassailable, the set of buildings covers a surface area of 161,000 square feet.

At the start of the fourteenth century Rome lost its role as papal city, and Avignon, the vassal city of the Holy See on the left bank of the Rhône River, became the religious, bureaucratic, and cultural center of Christianity.

To tackle the growing need for income, in 1296, the king of France, Philip IV "the Fair," imposed a tax (the *decima*) on the clergy, which appropriated one tenth of their income. This affront prompted a reaction by Pope Boniface VIII, but the temporal power of the Church was declining and Philip had no qualms about having the pope arrested on September 7, 1303. Boniface VIII died less than a month later as a result of the dreadful humiliation.

After a conclave lasting more than a year, Boniface was succeeded by Bertrand de Got, the Archbishop of Bordeaux, who took the name Clement V. In 1309, he gave in to the pressure imposed on him by the French king and abandoned Rome to transfer the papacy to Avignon. Initially, it was a proper exile, but soon the "Babylonian captivity" turned into a Byzantine exercise of power. Seven popes, all born in France, ruled there until 1377, in addition to the two anti-popes, Clement VII and Benedict XIII, who stayed in Provence while opposing their Roman antagonists for a further 25 years. The influence of the French monarchy was so overwhelming that 111 of the 134 cardinals nominated during this period were French.

Although Clement V was satisfied to live in the Dominican monastery, his successor John XXII, the former Bishop of Avignon, preferred to adapt the Episcopal palace to the requirements of a pontifical seat. However, it was Benedict XII who commissioned master-builder Pierre Boisson to build a fort that reflected the Spartan tastes of the Cistercian monk. Work began in 1335 on the Angel Tower, protected by a fortified wall, and the private apartments next door. Between 1338 and 1342, the wings of the palace were built, which enclosed a cloister and were protected by two solid towers. The Great Chapel was constructed parallel to the existing Romanesque cathedral of Nôtre-Dame-des-Doms, which was frescoed by the Sienese painter, Simone Martini, in 1340.

For Clement VI, an aristocrat and a lover of earthly pomp, this residence was too modest, so he invited the architect Jean de Louvres to build a new and better laid-out building next to the Old Palace,

143 top A corner of the cloister built by Pope Benedict XII (1334-1342) in the Popes' Palace. It is overlooked by the Benedictine Chapel and the rooms reserved for guests and staff. Note the severe-looking bell tower in the background.

PARIS

AVIGNON

144 top The ceiling of the Great Audience Room. From the start of his pontificate in 1343, Clement VI, an aristocrat who loved luxury, enlarged the Palace to make it more impressive and comfortable. The architect was Jean de Louvres and the decoration was by Matteo Giovannetti from Viterbo, who coordinated a group of artists from all over Europe.

144 bottom One of the many interiors of the Palais des Papes, adorned with funerary sculptures in Gothic style. Unfortunately, much of the magnificent fourteenth-century furniture was destroyed during the French Revolution.

to which was additionally added the Tower of the Wardrobe and the Great Audience Room. In the immense barrel-vaulted dining room (lined with blue silk studded with gold stars), banquets were given for important guests. The Great Chapel was substantially enlarged and redesigned in Gothic style and became the setting for masses. The first three spans are occupied by the altar, the pontifical throne, and the cardinals' benches; the other four spans are filled by the chapel's nave.

145 bottom right The Pope's Chamber on the main floor of the Angel Tower was decorated during the pontificate of Clement VI. It contains tempera paintings of vine and oak leaves, birds, and small animals on a blue background.

145 top The Grand Tinel is the banqueting room where the cardinals sat in conclave to elect the new pope. The walls are decorated with 17th/18th century tapestries of the French school.

145 bottom left A detail of the frescoes in the Great Audience Room. These and the frescoes in the Tower of the Wardrobe and chapels of

St. Martial and St. John reveal the quality of the Avignon school, besides giving a vivid insight into the pomp-filled life of the papal court.

In 1348, Clement's ambitions led him to buy the entire city of Avignon from Joan of Anjou, the Queen of Naples, and to encircle it with crenellated walls two-and-a-half miles long. He also had façades and interiors in the city rendered less severe with the construction of Gothic cross-vaults that made space for superbly carved walls. He commissioned Matteo Giovannetti to decorate the Tower of the Wardrobe, the chapels of St. Martial and St. John, and the Great Audience room. With these works, the Avignon Church ushered in the nascent era of Humanism, as the painted scenes of life in woods and gardens indicate.

The Popes' Palace, the cathedral, the Petit Palais – a thirteenth-century cardinals' residence – and the bridge of Saint-Bénézet form the heart of a city that played a decisive and strategic role in Europe during the fourteenth century. But the "Babylonian captivity" did not last much longer. Once the popes returned to Rome, Avignon remained the property of the Holy See, and the Popes' Palace remained the residence of the papal legates up until the French Revolution in 1791, when the enclave was forcefully restored to France and the papal treasures plundered.

In the nineteenth century, the Middle Ages came powerfully back into fashion and the great architect, Eugène Viollet-le-Duc, restored the residence to its original splendor. Often his interventions are clear travesties, but Avignon is inseparable from these nonetheless attractive deceits.

The Last Supper
ITALY

MILAN
REGISTRATION: 1980
CRITERIA: (I) (II)

CHURCH AND DOMINICAN MONASTERY OF SANTA MARIA
DELLE GRAZIE WITH "THE LAST SUPPER"
BY LEONARDO DA VINCI

146 top The "hut"-like façade of the brick church of Santa Maria delle Grazie, designed by Guiniforte Solari. The first stone was laid in 1463, but the building was not completed until 1490.

146 bottom left The longitudinal nave in Santa Maria delle Grazie bears the most important features of the fifteenth-century architectural innovations: side chapels in a unitary design systematically structured as part of the aisles.

After restoration work lasting 20 years, the refectory in the Monastery of Santa Maria delle Grazie in Milan was reopened to the public on May 28, 1999. The world's most famous fresco was once again avbailable to the eyes of the world with a splendor that not been seen for centuries.

It had been decided in the mid-fifteenth century that a new church should be built as a result of the refusal of the Dominican fathers in Sant'Eustorgio to adhere to the reform of the Order. The project was entrusted to Giuniforte Solari, and the first stone was laid in 1463. By 1490, the Late Gothic building and adjacent monastery had been completed, but two years later, Ludovico the Moor decided to have some modifications made to it so that it could hold the tomb of his wife, Beatrice d'Este. Donato Bramante was asked to demolish the presbytery and apse and build a superb Renaissance *tribuna* decorated with the coat of arms of the Sforza family, the lords of the city, and with marble medallions of the saints.

Bramante was probably assisted by Leonardo, to whom the fresco on the back wall of the refectory was entrusted. The refectory is a huge room with a vault and lunettes with umbrella-shaped tops. The master from Vinci set to work on the fresco in 1494-1495 and completed it in 1498. Although the Last Supper was a theme that was commonly represented in monastery refectories, Leonardo made it the symbol of Italian Renaissance painting. Jesus is shown in the center, isolated, while the Apostles, in groups of three, comment on the bad tidings Jesus has just given them that one of them will betray him. The table holds the remains of their frugal meal and the room is adorned with carpets, as remarked on in Saint Mark's Gospel. A magnificent central perspective appears behind the group that represents the imaginary continuation of the actual space in the refectory.

The dramatic scene inspired a plethora of works by painters not only of the

146 bottom right The dome of the church of Santa Maria delle Grazie is attributed to Donato d'Angelo Lazzari (known as Bramante) from Urbino. Its hemispherical structure is not visible from outside, where it appears as a 16-sided tiburio (crossing tower) typical of Lombard architecture.

146-147 Even before being finished, Santa Maria delle Grazie was profoundly renewed stylistically by Bramante for Ludovico the Moor so that it would contain the tomb of Beatrice d'Este. The transept and apse of the Solari were demolished and replaced by an extraordinary Renaissance-style tribuna.

147 bottom A detail of Bramante's tribuna. The 16 sides of the tiburio are adorned with a row of Corinthian columns.

Lombard school such as Titian, but also by Giorgione, Rubens, and Rembrandt. Numerous painters made copies of the "Cenacolo" (the fresco's Italian name); in 1503, Bramantino made one for a private client, followed by Giovan Pietro da Cemmo, Andrea Solario, and Marco d'Oggiono il Giampietrino, whose reproductions on canvas contributed to spreading the fame of the fresco.

Soon, however, the quality of the work began to deteriorate. Leonardo had made a surprisingly unforeseen mistake by using tempera and oil colors directly on a base,

compelling subject among Milanese cultural circles was the restoration of the "Cenacolo," but often such attempts were no more than a pretext for city governors and art curators to bring attention to themselves; for example, in 1770 an awkward stab was made at restoration by Giuseppe Mazza at the request of Count Carlo di Firmian, who had been charged with the task by the Austrian governors of Milan. An analogous episode occurred at the start of the twentieth century when Luigi Cavenaghi tried to secure the paintwork with hard resins as opposed to

which he himself had mixed, on the stone wall, a technique known as painting *a secco*. In traditional fresco painting, the colors are painted onto a fresh (hence, *a fresco*) layer of lime so that they would hold better. Leonardo preferred the former method, which allowed him to provide more detail, but the humidity in the refectory proved damaging. Serious harm was mentioned as early as 1517, and a century later, Cardinal Federico Borromeo commissioned Vespino to make a perfect copy of the fresco as a record of the masterpiece that had already been given up for lost.

Over the following centuries, the most

retouching the colors themselves. By World War II, the Last Supper was in very poor condition, but at least it was saved from the bomb that hit the refectory in August 1943. However, rebuilding work made necessary by the collapse of a wall and the ceiling produced dust and dampness that exacerbated the fresco's perilous state. In the 1950's, the paint was reduced to the minimum contact with the wall. The last restoration, begun in 1977, was the latest in a series of at least ten useless, or even damaging, attempts. Finally, the most ambitious option was taken, that of removing the added layers to find the true Cenacolo by Leonardo below.

148 On the wall of the refectory opposite Leonardo's "Last Supper" there is a 1495 fresco of the Crucifixion by Donato Montorfano. Artistically unremarkable in comparison, Montorfano's work has survived much better because the artist used the traditional fresco technique.

148-149 Leonardo painted the Last Supper between 1494 and 1498 for Ludovico the Moor, whose insignia appears in the central lunette above the fresco. The use of a central perspective gives the picture an exceptionally dramatic effect in which the real space of the refectory seems to continue into the painting.

The City of Vicenza and the Palladian Villas of Veneto

ITALY

VENETO
REGISTRATION: 1994, EXTENSION: 1996
CRITERIA: C (I) (II)

150 top Villa Almerico Capra, the most famous of Palladio's designs, was built for the prelate Pietro Almerico in 1570. It is called "La Rotonda" because it is the only one of Palladio's villas to have a dome; its design was inspired by the Pantheon in Rome.

150 bottom Built in 1542, Villa Godi in Lonedo di Lugo was one of Palladio's first works.

The White House, the homes of the tobacco barons in Virginia, and the country homes of the British aristocracy are a few examples of buildings all linked in architectural concept to the same origin. United by a thread that crossed seas and continents from sixteenth-century Vicenza, their common denominator is Andrea Palladio, his real name Andrea di Pietro della Gondola, who was born in Padua in 1508 but adopted Vicenza as his home, where he died in 1580. His genius and style prompted a revolution in architecture, and ever since then Palladianism has had a decisive influence on residential design.

Andrea's story began in 1535 with a fortunate encounter. The young boy was then a stonecutter, and came to know the poet and humanist Giangiorgio Trissino (the most illustrious intellectual in Vicenza at the time) while he was working on Villa Cricoli near Vicenza. A lover of ancient Greece, it was Trissino who gave the boy the nickname Palladio and took him under his protection, introducing him to the study of the classics and taking him on several occasions to Rome where he met Michelangelo, Giulio Romano, and Bramante.

In 1540, Andrea Palladio began his profession as an architect during a favorable period. Vicenza had been little more than a farming town since its foundation in the second century B.C. and part of the powerful Republic of Venice for a few decades. The local nobles competed to demonstrate their wealth at the court of the Doges, while the Venetians began to purchase land on the mainland for agricultural use.

Palladio first designed and built Palazzo Civena in Ponte Euro and Villa Godi in Lonedo, both just outside the city of Vicenza, but his official approval came in 1549 when his design for the reconstruction of the fifteenth-century Loggia del Palazzo della Ragione – the center of power in the city – was chosen over other submissions. The Basilica Palladiana, as the Palazzo was renamed, is a masterpiece, and from that moment on the nobility in the Serenissima contended for Palladio's services.

Although he designed public buildings, churches, monasteries, and bridges that altered the appearance of Vicenza, country houses were his preferred medium. The 70 or so that he built within a radius of 43 miles of

150-151 The Basilica is the most perfect example of Palladio's notion of architectural balance. Invited to enlarge the ancient Palazzo della Ragione, Andrea Palladio built two orders of loggias around it.

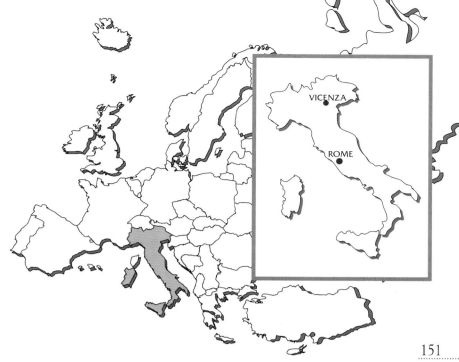

VICENZA

ROME

151 top The attractive but formal façade of Villa Barbarigo in Noventa Vicentina is crowned by obelisks and framed by two porticoes. The building is also known as the Villa of the Doges and perfectly matches the requirements of its clients, who wanted both a center from which they could control their agricultural activities and a building that would honor the glory of their family.

151 bottom Palladio died in 1580 a few months after designing the Teatro Olimpico in Vicenza. This Renaissance masterpiece contains a triumphal arch in honor of Hercules inside the proscenium, similar to the arches that were used to receive nobility and bishops.

Vicenza (not all of them still exist) were based on no particular model but displayed an astounding range of innovations that all shared the characteristics of being both functional and convenient.

The *summa* of his thought was a treatise entitled the *Quattro Libri dell'Architettura*, which he published in 1570. The chapter dedicated to villas contains a general introduction, his designs, and notes on the frescoes and statues that decorated the buildings. He did not hesitate to give practical advice, for example, relating to analysis of the land, checking of the nearby waterways, the health of the local population and animals, even testing the quality of the local bread, and the suggestion that an architect should never work in an office but on the spot.

Of those villas described in the treatise, 12 are still standing. The most famous is Villa Almerico Capra, known as "La Rotonda," not far from the center of Vicenza. Built around 1570 for the prelate Paolo Almerico, its structure is based on that of the Pantheon in Rome and is an interpretation of the classical theme of the sacred space in a temple. Palladio's design was that of a villa-cum-temple to celebrate his client's duties in the Vatican; it has a centralized layout and is topped by a dome.

His other villas were developed longitudinally, with porticoes and wings

used for storage purposes, which enclosed a court. Villa Pojana in Pojana Maggiore was modeled on the personality of his client. It was built in 1550 for a very old noble family traditionally related to the art of war that had only recently converted to agriculture. Here Palladio produced a structure of composite elegance that evoked the austerity of military life in its renunciation of loggias and decorative elements. Villa Pisani in Bagnolo di Lonigo was built for the aristocratic Venetian Giovanni Pisani. The façade that looks over the river has two towers that enclose a three-arched loggia topped by a tympanum. The inspiration for this design was the traditional Venetian shop known as a *fondaco*, as a reminder of the owner's vocation as a merchant. Villa Saraceno in Finale di Agugliaro is a perfect example of a villa-cum-farm, and Palladio used it as a model of functionality in his treatise.

From 1570, Palladio became the architectural consultant to Venice where he designed the churches of the Redentore and San Giorgio Maggiore. In the year of his death, 1580, he began the construction of another masterpiece, later completed by Scamozzi: the Teatro Olimpico in Vicenza, which was to be used for performances of classical tragedy. Featuring three dimensional perspective vistas, the Olimpico is Europe's oldest surviving covered theater.

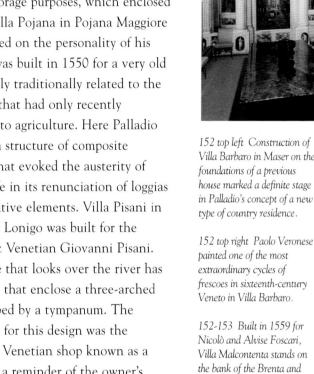

152 top left Construction of Villa Barbaro in Maser on the foundations of a previous house marked a definite stage in Palladio's concept of a new type of country residence.

152 top right Paolo Veronese painted one of the most extraordinary cycles of frescoes in sixteenth-century Veneto in Villa Barbaro.

152-153 Built in 1559 for Nicolò and Alvise Foscari, Villa Malcontenta stands on the bank of the Brenta and can be reached by boat from Venice. The clients were from one of the city's most powerful families and the villa was given a majestic, almost regal, character.

153 top left Attribution of the design of Villa Contarini is controversial, but in any case, the building was notably altered by the late seventeenth-century addition of two wings, and the large hemicycle square in front of the villa.

153 top right Villa Trissino in Cricoli was not designed by Palladio but he contributed to its construction as a stonemason. It was during construction of the building in 1534 that Palladio met his future patron, the nobleman from Vicenza, Giangiorgio Trissino.

Venice and its Lagoon
ITALY

VENETO
REGISTRATION: 1987
CRITERIA: C (I) (II) (III) (IV) (V) (VI)

154 top Built to hold the mortal remains of the Evangelist and consecrated in 1094, St. Mark's Basilica is the symbol of Venice. A unique monument in the history of medieval art, it has been adorned over the centuries with Byzantine, Romanesque, Gothic, and Renaissance art. Since 1807 it has been the seat of the Patriarchate, which was transferred here from the cathedral of San Pietro di Castello.

154 bottom The origin of the gilded bronze horses in St. Mark's Quadriga is uncertain. They arrived in Venice in 1204 as part of the booty taken from Byzantium (Constantinople).

A series of large mobile sluice gates have been designed to be anchored to the bottom of the lagoon across the entrances to Chioggia, Lido, and Malamocco. When the level of the Adriatic rises beyond a certain limit, the sluice gates will be raised to prevent the water entering the lagoon. That is a summary of the Moses Project, which, together with other steps being taken for the restoration of Venice, should protect the city and its lagoon from the "high water," the high tides that today strike the city on average 40 times a year.

If global warming raises the sea level as much as predicted, the phenomenon of high water may occur 100 times a year by the mid-twenty-first century, placing an inestimable cultural patrimony in jeopardy. It is inestimable and also unique because, as UNESCO emphasized when defining the entire city as a World Heritage site, the 118 islands on which Venice stands form an extraordinary masterpiece of architecture in which even the smallest palazzo contains works by great masters like Giorgione, Titian, Tintoretto, and Veronese.

Certain sources maintain that Venice came into being on March 25, 421, but this hypothesis is not supported by documentation. However, it is certain that in the middle of the fifth century, with the break-up of the Roman empire, the advance of the Huns under Attila forced many inhabitants from the Veneto mainland to take shelter in the lagoon areas along the Adriatic coast. Remaining in the sphere of the Roman Eastern Empire, the inhabitants of the lagoons obtained a wide degree of independence in 697 when the maritime tribunes sent by Byzantium were replaced by a *dux* (the first Doge), Paoluccio Anafesto.

The decisive moment arrived in 811 when the government under Doge Agnello Particiaco moved the area's administrative center from Malamocco to Rivo Alto (known today as Rialto) in the center of the lagoon. This is conventionally accepted as the moment the history of Venice began. A few years later, two artful sailors smuggled the body of Saint Mark

the Evangelist out of Alexandria in Egypt and took it to Rialto where, according to legend, the saint had taken refuge after a shipwreck. The body of the saint was buried in the Doge's chapel in the place where St. Mark's Basilica was later built. The church was consecrated in 1094 on the spot where two buildings had been built to hold and venerate Saint Mark's remains.

In the ninth century, Venetian sailors already enjoyed close relations with the Levant, and the young state had launched a series of military actions against rival ports in the Adriatic. During the early crusades, the plundering of conquered lands allowed the Venetians to accumulate great riches, but their increasing wealth was due more to the city's control of trade throughout a huge area of the Mediterranean. With the Fourth Crusade, Venice's power experienced a sharp upturn in quality. The taking of Byzantium in 1204 marked the conquest of a large part of the Roman Eastern Empire, with the result that the small city of sailors came to dominate islands, ports, and cities throughout the Aegean and Ionian seas. Besides political and economic gains, the sacking of Byzantium also brought Venice the four bronze horses (the Quadriga) that stand on St. Mark's church, the Golden Altar in the same basilica, and the many marble statues that adorn its façade.

155

155 top The Procuratorie that line the sides of St. Mark's Square are the offices of the nine public prosecutors of St. Mark. Next to the offices is the Clock Tower, built in 1493, at the top of which is the bell struck by two bronze Moors. They are called Moors because of the dark patina that formed on the metal after they were installed.

155 bottom The Ducal Palace was the Doges' residence and the seat of the institutions that governed public life was located. The Palace' current appearance is the result of many modifications made during the fourteenth and fifteenth centuries. To the left, St. Mark's bell tower was rebuilt after collapsing on July 14, 1902.

156 top The famous Pala d'Oro that adorns St. Mark's altar was placed in its current gilded silver Gothic frame in the mid-fourteenth century. The gold tiles are enameled and were probably manufactured in Byzantium between the tenth and twelfth centuries.

156 bottom left The iconostasis in St. Mark's presbytery was crowned by

statues sculpted by Jacobello and Pier Paolo Dalle Masegne in the late-fourteenth century. It is considered a masterpiece of Gothic Venetian sculpture.

156 bottom right The vault in St. Mark's. The five domes imitate the ancient church of Constantinople, and the frescoes that decorate them represent the life of Christ

and the path to man's salvation.

157 The interior of St. Mark's Basilica. Besides extraordinary works of sculpture, the church also

holds a treasury, consisting of 283 pieces of gold, silver, glass, and other precious metals that were largely looted during the sack of Constantinople by the Fourth Crusade.

Venice's greatness was soon rivaled by Genoa, the other great seafaring power in the Mediterranean. The first skirmishes between the two maritime states took place at Tiro. These were followed by over a century of wars in which, on one occasion, Venetians retired to the lagoon when the Genoese landed on the shore near Chioggia.

With the population struck down by the plague in the mid-fourteenth century, Venice was on the point of succumbing, but it managed to hang on. It searched for allies on the mainland and found one in Gian Galeazzo Visconti, the lord of Milan. At the start of the fifteenth century, St. Mark's Republic took the name of the "Serenissima" (The Most Serene Republic) and conquered cities in the Veneto region as far west as Brescia and Bergamo. The city's dominant commercial power led to great wealth that flowed into the coffers of the nobility, who then became patrons of the new schools of art that were flowering throughout Veneto. This period of exceptional prosperity produced painters like Vittore Carpaccio, Giorgine, and later, Paolo Veronese, Titian, and Tintoretto, whose masterpieces adorned the churches and private residences throughout the city.

During the age of this extraordinary artistic vitality, Venice began to lose its predominance. By 1453, the Turks had retaken control of Byzantium, and at the end of the fifteenth century, the French had invaded much of northwest Italy. The discovery of the Americas opened new routes, and national fleets such as those of the Turks and Spanish were gaining the upper hand. Even working at full speed, the Arsenale, the city's shipbuilding yard, was unable to keep up with the new and better organized sea powers.

In 1570, the Turks seized Venetian ships in the Dardanelles and the Bosporus, and then attacked Cyprus. Venice's reaction materialized in the resounding victory at the battle of Lepanto a year later, but by that time the city's fate was already decided. At the end of the seventeenth century, Venice lost Crete too. For a short period it

succeeded in taking the Peloponnese, but the region returned to Turkish rule in 1714.

By this time, Venice was alone. Foreign ships crossed the Adriatic without having to pay tolls to the Serenissima and the city's focusing of attention on the Mediterranean had distracted the government from the new routes of world trade. Commerce had definitively shifted to the Atlantic and Indian Oceans with the result that Venice's commercial traffic followed the wane of its military power. However, the city's political and commercial decline coincided with a golden period of art, and the Venetian

advance of Napoleonic troops. In an attempt to play its diplomatic cards once more, the Serenissima chose not to support the rebellion of the cities in the plain of the river Po, but Napoleon imposed harsh conditions on the city nevertheless. Worried only about losing their possessions on the mainland, the Venetian governors accepted the French terms on May 12, 1797, and a few days later Napoleon entered Venice with his troops and sacked it. These were the days that marked the end of the Serenissima Repubblica di San Marco.

158 bottom left Facing onto the Riva degli Schiavoni and the island of San Giorgio Maggiore, the Ducal Palace remained the center of political life in Venice until the fall of the Republic, caused in 1797 by Napoleon.

palaces were embellished with the magnificent frescoes of Giovanni Battista Tiepolo, Neo-Classical sculpture dawned in the workshop of Antonio Canova, and the theaters were filled with the irony of Carlo Goldoni and the music of Benedetto Marcello. Meanwhile, the increasingly numerous and well-to-do visitors to the city commissioned works by Venetian landscape artists like Francesco Guardi and Canaletto.

While Venice enjoyed its wealth in festivals and banquets as its power declined, Europe was shaken by the

Eight centuries of dominion of the seas and trade had made Venice unique. It is hard to propose any particular view of the city that is more beautiful than the rest, but without doubt the two-and-a-half miles of the Grand Canal are lined with Venice's most famous masterpieces. One begins in St. Mark's Square with the basilica – characterized by an amazing mixture of styles – and the bell tower, which collapsed on July 14, 1902 and was quickly rebuilt; the tower bears marks that record the worst episodes of high water. Next comes the Ducal Palace where the

Doges resided until 1797. The building is separated from the city prison by the famous Bridge of Sighs. Then we have the Procuratie, the porticoed buildings that enclose the square and contained the offices of the nine public prosecutors, the highest Venetian dignitaries after the Doge. The square is bordered on the lagoon side by the Riva degli Schiavoni and faces the island of San Giorgio Maggiore where the church of the same name designed by Palladio stands.

Right at the entrance to the canal there is the church of Santa Maria della

158 bottom right The Signoria (the Doge and his advisors) met in the Sala del Collegio inside the Ducal Palace. Its carved ceiling includes famous paintings by Pietro Veronese and Tintoretto.

158-159 A view of the Sala del Senato in the Ducal Palace, decorated with paintings by Tintoretto and Jacopo Palma the Younger. The 60-member Senate was also known as the "Consiglio dei pregadi" or "Consilium Rogatorium."

159 bottom The church of San Giorgio Maggiore stands on its eponymous island. It was rebuilt between 1565 and 1610 according to a design by Andrea Palladio. Before that time, the church was a fourteenth-century building with a nave and two aisles, and enclosed at one end by old buildings.

160 top The façade of the superb Gothic Ca' Foscari has two splendid eight-arched loggias on the first and second floors. Built for the Giustinian family at the end of the fourteenth century, it became the property of the Doge, Francesco Foscari, in 1453. Purchased and restored by the city, it is now part of the University of Venice.

Salute, then the Accademia, Palazzo Belloni-Battaglia, Palazzo Marcello (where the composer was born), Palazzo Vendramin Calergi (where Richard Wagner died), Ca' Foscari (the headquarters of Venice University), Ca' Dario, Ca' d'Oro, and Palazzo Grassi (where the city's most important exhibitions are held).

Further down the Grand Canal stands the church of Santa Maria Gloriosa dei Frari in which a monumental marble enclosure rings the 124 choir stalls and the sides of the nave are lined by an amazing array of paintings and sculptures. Further along comes Rialto Bridge with its

series of shops. It was first built as a pontoon bridge in the ninth century, then rebuilt in stone in 1591 following which it soon became a reference point in the heart of the city.

Even in its most remote areas, Venice does not cease to surprise with its artistic and architectural treasures. Today it is besieged by tourists and threatened by rising water levels, but with the passing of the years, knowledge of the dangers the city faces has resulted in the creation of hundreds of associations around the world whose aim is to safeguard Venice's patrimony.

160 center Despite its position behind the Rialto Bridge, the Ca' d'Oro is one of the most famous palaces on the Grand Canal. Built in the first half of the fifteenth century by Matteo Raverti and Giovanni and Bartolomeo Buon, its name is taken from the original decorations in gold leaf, vermilion, and ultramarine.

160 bottom right Ca' Dario is another of the extraordinary residences on the Grand Canal. It takes its name from the architect, Giovanni Dario, who designed it in 1487.

160-161 Rialto Bridge, with its famous shops, was built between 1588 and 1591 where there had previously been a pontoon bridge, later replaced by a wooden bridge. It took 70 years before it was decided how to build the Rialto, and in the end, the cost reached the astronomic figure of 250,000 ducats.

161 bottom This splendid polyptych by Bartolomeo Vivarini from the second half of the sixteenth century is one of the innumerable works of art in the church dei Frari.

The Early Christian Monuments and Mosaics in Ravenna

ITALY

EMILIA ROMAGNA
REGISTRATION: 1996
CRITERIA: C (I) (II) (III) (IV)

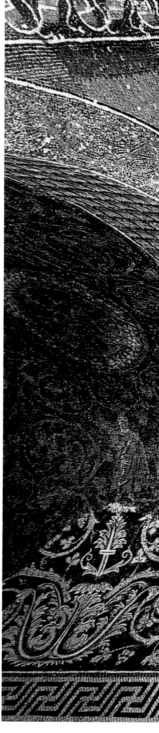

162 top The interior of the Neonian Baptistery. It was built in the late fourth and early fifth centuries, making it the earliest of Ravenna's monuments. Splendidly decorated with mosaics influenced by Hellenistic and Roman art, in the center it has an octagonal tank made from Greek marble and porphyry that was rebuilt in 1500 incorporating a fragment of the original.

Ravenna owes its fortunes to water. First mention of the city was made at the start of the first millennium B.C. when it was a village of stilted houses inhabited by the Umbri tribe. Experts do not agree on its name, which was probably of Etruscan origin. Some claim that it was called Navenna, from naves, while others opt for an etymology derived from *rhein*, meaning "place abundant with water."

162 center The lunette with the Good Shepherd in the Mausoleum of Galla Placidia. The iconographic themes in the mosaic decorations mostly represent the victory of life over death, in accordance with the funerary use of the building.

162 bottom The Mausoleum of Galla Placidia (386-452) is a small building in the shape of a Latin cross. Its mosaics (some of the oldest in Ravenna) cover almost all of the inner walls.

Whatever it was, Ravenna entered history because of its waters when the Roman emperor, Octavian Augustus, built the port of Classis there to accommodate the 250 ships that were to defend the Adriatic in his name. Water was also involved in one of the most important Roman monuments, a superb aqueduct, built by Trajan. The city's position on the sea served to win it the role of capital city when, in 402, Honorius transferred the capital of the Western Roman empire there. On his death in 423, an army arrived from Byzantium to place his sister Galla Placidia on the throne.

Even if officially the duties of the emperor were conferred on her son Valentinian, just six years old, the personality of this strong and profoundly devoted woman marked the start of Ravenna's golden age. Galla Placidia was present at the sacking of Rome by the Visigoths under Odoric, where she was abducted by the conquerors, but she succeeded in converting them to Christianity and transforming them into allies.

Although it has many similarities with pagan temples, the Mausoleum dedicated to her offers a perfect synthesis of paleo-Christian symbolism and a celebration of eternal life in its mosaics. Water, present once again, is used to represent this concept, with doves drinking from the springs of immortality and deer from river torrents. The figures of the Apostles, Evangelists, and Lorenzo (the Roman saint who emulated the martyrdom of Christ) are shown among motifs of flowers and acanthus leaves representing the dense vegetation that is

162-163 *A heavenly cross and the stars of eternal salvation cover the dome of the Mausoleum of Galla Placidia. Christ and saints look on from the sides among naturalistic motifs.*

163 top *Galla Placidia's mausoleum. Though similar in structure to analogous pagan buildings – a central plan, single entrance, roof topped by a cone – its decorations are strongly Christian in their symbolism.*

the result of the water of life.

The mosaics in the Neonian Baptistery, named after Bishop Neon, also date from the end of the age of Galla Placidia. Despite the poor restoration work of the last century, this octagonal structure covered by a dome has three registers of mosaics with representations mostly concerning the symbolism that unites water to eternal life.

In 476, Ravenna was the setting for the end of the history of the Roman empire, with the deposition of Romulus Augustolus by the eastern general

164 top left The Basilica of San Vitale is an octagonal church and one of the most important monuments in early Christian art.

164 top right Entirely built from Istrian stone, the structure of the Mausoleum of Theodoric is divided into two ten-sided orders. It is covered by a single slab of rock measuring 33 feet in diameter and weighing 330 tons.

Odoacer. In 493, it was the turn of the conquest of the Ostrogoths and the ascent to the throne of Theodoric. The ambitious sovereign was a follower of Arianism, a doctrine that negated the divinity of Christ; determinedly faithful to Arianism, he wished to build monuments in Ravenna that marked his religion's supremacy over the Orthodox church as well as exceeding the splendor of those built by Galla Placidia. He was responsible for the Baptistery of the Arians, his Mausoleum, the layout of an entire district where he established his palace, and the start of the construction of an Arian basilica which was converted to the Orthodox church 70 years later by the Byzantines with the name Sant'Apollinare Nuovo.

In its structure and its decorations, the basilica marked another fundamental moment in the history of Ravenna: the war between the Goths and the Byzantines that broke out on the death of Theodoric in 526. It ended with victory for the latter and the ascent to the throne of Justinian. The political stature and fervent Orthodoxy of the new ruler and his wife Theodora were expressed in the greatest splendor in the

164 bottom The mosaic on the left side of San Vitale's apse shows Emperor Justinian with Archbishop Massimian. The unity and perfection of the style combine with the meaning of the image: the celebration of the ruler's religious fervor and political power.

165 top In the mosaic decorations of the apsidal lunette in San Vitale, Christ Pantokrator is shown with the symbols of his power: seated on the world, he holds the Book of Wisdom in one hand. The archangels Michael and Gabriel, at the sides, represent the eternal celestial court, while the soldier-martyr Vitale and Bishop Ecclesius, who close the scene, link the Kingdom of Heaven with Justinian's empire.

165 center The superb mosaic in San Vitale portrays the Empress Theodora surrounded by her court.

165 bottom Dating from the fifth and sixth centuries, the mosaics in the dome of the Arian Baptistery articulate the theology of the Christian baptism.

Basilica of San Vitale in the most important series of mosaics in late ancient Christian art. The celebration of the power of the emperor – portrayed with Theodora and accompanied on either side by his court – is closely connected to the image of Christ Pantokrator, who is seated on a golden globe and in his left hand holds the Book of Wisdom that governs the world.

The style of the other decorations in the complex mark the powerful influence and arrival of oriental iconography. In the two succeeding centuries, this was to become the dominant model for all mosaic additions to pre-existing buildings and in the construction of new ones, for example, the Basilica di Sant'Apollinare in Classe. The mosaic on the hollow of the apse featuring Christ crowned by the glorious cross of the Resurrection was the work of art that sealed the glory of the Church in Ravenna, which in ancient times was second only to Rome.

166 top Glittering with gold, the outstanding representation of the three Magi offering gifts to the Virgin and Child is found on the left wall of Sant'Apollinare Nuovo.

166-167 A view of the artistically sublime mosaics in the Basilica of Sant'Apollinare Nuovo. They show Christ with 36 figures of saints and martyrs.

167 top In addition to its architecture and mosaics (including the large symbolic Transfiguration that fills the hollow of the apse), the Basilica of Sant'Apollinare in Classe is famous for the marble sarcophaguses of its archbishops that line the aisles.

167 center An elaborate capital is carved with naturalistic motifs in the Basilica of Sant'Apollinare in Classe.

167 bottom Sant'Apollinare in Classe was built by Julianus Argentarius on the orders of Archbishop Ursicinus during the first half of the sixth century. It is Ravenna's most famous religious building.

Piazza del Duomo in Pisa
ITALY

TUSCANY
REGISTRATION: 1987
CRITERIA: C (I) (II) (IV) (VI)

168 top left A detail of the fountain by Giuseppe Vaccà at the entrance to Piazza del Duomo. It shows three putti supporting the coat of arms of Pisa.

168-169 A view of the Duomo and its famous bell tower. Recently re-opened to the public after work to correct its lean, the tower is considered one of the most beautiful in the world for the uniqueness of its architecture.

On October 16, 1604, Galileo Galilei sent his friend Paolo Sarpi a letter in which he described the basis for the laws of motion. Some claim that the forty-year-old professor of mathematics had discovered those laws by dropping objects from the Tower of Pisa. In fact, Galileo did not have accurate enough timepieces to measure the time of the drop, but more compelling in the negation of this claim is the fact that he was teaching in Padua at the time. What is certain is that the story was inspired by the lean of the tower.

The bell tower of the Duomo (cathedral) in Pisa had begun to lean long before its construction was completed. Proof of this is given by the inscription above the entrance which commemorates the laying of the first stone on August 9, 1173 by the architect Bonanno Pisano, but just five years later, when builders had not yet finished the fourth level, he resigned from the job. This was due to a subsidence of the ground, inducing the tower lean an inch or so to the

169 top The huge galleried rectangular building borders the area that was once the graveyard. It was built at the end of the thirteenth century on the place where, tradition has it, Bishop Ubaldo de' Lanfranchi spread the earth taken from Golgotha, brought from the Holy Land by ship.

169 bottom left and right Views of the Duomo and Baptistery. The latter is the most impressive building of its kind in Italy. Its circumference is 351 feet and its height, 177 feet.

south, making the architect think he had made a design error.

Work began again in 1275 under the direction of Giovanni di Simone, who added three more levels carefully structured to balance the weight and – in vain – to correct the lean. In 1284, when the tower was only missing the bell housing and the lean had exceeded 35 inches, another sudden interruption was made: Giovanni di Simone died in the battle of Meloria between the seafaring republics of Pisa and Genoa. It fell to Tommaso Pisano to complete the job between 1350 and 1372. The tower stands 184 feet tall, is 51 feet in

170 left The 1260 Romanesque pulpit by Nicola Pisano is the Baptistery's most outstanding feature.

170 right Columns alternating with four pillars ring the interior of the Baptistery. The large octagonal font was carved by Guido Bigarelli da Como in 1246. The addition of the statue of St. John the Baptist on a capital dates from the sixteenth century.

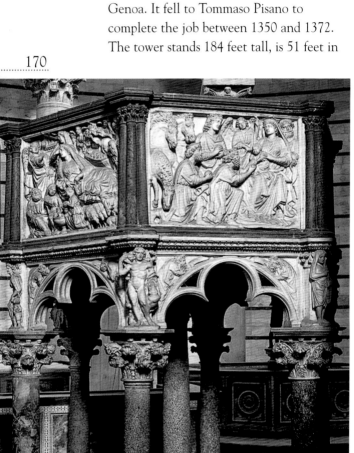

diameter at the base, and weighs 16,000 tons. It is decorated with 207 white marble and sandstone columns, 15 of which are at the base, 30 in each of the six round levels, and 12 around the bell-housing. A spiral staircase of 294 steps leads from the entrance, surrounded by two registers of bas-reliefs portraying monsters and animals, to the top floor where the ancient bells are hung.

The tower was the last work to be completed in the square of Pisa's Duomo. The square is called by many the "Campo dei Miracoli" (Square of Miracles), as it was considered a miracle that all the buildings necessary to religious life in the city had been grouped in a single area. The Duomo itself stands next to the tower and is a masterpiece of Romanesque architecture. Built on the site of a pre-existing Byzantine church, construction of the Cathedral of Our

Lady of the Assumption was begun in 1063 under the direction of Buscheto and was consecrated in 1118 by Pope Gelasius II. Despite the duration of the construction and the overlaying of Classical, Byzantine, Ravenna, and Arab style elements, its appearance is one of admirable unity. Its plan is that of a Latin cross, with a transept and egg-shaped dome. The façade, the front extension of the nave and its double-vaulted aisles, and the main apse were built during the second half of the twelfth century.

Originally the interior was to be decorated with large frescoes, but in 1595 a fire severely damaged the building. Fortunately, the generosity of the Grand Duke Ferdinando I de' Medici allowed the cathedral to be restored at a cost of 85,000 scudi, an enormous sum for that period. The three bronze doors and the caisson ceiling were rebuilt, and large paintings were hung on the walls, including those by Antonio Sogliani (a pupil of Raphael) and Andrea del Sarto (from the school of Leonardo da Vinci). The pulpit carved between 1302 and 1311 by Giovanni Pisano was disassembled after the fire. Some parts of it were placed in the Camposanto (cemetery) while others went to foreign museums. In May 1926, this extraordinary marble monument was reassembled and placed once more in the Duomo.

The Baptistery stands in front of the cathedral. It was begun in 1153 by Deotisalvi and completed in the fourteenth century. The magnificent round Romanesque building was later overlaid with Gothic decorations, white marble wall linings, with rows of serpentine stone. The structure is the most impressive of its kind in Italy, measuring 351 feet in circumference and 177 feet tall, with an internal diameter of over 115 feet. The interior is based on a peristyle of four pillars and eight columns

transported from Elba and Sardinia. Here too, the pulpit, by Nicola Pisano, is extraordinary; carved from different colored marbles, it is hexagonal in shape and supported by six outer columns, three of which stand on lions, and by a central column supported by human and animal figures.

The Camposanto lies on the north side of the square. Its buildings were the work of Giovanni di Simone at the end of the thirteenth century. The large frescoes – many of which were damaged in World War II – were begun around 1350 and continued for more than a century. Those that stand out in particular are the "Triumph of Death" and "Universal Judgement," both by anonymous artists. The Camposanto remained the city's burial place until the end of the eighteenth century.

During the last decade, the square was the setting of another miracle. On January 6, 1990, when the lean had reached 17 feet and one inch, the tower was closed to the public for reasons of safety. Three years later, consolidation work was undertaken in which 950 tons of lead were placed at its base and 18 steel cables attached to the first level. Samples of earth and water were taken on the north side so that the subsidence on the other side could be balanced. When the tower had been righted by nine inches, it was reopened to visitors.

171 The apse in the Duomo is richly decorated with mosaics and frescoes from different epochs. The hollow contains an immense

mosaic of the Redeemer Enthroned, flanked by the Virgin and Saint John, which was completed by Cimabue in 1302.

The Historic Center of Florence

ITALY

TUSCANY
REGISTRATION: 1982
CRITERIA: C (I) (II) (III) (IV) (VI)

After days of unyielding rain that had brought Italy to a halt, the floodwater of the river Arno reached Florence on November 4, 1966. The water level was 20 feet higher than that of the road, and a torrent of mud was sent through the historic center, raising fears around the world.

The damage was enormous but was limited by the dedication of the Italian army and volunteers of all nationalities who dug through the mud for days in the attempt to save the innumerable works of art that had been trapped in the lower stories of the buildings. For the whole world, Florence is the symbol of Renaissance art, the city where the painting of Masaccio, Piero della Francesca, Botticelli, Leonardo, Michelangelo, and Raphael flourished. This was the place in which Donatello sculpted his elegant bronzes and Leon Battista Alberti laid down the new directions in architecture that Filippo Brunelleschi followed in building his magisterial dome in the cathedral of Santa Maria del Fiore. Florence was the birthplace of Dante Alighieri, the father of the Italian language, and the city that welcomed the Pisan, Galileo Galilei, the inventor of scientific method and founder of the laws of motion. Florence was the city where 600 years of creativity have left an unparalleled heritage.

The city originated at the time of the Etruscans when a small settlement began to grow beside the Arno. It had its center in Fiesole, a village built on the hillside where it could best be defended. In 59 B.C., the Romans built a *castrum* on the site of Fiesole, which, in honor of the goddess Flora, they called Florentia. The town grew larger and richer during the Roman era and was consequently besieged by the barbarians. First came the Ostrogoths, then the Goths, and finally the Lombards, who were ousted by Charlemagne in the eighth century. The foundation of the Holy Roman Empire unleashed the violent conflict between the Church and the emperor over the rule of Italy.

With the death in 1115 of Countess Matilda of Canossa, a strong supporter of the Church, the town proclaimed itself a free community and thus initiated a period of prosperity for itself, despite the clashes between the Guelphs and Ghibellines throughout the 1200s. In the middle of the thirteenth century, the Florentine guilds enjoyed unrivaled power, perhaps thanks in part to the use of Arabic numbers, which the Pisan mathematician Lorenzo Fibonacci had introduced to speed up accounting and which revealed to architects the secrets of geometry. Merchants and craftsmen elected two lay advisors and a Captain of the People on the Podestà (chief magistrate and police chief selected only from among the major guilds).

In the meantime, the arts were flourishing in the city. Painters like Cimabue and Gaddo Gaddi and the sculptor Arnolfo di Cambio appeared, and the genius of Giotto and Dante were recognized. Gothic churches were built, like the superb Santa Maria Novella, and the political and religious center of the city was defined. Palazzo Vecchio, designed by

172 top The Cappella de' Pazzi was designed in 1430 by Filippo Brunelleschi. It is part of the complex of the Santa Croce Basilica and one of the purest examples of Renaissance architecture. The terracotta medallions in the walls were created by Luca della Robbia.

172 center An aerial view of Piazza della Signoria, which has been the political and social center of Florence since the fourteenth century. The Palazzo Vecchio and the bell tower, from which the citizens were called to public assembly, dominate the square. The fountain of Neptune was built in 1575 by Bartolomeo Ammannati to celebrate the naval ambitions of the Medici.

172 bottom The Baroncelli Chapel in Santa Croce is lined with superb frescoes. This is one of Florence's most famous churches, both for its works of art and the many famous people buried here.

172-173 The beautiful Salone dei Cinquecento in the Palazzo Vecchio was created in 1495-1496 by Antonio da Sangallo,

Cronaca, and Francesco di Domenico. The ceiling decorations are by Giorgio Vasari and his pupils, and some of the statues are by Michelangelo.

173 bottom left The carving of the Crucifixion in Santa Croce Basilica was made by Donatello in polychrome wood. The arms are hinged so that Christ can be placed in a tomb.

FLORENCE

ROME

Arnolfo di Cambio and completed in 1322, became the administrative center of Florence for all the fourteenth century and has remained the City Hall until the present day. The Gothic basilica of Santa Croce was built in 1294. The open, spacious interior was embellished with frescoes by Giotto, works like the Cappella de' Pazzi (a Renaissance masterpiece by

173 bottom right The square with the basilica of Santa Croce (1294). The façade of the magnificent Gothic church was lined with polychrome marble in 1836 thanks to the donation made by the Englishman Francis Sloane.

174 To build the immense eight-span dome of Santa Maria del Fiore, Filippo Brunelleschi used self-supporting bricks in different sizes, laid in herring-bone fashion, in a technique that had been used in the Pantheon in Rome. Next to the cathedral stands Giotto's bell tower, lined with white, green, and pink marble.

175 top The fresco that covers the interior of the dome in Santa Maria del Fiore shows the Last Judgment (1572-1579). It was painted by Vasari and his replacement, Federico Zuccari.

175 center right The court in Palazzo Medici-Riccardi was designed by Michelozzo di Bartolomeo and built in the mid-fifteenth century for Cosimo the Elder. The palace is considered the prototype of the patrician residences in Florence and today is the seat of the Prefecture.

Brunelleschi), Donatello's Crucifix (in the first Cappella Bardi), and the frescoes by Taddeo Gaddi in the Cappella Baroncelli. Santa Croce is the last resting place of the great geniuses of Florence, including Galileo (who was only buried here in 1737 because he had been excommunicated), Machiavelli, Michelangelo, and the humanist Leonardo Bruni. Dante Alighieri is missing, having died in exile in Ravenna, where his admirers built him a cenotaph during the nineteenth century.

Begun in 1296, construction of Florence's cathedral, Santa Maria del Fiore, took 160 years and involved the most exceptional talents. The fourth largest Christian monument, it was built by Arnolfo di Cambio on the site of the earlier church of Santa Reparata "so that the industry and power of man do not create, nor may they undertake anything so large or so beautiful." However, the most important sections of the cathedral were designed by two other artists. Giotto designed the bell tower in 1334, but it was only finished in 1356, 20 years after the artist's death. Standing 279 feet tall, the tower is a magnificent Gothic monument featuring terracotta panels at the base adorned with bas-reliefs by Andrea Pisano, and two- and three-light mullioned windows. The rest of the building is lined with white, green, and pink Tuscan marble. The dome of the cathedral, completed in 1436 by Brunelleschi, stands 20 feet higher than the bell tower. Inspired by the Pantheon in Rome, the architect built a vault of self-supporting bricks laid in herringbone fashion without the traditional wood reinforcements. During the sixteenth century, Giorgio Vasari painted a

memorable fresco of the Last Judgment on the inside of the dome.

At the start of the fourteenth century, Florence was the richest city in Europe, but just fifty years later various banks went bust and the plague began to strike the city. The economic crisis led to the Ciompi Revolt in 1378, and peace was only restored in 1434 when Cosimo de' Medici (the son of a powerful banker) managed to get himself appointed Signore (Lord) of the city. The era of Lorenzo il Magnifico, Cosimo's grandson, marked the economic upturn and cultural explosion of the city. Renaissance architects were invited to design houses for the rich of Florence, leading to the construction of the Palazzo Medici Riccardi (the residence of the Medici family for a

175 bottom left The superb Madonna with Child and Saints by Cosimo Rosselli (1439-1507) hangs in Palazzo Strozzi. Highly appreciated by Cosimo de' Medici, Rosselli was also a contributor to the frescoes in the Sistine Chapel.

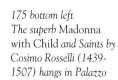

175 bottom right The vault of the gallery in Palazzo Medici-Riccardi, with its complex "Allegory of the Medici," was painted between 1682 and 1685 by Luca Giordano.

buildings. The central entrance leads into a porticoed court overlooked by the splendid Italian Renaissance garden, the Boboli, laid out by Niccolò Tribolo. It opens with the amphitheater, which was in fact the quarry from which the blocks were taken to build the palace. In the garden there are sculptural groups and architectural styles from various ages, such as the sixteenth century fountains of Neptune and Bacchus

176

176 top The façade of the Uffizi that faces onto the river Arno. Designed by Giorgio Vasari, the construction of the building (beginning in 1560) was the most drastic and monumental alteration to the city during the Medici era, and its construction represented the absolutism of the nobility.

176 center The ceiling of Room 23 in the Uffizi. Created in 1588, it is finely decorated with the interiors of five shops and grotesque faces.

176 bottom The Birth of Venus is displayed in the Uffizi Galleries. The work was painted by Botticelli around 1485 for Lorenzo di Pierfrancesco de' Medici, the cousin of Lorenzo the Magnificent.

176-177 The Iliad Room in the Pitti Palace was named after the ceiling frescoes by Luigi Sabatelli illustrating episodes from Homer's poem. The palace exhibits include works by Raphael, Ghirlandaio, and Andrea del Sarto.

177 top The Ocean fountain by Giambologna is located in the center of the square in Isolotto di Boboli. The square is late-Mannerist in conception and surrounded by statues and tall boxwood hedges.

century), Palazzo Strozzi, and Palazzo Rucellai, where bankers and merchants lived. However, the most magnificent private residence was the one that the banker Lucio Pitti commissioned from Brunelleschi in 1458, almost as a challenge to the Medici. However, the bankruptcy of the bank brought construction to a halt, and the palace was only completed a century later by Bartolomeo Ammannati, when the Medici made it their own home.

The body of the original large-windowed building is a perfect cube built from massive rusticated stone blocks. To this were added the wings and other

and the Rococo Kaffeehaus Pavilion built in 1776.

Inside the Pitti Palace, the Palatine Gallery deserves mention for its frescoes by Pietro da Cortona from the mid-seventeenth century. Also on display are the art collections of the Medici with works by Perugino, Titian, Andrea del Sarto, Pontormo, Tintoretto, Caravaggio, Rubens, and Van Dyck. The 14 rooms in the Royal Apartments can also be visited; they are finely furnished in the taste of the Medici and their successors, the Dukes of Lorraine.

The largest and most valuable artistic

legacy collected by the Medici over a period of three centuries can to be seen in the Palazzo degli Uffizi.

This palace was built by Vasari to house the offices of the magistracy under Grand Duke Cosimo I. It stands next to the Palazzo Vecchio to which it is connected by a famous corridor. From 1581 on, the heirs of Cosimo used the light-filled building to exhibit their art treasures. The family collections include exceptional works of Tuscan art from the twelfth to sixteenth centuries by artists such as Giotto, Botticelli, Beato Angelico, Leonardo, Simone Martini, and Masaccio. In the years that followed, these were added to with Italian works by Titian, Tintoretto, and Caravaggio and European paintings by Albrecht Dürer, Rubens, Rembrandt, and Goya.

In 1737, Florence passed to the Austrian house of Lorraine but was then conquered – and sacked – by the armies of Napoleon at the end of the eighteenth century. In 1865, it became the temporary capital of the Kingdom of Italy, but that honor passed to Rome in 1871. Before the history of the Grand Dukedom of Tuscany was brought to an end, Anna Maria Luisa – the last of the Medicis – donated the Uffizi Gallery to the people of Florence. In doing so, she gave the city the oldest museum in modern Europe and, without doubt, one of the greatest legacies of Italian culture.

Assisi, the Basilica of San Francesco, and other Franciscan Sites

ITALY

Umbria
Registration: **2000**
Criteria: **C** (I) (II) (III) (IV) (VI)

178

The tragic earthquake that struck the provinces of Umbria and Le Marche at 11:42 a.m. on September 6, 1997 caused 13 deaths and 20,000 homeless. Apart from the human drama, Italy wept at the damage suffered by the Basilica Superiore in Assisi, one of the most important examples of medieval art. The collapse of part of the roof cost the lives of four Franciscan monks, irreparably

damaged the frescoes painted by Cimabue, and seriously compromised the stability of the Sacro Convento. Yet just two years later, thanks to prompt restoration work (to which many volunteers contributed) the Basilica was reopened to the public and Assisi was able to continue the tradition that had turned it into an ecumenical center since the thirteenth century.

Francis was born into a well-to-do family in Assisi in 1182. In 1206, as he was praying, he was asked by God to establish an ecclesiastical body. Just two years later, he had gathered his first followers around

him with whom he settled in the Porziuncola chapel; here Francis dedicated himself to the cure of lepers and the setting up of an apostolate. In 1233, the papal bull, *Solet annuere*, issued by Honorius III, approved the rule proposed for the founding of the new Franciscan monastic order. In 1226, after an intensely busy life dedicated to asceticism and charity, Francis died at the age of 44 following a serious illness.

For Francis, the Passion of Christ was a model to imitate, and in consequence, he chose the "hill of hell" where capital executions were carried out, next to the town of Assisi, for his place of burial. In 1228, the year of his canonization, a church was built on the hill on the orders of Pope Gregory IX to hold Francis' remains, in imitation of the Holy Sepulcher in Jerusalem. The body of the saint was buried below the high altar in the center of the church, built in Romanesque style. Then, another church was built over the Romanesque one, this time in Gothic style, and both were

consecrated in 1253.

A tradition says that mosaic decorations are chosen for the most important places of worship, however in tribute to the rule adopted by Saint Francis, "humble" frescoes were chosen instead. Coincidentally, the greatest artists of the period were working in Assisi during the thirteenth and fourteenth centuries, and their work in the church inaugurated a new phase in Italian painting that was to revolutionize late Medieval European art.

In the Upper Basilica, the Florentine

178 top left Detail of the wood gateway of the Lower Basilica that was carved in the second half of the sixteenth century.

178 bottom Seriously damaged by the 1997 earthquake, the portico in the lower square was built in 1474 to provide pilgrims and peddlers with shelter.

178-179 The Upper Basilica of St. Francis. The simple Gothic architecture in French style is divided horizontally in three sections by moldings and is topped by a triangular pediment. The massive four-sided bell tower, on the other hand, is in Umbrian Romanesque.

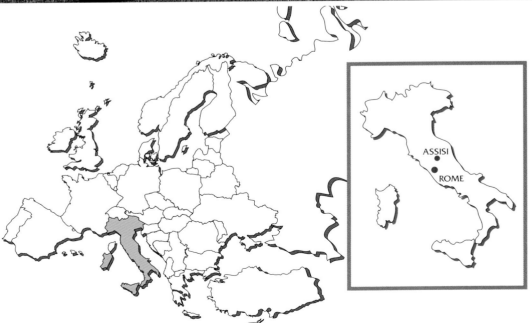

179 top left The hill of Assisi is dominated by the Basilica. The imposing complex consecrated in 1253 is one of the most important in the Christian religion and is formed by two churches, one built above the other. In his spiritual testament (1226), Saint Francis left instructions for the construction of the churches, insisting that they should not contradict the rule of holy poverty.

179 top right The basilica seen from the lower square. Designed for social purposes, it was modeled after a medieval cloister lined with porticoes.

180 *The interior of the upper basilica has a four-span nave, a transept, and a polygonal apse. The interior is completely frescoed with images of the life of Saint Francis as interpreted by his disciple Saint Bonaventura.*

painter, Cimabue, illustrated the lives of Saints Peter and Paul on the north transept, the life of the Virgin on the apse, five scenes of the Apocalypse and the Crucifixion on the south transept, and in the webs of the cross above the altar, the four Evangelists. In the landscapes behind the Evangelists, Cimabue added a view of Assisi to symbolize the region in which

the Franciscans had preached the word of Christ. The innovation in these pictorial cycles was their three-dimensionality, a characteristic expanded upon by the young Giotto, who, beginning in 1296, decorated the lower part of the nave with episodes of the life of the saint. In the second decade of the fourteenth century, a number of chapels were built into the

181 top left *The cross of the apse in the upper basilica was frescoed by Cimabue (1240-1302) with the four Evangelists, each in the act of writing under the inspiration of an angel, with the evangelized lands before them: Matthew in Judea, John in Asia, Luke in Greece, and Mark in Italy.*

181 top right *Detail of a fresco of "Saint Peter healing the sick" on the left aisle in the upper basilica. Giorgio Vasari attributed the pictorial decorations to Cimabue, however recent studies have suggested many of these may have been painted after the death of the Florentine master.*

181 bottom *This is part of a cycle of 28 frescoes that illustrate the life of Saint Francis below the gallery in the upper basilica. They are attributed to Giotto who, according to Vasari, painted them between 1296 and 1300.*

182 top A detail of the frescoes in the right arm of the cross. Note Giotto's superb Crucifixion scene on the left. The other

frescoes are attributed to Cimabue, Simone Martini, and to pupils of Giotto and Pietro Lorenzetti.

182 bottom "St. Francis giving his cloak to a poor man" is one of the episodes in Giotto's cycle of the saint's life in the upper basilica. Note the view of

Assisi, seen from Porta Nuova, in the background, with St. Benedict's Abbey on Mount Subasio to the right.

nave of the Lower Basilica and decorated by Simone Martini and Pietro Lorenzetti, painters from the Sienese school.

While the Upper Basilica was being built, Gregory IX also prompted construction of the monastery next door. The first Franciscans lived in cells dug out of the rock, but in the mid-fifteenth century, the building was laid out on a more organized basis. Construction of the Sacro Convento was completed at the end of the fifteenth century thanks to the generosity of Pope Sixtus IV, who made certain the complex was strengthened with two solid corner bastions and that the cloister was given an upper open gallery. Sixtus IV was also responsible for the immense arcade that encloses the lawn in front of the Lower Basilica.

Concerned for the fate of the relics of the saint in an age of frequent plundering, Sixtus IV ordered that the narrow passage to the crypt be walled up. Despite this measure, the treasure that had been accumulated over the centuries by donations from the faithful was subject to a number of thefts, the last of which was committed by the Napoleonic troops. What remains of the treasure today is kept in the museum located in the dormitory of the monastery.

182-183 The right arm of the cross in the lower basilica leads into the chapel dedicated to Saint Nicholas. Since 1292, it has held the remains of Giovanni Orsini and is decorated with frescoes by the Giotto school.

183 bottom left The semicircular apse in the lower basilica with its superb wooden choir and a cycle of frescoes with the Last Judgment. This was a seventeenth-century work that replaced an earlier decoration of Heavenly Glory, attributed by Vasari to Stefano Fiorentino.

183 bottom right Another detail from the lower basilica frescoes. The earliest, the "Stories of Christ and Saint Francis," were painted in 1253 at the time the complex was consecrated, but they had already been mostly destroyed and replaced by the sixteenth century.

The Vatican City and San Paolo fuori le Mura

ITALY

HOLY SEE, ROME
REGISTRATION: 1984
CRITERIA: C (I) (II) (IV) (VI)

On February 11, 1929, the Lateran Treaty, signed by Pope Pius XII and Benito Mussolini, ratified the existence of the sovereign State of the Vatican City, governed by the Pope and completely independent of the Kingdom of Italy. The treaty therefore put an end to the controversy begun on September 20, 1870 when the troops of King Vittorio Emanuele II entered Rome and put an end to the papal state.

In the first centuries of the existence of Rome, the *Ager vaticanus* was a peripheral area that covered the land between the right bank of the Tiber and the Vatican hills, the land as far as the Milvius Bridge to the north, and all of the Gianicolo Hill to the south. Around the first century B.C., these marshy areas were gradually transformed into a residential area where important Roman families built *horti* (luxurious residences). At the time of Augustus, the area was covered by the gardens of Agrippina, and when Caligula became emperor, by a circus – the Gaianum – of which some parts remain in the colonnade in St. Peter's Square.

The history of the Vaticanum changed radically in the fourth century. Emperor Constantine I proclaimed toleration of the Christian religion with the Edict of Milan in 313 and began construction of a church on the place where Saint Peter was supposed to have been buried. Peter had come to Rome with Paul in 42 A.D. to preach the Word of Christ, but the two are thought to have been martyred in 67. Large building works were undertaken so that the new church could be built. The slope of the Vatican hills was leveled, the

burial ground was covered over, and the center of the apse in the Basilica was built right over Saint Peter's tomb. The huge church was built with a nave and four aisles, a wide transept, and a four-sided porticoed atrium but was not completed until 329.

The basilica soon became an important focus of city life. Civil buildings, churches,

monasteries, and hospices for pilgrims began to be built around it. To the south of the city along the Via Ostiense, the large basilica of San Paolo fuori le Mura was constructed, also in the fourth century. Like all early Christian temples, it had an oblong plan, a nave, and two aisles, each of which ended in an apse. Although the original basilica was destroyed in a fire on July 15, 1823, the

184 top Designed by Carlo Maderno in 1629, San Lorenzo's Chapel in San Paolo fuori le Mura is also known as the Chapel of the Choir. The wooden stalls were remade in 1928 according to a design by Guglielmo Calderini.

184 bottom San Paolo fuori le Mura is a Benedictine abbey that stands on a former site of Christian churches from the first centuries A.D. It was destroyed by fire on the night of July 15, 1823, and the reconstruction – which lasted more than a century – was completed in 1931 with the installation of the monumental bronze central door.

reconstruction was in full respect of the original, though little remained of the original structures. A fifth century mosaic decorates one side of the triumphal arch that separates the apse from the nave. The apse mosaics of Christ with Saints Peter, Andrew, Paul, and Luke were Venetian from the thirteenth century. The *Confessio*, the tomb in which Saint Paul is said to be buried, lies below the altar.

185 top left The basilica of San Paolo fuori le Mura was built between 1831 and 1854 with a nave and four aisles. Pasquale Belli designed the reconstruction on the same plan as the original. The ceiling is decorated with the coats of arms of the popes that contributed to the costs of reconstruction.

185 top right The chapel of the Most Holy Sacrament in San Paolo fuori le Mura was built in 1725. Its fame comes from the twelfth/thirteenth-century mosaic of the Virgin and the thirteenth-century Crucifixion attributed to Pietro Cavallini, whose remains are buried in the chapel.

184-185 In the twelfth and thirteenth centuries, San Paolo fuori le Mura enjoyed a period of spiritual and economic prosperity. This was the period in which the lovely mosaic that decorates the apse was installed by the best mosaicists from Venice.

ROME AND
THE VATICAN
CITY

While Rome survived through the dark ages of the barbarian invasions, a new popular district arose around St. Peter's. Between the eighth and ninth centuries, with the consent of Charlemagne, Pope Leo III decided to protect the area by building an encircling wall with only one entrance at Castel Sant'Angelo. Upon the death of the pope, however, the walls were pulled down by the Romans, and in 846 the city was sacked by the Saracens who devastated the Christian places of worship. It was Leo IV who once more protected the Vatican with new walls, and from that moment on the district was considered to be independent. Nonetheless, the popes continued to live for centuries in the Lateran District of Rome. The first to reside in the Vatican was Nicholas III in 1277, who also set about strengthening the city walls. Before the Vatican was to become the permanent residence of the papacy, however, the Church moved its court to Avignon, which led in turn to the "Babylonian captivity" of the pope by the French monarchs.

During the fourteenth century, the Vatican became run down, and in the fifteenth Constantine's basilica was falling into ruin. In 1452, Nicholas V planned restoration work, which was put into the hands of Bramante 50 years later by Julius II. In 1506, the first stone was finally laid in the new church. The St. Peter's that was to rise from the ruins of the former church was designed to be the beacon of Christianity. To build the immense basilica – the largest religious building in the world with its nave measuring 611 feet and dome 448 feet tall – took more than a century to build, and the project involved

186-187 St. Peter's basilica and its square surrounded by the unusual elliptical colonnade were designed by Gian Lorenzo Bernini in the mid-seventeenth century. The obelisk in the center of the square was brought from Egypt by the Roman emperor, Caligula, and raised in the square on September 10, 1586.

the greatest engineers of the Italian Renaissance and Baroque periods. Bramante was succeeded by Raphael, Antonio da Sangallo the Younger, Michelangelo, and Carlo Maderno, who completed the façade in 1614. Inside, there are eleven marble-lined chapels, five altars, and innumerable works of art, many of which were recovered from the original basilica; the rest were commissioned from artists during the sixteenth and seventeenth centuries.

The interior is dominated by the papal

altar that stands below the dome. Made from a simple slab of marble taken from Nerva's Forum, it was designed by Michelangelo though he did not live to see it completed at the end of the sixteenth century during the pontificate of Clement VIII. The magnificent gilded-bronze canopy above the altar was designed by Gian Lorenzo Bernini and stands on spiral columns 66 feet tall. All around, the basilica is adorned with superb works of art. First and foremost is the white marble sculpture of the Pietà by Michelangelo, which stands in a side

187 top Built between 1624 and 1633, the colossal bronze canopy designed by Bernini weighs 81,400 pounds. It stands over the papal altar below the dome of St. Peter's and is the largest bronze monument ever built.

187 bottom The Pietà was begun by Michelangelo when he was just 22 years old. Today it is one of the most famous sculptures in the world. Commissioned by the Vatican legate of the French king Charles VIII, it was supposed to be completed within one year and to be placed in the St. Petronilla Chapel, also known as the Chapel of the French Kings.

186 bottom The original Basilica of St. Peter in the Vatican was built between 324 and 329 by Constantine over the tomb of the Apostle on the former site of Caligula's and Nero's circus in which he was crucified. The current basilica was begun in 1506 during the pontificate of Julius II according to a design by Donato Bramante.

chapel near the Holy Door and was finished by the artist in 1499 when he was just 25 years old. Other works by Bernini include the throne of St. Peter in the apse on the right side of the basilica and the monuments dedicated to popes Urban VIII and Alexander VII. The latter was his last work, completed in 1678. Bernini was also the architect of the vast square in front of the basilica, which is faced onto by St. Peter's modest parvis. Designed between 1656 and 1667, the square is enclosed by a curved colonnade and, at its

center, has the Egyptian obelisk moved there in 1586 by Sixtus V.

Next to the basilica stand the Vatican palaces, designed as residences for various popes. The first papal palace was built in 1198 for Innocent III, but the structures were ornamented during the Renaissance. In 1473, Sixtus IV had the Sistine Chapel built. At the end of the century, Innocent VIII commissioned Bramante to build the Belvedere, and this was later subjected to a number of enlargements, particularly during the eighteenth century. These palaces represent an enormous artistic heritage: the Sistine Chapel is decorated by frescoes by Botticelli, Perugino,

Ghirlandaio, and of course, Michelangelo, who painted the extraordinary "Last Judgement" behind the altar in 1541. In the four year period between 1508 and 1512, he concentrated on the ceiling where he painted a cycle containing more than 300 figures in episodes taken from Genesis and other books of the Old Testament. During the same period, Raphael was decorating the four rooms in the private apartments of Pope Julius II. The work was commissioned by Julius to renovate the rooms where his predecessor and rival, Alexander VI, had lived. It took 16 years and Raphael did not live to see it finished.

In the mid-eighteenth century, with the

188

188-189 It was Pope Julius II della Rovere who commissioned Michelangelo in 1508 to paint the ceiling of the Sistine Chapel. In four years, the Florentine artist produced an astounding pictorial cycle showing episodes from Genesis and the Old Testament.

189 top and center Two details from the ceiling of the Sistine Chapel illustrating episodes from Genesis. At the top, the Creation of Adam; in the center, the Expulsion from Paradise.

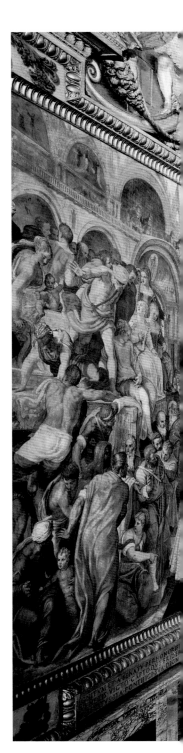

190 The room containing the fresco of the "Fire in the Borgo" was the last in the Vatican to be supervised personally by Raphael, who only painted the lunette that shows the fire in the Roman district. Perugino painted the vault, shown here, in 1508.

190-191 The Sala Regia was built after the sack of Rome in 1527 and decorated with large frescoes by Giorgio Vasari and other Mannerists. The relief stucco ceiling was the work of Perin Del Vaga, completed in 1549 during the pontificate of Paul III.

191 top left The Chiaroscuri Room – with the wooden carving of the Flagellation – was decorated by pupils of Raphael and used by the Pope as a bedroom.

191 top right The Court of the Pinecone is named after the large bronze pinecone in the niche above the landing of the staircase. Found in Agrippa's Baths, the pinecone used to decorate a fountain. The bronze work, "Sfera con sfera" by Arnaldo Pomodoro, stands in the center of the court.

191 bottom The richly frescoed ceiling in the Map Gallery. The name comes from the 40 maps that show the regions of Italy and the possessions of the Church.

foundation of the Sacred Museum and the Museum of Pagan Antiquities, the popes opened their collection of sacred treasures to the public. The first collections to be exhibited were the Greek and Roman antiquities, then, from 1837, works of Egyptian, Assyrian, and Etruscan art. Although most of the Vatican Museum is dedicated to Greek and Roman art, the popes during the Renaissance period commissioned artists like Raphael, Beato Angelico, and Pinturicchio to decorate the walls, and their frescoes are unquestionably considered part of the masterpieces on display.

The art gallery contained a small but extraordinary collection of paintings with works by Leonardo, Raphael, Titian, Domenichino, and Caravaggio. There is also a collection of modern art that was begun by Paul VI in 1973 and which includes works by Georges Braque, Paul Klee, and Edvard Munch and ceramic works by Pablo Picasso.

Flanked by the two large courts of the Belvedere and the Pigna, the Vatican Library holds an extraordinary collection of texts with over 1.6 million ancient and modern printed works, 8,300 incunabula (65 of which are on parchment), 150,000 illuminated manuscripts and archive papers, and 100,000 prints. In addition to these are the extensive collections of the secret archives that contain letters, codices, and declarations that encompass the history of the Catholic Church.

The Royal Palace in Caserta, Vanvitelli's Aqueduct, and San Leucio

ITALY

CAMPANIA
REGISTRATION: 1997
CRITERIA: C (I) (II) (III) (IV)

Seated at a massive Baroque desk on September 20, 1860, Giuseppe Garibaldi signed the letter in which he handed over his supreme power to Victor Emanuel II of Savoy, together with the most dazzling symbol of Bourbon power in Italy. Just a century earlier, Charles Bourbon had had inscribed on the first stone laid in the residence, "May the palace, its threshold, and the Bourbon family remain while this stone does not fly under its own power."

took the project over from his father – created a unique monument that merges the Baroque and the Neo-Renaissance in an order governed by the rationality of the Enlightenment. Standing 118 feet tall, the building is built partly with brick and partly with travertine stone from San Iorio; the decorations, on the other hand, are carved out of marble from southern Italy and Carrara. The five floors contain 1,200 rooms, 34 staircases, and almost 2,000 windows. Starting from the superb atrium

192 left The superb main staircase that leads from the lower vestibule to the royal apartments. Note the two white marble lions by Pietro Solari and Paolo Persico on the first landing. The staircase has a double elliptical vault where musicians signaled the arrival of the king and other important guests at official receptions.

It was January 20, 1752. To complete the construction of the palace that was to rival Versailles, 22 years, more than six million ducats, and thousands of workers were required. The overall project was awarded to Luigi Vanvitelli, with design of the hydraulic works entrusted to Francesco Collecini. The fountains were to be sculpted by Paolo Persico and Pietro Solari, layout of the park by the Parisian Marcel Biancour, and design of the English garden by John Andrew Graefer, the botanist responsible for the cultivation of the first camellias in Europe.

The palace is extraordinary. Luigi Vanvitelli – and later his son Carlo, who

that faces the main staircase, the interiors contain artistic masterpieces such as statues from the excavations at Pompeii and Herculaneum, a small court theater where performances were given of dramatic operas plays by Paisiello and Cimarosa, and the Christmas manger, or crèche, with more than 1,200 figures of shepherds and animals by the most famous eighteenth-century masters from Naples. Furthermore, the royal apartments hold endless collections of paintings, furniture, and furnishings from the late eighteenth and early nineteenth centuries.

The huge park covering 296 acres, contains an assortment of meadows,

192 right The ceiling of the Throne Room with the fresco of the "Laying of the Palace's first stone" by Gennaro Maldarelli. Measuring 49 by 43 feet, this is the palace's largest room (it originally had a total of 1,200) as well as the last, inaugurated in 1854.

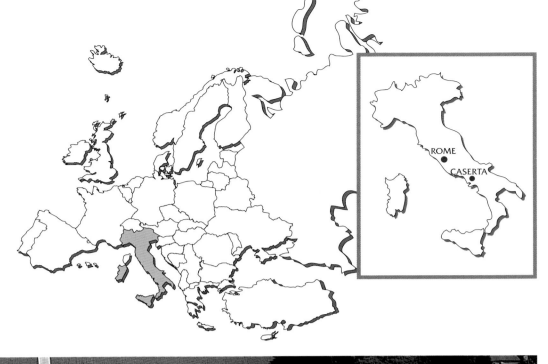

192-193 An aerial view of Caserta Palace. The superb building is rectangular in plan and measures 810 by 604 feet. It has four large internal courts and stands five stories high. In his memoirs, the architect, Luigi Vanvitelli, confessed he had only put onto paper the ideas of Charles Bourbon III, who wanted a palace modeled on Versailles and the Buen Retiro in Madrid.

193 top The Mars Room in the New Apartments was built in 1810 by Antonio de Simone. In Emperor style, it has 12 marble bas-reliefs by Valerio Villareale, Claudio Monti, and Domenico Masuci illustrating episodes from The Iliad.

193 bottom Another view of the gilded and stuccoed Throne Room. Other important rooms in the palace are the ten rooms of the Art Gallery and, on the ground floor, the Court Theater, one of the best examples of eighteenth-century theatrical architecture.

hedges, gardens, and woods crossed by two avenues roughly two miles long. A succession of 12 waterfalls and pools create the waterway that joins the splendid fountain of Venus and Adonis to the palace. Behind the palace, the great waterfall, 256 feet high, marks the arrival of the waters carried by the Caroline Aqueduct. This extraordinary piece of engineering (also by Vanvitelli) collects the waters flowing from mountain springs and transports them 25 miles. The most spectacular section of

the aqueduct is the Ponti della Valle viaduct, which is 1,736 feet long, 184 feet high, and composed of three orders of arch.

Charles Bourbon was unable to enjoy this phenomenal complex because, in 1759, he was nominated to the Spanish throne. His son Ferdinand, who was then only eight years old, took his place. First, the boy was king of Naples as Ferdinand IV, then, from 1816, he was king of the Two Sicilies under the name Ferdinand I. An enlightened ruler, he loved to throw

parties and go hunting; he was the life and soul of Caserta, which soon became a center for the most famous intellects of the age.

Inspired by the Utopian doctrines of Gaetano Filangieri, the king founded Ferdinandopolis, a "town of happiness," in the nearby village of San Leucio. The setting up of silk and fabric factories was supposed to ensure the economic autonomy of the village. The laws of the community were based on principles of equality and mutual support, and the

194

194 top The pool of the Great Cascade, also known as the Fountain of Diana, has four statuary groups that represent episodes linked to the mythology of the goddess of hunting. In this one, Actaeon has been transformed into a stag and is being attacked by his own dogs.

194 bottom The harmonious figures of Diana and Actaeon stand in the center of the Great Cascade, the work of Paolo Persico, Angelo Brunello, and Pietro Solari.

194-195 The landscaped park measures 296 acres. It features fountains and stepped waterfalls in the form of water terraces. In

the picture, cupids, nymphs, and dogs surround the Fountain of Venus in the lovely statuary group by Gaetano Salomone, depicting the goddess as she pleads with Adonis not to go hunting.

195 top left The viaduct of the Ponti della Valle is the most monumental work in the Caroline Aqueduct designed by

Luigi Vanvitelli. Construction began in 1752. Twenty-five miles long, it was opened on June 27, 1769.

195 top right A lovely view of the water terraces in the palace park, seen from the top of the Great Cascade. Fed by the water from the aqueduct, this waterfall drops 256 feet.

village prospered until the factories were bought by private individuals when the assets of the Bourbons were confiscated by the Savoys.

From Ferdinand I's reign there remains the highly attractive urban layout designed by Collecini and the Casino Reale di Belvedere featuring a ceiling frescoed by Fedele Fiaschetti with magnificent views of the palace and park of Caserta. San Leucio is still the site of silk factories that produce fabrics of excellent quality.

Parc Güell, Palau Güell, and Casa Milá

SPAIN

BARCELONA, CATALONIA
REGISTRATION: 1984
CRITERIA: C (I) (II) (IV)

As winter approached, Eusebi Güell y Bacigalupi, a rich businessman in the textile industry, a huntsman, and a lover of Wagner, headed for the Passeig de Gracia in Barcelona to buy a pair of gloves. Having reached the shop, he remained impressed by the attractiveness of the window. He entered and asked who was responsible for such an imaginative display. Eusebi Güell, naturally, forgot to buy his gloves, but he made a much more important purchase that was to mark a turning point in the history of architecture. The window-dresser turned out to be a recent graduate from the University of Barcelona. He came from Reus, near Tarragona, and his name was Antoni Gaudí

196 top Detail of a fountain in which the water spurts from the mouth of a dragon. Gaudí designed a water system for Palau Güell, and some of the oddest forms in the park hide valves and faucets.

196 bottom The entrance to Parc Güell. What was actually completed was only a small part of the original project. The client intended the complex to become a garden city with 60 detached houses situated at the gates of Barcelona.

y Cornet. Thus began a relationship between a patron and artist that was to be one of the most successful creative associations in history.

After a few minor commissions, in 1886 Güell asked Gaudí to design him a house in the city center on a small plot of land in Calle Nou de la Rambla. Just 34 years old, the architect built his patron his first masterpiece. The heart of the Palau Güell is the central reception room that

rises three floors. It is topped by a dome, inspired by Arab architecture, with small holes to give the impression of a night sky. Swept away with enthusiasm, Gaudí oversaw every detail of the project; he made the lamps, railings, and gates by bending wrought iron into improbable shapes, designed the furniture, and dreamed up a roof on which fairy-tale chimney pots covered with pieces of ceramic sprouted like mushrooms.

This visionary design was talked about by all of Barcelona, and Gaudí made his triumphal entry into the most important drawing rooms, receiving praise and commissions. With the passing of time, he perfected his style and, during that period, began his most famous work, the Sagrada Familia, which, more than a century later, has not yet been completed. In 1900, Güell once more commissioned Gaudí with what was to be his most original work.

196-197 Some of the domes in Parc Güell. Color is the distinctive element in this extraordinary development. Most of the architectural elements are lined with majolica fragments that were found in the waste area of a ceramics factory.

197 top right Another architectural detail in the park. For the businessman Eusebi Güell y Bacigalupi, Gaudí also designed the equally imaginative Palau Güell.

197

197 bottom left What is most striking throughout the park is how luxuriant it is, both in terms of vegetation and architecture. Antoni Gaudi's outlandish figures were inspired by natural forms.

197 bottom right An attractive passage in Parc Güell featuring Doric-inspired columns.

198 top Casa Milá is better known as la Pedrera (stone quarry). It has a surface area of 10,760 square feet and stands on the corner of Passeig de Gracia and Calle Provenza in the central district of Eixample.

198 center Gaudí also designed the monumental fireplace in the dining room of Palau Güell in his typical style.

198 bottom The large central salon seen here in Palau Güell is three floors high and topped by a dome in which Gaudí put small holes to give the sensation of a starry night sky.

199 The façade of the Pedrera. The undulating rhythm of the projections and recesses resembles sand dunes. In the building, the slight link with Catalan Modernism is represented by the cast iron inserts of the load-bearing columns and balconies, which have also been twisted into bizarre shapes.

The intention of the client was for Parc Güell to be a huge neighborhood/garden in an isolated area on a hill that overlooks Barcelona. The site was to have 60 plots, each of which was to be built with a single family home. The villas were in fact never constructed, but Gaudí laid out the street design made up of five elements: a main street, an avenue, a square, streets for vehicles, and paths for pedestrians. At the entrance there was to be a sort of Greek temple with Doric columns and ceramic rosettes that hung from the ceiling. The whole park is populated with fantastic creatures and splashes of color because Gaudí covered everything with small pieces of ceramic that had been thrown out as waste by a ceramics factory. The style was represented best by the wavy balustrade/bench that bounds the large panoramic terrace.

In 1906, Pere Milá Camps, another successful Catalan businessman, commissioned Gaudí to build a block of apartments on a plot measuring nearly 11,000 square feet on the corner of Passeig de Gracia and Calle Provenza. Here the brilliant architect let his imagination run wild: the house he built was made of stone sculpted into wave-like forms that seem to expand and contract with life. The load-bearing structure is made from wrought iron girders and vaults supported by brick and metal architraves. The construction of the façade was carried out somewhat like a ritual. Gaudí worked on rough sketches, then the blocks of stone were brought to the site to be cut, shaped, and laid in place. At this point he would modify the curves and shapes as the feeling took him. To passers-by, the street increasingly resembled a stone quarry, la *pedrera*, which is the name Casa Milá has always been known by in Barcelona. The final touch came with the addition of the roof on which the chimneys were given the appearance of masked warriors.

Due to delays caused by the architect's exuberance, construction lasted four years. When it was completed, the enthusiastic client, Pere Milá, moved into the first floor of the building. His wife, Señora Rosario, did not appreciate Gaudí's somersaults of the imagination but put on a good face. Casa Milá was Gaudí's last civil building as, from that time until his death in 1926, he thought of nothing other than the Sagrada Familia. After his death, the Señora Rosario took advantage of the situation to transform the entire first floor of "The Pedrera" into an elegant but banal apartment in Louis XVI style.

The University and Historic Precinct of Alcalá de Henares

SPAIN

AUTONOMOUS COMMUNITY OF MADRID
REGISTRATION: 1998
CRITERIA: C (II) (IV) (VI)

In a stately ceremony held on April twenty-third each year, the monarchs of Spain award the Cervantes Prize, the country's most prestigious literary honor. The setting for the evening ceremony is the Paraninfo, the former Great Hall of the University of Alcalá de Henares. The room stands in a building constructed between 1516 and 1520 and is a masterpiece of mudéjar art, with a roof decorated with geometric patterns of red, blue, and gold and the floor covered with elegant *azulejos*. But, aside from the beauty of the hall, the place itself is highly symbolic. On one hand, in 1547 Alcalá de Henares was the

birthplace of Miguel de Cervantes Saavedra, the author of *Don Quixote* and father of Spanish literature; on the other, it was the first university city in history.

Created by Cardinal Francisco Jiménez de Cisneros and instituted by Pope Alexander VI with the papal bull *Inter Caetera* on April 13, 1499, the University of Alcalá de Henares could be termed the first large cultural manifestation of the Renaissance. Although other universities like those in Paris and Salamanca boast a longer history, the novelty of Alcalá de Henares lies in the fact that it was not a center dedicated exclusively to learning in the seclusion of a monastery. Here, for the

first time, there was interaction between culture and society. Moreover, it was codified that culture was the fundamental requirement for the exercise of power.

This was the period during which the outlines of the modern state began to take form in Europe, and Catholic Spain, which began its expansion into the Americas, needed individuals from the ranks of the Church who were able to perform political roles. Cisneros understood and interpreted this moment in history perfectly. He appreciated the need to adapt theological principles through the renovation of both the intellectual education of the ecclesiastical elite and the doctrinal texts. He conceived his Colegio Universidad as a *Civitas Dei*, laid out and equipped with a good infrastructure.

The nucleus of Alcalá de Henares was the Colegio Mayor dedicated to San Ildefonso. It was the seat of theological studies and the residence of the rector who, appointed on an annual basis, enjoyed wide-ranging academic, judicial, and economic power. Around the Colegio Mayor, Cisneros founded five smaller colleges: Santa Catalina for the study of Aristotelian physics, San Eugenio for grammar, Santa Balbina for logic, San Isidoro for Greek, and Madre de Dios for medicine.

Expanded until it comprised 33 colleges, Alcalá de Henares numbered among its students Sant'Ignacio di Loyola, Lope de Vega, Francisco de Quevedo, Tirso de Molina, and Calderón de la Barca. In the eighteenth century, the university began a slow decline until, in 1836, the chancellorship was transferred to Madrid and the city's population declined. In 1977, however, the university reopened and today it is an avant-garde campus. The departments of the humanities have been joined by a variety of experimental

200 left The Plateresque style of the Colegio Mayor de San Ildefonso, the seat of the Rector. Rodrigo Gil de Hontañon built it in 1553 in golden stone from Tamajón in the province of Guadalajara. Note the fine sculptures on the windows and the large shield with the coat of arms of Charles V.

200 bottom right The benches and mudejár decorations in the Paraninfo, the old Great Hall of the university. On April twenty-third each year, the king of Spain awards the prestigious literary prize named after Miguel de Cervantes in this room.

sciences that have inherited the legacy of the Hospital de Antezana, the oldest health institution in Spain, founded in Alcalá de Henares in 1483.

Buildings of great architectural value are enclosed within the ring of walls and rectangular towers constructed in 1380 on the wishes of Pedro Tenorio, the archbishop of Toledo. Next to the Paraninfo, the Capilla de San Ildefonso (1510) boasts mudéjar decorations and the tomb of Cisneros himself, designed by Domenico Fancelli and Bartolomé Odoñez and decorated with marble sculptures. The university colleges that merit closest attention are the Colegio Mayor with its superb façade in plateresque style adorned with statues (1553), the Colegio de San Pedro y Pablo, and the Colegio de Malaga. Also notable is the Convento de San Bernardo with internal frescoes by Angelo Nardi and the 1694 Oratorio de San Felipe Neri that contains a collection of wooden sculptures.

The Cathedral was also built on Cisneros' wishes; it is in late Gothic style and shares the title of Magistral Church (a sixteenth century papal honorific) with only the church of Lovanio in Belgium due to the fact that its canons were members of the university teaching staff. Unfortunately, the high altar and many of the chapels were almost completely destroyed by a fire during the Civil War.

The medieval Archbishop's Palace, arranged around five cloisters, also suffered a great deal of damage during that period. Inside there is the Sala de la Entrevista, so called because this was where the first and decisive meeting took place between Christopher Columbus and Queen Isabella of Castile, yet another example of the important role Alcalá de Henares has played in the history of Spain.

200-201 The main patio with three orders of galleries of the Colegio Mayor. Dedicated to San Tomás de Vilanueva, this large open area was designed by Gómez de Mora and completed in 1662.

201 bottom The municipal hall of Alcalá de Henares in Plaza Cervantes. The author of Don Quixote was born here in 1547 and became a physician in Antezana hospital, the oldest health institution in Spain.

The Alhambra, Generalife, and Albaicín in Granada

SPAIN

GRANADA, ANDALUSIA
REGISTRATION: 1984, 1994*
CRITERIA: C (I) (III) (IV)
*EXTENSION OF THE REGISTRATION TO
INCLUDE THE ALBAICÍN DISTRICT

Beating a retreat from his beloved Granada on January 2, 1492, abu Abdallah, the last ruler of the Nasrid Dynasty, stopped for a final look at the Alhambra. The story goes that his cheeks were lined with tears, which brought him the rebuke from his mother, "You cry like a woman because you could not defend your kingdom like a man." Today, an anonymous gas station stands on the site, but the Spaniards continue to call it "El Suspiro del Moro" (The Moor's Sigh) to remember the sad and defeated ruler.

The dynasty named after Muhammad ibn Nasr was never renowned for its military skills, but thanks to diplomacy, it succeeded in surviving the Christian Reconquest of Spain for two centuries longer than all the other Muslim possessions in Andalusia.

The history of the Nasrid Emirate – which extended from Granada to the Mediterranean and from Tarifa to Almería – began in 1245 when ibn Nasr was chased out of his native Jaén by the troops of Ferdinand III of Castile; having taken refuge in Granada, he moved his capital there. On the one hand, threatened by the increasingly powerful Christian kings, and on the other, exposed to attack by the Marinid Dynasty in Morocco, the emirate of Granada did not have an easy life. To ease Spanish pressure, ibn Nasr was soon forced to sign a peace treaty with Ferdinand III, to pay him an annual tribute, and to agree to assist him in the event of war. The terms of the treaty put the Muslim leader in the unenviable position of having to send troops when Seville was under siege by Ferdinand in 1248, which showed ibn Nasr in a very bad light to his Muslim brothers. This was emphasized when he and his son, Muhammad II, were forced to ask for aid from the Marinids to resist the unsupportable requests from the Castilian throne.

The inappropriate alliance could have unleashed a military reaction by the Spanish, but they restricted themselves to neglecting the small territory on the slopes

of the Sierra Nevada and instead increased their pressure on the Muslim territories that had already been taken back from the Moors. Thus Granada became a historical, religious, and political paradox: it had 150,000 inhabitants, all of whom were either Muslim or Jewish, but had to recognize the supremacy of the Christians who surrounded it. Inside the city walls, the motto of the Nasrids, "*laa gha'liba illa-llàh*" (there is no winner who does not follow Allah) was seen everywhere and repeated

202 top left *The superb fountain resting on 12 marble lions and symbolizing the signs of the zodiac inspires the name of the Patio de los Leones in the Alhambra.*

unendingly on the walls of the Alhambra.

Despite its mixed fortunes, in the fourteenth century Granada was a city in which the arts and sciences flourished and where there were schools, hospitals, and public baths. The silk trade with Italy raised a handsome income, and agricultural labor produced plentiful foodstuffs that were sent to the port of Malaga for export.

In 1238, when the Nasrid court was still in Jaén, Muhammad ibn Nasr began construction of a palace on the top of a hill where the Berber fort Alcazaba had once stood. His ambitious aim was to transform the ruins of the military outpost into the terrestrial paradise described in the Koran, in which a luxuriant garden is watered by streams. His engineers changed the courses of the streams flowing down from the Sierra Nevada to feed canals, tanks, and fountains, and to irrigate the gardens. Muhammad's plans ended there and it was the task of his successors, Yussuf I (1333-1354) and Muhammad V (1354-1391), to complete what was to become the most extraordinary work of Islamic architecture in the West: the Alhambra. The name comes from the Arabic *al-Hamrà* (the Red One), which described the color of the clay with which its walls were built.

The Nasrid Palace is entered through the 1348 Puerta de la Justicia. The keystone of the vault in the external arch is carved with the image of an open hand, the five fingers symbolizing the pillars of Islam: the profession of faith, prayer, fasting, charity, and the pilgrimage to Mecca. One then enters the Patio de los

202 bottom The Patio de los Arrayanes lies in the center of the buildings in the Alhambra. It has an enormous fish tank surrounded by hedges of myrtle and arcades. The pool creates a scenic effect and reflects the light into the surrounding rooms.

202-203 An aerial view of the Alhambra Hill. Charles V added the solid Renaissance-style building in the center of the picture to the complex in 1526.

203 top right The skilful and sensual use of space, light, and water typifies the architecture of the Alhambra, which was designed by the Nasrid caliphs as an Islamic paradise on earth. The photograph captures the play of light and shade of the slender columns in the Patio de los Leones.

203 bottom right The ceiling of the Sala de los Reyes boasts magnificent fourteenth-century paintings on leather of knightly and hunting scenes.

themselves far from the demands of government. Therefore, the Generalife was built in 1318 on a hill to the north of the Alhambra under the supervision of the architect Aben Walid Ismail. The name of the building comes from the Arabic *Yannat al-Arif* (Garden of Sublime Paradise). Today only two pavilions of the palace remain, and they face each other across the Patio de la Acequia, an oriental garden around a long tank with arcing spouts of water. Other gardens extend all around which were originally planted with fruit trees or provided animal pasture land. Above all,

Arrayanes (the Court of the Myrtles) where there is a large fish pond. The courtyard is in turn dominated by the Salón de Embajadores (the Ambassadors' Hall). Constructed between 1334 and 1354, it is the largest room in the Alhambra and features a filigree ceiling that represents the seven heavens in Muslim cosmology.

To the right lies the harem (the women's private quarters) that looks onto the Patio de los Leones (Court of the Lions); the name is derived from the 12 marble lions that symbolize the signs of the zodiac and support the fountain in the center of the court. The fountain has a single alabaster basin where the water is collected before gushing from the mouths of the lions; it is fed by four canals aligned with the points of the compass to represent the rivers of heavenly paradise. The patio is surrounded by a portico composed of 124 slender columns. The palace's two most beautiful rooms stand on either side of the court: they are the Sala de las dos Hermanas (Room of the Two Sisters), named after the two marble slabs embedded in the floor, and the Sala de los Abencerrages (Room of the Abencerrages), which is named after a rival noble family that is said to have been massacred during a banquet in the hall. The walls of both rooms are lined with *atauriques*, exquisitely painted and glazed majolica tiles; the stucco ceiling in the latter is decorated with stalactites that create 5,000 niches rather like a honeycomb.

The nature of the Alhambra as an official residence meant that it was soon necessary to build a summer palace in which the Nasrid rulers could refresh

however, they were the location for trysts between the rulers and their favorites.

In the fatal year 1492, Ferdinand II of Aragon and his queen, Isabella of Castile, took possession of the Alhambra and the Generalife, which the Nasrids had let fall into a state of disrepair. The Spanish monarchs' wish to infuse the city with a Catholic atmosphere was mitigated by their admiration for the Alhambra. Willingly, they accepted the style of Islamic life and initiated a restoration of the site using Muslim craftsmen, wishing to return the palace to its former splendor. They did no more than build a Franciscan monastery nearby and to convert the palace mosque into a church. The most evident modifications made were by Pedro de Machuca, architect to Charles V, who, at the start of the sixteenth century, demolished a number of rooms to make space for a royal palace.

The best view of the hills on which the

Alhambra and Generalife stand is from Albaicín, the main residential district during the Muslim era, at dusk. Here Ferdinand and Isabella only built a small monastery so as not to intrude upon the harmony of the Arab architecture. Although the district has since been greatly rebuilt, it has only emphasized its original character, which is one of the reasons that UNESCO decided to make it a World Heritage site in 1994, in addition to the Moorish era's two more representative monuments. Among the district's many flights of steps, white-washed walls, and twisting alleyways, there are still houses built using traditional Moorish architecture, hanging gardens, old mosques, tea rooms, and public baths. Recently, with the increase in immigration, a community of Sufis, a mystical branch of Islam, has transferred to the district, and there are those in Granada who speak of a new invasion of the Moors.

204 top left The majestic entrance of Charles V's palace, designed by Pedro de Machuca, is bounded by pairs of Doric half-columns and sculpted medallions.

204 top right The round court with its colonnaded gallery is overlooked by the apartments in Charles V's palace.

204 bottom A view of the Albaicín, the attractive, originally Muslim quarter that has been a World Heritage site since 1994.

205 left A perfumed oriental garden in the Patio de la Acequia flanks the long tank topped by arcs of water jets. This is one of the loveliest spots in the Generalife, whose name is derived from Yannat al-Arif (garden of sublime paradise).

205 right A detail of the perimeter wall in the Generalife. Built in 1318 under the supervision of the architect Aben Walid Ismail, it was the country residence of the Nasrid rulers.

The Historic Center of Cordoba

SPAIN

CORDOBA, ANDALUSIA
REGISTRATION: 1984, 1994*
CRITERIA: C (I) (II) (III) (IV)
* IN 1984, THE MEZQUITA WAS REGISTERED
AS A WORLD HERITAGE SITE WITH UNESCO;
TEN YEARS LATER, THAT RECOGNITION WAS EXTENDED
TO THE WHOLE OF THE HISTORIC CENTER.

Built on the northern bank of the Guadalquivir, Cordoba became famous during the Roman era for having been the birthplace of Seneca and Lucan in the first century A.D. At the time it was the provincial capital of Betica and the largest city in Iberia, but the time of its greatest prosperity lay many centuries in the future.

In the eighth century, while Christian Europe was still living in its darkest age,

Cordoba became the capital of al-Andalus (Andalusia) under the Umayyad emir, Abd el-Rahman I. Chased out of Damascus by the Abbasids, the Umayyads conquered Spain with the aim of creating an economic and military power large enough to rival those of Damascus and Baghdad.

The boundaries of the emirate were rapidly extended to run from Gibraltar to the Pyrenees, and the tolerant spirit of the emir ensured his dominion long-lasting prosperity. The basilica of St. Vincent was shared between the Christians and Muslims, and the city was peacefully inhabited by Arabs, Berbers, Jews, and Visigoths. Cordoba became the center of a flourishing farming region, responsible for the introduction to Europe of oranges, apricots, rice, and eggplants, and the city also

established itself as a center for the production of fabrics.

To give thanks to God, in 785 Abd el-Rahman I decided to found a mosque that would become the symbol of the magnificence of the Umayyad Emirate. He purchased a basilica from the Christians and, in its place, built what was to become the nucleus of the Mezquita Mayor. It was built on the model of the mosque in Damascus but soon exceeded it

206 top left The wooden stalls of the choir in Cordoba Cathedral were produced in 1758 by Pedro Duque Cornejo in the elaborate Churringueresque style.

206 center left The elegant arcade that rings the Patio de los Naranjos at the north end of the Mezquita Mayor. The Muslims performed their ritual ablutions in the four tenth-century fountains in this wide courtyard embellished by orange trees.

206 center right The interior of the Mezquita Mayor features 1,293 columns made from granite, jasper, and marble, arranged to form 19 corridors. The columns support horseshoe-shaped arches made from alternate rows of white stone and brick.

206 bottom right A lovely internal view of the cathedral dome, designed in 1523 by the Hernán Ruiz family of architects. They used domes from the Italian Renaissance as their model.

206-207 From above, the view embraces the entire Mezquita Mayor complex. Much of the Umayyad construction (covering an area of 591 by 427 feet) has remained unaltered. In the sixteenth century, the center of the mosque was destroyed for a cathedral to be built, and the Alminar Tower was raised to the south where the minaret once stood. In the background there is the Roman bridge over the Guadalquivir.

207 right The nave of the cathedral in which late-Gothic Christian elements are merged with the original Umayyad architecture.

in splendor. In four stages of expansion over two centuries, the Mezquita slowly reached its full size; the *haram* (sacred area) measured 590 by 430 feet and covered nearly four acres. Inside, a forest of 1293 columns made from granite, jasper, and marble were arranged to form 19 corridors. Built using materials taken from Roman and Visigoth buildings across southern Spain, the columns support horseshoe-shaped arches made from alternating brick and white stone. In this immense space, which was gradually covered with beautiful mosaics, it is difficult to identify the *mihrab*, or niche that faces Mecca.

Bounded to the south by the river Guadalquivir, the building, enclosed by high crenellated walls, opens to the north onto the Patio de los Naranjos, the courtyard in which the faithful perform their ritual ablutions in the four fountains that were built among the orange trees in the tenth century.

Cordoba enjoyed its greatest glory in the eleventh and twelfth centuries. It had almost a million inhabitants and was divided into 21 districts, each of which had its own mosques, markets, and public baths.

The city was also a flourishing center for the arts and sciences. In 1126, it was the birthplace of ibn Rashid (the great Arab philosopher known as Averroes), and less than 10 years later, of the Jew, Moses Ben Maimòn, who became the physician and theologian known as Maimonides. Jewish merchants were leading figures in the life of the city. Today, their quarter, the Judería,

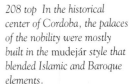

208 top In the historical center of Cordoba, the palaces of the nobility were mostly built in the mudejár style that blended Islamic and Baroque elements.

208 center left One of the many flower-filled patios in the Barrio Judio, the district originally inhabited by the city's Jewish community.

208 center right Three hundred and five feet high, the Alminar Tower in mudejár style tops the Puerta del Perdón, so called because this is where penitents were absolved.

behind the Mezquita, has remained pretty much intact. The alleys are lined by white walls behind which there are splendid town houses, flowered patios, wrought iron gates, and tanneries, for which Cordoba has always been famous. After the Reconquest of Spain by the Christians, in 1236 the Mezquita was reconsecrated as a Christian church and the city endowed with fortified palaces like the Alcázar de los Reyes Cristianos and the Torre de la Calahorra. The lines of the Mezquita, however, remained unaltered until the end of the fourteenth century when the minaret was demolished to make room for the Puerta del Perdón, a majestic entrance in *mudejár* style topped by the Torre del Alminar, a bell tower 305 feet tall that affords a view across the whole city. In the

same period, the first Christian chapel, the Capilla de Villaviciosa, was built inside the Mezquita. In the sixteenth century, the Holy Roman Emperor, Charles V, authorized construction of a cathedral in the heart of the Mezquita. Designed by the Hernán Ruiz family of architects, its structure mixes late Gothic and Renaissance elements to which, in the nineteenth century, an intricate wooden choir was added.

The Cordoban nobility also built magnificent palaces such as the Palacio de Viana, but these have not affected the spirit of the Moorish city. Today Cordoba is an extraordinary account in stone of the harmonious cultural and economic co-existence of the three great monotheistic religions.

208-209 The lovely gardens of the Alcázar de los Rejes Cristianos, a palace-fortress built in 1328 by King Alfonso XI. Ferdinand II and Isabella of Castile stayed here during the campaign to chase the Moors out of Granada.

209 top The massive Calahorra Tower was built at the end of the Puente Romano for defensive purposes in the fourteenth century.

The Cathedral, the Alcázar, and the Archivo de Jndias, Seville

SPAIN

SEVILLE, ANDALUSIA
REGISTRATION: 1987
CRITERIA: C (I) (II) (III) (VI)

After two years of patient siege, on November 23, 1248, Ferdinand III of Castile forced the Moors in Seville to surrender and he made his triumphal entry into the city. The Catholic king found a beautiful city strongly characterized by the Islamic architecture of the flourishing region of al-Andalus. The return of the Christians also marked the return of their religious ceremonies, and as there were no churches to perform them in, the archbishop blessed the Almohad mosque that been built just 50 years prior.

It was necessary to wait until 1401 for construction of a cathedral to begin. Founded on the site of a former mosque, the cathedral measured 381 by 249 feet, with a nave, four side aisles, and 25 chapels. Known as the *Magna Hispanensis*, it was the second largest church in the world after St. Peter's. It took 100 years to complete the structure and more than 300 for the internal decoration to be finished. After the discovery of the New World by Christopher Columbus (whose body is buried here), the riches that flowed into Seville allowed the cathedral to be adorned with large windows, *retablos*, and magnificent paintings by artists such as Murillo, Zuburán, Pedro de Campaña, and Goya. Besides its many paintings, other artistic masterpieces in the cathedral include the high altar dating from 1482, considered the most intricate in Spain, and the impressive, elliptical Chapter Room.

The cathedral has nine doors. The main one, Puerta Mayor, is on the west side; the north door, the Puerta del Perdón, is a perfect example of *mudejár*

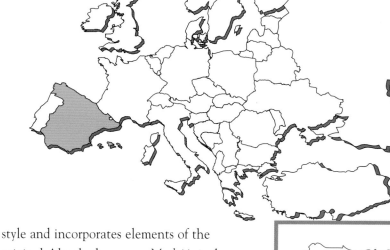

style and incorporates elements of the original Almohad mosque. *Mudejár* is the result of the syncretism of Islamic and Christian architecture, and the term was originally used to define Muslims who decided to remain in Spain after the Reconquest, though without converting to Catholicism (the word is derived from the Arabic *mudayyan*, which means "one allowed to stay"). The Puerta del Perdón leads into the Patio de los Naranjos (Court of Oranges), a garden laid out under Islamic criteria (it includes a fountain for performing ablutions). Similarly, the Giralda, an elegant minaret built between 1172 and 1195, was transformed into a bell tower and given two bells at the end of the

210 left Masterpieces by Goya, Murillo, and Zuburán are kept in the extraordinary elliptical dome of the Chapter Room.

210 right The sarcophagus of Christopher Columbus (1890) in the cathedral is supported by figures representing the kingdoms of Castile, León, Aragon, and Navarre.

210-211 This aerial view
of the historic center of
Seville embraces the three
monumental complexes
under the protection of
UNESCO. In the center,
the cathedral with its
famous Giralda, the
minaret that was built in
1198 and later turned into
a bell tower. To the right
there is the Alcázar and, in
the background to the left,
the building that holds the
Archives of the Indies.

211 bottom left The
elaborate columned vault of
the Capilla Mayor. Access
to the chapel is gained
through a large grill beyond
which lies the largest retablo
in the Christian world.

211 bottom right The Patio
de los Naranjos next to the
cathedral, along with the
Giralda, is what remains of
the earlier Moorish building.
In the center of the patio
stands the fountain Muslims
used to perform their ritual
ablutions.

212 top Azulejos and elaborate stucco work decorate the Ambassadors' Room with its three symmetrical horseshoe-shaped arches. This is one of the most dramatic rooms in the Alcázar.

212-213 A picture of the Alcázar from the top of the Giralda. Originally, this was the site of the palaces built for the Almohad rulers. In 1346, after the Reconquest, Pedro I ordered their restoration in accordance with his own tastes to create a magnificent royal residence.

212 center Inside the Alcázar, the apartments of Charles V are embellished by spirited sixteenth-century azulejos and large wall hangings.

212 bottom left A view of the patio that leads to the magnificent apartments built in the first half of the sixteenth century by Charles V in the Alcázar.

212 bottom right A room in the Archivo General de Indias, created by Charles III in 1778. Housed in what was originally the Lonja, the merchants' loggia, it holds roughly 40,000 documents relating to Spanish holdings overseas from the time of the discovery of America to the independence of various states.

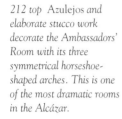

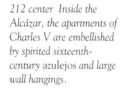

sixteenth century.

Opposite the cathedral stands the Alcázar, the fortified palace built in 913 by the Almoravid caliph, Abd el-Rahman III, which was transformed into a royal residence by Pedro I "the Cruel" in 1350. The modifications he made represent the height of *mudejár* style in Seville, but Pedro was not the only one to make alterations on the building, and now it comprises various styles that include Renaissance and Neo-Classical. The same mix is to be seen in the gardens, for example, Charles V's sixteenth century pavilion, which combines Moorish elements with statues of classical mythological figures, humorous hydraulic

objects typical of the Italian Renaissance like an organ that spouts water, and the eighteenth-century Jardín Inglés, in the landscaping style of the British Isles.

All trade in Seville took place in front of the Alcázar, between the steps of the cathedral and the Patio de los Naranjos, until 1572 when Archbishop Don Cristóbal de Rojas y Sandoval sent an indignant letter to King Philip II, who immediately initiated construction of a Lonja (a loggia for merchants) that faces onto the same square. The architect responsible was Juan de Herrera, who had designed the royal monastery of San Lorenzo de El Escorial. The building is square with a dual-colored façade softened by pillars and vaults.

Less than a century later, however, the commercial fortunes of Seville began to decline. In 1660, the building was converted to house Murillo's school of painting and then slowly left to fall into ruin. The idea of using it to house all the Spanish documents relating to the Indies was approved in 1778 by Charles III. Restoration of the Lonja, renamed the Archivo General de Indias, was completed in 1789. Today it holds about 40,000 documents divided into 16 sections, and includes handwritten letters by Christopher Columbus, nautical and land-registry maps, and even the request by Miguel de Cervantes for a shipload from the Indies.

The Convent of Christ in Tomár

PORTUGAL

DISTRICT OF SANTARÉM, RIBATEJO

REGISTRATION: 1983

CRITERIA: C (I) (VI)

Qn the night of October 13, 1307, the king of France, Philip the Fair, ordered the first police operation in history. In the round-up, all the Knights of the Order of the Temple of the Holy Sepulcher were arrested.

The Knights Templar were spread across the whole of medieval Europe and played a leading role in the Crusades and in chasing the Moors out of Spain and Portugal. However, once external dangers had been removed, their influence threatened the political power of the monarchies, and therefore, once the French operation had been completed, the hunt spread to Spain. In 1312, Pope Clement V suppressed the Order and ordered the confiscation of all their goods. The Knights Templar found refuge at the court of Dom Dinis in Portugal, who reconstituted the Order in 1320 with a new name, the Order of Christ, and transferred all the Portuguese properties of the Templars to the new organization, beginning with the district of Tomár.

The Convent of Christ had been founded on top of the hill that overlooks the village of Tomár in 1162 by Gualdin Pais, the first and supreme Master of the Templars, who made it a religious and military center. The heart of the complex was the Charola, also known as the apse or rotunda of the Templars, which is a 16-

214-215 *The complex of
the Convent of Christ.
The fortifications are one
of the few sections
remaining from the twelfth
century.*

sided church with the high altar positioned
in the center. Like other religious buildings
of the age, its form was inspired by the
Church of the Holy Sepulcher in Jerusalem,
which the Order of the Knights Templar
was originally established to defend. The
military role of the place was reflected in
the simplicity of the Romanesque
architecture and its size, for it seems that
the Knights participated in functions on
horseback.

The link between the royal dynasty and
the Order of Christ characterized, in the
fifteenth and sixteenth centuries, the era of
the Portuguese conquests overseas. From
1417 to 1460, Henry the Navigator was the
Grand Master, and the Knights were
guaranteed spiritual jurisdiction over all
new lands. This was why the sails of the
caravels bore the sign of the Cross, as that
was the symbol of the Order. Henry built his
palace in Tomár, though today it is only a
ruin, and two cloisters, the Claustro do
Cemitério and the Claustro do Lavagem.

215

*215 bottom left A detail
of a balustrade in the
Great Cloisters, built by
Dom Joao III in 1557.*

*215 bottom right The
heart of the Convent is
the round Romanesque
temple of the Carola, also
referred to as the
Templars' Rotunda. The
building imitates the form
of the Holy Sepulcher in
Jerusalem.*

TOMÁR

LISBON

*215 top Crowned by
elaborate sculptures, the
entrance to the Convent of
Christ is of unusual size,
probably because the
members of the Holy
Order of Templars entered
on horseback.*

216 left One of the
enormous windows
decorated with tree trunks,
roots, acanthus leaves,
rose fruits, artichokes,
seaweed, and fantastic

creatures, all bound together
by ropes and chains. These
exuberant motifs gave rise to
a style known as Manueline
after the sovereign, Dom
Manuel.

216 right The large,
severe Chapter Room was
designed by Diogo de
Almeida and built in the
late fifteenth and sixteenth
centuries.

216

The most extensive alterations to the complex in Tomár were made by Henry's successor, Dom Manuel, who hired the architect Diogo de Almeida to build a large rectangular aisle on the west side of the Charola to hold the choir and the sacristy. Today this aisle is known as the Chapter Room.

The extensive sculptural decorations in this new construction, and above all the large windows, represent the mystique of the Knights and their mission in the age of overseas exploration. The many figurative motifs include tree trunks, roots, acanthus leaves, rose fruits, artichokes, seaweed, and imaginary animals, all of which are linked by ties, cords, chains, fire, and waves in a clear reference to the unity of life. This sculptural work can be considered the template for the Manueline architectural style seen in many Portuguese buildings of the era.

In 1521, Dom Joao III succeeded Dom Manuel, and in accordance with

the dictates of the Council of Trent, he made far-reaching alterations to the Order, changing its rule so that it was transformed into a monastic community devoid of political power or a military role. This "revolution" was reflected in the architecture of the complex. Joao III built dormitories, kitchens, and the plain, two-story building decorated with columns known as the Great Cloisters. These buildings were completed in 1557 in the pure Italian Renaissance style of which the king was an enthusiastic connoisseur. The final alterations were made during the dynasty of the Philips (1580-1640), this time in the Mannerist style.

In 1789, Pope Pius VI issued the bull *Qualqunque a majoribus* that allowed the queen, Mary I, to reform the Order of Christ. From then on, the privilege of being a Knight Templar was relegated to simply that of an honorific. Today, it can be awarded by the President of Portugal, whose position qualifies him as Grand Master.

216-217 A view of the galleries of the Great Cloisters. The memory of the Knights of the Order has been preserved as an honorific title that can be bestowed by the President of Portugal.

217 top left The superb architecture of the Great Cloisters is in the purest Italian Renaissance style. The Convent's kitchens and refectories also date from the mid-sixteenth century.

217 top right Built for King Henry the Navigator, Grand Master of the Order, the Claustro do Lavagem, together with the Claustro do Cemitério, is one of the few sections of the palace built by the king.

The Cultural Landscape of Sintra
PORTUGAL

REGISTRATION: 1995
CRITERIA: C (II) (IV) (V)

"**P**alaces and gardens stand amongst high, craggy hills, waterfalls, and precipices, [along with] the monasteries on splendid heights [and] a distant view of the sea and the Tago, combining the wildness of the western Highlands with the greenery of southern France." Thus the 21-year-old George Byron described the wonders of Sintra in a letter to his mother. It mattered little that he had not seen either the Highlands or Provence, yet his words were a faithful portrait of this semi-mountainous area, not far from Lisbon, that looks out onto the Atlantic from Cabo da Roca, the westernmost point in Europe.

Byron had withdrawn here in 1809 to write *Childe Harold's Pilgrimage*, the epic poem, some of which describes the landscape of Sintra. Considered during the Romantic age as "the Eden of Europe," Sintra was the destination of the rich and noble of every nationality for the summer period. The origin of Sintra, however, is much older.

Its geographical position and the picturesque views from the Sintra mountains aroused the interest of the Moors who, in the eighth and ninth centuries, built a fort there known as the Castillo dos Mouros. Conquered in 1147 by Dom Alfonso Enriques, the castle remained a residence of the Portuguese royal family until the fourteenth century when it was abandoned, later to be restored during the Romantic age.

At that time, Dom Joao I ordered the construction of a palace in Chao da Oliva, what today is the historic center of Sintra and probably the site of an earlier Moorish building. Sintra's Gothic touch,

taken up in many other Portuguese buildings, was the work of another king, Dom Manuel, after whom the style Manueline was named. Renovated mostly during the Renaissance, today the Paço Real complex features extravagant architectural forms such as the two conical chimneys above the kitchens that have become the symbol of Sintra. The palace attracted a circle of artists and men-of-letters, and according to tradition, this was where Luis de Camões gave the first public reading of his poem The *Lusiads*.

In the centuries to come, the Portuguese royal family made Sintra their *buen retiro* (favorite country residence).

218 top The style of the Paço Real is predominantly Gothic, though a Moorish influence and extravagant Manueline forms can be identified. The most evident feature is the two cone-shaped chimneys over the kitchens.

219 top *The ramparts of the Castillo dos Mouros, the first building constructed in the area. The Moors built the fort in the eighth and ninth centuries, but when it was conquered by Dom Alfonso Enriques in 1147, it became the residence of the Portuguese royal family until the sixteenth century.*

218-219 The Sala das Armas is the most dramatic in the Paço Real. Its walls are lined with azulejos and the barrel-vaulted ceiling is decorated with the coats of arms of 72 Portuguese noble families.

219 bottom The Sala dos Cisnes is named after the elegant swans that decorate the ceiling. On the first floor of the Paço Real, it is one of the plainest rooms.

220 top The lovely Sala
do Trono in the Palácio
Queluz was designed by
the architect Jean-Baptiste
Robillion. The mirrors
hung on all the walls
increase the sense of
spaciousness. Silvestre
Faria Lobo carved their
gold-leaf wood frames.

220-221 Though smaller, Palácio Queluz is often compared to Versailles. Jean-Baptiste Robillion and the Dutch gardener José Van der Kolk designed its gardens, filled with statues and fountains, according to French tastes in the eighteenth century.

221 top Detail of the elegant statue of a sphinx in the Queluz garden. The garden was designed for the royal family to relax in with cages for exotic birds, and pools and fountains inhabited by black and white swans.

In 1747, Dom Pedro bought the country estate of the Marquis of Castelo Rodrigo and built the Palácio Queluz there, an elegant building surrounded by a park adorned by Rococo statues, a navigable canal decorated with azulejos, a pavilion designed by the French architect Jean-Baptiste Robillion, and fountains, one of which, the Fonte de Neptuno, has been attributed to Gian Lorenzo Bernini.

Perhaps Sintra's most surprising building is the Palácio da Pena. Situated high on the rocky peaks of the Sintra mountains, it arose from the ruins of the

221 bottom The marvelous statuary group of the Fonte do Neptuno stands in front of the main entrance to the Palácio Queluz. The sculpture has been attributed to the Italian master, Lorenzo Bernini.

Jeronymite monastery of Nossa Señora da Pena, built in the sixteenth century to celebrate the deeds of Vasco da Gama. The palace was commissioned by Ferdinand II of Saxe-Coburg in 1839 for his wife, Queen Maria II of Portugal, from Ludwig von Eschwege. The architect created a magnificent concoction of domes, ramparts, passageways, and decorations partly inspired by Ludwig II's castle in Bavaria and partly by the works of Schinkel in central Europe.

Besides the royal residences, Sintra is also the site of churches, monasteries, and aristocratic *quintas*. One of these is the astounding Victorian residence of Monserrate. Its history began in 1793 when William Beckford, the richest self-made Englishman of the period, rented the estate and began to decorate its interiors and gardens in his refined personal taste. Half a century later, Monserrate was bought by another Englishman, Sir Francis Cook, who rebuilt the house taking his inspiration from the Mogul palaces of India.

With the opening of the railway between Lisbon and Sintra in 1887, the delights of this area became accessible to one and all, but notwithstanding the prod towards progress, the romantic charm of the place has remained unaltered.

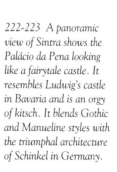

The Old City of Dubrovnik

CROATIA

DALMATIA
REGISTRATION: 1979
CRITERIA: C (I) (III) (IV)

Between November 1991 and May 1992, the Yugoslav army subjected the city of Dubrovnik to an incessant bombardment, reducing its population to their final resources and damaging roughly 70 percent of the buildings in the historic center. Today Dubrovnik has conserved the spirit of that dreadful siege, but thanks to a large scale restoration program coordinated by UNESCO, its walls, churches, and limestone buildings have been returned to their past splendor.

At the start of the war that led to the break-up of Yugoslavia, in undervaluing the symbolic value of the "Pearl of Dalmatia," the Croats did not think that Dubrovnik would become a theater of war. During its history, the city had distinguished itself as a model of freedom, independence, and civic tolerance and had never been forced to resort to arms.

Founded on a small island in 614 with the name Lus, it was turned into Ragusa by the peoples arriving from the nearby Epidaurus (modern Cavtat) who had fled the raids and plundering of the Slavs and Avars; the new city was soon given solid defensive walls.

From the seventh to twelfth centuries, it enjoyed the protection of the Byzantine Empire and became an important trading city in the eastern Mediterranean. By 1205, it had peacefully fused with nearby Slav settlement on the mainland from which it took the name Dubrovnik (from *dubrava* meaning holm oak, a tree that covers the surrounding hills), but in that same year it was conquered by Venice. Nonetheless, under the rule of the Serenissima, it continued to trade without external interference.

Independent once more in 1358 but aware that it could not defend itself from future attacks, the city requested the protection of the kings of Croatia and Hungary in return for an annual tribute. Free, therefore, to concentrate on its own affairs, the *Republica Ragusina* assured itself of the monopoly of the salt trade in the Balkans and entered a long period of splendor. In spite of the earthquake of 1667 that razed it to the ground and killed 5,000 people, it prospered to such an extent that in the seventeenth century it had consulates in 80 countries. Furthermore, it considered diplomacy so important that it was the first European country to recognize the United States of America. The end of the city's independence came in 1806 when Napoleon incorporated Dubrovnik into the Illyrian Provinces.

Dubrovnik's fortunes are reflected in its architecture and town plan. Its walls – 82 feet high and, in some places, 20 feet thick – are adorned with Gothic towers and Renaissance semi-circular ramparts. Enclosing remarkable religious and civil buildings, when one arrives from the sea, they appear like a crown rising out of the water. The main city street is the Stradun, the broad cobbled road that follows the

line of the canal, which separated the island from the mainland in ancient times. The Stradun is lined with Baroque buildings constructed after the earthquake and leads into Luza Square, where there stands the sixteenth-century Sponza Palace, built in a harmonious mix of Gothic and Renaissance styles, and which was once home to the Customs and the Mint.

224 top left The cathedral of Santa Maria Maggiore (Velika Gospa) overlooks the old city. It is a beautiful example of Baroque architecture built between 1672 and 1713 over the ruins of a Romanesque church that, it is said, had been constructed thanks to the generosity of Richard the Lionhearted.

224-225 The aerial view of Dubrovnik shows the city's unusual urban layout. The late-thirteenth-century walls were strengthened in the sixteenth century with semicircular bastions.

224 bottom Always crowded, the Stradun is the wide cobbled road that runs along the canal that, in ancient times, separated the island from the mainland.

225 top The heart of city life, the Luza (City Hall Square) lies at the east end of the Stradun.

225 bottom The unusual architectural harmony and uniformity of the city is due to the massive reconstruction that took place after the 1667 earthquake. The picture shows the nearby and wild island of Lokrum.

226-227 Founded in the late thirteenth century and rebuilt after the 1667 earthquake, the Convent of the Poor Clares housed one of Europe's first orphanages from 1432.

226 bottom The aerial view of the church of St. Biagio (Sveti Vlaho) is dedicated to the city's patron saint. It was built in Venetian Baroque by Marino Groppelli between 1707 and 1717. The statue of the saint on the high altar is from the fifteenth century and is a local example of the goldsmith's art.

227 top The Small Fountain stands on the east side of the Luza. Its lovely relief decorations are by Pietro di Martina, a Milanese sculptor who worked in Dubrovnik in the mid-fifteenth century.

In front of the palace stands the church of St. Biagio. The present building dates from the first half of the eighteenth century and has an elaborate Baroque façade and richly decorated interior with statues and gilding. The Cathedral of Santa Maria Maggiore is also Baroque, and was completed in 1713 on the ruins of a Romanesque church that, it seems, had been built as a result of the generosity of Richard the Lionhearted, whose ships had found asylum in the port after a storm.

Among the other monuments, there is the Franciscan monastery of Mala Braca that includes a Baroque church and an elegant fourteenth-century cloister ringed by 60 slender twin columns each with unique capitals that mark the transition from the Romanesque to Gothic architectural style. In 1317, Europe's oldest known public pharmacy was founded here. Lastly, the Rectors' Palace, begun in 1460, is also an architectural masterpiece. The exterior is decorated with a portico with finely sculpted capitals, while the Renaissance entrance leads into the rooms

227 center A masterpiece of balance and proportions, the Rectors' Palace was begun in 1460. The façade has a portico of six arcades supported by columns with finely sculpted capitals.

227 bottom The lovely pharmacy inside the Franciscan monastery of Mala Braca. Operative since 1317, it is one of the oldest in Europe.

of the City Museum. At the time of the Republic, it was used as the residence of the noble who was elected every month to represent, though only nominally, administrative power. In fact, this prestigious appointment carried with it one major drawback: a gilded seclusion. The noble in question was not allowed to leave the palace without the consent of his electors. Perhaps this strange custom of "imprisoning" power was the foundation of the libertarian tradition of this ancient coastal state.

228 top left The entrance court at the Budavári Palota (Royal Palace). The buildings now house four museums, the most important of which are the National Gallery of Hungary and the Budapest History Museum.

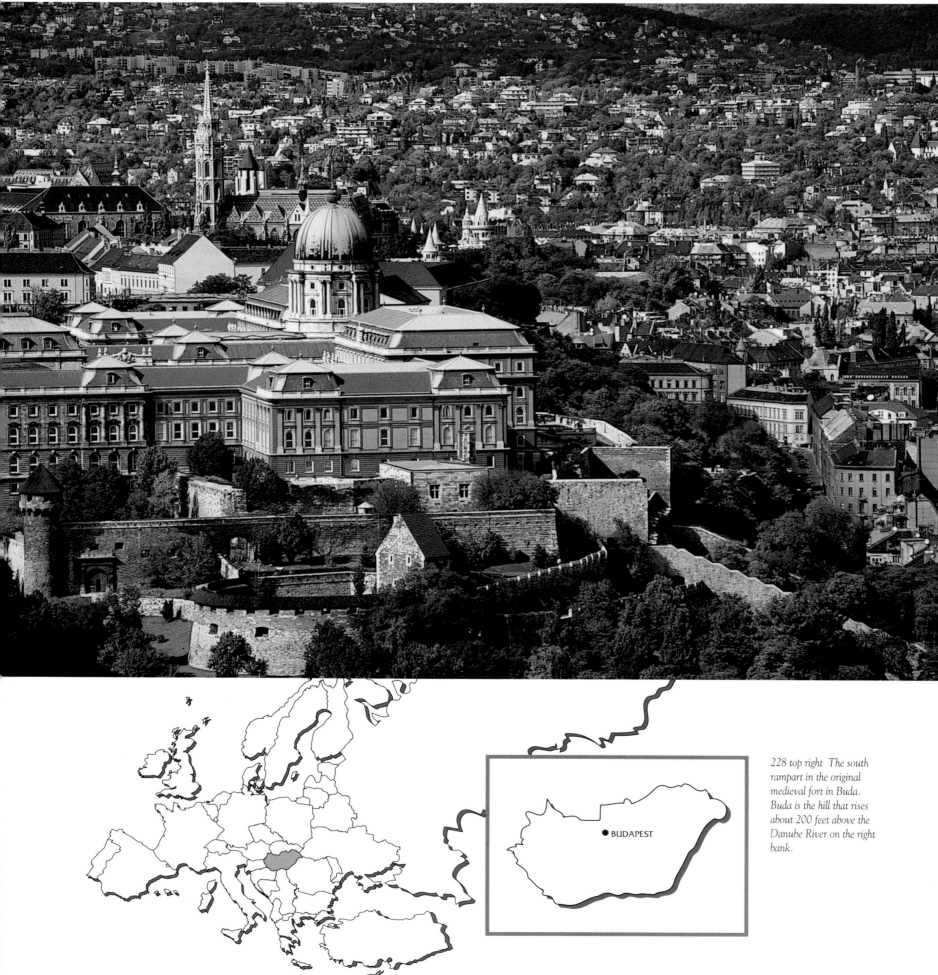

BUDAPEST

228 top right The south rampart in the original medieval fort in Buda. Buda is the hill that rises about 200 feet above the Danube River on the right bank.

Budapest, the Banks of the Danube and Buda Castle

HUNGARY

BUDAPEST
REGISTRATION: 1987
CRITERIA: (II) (IV)

At the end of the nineteenth century, when the Austro-Hungarian empire had a strong influence over international affairs, Budapest enjoyed a moment of glory. Gustav Mahler and the young Béla Bartók performed at the Academy of Music, and Art Nouveau buildings sprang up like mushrooms in the residential areas. The city was illuminated at night by an electric lighting system, and in 1896 continental Europe's first underground train system was opened. The occasion being celebrated was the thousandth anniversary of the Hungarian state, but the city's history went back further than that.

The first settlement on the Gellert hills named Ak Ink, meaning "rock rich with water," was built by the Celts in the first century B.C. At the start of the Christian era, it became the capital of the Roman province of Pannonia Inferiore with the name Aquincum, but it was soon invaded by the Huns. After the Hun empire was dismantled, it was the turn of the Gepids, the Lombards, the Avars, and other Germanic and central Asian peoples. The Magyars first appeared around the ninth century and settled their own capital at Esztergom; later, in the thirteenth century, they moved it to Obuda, (the Roman Aquincum) near Pest, a trading town inhabited by Germanic and Hungarian peoples.

In the mid-thirteenth century, following the invasion of the Tatars, King Béla IV began construction of the royal palace and fortified walls on a terrace elevated about 200 feet above the right bank of the Danube. This side of the river could be more easily defended than Pest, which was situated on a plain. Buda, which grew up around the fort on the hill, was the third city founded in that area, and it soon grew. The country's second university was established there in 1395 and, in 1473, the first Hungarian book, *Budai krónika* (*The Chronicles of Buda*) was printed.

The political, economic, and cultural capital, Buda enjoyed its greatest splendor in the late fifteenth and early sixteenth centuries when it was visited by travelers from all parts of Europe. At the start of the sixteenth century, the city's ramparts were strengthened, but they could not withstand the Turks, who succeeded in taking the city by cunning. The Ottoman occupation marked a long period of decline and came to an end in 1686 after a long siege. Having lost almost all its inhabitants as a result of the hostilities, Buda was relegated to the role of a small provincial city in the Hapsburg Empire until the mid-nineteenth century.

228-229 A view of the city with Buda Hill and the royal palace in the foreground. Built in the thirteenth century and seriously damaged in the bloody battle for independence against the Turks, the palace was enlarged in the eighteenth century and renovated in Neo-Baroque style in 1890.

229 top right The Baroque fountain dedicated to Mattia Corvino, the enlightened ruler and general who reigned over Hungary in the second half of the fifteenth century. With an army of 30,000 mercenaries – known as the "Black Army" – he was able to halt the advance of the Turks.

229 bottom The entrance to the Royal Palace from the Fishermen's Rampart. Note the bronze equestrian statue of King Stephen the Holy, the legendary founder of Hungary by Alajos Strobl.

Having also been seriously damaged during the Nazi occupation, Buda's appearance today is composed of a variety of styles. Its streets – dominated to the north by the Fort and its residential district, and to the south by the royal palace – are lined with Gothic, Renaissance, and Baroque buildings. The Turkish domination is also seen in buildings like the Király public baths, built between 1566 and 1570, later enlarged with Neo-Classical wings.

The city's most interesting building is the Church of Our Blessed Lady, also known as the Matthias Church because it

contains the armor of Matthias Corvinus who reigned from 1458 to 1490. The history of this church is one of suffering, like that of the city: the first religious building was raised on this site in the thirteenth century but was soon replaced by a Gothic cathedral that was never completed. During the Ottoman era, the building was converted into a mosque, and during the siege of 1686 the tower and roof collapsed. Reconstruction included Baroque elements, but in the nineteenth century, the Gothic building was rebuilt following excavation of the remains of the medieval church. Especially interesting are the Neo-Gothic bell tower and the south door; the latter was frescoed with a scene of the "Death of the Virgin" and the interior enlivened with stucco-work and paintings with ornamental motifs.

Behind the church stands the Fishermen's Rampart, in a style somewhere between Neo-Gothic and Neo-Romanesque, from where one can admire the whole city. Its name is taken from the district over

which it looks, where the fishermen used to live, and from the fact that a fish market was held there in ancient times because the placid waters of the Danube that separates the two halves of the Hungarian capital flow nearby.

Shortly afterwards the stubbornness of the aristocrat István Széchenyi proved useful: blocked on the east bank while the funeral of his father was being held on the west bank, he spared no effort until finally the river was crossed by a bridge. Thanks to him, in 1848, the Széchenyi Lánchid, a magnificent chain bridge, was completed, and for the first time, the two banks of the great river were joined.

230 bottom Fishermens' Rampart. Built in sandstone in the nineteenth and twentieth centuries in a style somewhere between Neo-Romanesque and Neo-

Gothic, the bastion is decorated with statues of medieval heroes and towers in the shape of a helmet, which symbolize the Magyar tribes.

230-231 View of the Danube and Pest. In the center, there is the famous Bridge of Chains, also called Széchenyi Lánchid after the ambitious person who commissioned its construction in 1839 from

the English engineer Adam Clark. The left bank of the river is dominated by the huge Parliament building designed in the late nineteenth century in Oriental Neo-Gothic by the architect Imre Steindl.

231 top left Detail of an old house in Buda, with a shrine showing Mary and Jesus.

231 top right An imaginative decoration on a Jügendstil palace in the

Várhegy district. There are many examples of this eclectic style that flourished in the late nineteenth and early twentieth centuries. Odon Lechner was Hungary's greatest architect in this style.

The Rock-hewn Churches of Jvanovo

BULGARIA

REGION OF RUSE
REGISTRATION: 1979
CRITERIA: C (II) (III)

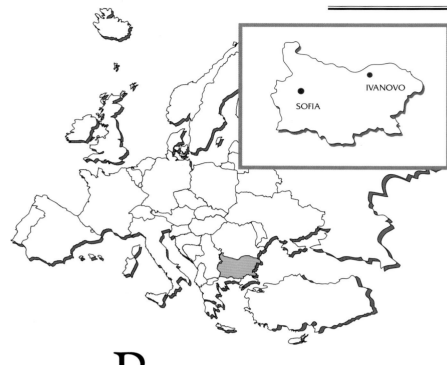

Born to a noble Bulgarian family, Gioacchino grew up with a disregard for human vanities, and as soon as he reached adulthood he left for Mount Athos where he conducted a life of prayer, fasting, and vigil. Once his pilgrimage to the sacred mountain was completed, he returned home and withdrew to a cave on the banks of the river Rusenski Lom, a tributary of the Danube. Soon he was joined by three disciples – Diomedes, Athanasius, and Theodosios – with whom he founded a small rock-hewn church dedicated to the Transfiguration.

His fame spread through Serbia and Bulgaria and reached the court of Czar Ivan Asen II, who reigned over the region during the first half of the thirteenth century. Moved by curiosity and religious fervor, the czar went to visit the ascetic, and after spending a little time with Gioacchino in retreat, decided to donate a large sum of gold so that his followers might be offered hospitality. This was the origin of the Monastery of the Archangel Michael, built between 1218 and 1235, a sacred complex dug out of the limestone to which other chapels, churches, and cells were added over the following four centuries.

Today, this settlement is one of the best examples of Orthodox Christianity in

232-233 The smoothed walls of the Zatrupanata tzarkva (the lavra of the Monastery of the Archangel Michael). The ceilings are perfectly conserved, but the paintings on the walls are suffering. One of these is a portrait of Ivan Asen II, the czar that sponsored the construction of the monastery.

234 top *The limestone wall on the Rusenski Lom in which the entrances to the rock churches of Ivanovo are carved out. The difficult access allowed the monks to dedicate themselves to spirituality and studies.*

eastern Europe. During the late Middle Ages, St. Gioacchino's complex was elevated to a Patriarchate and became an important reference point for a large circle of grammarians and other learned followers of Hesychasm. This religious doctrine, which arose during the last period of the Byzantine empire, is based on the renunciation of earthly passions in order for the individual to be reunited with God.

Today the three miles of the Rusenski Lom Gorge, near the village of Ivanovo, numbers about 300 caves of which 40 still boast religious iconography. It is thought that the monks lived in at least 60, but many of the caves have been destroyed by the erosive force of the river and by raids made during the Ottoman occupation of the country. The oldest caves are on the right bank of the river, which, with seven churches, make up the original Monastery of the Archangel Michael. This construction, known as the *Zatrupanata tzarkva* (Covered Church), is the hub (*Lavra*, in the Orthodox terminology) of the religious center. It covers a surface area of 296 square feet (about 16 by 16 feet) and the walls are perfectly smoothed. On one wall there is an icon of Ivan Asen II, the pious ruler whose generosity was responsible for the foundation of the monastery.

The Ivanovo settlement has many other frescoes, most of which date from the thirteenth century. The best preserved church, the *Krasalnjata* (baptistery) lies to the east of the Lavra, and its walls and

ceiling are decorated with episodes from the Passion of Christ: the entry into Jerusalem, the Last Supper, the betrayal and hanging of Judas, the denials of Peter, and Christ before Pilate. The *Tzarkvata* (the church) contains the image of another of the monastic community's patrons, Czar Ivan Alexander (1331-1371), who, with his wife, consigns a model of the church to the Virgin. The most recent frescoes date from the fourteenth century and are to be seen in the *Saborenata tzarkva* (demolished church) where we see Theodora, the first wife of Ivan Alexander, who founded many monasteries and eventually became a nun.

The frescoes in Ivanovo mark the apex of Bulgarian religious painting. Inspired by a humane approach to dogma, they demonstrate great intensity and are typified by expressive elements that link religious painting to the aesthetic and moral codes of the nascent Humanism. It may have been due to the spiritual, artistic, and cultural vitality of the monastery that the region of Ruse enjoyed a period of great prosperity in the sixteenth and seventeenth centuries. Accounts of the era written by a Franciscan monk, Peter Baksic, tell of a town of extensive trading and cultural exchange in which there were 3,000 Orthodox churches, 200 Turkish homes, and 200 of other nationalities. Many years later, the writer Elias Canetti, a Jew born in Bulgaria, noted, "Everything I have known in my life, I had already seen in Ruse."

234-235 Krasalniata (the baptistery) is the best conserved church in the monastic complex of Ivanovo. The thirteenth-century frescoes on the walls show scenes of the Passion of Christ.

235 right Ivanovo's most recent frescoes, which date from the fourteenth century, are to be seen in the Saborenata tzarkva (demolished church). The wall paintings in Ivanovo represent the apex of Bulgarian religious art.

Mount Athos

GREECE

CHALCIDIAN PENINSULA
REGISTRATION: 1988
CRITERIA: C (I) (II) (IV) (V) (VI);
N (III)

The Greek Constitution of 1927 contained an appendix dedicated to Mount Athos in which it defined the independent nature of the monastic community that lives there, the relationships between it and the State and Church, and the administrative responsibilities and hierarchical relations within the community itself. The document confirms that Mount Athos depends on the Ministry of Foreign Affairs for political questions and on the Patriarch of Constantinople for religious ones, thereby sanctioning the peninsula's semi-autonomous nature that comes from a

long history of independence.

In mythology, Athos was a giant Thracian who attempted to hurl an immense boulder at Poseidon, but the rock slipped from his fingers and formed the mountain that has taken his name. Another myth says that Mount Athos, also known as Aghion Oros (holy mountain), was requested as a gift from Jesus, who had been shipwrecked there while visiting Lazarus.

During the classical era, the place was cited in the works of Homer, Herodotus, and Strabo before it fell into Roman hands.

The date of the first religious settlement there is uncertain, but records exist of monks and hermits on the northernmost promontory of the Chalcidian Peninsula – dominated by Mount Athos at 6,690 feet high – since the eighth century. It is known that a delegation of monks was present at the Ecumenical Council of 843 called by the Byzantine empress, Theodora. And in 885, Emperor Basil issued an edict that officially recognized Mount Athos as an area governed exclusively by monks and hermits who had chosen to pass their lives in prayer and contemplation.

At the end of the ninth century, the community was already sizeable. The monks lived ascetically in makeshift shelters and without any general organization with the

236 Detail of a fresco in the Katholikon in Iviron Monastery. Dating from the sixteenth century, it was probably the work of the Theban artist, Frangos Katelanos.

236-237 Founded in the late tenth century by hermits from what is today Georgia, Iviron Monastery stands on a rocky promontory overlooking the sea. Besides the Katholikon, 16 other chapels face onto the monastery's main court, one of which contains the miraculous icon of the Virgin Mary.

237 top left Frescoes in Iviron Monastery. The iconography and dating suggest that artists from the Cretan school, influenced by Hellenistic art, worked here.

237 top right Dedicated to the Nativity, Simonopetra Monastery was named after Saint Simon who lived on Mount Athos in the mid-fourteenth century. With seven stories, it is the largest of the monastic buildings in the area.

238 top A view from the top of the Great Lavra Monastery. Founded in 963 by Saint Athanasios with the help of Emperor Nikephoros Phokas, it is the earliest of the monasteries on Mount Athos and the only one not damaged by fire.

238-239 The entrance to the church of the Great Lavra, with frescoes from 1535 by the Cretan, Theophanis Strelitzas. The artist admirably combined forms from Hellenistic art with iconography strictly linked to Orthodox Christianity.

239 left One of the buildings in the Great Lavra. During its ten centuries of activity, this was always considered the most important of the Mount Athos monasteries for its splendor and the great number of sacred texts it held.

239 right Some of the high, elaborate domes of Agios Panteleimon, also known as the Rousikon because a large community of Russian monks settled there in 1875.

exception of the Monastery of Kolobou founded in 872 in Ierissos. At the end of the next century, the destiny of Mount Athos was altered with the arrival of Athanasios, a monk from Trebisond. The son of a well-to-do family, he embraced poverty but took advantage of his friendship with Emperor Nikephoros Phokas to build the Great Lavra, the monastery that is still at the heart of the community. The central church, the Katholikon, with the chapels dedicated to Saint Nicholas and the Forty Martyrs, is still the site of the refectory, the kitchen, and the library. The monks' cells are distributed throughout the four wings that surround the monastery.

Athanasios did not have an easy life. The hermits most inclined to private meditation objected to the advent of an organized monastic community, but the emperor agreed with Athanasios, and in 971, he issued an imperial bull, the *Tragos*, that laid down the first rules to be followed on Mount Athos. With the support of Byzantium, at least 40 monasteries were built by the fourteenth century, despite pressure from the Roman Church for the reconciliation of the Catholic and Orthodox faiths.

The peninsula's prosperity was about to end, however. When Constantinople fell to the Turks, Mount Athos passed under Ottoman influence, which lasted 400 years. The Turkish sovereigns never changed the law but imposed increasingly large taxes on the monasteries, with the result that the number of monks gradually declined and aid had to be asked from the Russians, Wallachians, and Moldavians. With the independence of Greece in the nineteenth

century, Mount Athos became a destination for monks from all over eastern Europe, in particular, Russians. They established themselves in 1875 in the large monastery known as Aghios Panteleimon, characterized by the onion-shaped domes that were typical of the Orthodox Church in czarist Russia.

Today Mount Athos includes 20 monasteries inhabited by 1,500 monks. Their architecture is a curious mix of styles created by continual additions and rebuilding that has gone on since the Byzantine epoch. Each monastery is composed of a maze of buildings huddled against one another and a sequence of chapels, each of which has a particular function. Few, however, of the original frescoes have survived. Those in the Great Lavra are from the thirteenth century, and there are fragments of mosaics dating from the eleventh in Vatopedi Monastery. The heads of Saints Peter and Paul frescoed in the refectory were painted just a little later. Each monastery has its icons, some dating back to the Byzantine period, and the libraries are filled with important Greek and Slavic manuscripts.

Despite the unceasing changes in fortune suffered by the monasteries, the natural appeal of Mount Athos still attracts mystics from all over Europe, and the strict rule still survives that prohibits women from all of the peninsula, so that the monks can remain far from temptation.

Meteora
GREECE

PREFECTURE OF TRIKALA, PROVINCE OF
KALAMBAKA, THESSALY
REGISTRATION: 1988
CRITERIA: C (I) (II) (IV) (V); N (III)

At the beginning of the fourteenth century, the Byzantine Empire was on its last legs. Because of the inefficient military protection being provided, the monks of Mount Athos began to suffer raids by Turkish pirates, and following the umpteenth such encounter, three monks – Athanasios, Gregory, and Moses – decided to leave the monastery of Iviron in search of a different and safer abode.

Following the echo of ancient legend, they headed into Thessaly as far as the Kalambaka Valley. Here the river Pinios had eroded the rock leaving immense stalagmites that rise hundreds of feet from the base of the valley. The three arrived at Meteora. In Greek, *metéoros* means "suspended in the air," and Athanasios and his companions climbed one of these spires to build themselves a wooden shelter. A few years later, in 1336, 14 monks lived on the 2,044-foot-tall rock of Megálo Metéoro, while a chapel dedicated to the Virgin had been built at the base.

Hermits had lived in the caves of Meteora since the eleventh century, but it was Athanasios who initiated an organized community life regulated by strict rules and marked by asceticism. Women were not allowed entry as they were considered to be "a punishment" for mankind.

The surrounding landscape offered, and still does, strong symbolism. Being founded on the immensity of God, the "suspended" community received stability from above and transferred it to humanity through the monks' prayers.

Good fortune came to Megálo Metéoro in 1356 when the king of Serbia, Simeon Uros Paleologue, proclaimed himself

240 top left Megálo Metéoro (Monastery of the Transfiguration) is the largest and most important of the monastic centers in Trikala in Thessaly. It was founded by Saint Athanasios, who is buried here. A museum based on the monastic religious life is housed in the refectory of this building.

240 bottom Perched on a steep spire of rock, Rousánou, dedicated to Saint Barbara, is the most spectacular of the Meteora monasteries. Although traditionally women were not allowed to enter these places, Rousánou currently houses a community of nuns.

240-241 A panoramic view of the bare landscape of rock stalagmites created by the erosion of the river Pinios. For the hermits that came here in the fourteenth century, these rock spires must have had a strong symbolic value, for which reason they formed communities "suspended in the air," founded on the immensity of God.

241 top Still inhabited, the monastery dedicated to the Most Holy Trinity is the least accessible in the area.

emperor of Thessaly, placed the monastery under his protection, and built a church (*katholikón*) dedicated to the Transfiguration. In 1373, John Uros, Simeon's son, became a monk, and 10 years later, on the death of Athanasios, he was bequeathed the leadership of the community. The good fortune of the monastery was short-lived, however, because just 40 years later the Serbian dynasty of the Uros family was defeated in battle, and Thessaly became the setting for war between the Turks and Wallachians.

The monks were forced to leave the monastery for a century and were only able

242 top The vestibule that leads into the church of the Transfiguration in Rousánou Monastery is remarkable for its Cretan school frescoes painted around 1560. Some of them portray cruel scenes of war inspired by the events in Thessaly of the previous centuries.

242-243 Built in 1475-1476, the cross-shaped katholikón of the monastery of the Most Holy Trinity was decorated with an elaborate iconostasis in the mid-eighteenth century.

to return when the region was under the dominion of the Ottomans. Though places of Christian worship had been sacked by his emperor predecessors, under the enlightened Suleyman the Magnificent, they were finally allowed to be rebuilt. By the mid-sixteenth century, therefore, another 23 monasteries had been built, each clinging to its own rock out-cropping. Masters of the Cretan school were invited to decorate them with frescoes and icons. It was here that Theophanis Strelitzas and his sons Symeon and Neopytos produced the best of Greek Byzantine art. The Cretan school reconciled the late-Gothic and Renaissance artistic

243 top The detail on Christ's perfect face, created by the Cretan artist Frágkos Katelávos in the sixteenth century, is one of the most outstanding examples of late-Byzantine art. The fresco is in Varlaám Monastery, which boasts many three-dimensional pictorial effects.

243 center A detail of the large and brightly colored fresco of the Universal Judgment in Rousánou Monastery.

elements with those of the Orthodox Church to produce austere figures with faces of great expressiveness. They used bright colors and created attractive compositions.

After Suleyman, Meteora prospered as a place of prayer and a center for study in spite of the harshness of the Ottoman policies towards Christians until the mid-eighteenth century. Many lay Christians took refuge there to escape Turkish persecution as the difficult access to the monasteries worked in their favor; the only method of reaching them was to be hoisted up in a basket on a complicated system of cables and pulleys.

Slowly but inexorably the buildings began to deteriorate and many monks left to return to Mount Athos. In the nineteenth century, the monasteries

provided valuable shelter for Greeks in the war of independence against the Turks, and during the Nazi and Fascist occupation of World War II, many of the buildings were raided and partly destroyed.

Today only six of the 24 monasteries have survived with small communities of monks. They are responsible for the care of the frescoes, the icons, and a valuable collection of illuminated manuscripts that date from the founding of the settlement.

Their ancient beauty can still be seen in the candlelit churches and modest cells dug out of the rock, but here too progress has made inroads. Steep flights of steps have been cut so that the risky pulley system is no longer required, and two monasteries, Rousánou and Agios Stéfanos, are inhabited by nuns in blatant violation of the rules laid down by Patriarch Athanasios.

243 bottom Today the faithful leave their offerings in the niche that contains the fresco of Christ the Redeemer in the monastery of Megálo Metéoro.

The Painted Churches in the Troodos Region

CYPRUS

REGION OF TROODOS,
DISTRICTS OF NICOSIA AND LIMASSOL
REGISTRATION: 1985 (2001)
CRITERIA: C (II) (III) (IV)

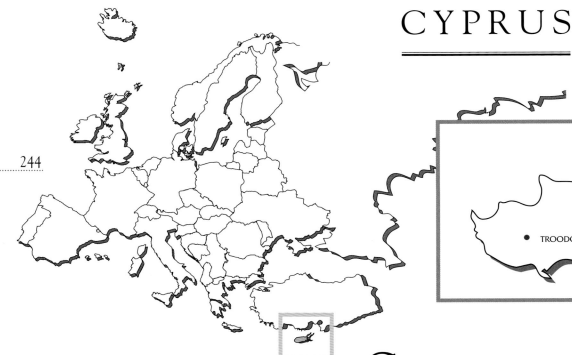

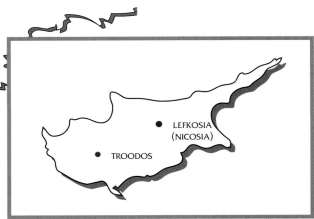

LEFKOSIA
(NICOSIA)

TROODOS

244 top left An outstanding Nativity scene in the wall fresco of the church of Aghios Nikolaos tis Stegis in the village of Kakopetria.

244 bottom right Panaghia Phorbiotissa in Asinou, in the Cypriot region of Troodos, has maintained intact the greatest number of frescoes of any church in the area, all painted between the twelfth and sixteenth centuries. This is Christ walking on the waves, surrounded by angels.

Situated so close to the Holy Land, it was inevitable that Cyprus would be one of the first lands to receive the Christian teachings, and it thus became a refuge for persecuted Christians and a safe haven for the artistic treasures threatened by iconoclasm. In A.D. 45, Saint Paul journeyed around the island with Saint Barnabas, the converted Jew of Cypriot origin who had been accepted by the Apostles to take the place of Judas Iscariot. On his travels, Paul founded the church dedicated to Heraclius, the saint who had led him as far as the mountains in the region of Troodos.

The dense forest of cedars and pines and the slopes scorched by the sun provide an unexpected landscape to those arriving from the nearby coast. In this area halfway between Nicosia and Limassol that reaches a height of 6,398 feet, the spread of Christianity has left important traces. Nine of the Byzantine churches in Troodos – Stavros tou Ayiasmati, Panayia tou Araka, Timiou Stavrou a Pelendri, Ayios Nikolaos tis Stegis, Panayia Podithou, Panayia Asinou, Ayios Ioannis Lampadistis, Panayia tou Moutoula, and the Church of the Archangel Michael at Pedhoulas –

have been included in UNESCO's list of World Heritage sites. In 2001, the church of Ayia Sotira tou Soteros in Palaichori was added to the list.

Built between 1100 and the end of the fifteenth century, all the churches are surrounded by peaceful countryside and share a plain exterior that offers no hint of the richness of the frescoes and icons inside. Often it is necessary to ask the inhabitants of the nearby houses to unlock the church doors. The most magnificent is probably the Church of Panayia Phorbiotissa di Asinou – the name is derived from the ancient Greek city of Asine, founded here in the eleventh century B.C. – that lies a few miles to the south of the village of

Nikitari. Inscriptions suggest that the church was built between 1099 and 1105.

The building is rectangular with vaults and niches at the sides and has a sloping, flat-tiled roof. At least two thirds of the original frescoes have survived and explain that Asinou was built as the family chapel of the Byzantine strategist Nicephoros Magistros, who died in 1115. Later, the church became one of the possessions of the nearby monastery at Phorbia. The church was further decorated up until the seventeenth century.

Byzantine chapel. It is decorated with frescoes from around 1280. Continuing up the mountain along a road lined with cherry trees, one comes to the village of Pedhoulas and the church dedicated to the Archangel Michael. It was built in 1474 in post-Byzantine style. The larger church of Panayia Podithou nearby is slightly younger (1502) and was once annexed to a monastery and features frescoes in a curious mixture of Italian and Byzantine styles.

Cyprus's early conversion to Christianity means that it has maintained a certain independence within the

Orthodox Church. The archbishop still enjoys certain privileges conceded to him in the fifth century by Emperor Zenon. One of these is the right to wear a purple cassock, to carry a scepter instead of a crook, and to sign his name with red ink.

Recently, the Turkish occupation of the northern half of Cyprus has resulted in a standstill in conservation efforts of the island's Byzantine heritage. Without adequate protection, many of these churches have been systematically looted, and unscrupulous dealers have been able to trade their works of art freely on the black market.

245

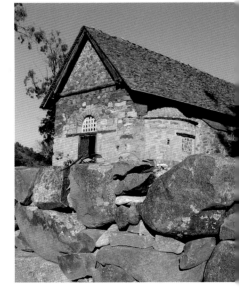

245 bottom left Comprising two churches and a chapel, the complex of Aghios Ioannis Lampadistis is located in the village of Kalopanagiotis. On St. John's Day (October fourth), this is the setting for one of the most important religious festivals in Troodos.

245 bottom right The church of Panaghia Phorbiotissa in Asinou. Probably built between 1099 and 1105, it is rectangular with vaults, side niches, and a steeply sloping roof covered with flat tiles.

The village of Kalopanagiotis, famous for its sulfur springs, is the site of the complex of Agios Ioannis Lampadistis. It is comprised of two churches and a chapel and is decorated with lovely frescoes from the thirteenth to fifteenth centuries. On St. John's Day, October fourth, it is the setting of one of Troodos' most important religious ceremonies. Barely a mile away stands the small Panayia tou Moutoula, which is one of the first examples of a wooden-roofed

244-245 Painted in brilliant colors, the twelfth-century frescoes on the dome of Panaghia tou Araka have the majestic figure of Christ Pantokrator at their center.

The Historic Areas of Istanbul

TURKEY

PROVINCE OF ISTANBUL
REGISTRATION: 1985
CRITERIA: C (I) (II) (III) (VI)

On May twenty-ninth each year, Istanbul celebrates the conquest of Byzantium by the Ottomans and, consequently, the conversion from Christianity to Islam in 1453. It is said that Sultan Mehmet II, who in honor of the occasion was given the title "Conqueror," thanked Allah for having guided him in the taking of what he called "the greatest and most splendid city in the world."

Accounts of the grueling siege of Byzantium feature many dramatic turns of events and astonishing acts of heroism, plots, betrayals, and ruses. For example, it was suggested to transport the Ottoman ships over land to a bay to the south of the city so as to surprise the Byzantines who, in order to protect the Golden Horn from the north (logically the only route available), had stretched an iron chain across the Bosporus. A decisive fact in the taking of the city was the "largest cannon in the world" that created large breaches in the walls. The weapon was sold to Mehmet by a Hungarian mercenary who had, in fact, arrived on the shores of the Bosporus as an ardent supporter of Christianity hoping to offer it to the Byzantines. But the power of money was more persuasive than that of his faith, and having understood that the Byzantines could not afford it, he turned to the wealthier Muslims.

The greatest and most splendid city in

the world was at that time little more than a ruin ravaged by debt, depopulation, and general, wide-spread decline since its capture by their supposed Christian friends in the Fourth Crusade. But the crusaders, instead of continuing east to wrest Palestine and Syria from the infidels, found it more convenient to sack Byzantium of its treasures and to hold it in check for more than half a century.

After three days of looting in the districts that had provided resistance (this was traditional Ottoman practice), Mehmet entered the church of Hagia Sophia. It is said that, before passing through the heavy entrance doorway, he covered his head with ashes as a sign of respect for the extraordinary building,

which was the largest basilica in Christendom at the time. Yet his respect did not prevent him from converting it into a mosque, thus putting an end to over 1,000 years of tradition. Today Hagia Sophia has become a historic monument and has lost its religious significance, but upon entering it, one cannot ignore the symbolic importance of this magnificent building that was constructed by Justinian between 532 and 538 in celebration of the glory of God and to restore the grandeur of the Roman Empire.

Also known as the Church of Holy Wisdom, Hagia Sophia stands on the site of an earlier basilica (destroyed during a revolt) built during the age of Theodosius that, in turn, had been built over the

remains of the Acropolis from the Hellenistic period. Construction of Hagia Sophia was commissioned from two Greek architects – Anthemius of Tralles and Isidore of Miletus – who conceived the structure as a synthesis between early Christian basilicas and imperial palaces. To build the dome, which was at that time a challenge to the laws of gravity not yet fully conquered, they used hollow bricks made from particularly porous, light clay that they imported from Rhodes. To decorate the interiors, where precious materials were used, Justinian ordered a sequence of mosaics that became the object of disputes between the Church and the Byzantine State for their very splendor. The former claimed that the realistic images that shone with gold were impious and wanted them to be replaced with more ascetic versions. The governors of the state, however, supported by the people of the city who formed large, admiring crowds around the building, won out against the wishes of the Church. Despite surviving this battle, many of the mosaics were destroyed by the iconoclasm of the Muslims. Of those that remain (restored following the removal of a layer of lime applied by the Ottomans), the most important are the one known as the Deisis (Christ between the Virgin and Saint John the Baptist on the south gallery), Christ

246 top The face of Christ in the mosaic in the eastern gallery in Hagia Sophia. When they were produced in the sixth century, the decorations in the basilica were considered impious by representatives of the Byzantine Church for the quantity of gold and precious materials they used.

246 bottom The interior of Hagia Sophia, also referred to as the Church of Holy Wisdom. The picture shows the imperial cloister and the central dome, which has a diameter of 105 feet.

247 The grandeur of Hagia Sophia seen from an aerial view. When Sultan Mehmet II conquered the city in 1453, the basilica was converted into a mosque and remained that way until 1932. Since then, the Turkish state has withdrawn its religious status and made it a museum.

248 top Built between 1459 and 1465, Topkapi Palace was the symbol of the Ottoman empire for almost 400 years. In keeping with Islamic tradition, the palace consists of a number of pavilions laid out around an equal number of courts.

248-249 The bulk and six minarets of the Sultan Ahmet Camii Mosque are visible from a great distance. The mosque was built in 1609 near the equally imposing Hagia Sophia.

249 top Süleymaniye Camii overlooks the Golden Horn. It was designed and built by Sinan between 1550 and 1557.

Pantokrator above the third door, and the portraits of the saints in the upper galleries that were originally reserved for women.

To the Ottomans, Hagia Sophia was both a model and a challenge. To build a mosque that equaled it in magnificence was a categorical imperative from the time of Mehmet II, but it took 100 years of Muslim rule over the city before this goal was achieved. Sultan Suleyman the Magnificent commissioned his janissary and military genius Sinan to build a mosque dedicated to the ruler himself to be built in a dominant position over the

Golden Horn. Sinan had previously overseen consolidation and restoration works in Hagia Sophia and had become obsessed by the building. To demonstrate his capacity to "outdo the Greeks," between 1550 and 1557 he produced a massive domed building, the Suleyman Camii, that is surprisingly geometrical and features a perfect balance between light and shade and elegantly minimalist decoration. At the corners of what was to become the symbol of Ottoman Istanbul (and which earned Sinan the nickname "the Turkish Michelangelo"), there are

four slender minarets.

The Hagia Sophia's second rival, the mosque of Sultan Ahmed Camii, was built at the start of the seventeenth century facing the former Christian church. Better known as the Blue Mosque, the forms of the domed building are extraordinarily harmonious. Its name is derived from the blue majolica tiles manufactured in the city of Iznik that entirely cover the walls of the mosque.

Istanbul has many other monuments from the Ottoman period, the most important of which are Topkapi palace,

249 center left Sultan Ahmet Camii is better known as the Blue Mosque due to the 20,000 blue majolica tiles made in the city of Iznik that completely cover its walls.

249 center right A richly decorated room in the Topkapi harem. Over the centuries, many western travelers have been fascinated by this mysterious place. It is said that, at the time of Mehmet II, 688 odalisques lived here. The most famous woman in the harem was Roxelana, the powerful concubine of Suleyman the Magnificent.

249 bottom The entrance to Sultan Ahmet Camii. Note the gilded arabesques and the enormous hanging light typical of Turkish mosques.

the Great Bazaar with its han (caravanserai), and the city's dozens of mosques. UNESCO's attention, however, is focused on the more ancient monuments from the age of Constantinople and Byzantium, which are in need of more extensive restoration. Their importance lies in their contribution to the revelation of the spirit of a city that, over its long history, has seen many great civilizations flourish and pass. Above all, the city has always

managed to rise from its ashes, changing name in the process, from Constantinople to Byzantium to Istanbul, with each new version more magnificent than the former.

A perfect example of this continuity, and a warning for the governors, was the ancient Hippodrome (horse-racing track), which today is covered by the huge esplanade that lies between the Hagia Sophia and the Blue Mosque, and below which lies the most famous of the many cisterns built to guarantee water supplies during a siege. The Hippodrome was built on Constantine's orders and included a Greek column that had been raised in front of the Temple of Apollo at Delphi that Constantine had transported to the new city in 330. The place quickly became a meeting point in the city, a role that it still plays. During the Byzantine epoch it was used for chariot races, the results of which often caused riots that had a political fallout and could lead to the destitution of the emperor. Many centuries later, in 1826, during the troubles that marked the decline of the Ottomans, the Hippodrome was the setting of the famous massacre of the Janissaries by Mahmud II.

Another important indication of the history and power of the city is the elaborate defensive system built in the fifth century to protect it from the mainland. It comprises 96 towers, 13 gates, and a further eleven gates protected by lookout bastions. The walls were knocked down once by the Crusades and later by the powerful Hungarian cannon belonging to Mehmet II, but they were then kept in perfect condition until the nineteenth century when, having become redundant, they were left to fall into ruin. Restoration work was begun in 1980 and has been the source of bitter argument as it has not been faithful to the original design.

Istanbul has experienced enormous demographic growth in the last few decades and is now a metropolis of ten million inhabitants with uncontrolled urban development. Many ancient architectural treasures have been surrounded by ghetto areas and their

safeguarding is now a desperate task. One such example is the twelfth-century monastic complex of Christ Pantokrator, which contains three churches decorated with refined mosaics and was the resting place of the Byzantine emperors for more than 200 years. Following the Ottoman conquest, the complex was turned into a Koranic school and then a mosque with the name Zeyrek Camii. Still used for Muslim worship, it is considered by UNESCO one of the hundred sites at risk throughout the world.

250 left An Egyptian obelisk stands in the center of the Hippodrome, an area now covered by the esplanade between Hagia Sophia and the Blue Mosque. Originally 197 feet tall, it broke during transportation. The same esplanade contains a column from Apollo's Temple in Delphi.

250 right Probably built during the reign of Emperor Constantine, the Yerabatan Saray (the basilica's water tank) is the largest of the city's ancient water storage containers. The container stands on 336 Corinthian columns and could hold 2,825,000 cubic feet of water.

250-251 Stuffed with carpets and other goods, this is one of the main galleries in the Great Bazaar. The entire complex contains more than 5,000 shops.

251 top left Built in the fifth century during the reign of Theodosius II, Constantinople's walls measure 21,820 feet in circumference. Now in ruins, they are at the center of a much-debated restoration project.

251 top right This is the Monastery of Christ Pantokrator. Empress Irene founded its church in the twelfth century.

The City of Safranbolu
TURKEY

CENTRAL ANATOLIA, BLACK SEA REGION
REGISTRATION: 1994
CRITERIA: C (II) (IV) (V)

During the rebellion to overthrow the sultanate, it was the *yemeniciler*, the shoemakers of Safranbolu, who sewed the shoes for the fighters who supported Mustafa Kemal Atatürk. The best hides were supplied to them by the eighty or so tanneries in the city. Few of the inhabitants left for the front as they were a peaceful people who had always been dedicated to commerce, handcrafts, and agriculture.

The name of the town (numbering about 25,000 inhabitants and situated at an altitude of 1,150 feet) celebrates the area's most valuable local product; Safranbolu means "city of saffron" (the suffix "-*bolu*" is of European origin and is derived from "burg," meaning castle or fortified city). During the months of September and October, the flowers of this plant of the Iridaceae family were collected for use in medicine, as a colorant for fabrics, or as a spice in foods. To produce one pound of saffron required 50,000 flowers.

Whereas "red gold" was the basis of Safranbolu's fortunes, the rest was the result of the industry of the local guilds who organized a commercial network that reached into Europe and the Middle East during the Ottoman empire. Safranbolu was located in a strategic spot and had become a stop on the caravan route

heading for the Black Sea Coast as early as the thirteenth century.

Although the town was established around 2000 B.C. and was conquered by the Hittites, Persians, Lydians, Romans, and Byzantines, there are no traces in the city itself of the passing of these peoples. The earliest architectural remains date from the start of the fourteenth century and were left by Turkish sovereigns, first from the Çandaroglu Dynasty and, from 1354 on, by the Ottomans.

This was the era of the construction of the first mosque, the Süleyman Pasha Camii, and the first *hammam* (public baths), which were rebuilt in the seventeenth and eighteenth centuries when Safranbolu took on its modern day appearance, one that it has miraculously preserved. The city contains about 2,000 historical buildings, 30 mosques, 150 fountains, and 15 bridges. The mosques most worthy of mention are the large Köprülü Camii, built in 1662, and the Izzet Pasha Camii, from the end of the eighteenth century.

The most attractive and impressive building is the Cinci Han, the caravanserai built in 1645 to accommodate the merchants visiting Safranbolu for business, and its annex, the magnificent Cinci Hammami. This yellow marble building, with its dome interspersed with small windows, was built in perfect Ottoman style and is still the most popular of the city baths. Inside the *hammam* and caravanserai complex stands the bazaar, and it is in the bazaar's loveliest section, the ancient arasta, that the shoemakers' workshops stood. Most of the inhabitants of Safranbolu

owned a winter home in the Cinci (the city center situated in a hollow sheltered from Anatolia's cold winds) and a summer home in the nearby countryside of Baglar, where there is a cooler climate and agriculture and stockbreeding were the main economic activities. Today the area of Baglar has undergone aggressive industrial expansion and is only a shadow of what it was up until a century ago.

What keeps the links with the past and tradition alive are the manor houses in Cinci, which mostly date from the eighteenth and nineteenth centuries. Their complex architectural design has inspired the nickname "the houses with five façades." Built in stone, brick, and wood, they are arranged around a large square courtyard with a fountain in the center. They have three floors, each divided into six to eight rooms, and the walls are made from *küfünk*, a porous stone. Traditionally, the animal stalls, storage areas, and kitchens were housed on the ground and first floors, while the living areas were located on the second and third floors. The most important of these would contain the *sofa*, have walls and ceilings covered with finely carved wooden panels, and be used to entertain guests.

Each house was divided into separate areas for men and women, and ingenious solutions were used to prevent guests from being subjected to the gaze of the women, for example, the revolving sideboard that allowed dishes to be transported from the kitchens to the dining room. In this way, the men were only able to tell far-fetched stories about the women who produced the delicacies.

252 top The Kausalar House, one of the oldest summer homes built by the wealthy merchants of Safranbolu in the rural area of Baglar.

252-253 A view of the Cinci (city center) of Safranbolu, which contains more than 2,000 historical buildings and 30 mosques. Two of the most famous mosques are the Köprülü Camii, built in 1662, and Izzet Pasha Camii, from the late eighteenth century.

253 center right A pretty corner of the historic center of Safranbolu. The entire city has been placed under the protection of UNESCO as it represents a compendium of the architectural styles of the Ottoman era.

253 bottom right A detail of the Curtlar House in the suburb of Baglar. Note the original layout of the second floor, built with alternating layers of porous bricks and wooden beams.

List of the Sites

Asia

Although communications have gradually improved over the centuries and trade between China and Asia Minor has existed since pre-Christian times, the huge size of Asia has meant that the continent has been home to very diverse civilizations even in recent times. An example of this extraordinary cultural diversity is seen in the different religions that sprang up in various parts of Asia: Zoroastrianism in Persia, Judaism and Christianity in the Middle East, Islam in the Arabian peninsula, Buddhism and Hinduism in India, and Shintoism in Japan. The same principle is true of the methods of writing and their alphabets, from Arabic and Sanskrit to the ideograms of Chinese and Japanese.

A similar richness was seen over the centuries in heterogeneous architectural and artistic styles, stamped naturally by local traditions but also influenced by the information that arrived, together with goods and religions, along the tangle of trading routes generically known as the Silk Road. As in Europe, much of Asia's architectural heritage is profoundly bound up with the development and diffusion of religion.

Islamic architecture achieved its greatest splendor in the Middle East and the Arabian peninsula, but is also present in the Caucasus, Iran, India, Pakistan, and the former Soviet republics like Turkmenistan

and Uzbekistan. Cities that have been established for thousands of years, such as Damascus, exemplify its development, as do unique monuments of inestimable value such as the Meidan Imam in Isfahan and the Taj Mahal in Agra. Buddhism, on the other hand, arose in north India around the sixth century B.C. and spread throughout eastern Asia, from Korea to Vietnam.

Asia's heritage is not limited to religious architecture. Political and military power, rather than economic wealth, have produced a similar number of architectural marvels. The Chinese empire was perhaps the most striking, with the Forbidden City in Beijing and the immense engineering feat of the Great Wall. Empires in Japan, Vietnam, and India left their marks too.

Lastly, but no less important, the architectural legacy of the colonial era left notable traces in the churches of Goa in India, Galle fort in Sri Lanka, French and Chinese architecture in Indochina, and, in an unusual symbiosis, the splendid Vietnamese city of Hoi An.

Although Europe has produced the greatest number of monuments, there is no doubt that the vastness of Asia has contributed to the development and evolution of an exceptional variety of architectural styles, all of which are adequately represented in the list of UNESCO World Heritage sites.

The Ancient City of Damascus
THE ARAB REPUBLIC OF SYRIA

ADMINISTRATIVE DISTRICT
OF DAMASCUS
REGISTRATION: 1979
CRITERIA: C (I) (II) (III) (IV) (VI)

It has been said that every man of culture must feel that he is the son of two homelands, his own and Syria. This country has been the setting for the birth of agriculture, the alphabet, the three great monotheistic religions, philosophy, trade, and the art of diplomacy. Damascus even contends with Aleppo for the title of the world's oldest city. Nonetheless, recent excavation has brought to light an older urban center, Hama, exactly halfway between the two great cities. The debate remains open.

Dimashq-ash-Sham, or *Sham* – as it is known to its inhabitants – gets its name from Noah's eldest son who, according to the Bible, settled here after the Flood. The first written reference to the city has been found at Mari, on the Euphrates, engraved on a clay tablet during the Neolithic period, and a papyrus document proves that Damascus traded with Egypt as early as the ninth millennium B.C.

These fragments do not indicate who the governors of Damascus were during those remote epochs, but it is certain that, in the second millennium B.C., the city

was the capital of the kingdom of the Aramaeans, who had been chased out of their lands after the Assyrians landed on the Phoenician coast of Syria. After a 30-year period under the control of the Babylonian king, Nebuchadnezzar, in 538 B.C. the city was conquered by Cyrus, the king of Persia, who made it his capital. However, it was under Alexander the Great in 333 B.C. that Damascus became the heart of an immense empire that stretched from the eastern Mediterranean to Afghanistan.

64 B.C. signaled the beginning of Damascus' golden age with the arrival of the Romans. They built a magnificent city on the foundations of earlier versions and it soon became one of the empire's ten most important centers. The Roman trading aristocracy was composed of Damascenes, who formed the commercial bridgehead

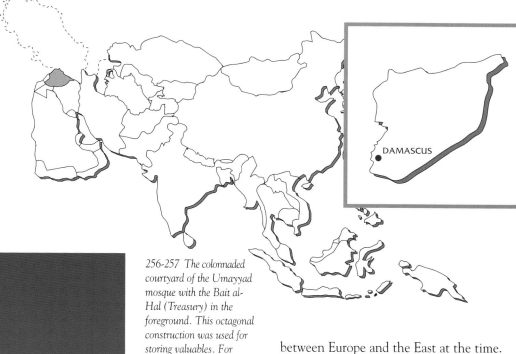

256-257 The colonnaded courtyard of the Umayyad mosque with the Bait al-Hal (Treasury) in the foreground. This octagonal construction was used for storing valuables. For reasons of security, it stands on eight Corinthian columns taken from Roman temples.

257 center left An overall view of the Umayyad mosque surrounded by the buildings that comprise the Suq al-Hamadiyyeh.

257 center right In the center of the huge prayer hall in the Umayyad mosque stands the marble monument erected in the nineteenth century on the site where, according to tradition, the head of St. John the Baptist was buried. John the Baptist is numbered among the holy men of Islam.

256 top The west tower (al-Garbiyya minaret) was built by the Mameluk sultan Qait Bey in 1488 in Egyptian style.

256 bottom Byzantine artists produced the mosaics on the south wall of the Umayyad mosque. Despite the destruction of many of the decorations over the centuries, this is one of the largest mosaics in the world. This particular mosaic shows the gardens of Paradise.

between Europe and the East at the time. The swords and fabrics produced in Damascus were sought after in even the remotest of regions.

In A.D. 34, as Saul of Tarsus, a Roman dignitary better known as Paul, was traveling on the road that brought Damascus so many riches, he was blinded by a dazzling vision, as a result of which he converted to the new Christian religion that was creating such turmoil in the empire. Because of the convergence of the sacred and the profane in the city, within a century the power of the bishop of Damascus grew to be second only to that of the Patriarch of Antioch.

The Roman empire was replaced by the Byzantine version in A.D. 395, but the real turning point for Damascus was to come after nearly 1,000 years of western rule when the troops of the Umayyad caliphs arrived in Syria from the Arabian peninsula and made mass conversions, at times forcibly, to yet another recently-created religion: Islam. The powerful new rulers were astounded at the city's beauty and made it the first great capital of the Muslim world, which, only a century later, was to

stretch from the Atlantic to the Indus.

Today the old city of Damascus, enclosed by high walls, is an extraordinary mix of Umayyad, Roman, paleo-Christian, and Byzantine remains that were combined to a surprising degree. For instance, the center of the Umayyad city was the Great Mosque; this stood on the site of a church dedicated to Saint John the Baptist, which had been built over a Roman temple dedicated to Jupiter, which in turn occupied the site of an earlier temple dedicated to the Aramaic god Hadad.

To glorify the power of the dynasty, in 705 Caliph al-Walid ibn-Abdul Malik began the construction of a new building. The work cost the fabulous sum of eleven million gold *denari*, lasted ten years, and required 1,200 laborers. The austere walls give no indication that the interior is one of the grandest glorifications of the power of Allah. The Gate of Paradise (the main entrance to the Great Mosque) leads into a huge court ringed with columns. Originally, mosaics covered well over 48,000 square

feet, lining all the outer walls, but in the catastrophic fire of 1893 most of these were lost. However, enough remains to indicate the quality was only equaled by the mosaic art in Santa Sofia in Istanbul or the basilicas in Ravenna. The Byzantines were accustomed to producing figurative works and their art was so perfect that the caliph devised a way to avoid the Islamic principle of not reproducing human figures and works. He decided that the decorations on the walls of the Great Mosque would represent the "City of God," with the result that gold and 30 shades of green were used to contrast the lapis lazuli and aquamarine of the rivers of Paradise.

Al-Walid also appreciated Roman

architecture and ordered that the columns in the temple of Jupiter be used in the construction of the mosque. They can be seen with their Corinthian capitals supporting the octagonal structure covered with luminescent mosaic tiles known as the *Bait al-Hal* (Treasury) where the Damascenes used to keep their valuables and documents.

Syncretism between Islam and Christianity is evident in the presence of the

Saint Paul and who was later canonized, is of great symbolic value to Christians. A few ancient houses belonging to Jews survive near the streets where Christians still live.

In 750, the honor of being the Islamic capital was transferred from Damascus to Baghdad when the Umayyads were overthrown by the Abbasids. Nonetheless, Damascene architecture continued to be used as the model for the construction of

by a high vaulted metal structure, like most of the city's souks. Passing by the remains of a Roman arch, one comes to the Great Mosque, and then enters a tangle of alleyways. These contain many *hammam* (public baths) and *khan* (caravanserai), including the large and magnificent one built in *suq al-Bizurieh* (the spice market) by Assad Pashà al-Azem, the governor of Damascus in the mid-eighteenth century. He

tomb of Saint John the Baptist in the prayer room, and in the fact that one of the minarets is dedicated to Jesus. Muslims believe that on the Day of Judgment, Christ will descend to Earth by placing his foot on this massive tower.

Damascus is one of the four Islamic holy cities and it is said that a prayer recited in the Great Mosque of the Umayyads is worth 10,000 elsewhere. The bodies of famous individuals are conserved in mausoleums and mosques, like that of Saladin, the holy man and army leader who defeated the Crusaders in the twelfth century, and that of Saida Ruqqaya, the granddaughter of the Prophet worshipped by Shiites.

The humble underground church of Ananias, the ascetic who gave refuge to

Arab cities in Andalusia, Cordoba in particular, and the roses of Damascus, for example, were used in Granada as a decorative motif in the Alhambra. After a long period in which trade prospered, the city grew weaker during the Crusades and in 1400 was sacked by the Mongol troops led by Timur, as known as Tamerlane.

In 1516, the Ottomans arrived and remained in power until the end of World War I. Under the Turkish empire, Damascus was enhanced with magnificent buildings and enjoyed a second golden age. Lovers of beauty and earthly pleasures, the Ottomans restored the Great Mosque and turned the city into a flourishing commercial center.

Little has changed inside the walls since that time. From Bab al-Faraj, the main gate, one enters the Souk al-Hamadiyyeh covered

was also responsible for the construction of the Azem palace, an enchanting residence built around a series of flower-filled patios and home to the Museum of Arts and Traditions where thousands of objects are displayed in boiserie-lined rooms.

This was the building that inspired the construction by Ottoman nobles of houses that sing a hymn of joy. Two of these, Bait Siba'i and Bait Nizam, have been returned to their original beauty with the restoration of frescoes, wood carvings, stuccoes, and marbles. Upon entering, it is easy to understand the words of an anonymous Damascene poet who claimed that the city's houses were made with mud, water, wood, straw, colors, stone, marble, glass, poetry, and love.

258 left The Mausoleum of Saida Ruqqaya was built in the nineteenth century in Persian style in honor of the Prophet's granddaughter, who is worshipped by the Shiites. The tomb of the young martyr is a place of pilgrimage for hundreds of thousands of women.

258 right Built in 1196, the tomb of Saladin, the hero of Islam, was neglected for centuries until 1898 when Kaiser Wilhelm II had it restored as a tribute to the Ottoman sultan, Abdel Hamid II.

259 top Built in the mid-eighteenth century, Bait Azem was the splendid residence of the Ottoman governor in Damascus. Its magnificent interiors and patios have been converted into a museum for popular arts and traditions.

259 bottom left These are the elaborate multicolored marble decorations of the walls and the fountain in one of the iwan (rooms) in Bait Nizam, one of the loveliest and best conserved Ottoman houses in the Old City.

259 bottom right Bab Sharqi (the East Gate) is the oldest existing monument in Damascus. It is the only one of the seven or eight gates built in Roman times to have retained its original form.

Jerusalem and its Walls
ISRAEL

JERUSALEM DISTRICT
(SITE PROPOSED BY JORDAN)
REGISTRATION: 1981
INSCRIPTION IN THE LIST OF WORLD HERITAGE
SITES IN DANGER: 1982
CRITERIA: C (II) (III) (VI)

In 1947, the United Nations passed a resolution defining Jerusalem as a *corpus separatum* that did not belong to either Israel or Palestine. Over half a century later, however, the parties involved – often using weapons rather than diplomacy – have yet to agree on the status of the city, which stands as the symbol of a seemingly endless conflict. Jerusalem's registration in UNESCO's list of World Heritage sites in 1981 was followed by its inscription a year later on the list of World Heritage Sites in Danger. In addition to the direct effects of Arab and Israeli extremism, Jerusalem also suffers from unbridled urban development, the negative effects of tourism, and negligence toward its monuments. Its status as "everyone's city" is by definition unfortunately turning it into

"no one's city."

Jerusalem is considered the holy city of the three great monotheistic religions, Judaism, Christianity, and Islam. For Jews, it is the site of Abraham's sacrifice. For Christians, it is where Christ was crucified and resurrected. According to Muslims, the prophet Muhammad ascended into heaven from this city.

Although Jerusalem currently looks like a modern city, the Old City – an area of less than one-half of a square mile circled by 39-foot-high walls two and a half miles long – bears witness to its troubled history spanning 5,000 years.

Founded by the Canaanites in the third millennium B.C., Jerusalem forcefully earned its place in eternity in about 1,000 B.C. when the biblical King David conquered the city and King Solomon built the Temple there. In 586 B.C., King Nebuchadnezzar devastated it, destroying the Temple and sending the population into exile in Babylonia. Fifty years later, the Persian king, Cyrus the Great, conquered Babylonia and allowed the Jewish population to return to Jerusalem and rebuild the Temple. The Persians held the city until 333 B.C. when Alexander the Great added Palestine to his empire, only to lose it a few years later to Ptolemy I of Egypt.

In 198 B.C., the Seleucid king Antiochus III conquered Judea – of which Jerusalem was a part – and made it one of Syria's tributaries until the Judeans rebelled against their rulers. The Temple was re-consecrated in 168 B.C. and the city prospered, led by the Jewish dynasty of the Maccabees until the Roman conquest in 63 B.C. Jerusalem was rebuilt under Herod, the sovereign installed by Rome, but power was still exercised by the Roman governors, and it was one of these, Pontius Pilate, who authorized the crucifixion of Christ.

From then on, the Jews repeatedly attempted to break away from Roman rule. Following the revolt in A.D. 70, the second Temple was burned, and after the revolt in 135, the Jews were banished from Jerusalem. During the fourth century, the Christian religion was legalized in the Roman world and Jerusalem became an important place of pilgrimage. Many

260 bottom left Bab al-Rahmeh (the Golden Gate) is cited by all the ancient texts of the three monotheistic religions. For Jews, it is where the Messiah will enter Jerusalem; for Christians, it is where Jesus entered the city for the last time; for Muslims, it is the Gate of Mercy through which the just will pass on Judgment Day.

260-261 A view of Jerusalem with the Dome of the Rock in the foreground. As a result of a continually growing population (now roughly 700,000), mass tourism, and the interminable Palestinian-Israeli conflict the fragile and ancient equilibrium of the city is at serious risk.

261 top The labyrinthine old city that lies within the two-and-a-half-mile-long walls contains over 100 streets and more than 1,000 shops.

261 bottom Suq Khan az-Zait is the most crowded street in the Arab quarter of Jerusalem and the most densely populated area of the old city.

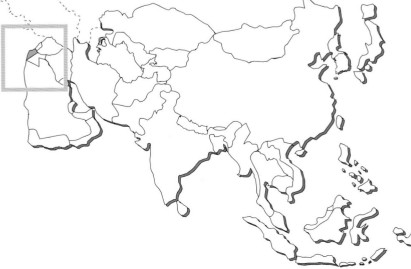

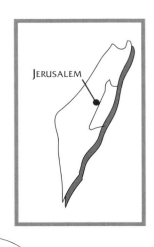

JERUSALEM

churches were built, including the Holy Sepulcher, the site of the resurrection of Christ.

With the exception of the brief Persian rule between 614 and 628, the city was governed by the Romans and, upon Rome's downfall, the Byzantines. In 638, it was conquered by the Arabs, who built the Dome of the Rock over the site of the Temple. Despite this affront, the Jews, Christians, and Muslims continued to live together peacefully until 996 when the Fatimid caliph al-Hakim began to persecute the non-Muslim population. Christian Europe responded swiftly, embarking on a campaign to regain the city, and after an extended siege, the victorious Crusaders entered Jerusalem in 1099. Nevertheless, a little less than a century later Saladin returned the city to

Islamic domination. Under the Ayyubids, Mamlukes and Ottomans, Muslim rule continued until the British occupation in 1917, and Jerusalem remained the capital of Britain's mandate over Palestine until 1948. The plan to internationalize the city failed with the Six-Day War between Egypt and Israel in 1967, and the rest is a painful part of history.

The walls of the Old City, built by the Ottomans at the end of the sixteenth century, circle an area divided into three districts: the Hebrew quarter, the Muslim quarter, and the Christian quarter that includes an area for Armenians. In addition to the colorful souk and white stone houses, there are numerous religious buildings that have survived destruction and transformation, revealing the plurality of Jerusalem's religious life. Among these,

the Wailing Wall, the Holy Sepulcher, and the Dome of the Rock are the sublime symbols of the three monotheistic religions, and they expression a powerful cultural and political identity.

The texts of the Jewish mystics indicate Mount Moriah, along the western section of the wall, as the center of the universe. This was where Abraham, the patriarch of the people of Israel, prepared to sacrifice his son Isaac. This was also where Solomon built *Beth-El*, the Temple, to hold the tablets of the Ten Commandments. When the second Temple was destroyed in A.D. 70, it was commemorated by what the Jews refer to as *Ha-Kotel Ha-Ma'aravi*. This was the wall built by Herod and later incorporated into the Ottoman fortification. For centuries, the "Chosen People" have come here day and night to

262 top left, center and right The Wall is more famously known as the Wailing Wall because the Hebrews here came to weep when the second Temple was destroyed in A.D.70 following a popular rebellion. Believers place prayers written on slips of paper in the cracks in the wall.

262 bottom The tradition of making a pilgrimage to the Wall began during the Ottoman era when the buildings in the Old City huddled almost up to the wall, leaving only a narrow space for prayer. The Arab district in this area was demolished in 1967 during the Six Day War.

263 Ha-Kotel Ha-Ma'aravi (the Wall) was built by Herod in 20 B.C. to contain the embankment on which the second Jewish temple stood. Today, the Dome of the Rock, practically a symbol of the difficult co-existence of Islam and Judaism, stands just beyond the Wall.

weep over the fate of the Temple, leaving folded notes with their innermost prayers and confessions to God in the cracks between the stones.

Overlooking the Wailing Wall is the *Qubbat as-Sakhrah*, or the Dome of the Rock, the oldest masterpiece of Islamic art. Its construction, which lasted from 685 to 691, can be considered a political act. The caliph Abd al-Malik built it to affirm his supremacy over rival sultans from the Arab peninsula. Interpreting the seventeenth *sura* of the Koran to suit his needs, he identified the site of the ruins of the Temple of Israel as the place where Muhammad ascended into heaven. Thus, an extraordinary building was constructed around the rock bearing the prophet's footprint. Rising from a stone platform are two concentric colonnades, the first octagonal and the second circular,

supporting a dome with a diameter of 66 feet and a total height of 98 feet. The interior is richly decorated with mosaics of geometric, calligraphic, and floral motifs, the oldest of which were made by Byzantine craftsmen. The mosaics cover an area of 13,800 square feet. Following the conquest of Jerusalem, the Crusaders consecrated it for Christian worship and on top of the dome they mounted a golden cross that was later removed by the Ottomans. In the sixteenth century, Suleyman the Magnificent decorated the dome and the exterior walls with 45,000 faience tiles in blue, the color of the sky and thus of infinity, and gold, the symbol of Allah's power. In the early 1990's, King Hussein of Jordan paid homage to the third most important site of Islam by covering the entire dome of the *Qubbat as-Sakhrah* with sheets of pure gold.

264 top left Two concentric colonnades, one octagonal and the other circular, support the 66-foot-high dome of the mosque.

264 top right The dome of the mosque was lined with sheets of pure gold at the start of the 1990's by King Hussein of Jordan, whose family is directly descended from the prophet Muhammad.

264 bottom Underneath the Dome of the Rock is the sacred rock on which Abraham prepared to sacrifice his son, and from which Muhammad ascended to heaven to take his place next to Allah.

264-265 Built between 685 and 691 by Sultan Abd al-Malik, the Qubbat as-Sakhra (Dome of the Rock) is the earliest masterpiece of Islamic art. To affirm the supremacy of Islam, the sultan ordered his architects to use the rotunda of the Holy Sepulcher as a model.

265 top Suleyman the Magnificent decorated the outer walls and the vault of the Dome of the Rock with 54,000 blue and gold majolica tiles, which represent the color of heaven and the power of Allah.

266 top The court that leads to the Church of the Holy Sepulcher is lined on the left by the Chapel of the 40 Martyrs, the Greek Orthodox Chapel of St. John, and the Chapel of St. James. The façade of the church was built during the Crusader era in the twelfth century.

266 bottom The Church of the Holy Sepulcher. Surrounded by houses, the church has practically been suffocated by Jerusalem's urban sprawl.

The Church of the Holy Sepulcher is located further away from the sacred Jewish and Muslim sites, at the end of a road that is traditionally indicated as the Via Dolorosa, where the Passion of Christ took place. Emperor Hadrian built a temple dedicated to Venus here. It is said that the mother of Emperor Constantine came to Jerusalem in 326, found the Holy Cross here, and ordered that a church be built on this site. To avoid copying the structure of pagan temples, the model of the basilica, a civil building used for meetings and trade,

was chosen. The Church of the Holy Sepulcher was repeatedly destroyed, but its current form, which dates to the era of the Crusades, is a faithful copy of the first Constantinian church. The *Rotunda*, which has a diameter of 131 feet, is the accepted site of the crucifixion, burial, and resurrection of Christ. Another basilica, with galleries and colonnaded courtyards, was built over it. Representatives of the six Christian Churches take turns each day to keep watch over Christianity's most sacred complex.

In addition to these mainstays of the three monotheistic religions, each corner of the Old City contains monasteries and churches of the different Christian cults, including St. Anne's, built over the site of the Virgin's home, as well as synagogues, Talmudic colleges, mosques, and civil buildings from the Mamluke and Ottoman periods. Nevertheless, the most astonishing and moving sights are the throngs that flock here from all over the world, bearing a message of peace for the Holy Land.

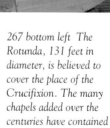

267 top left The Katholikon, the Greek choir in the Holy Sepulcher, contains representations of all six faiths of the Christian religion.

267 top center The Altar of the Virgin stands on the site of Calvary where the Crucifixion took place.

267 top right The Unction Stone, at the entrance to the Holy Sepulcher, is said to be where the body of Jesus was anointed once he was taken down from the Cross.

267 bottom left The Rotunda, 131 feet in diameter, is believed to cover the place of the Crucifixion. The many chapels added over the centuries have contained the remains of people who have played an important role in the defense of the Holy Sepulcher such as the Crusader kings Baldwin I and Goffredo of Buglione.

267 bottom right Christ Pantokrator is frescoed on a vault in the Church of the Holy Sepulcher.

The Old City of Sana'a

YEMEN

Territory under a governor
in the capital, Sana'a
Registration: 1986
Criteria: C (IV) (V) (VI)

268-269 Built by the
Ottoman occupying forces
in 1870, the majestic Bab
al-Yamn (the Gate of
Yemen) is the main
entrance to the old city of
Sana'a.

269 top left The Suq al-
Milh lies right behind the
Bab al-Yamn and is the
most crowded of the city's
40 or so markets. Its name
means "salt market" even
though today it sells all
kinds of goods.

269 center right A view of
the old city where almost 20
percent of the capital's
250,000 population live. In
recent years, the migrants
from the provinces have
been replacing the original
families, who have now
chosen to live outside the
walls in more modern
houses.

269 bottom Street scene in
Sana'a. Inside the walls
there are roughly 6,500
houses built before the
eleventh century, 106
mosques, and 12
hammam.

The souk in Sana'a is divided into forty or so smaller markets, each one representing a particular set of goods. Each sector is overseen by a mediator, the *aqel*, whose duty it is to resolve disputes between traders and those no less frequent between traders and their customers. The *aqel* is also responsible for directing production towards particular goods and, in some cases, of distributing raw materials and selling products. Lying outside of his jurisdiction are the Samsara, the 33 commercial "agencies" that played an important role in ancient times, when Sana'a was a terminal on the Incense Road, which caravans followed on their journeys between the Arabian peninsula and the Mediterranean.

The capital of the Yemen Arab Republic, Sana'a lies in the mountainous interior of the country at an altitude of 7,200 feet. It stands in a hollow crossed from east to west by the dry river bed of the Wadi Saylah, which is turned into a powerful torrent during the rainy season. According to legend, the city was founded by Sem, one of Noah's three sons, but the Yemeni are happy just to note that it is the oldest continuously inhabited city in the world. Historians consider Sana'a to be at least 2,500 years old, and in the second century B.C. it was referred to in chronicles as the most important garrison in the mountain area of the Kingdom of Saba. The name Sana'a actually means "fortified city," but it was unable to withstand the two invasions of the Persian armies, and was later governed by the Abyssinians who, during the reign of the Roman emperor Justinian, built there the largest cathedral south of the Mediterranean. The turning point came in A.D. 628 when Yemen embraced Islam and

the existing religious buildings were demolished to make space for mosques. Chronicles report that it was the prophet Mohammed himself who laid down strict instructions on the place where the main mosque was to stand.

During the Islamic expansion, Sana'a enjoyed a thousand years of peace and prosperity and became one of the largest political and religious centers in the Muslim world. A legacy of that fertile period are the 106 mosques, 12 *hammam* (public baths), and 6,500 houses built prior to the eleventh century that have survived to the present day.

At the end of the sixteenth century, however, the city was conquered by the Ottoman Turansha, the brother of the

270 top The court in the National Museum. The museum is a fine three-story building that illustrates the history of the kingdom of Saba (Sheba) through archaeological objects and ornaments that once belonged to ancient Yemeni kings.

famous Salah ad-Din (Saladin). Turkish domination lasted a century, but at the end of the seventeenth century, power was returned to the Imam who launched the city on a second period of rebirth. Within the city walls, there was an extraordinary burst of urban development, and the fame of the legendary Sana'a reached as far as Europe. Consequently, the first Western travelers arrived in a Danish scientific expedition that published detailed reports in the newspapers of Europe. Other trips were made, as sporadic as they were daring, since the governors of Sana'a discouraged

non-Muslim visitors. Recent history saw another Turkish invasion, lasting from 1872 to 1919, which was followed by a further half century of government led by the Imam, until the establishment of the Republic in 1969.

Sana'a is a priceless treasure-house of Islamic architecture, with houses made from brown basalt and magnificently decorated with elegant patterns of white lime and stucco around polychrome windows. The advent of modern building techniques and the invasion of the motor car have resulted in conspicuous damage,

but the pride of the Yemeni has ensured that Sana'a continues to be enriched with new buildings using traditional construction methods. The extraordinary pearl of the Roman Arabia Felix continues to be preserved, thanks to the providential projects run by UNESCO in collaboration with the government, and financed by many foreign countries.

One of the most fascinating places is the Suq al-Milh, the salt market, now invaded by other products, such as spices, qat, vegetables, and handcrafts, which buzzes with activity starting in the early

hours of the morning. Another gem, which stands close to the mosque of al-Mutwakil, is the former royal residence, the Dar as-Sa'd, (House of Fortune), which now hosts the National Museum.

Unfortunately, the many marvelous mosques like the Jami' al-Kabir (Great Mosque), the Salah ad-Din, the Ottoman influenced Qubbat Talha, and the small al-Aqil close their doors to non-Muslims. However, as the Arabs say, "Ma labod min Sana'a Wae'en tal as-safar," meaning "You must see Sana'a, even if the journey is long and difficult."

270 bottom
A view of the city's buildings illustrates the Yemeni architects' technical and decorative ability.

271 top left The white minarets rise above al-Jami'al-Kabir (the Great Mosque), one of the oldest in the Muslim world. It was built while the prophet Mohamed was still alive, and was enlarged in the year 705.

271 top right The white lime-covered domes of al-Mutwakil Mosque contrast with the brown houses built from basalt.

271 bottom A detail of one of the splendid multicolored glass windows in the Dar al-Shukr (Palace of Gratitude) where the Museum of Yemeni Traditions is to be found.

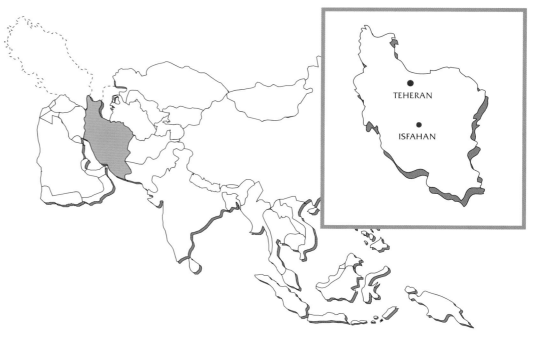

272 top Once the symbol of the power of the Safavid empire, Meidan Imam (Royal Square) measures 1,640 feet by 591 feet. It is lined by the Royal Mosque, Sheikh Lotfollah mosque, Ali-Qapu royal palace, and the entrance to the city's Grand Bazaar.

272-273 The superb central court of the Royal Mosque. The eivan (portals) and porticoes decorated with turquoise and gold majolica tiles are reflected in the large pool. Built in the early seventeenth century, the Royal Mosque marks the apotheosis of Persian architecture.

273 top right The interior of the Royal Mosque is lined with elaborate floral motifs and calligraphic decorations by the artist Ali Reza Abbassi. From the city of Tabriz and of Safavid origin, he was the best-known artist of his time in Persia.

Meidan Imam in Isfahan

IRAN

PROVINCE OF ISFAHAN
REGISTRATION: 1979
CRITERIA: C (I) (V) (VI)

Esfahan nesf-é jahan, meaning "Isfahan is the center of the world," was the phrase on the lips of everyone who visited the city in the seventeenth century, impressed as they were by the magnificence of its buildings and extent of its commercial activity. Yet, this marvelous city was created in just 30 years by an ambitious ruler who had successfully made use of the services of two mercenaries.

For all of the sixteenth century, the Safavid Dynasty, which had reigned over Persia for 150 years, watched its territory shrink at the hands of Ottoman troops. This situation continued until Sir Anthony Sherley and his brother Robert knocked at the door of Shah Abbas I. The two English adventurers had offered to the European courts to undertake diplomatic exploits – in return for payment and honors – to provide the Safavids with support against the Ottomans. Moreover, the pair offered to initiate the Persians into the "magical" powers of a new invention, gunpowder, and to teach them to build cannons. An agreement was reached with the result that, in less than two years, Shah Abbas was able to win back much of Persia.

Having entered Isfahan in triumph in 1598, the ruler decided to make the city his new capital and he began to construct buildings to celebrate its greatness. Using the modest Turkish palace as the basis, he had the six-story Ali Qapu, the royal palace, built looking onto the ancient esplanade of Nagash-e-Jahan that measured 1,640 by 490 feet. On the east side of the square, which he renamed Meidan Shah but that was later to become Meidan Imam, he began construction of the Royal Mosque (*Masjed e-Shah* or *Masjed e-Imam*).

The building was completed in 1628, one year after the death of Shah Abbas I, and is considered one of the greatest examples of Persian art. It has been estimated that its construction required 18 million bricks and 472,500 blue and turquoise majolica tiles to cover its surface. It had been the tradition to use monochromatic tiles on which motifs were carved at the moment of application, but Shah Abbas was impatient to see the finished effect and ordered the process to be accelerated by laying tiles already decorated with floral motifs, known as *haft rangi* (seven colors).

The entrance gate stands 89 feet tall, and it is topped by a superb dome and flanked by two round minarets. To keep the entrance to the mosque on the same axis as the square and, at the same time, to allow the *mihrab* to face Mecca, the architect, Abu'l Qasin, "rotated" the complex by 45 degrees. The complex includes several vestibules, the great domed prayer hall, and the Koranic school, all arranged around a colonnaded court.

In 1602, Shah Abbas had another mosque built, this time on the west side of Meidan Imam, dedicated to his father-in-law Sheikh Lotfollah, a famous Shiite theologian. More modest in size and with no minarets (as it was built for the exclusive use of the royal family), it rivals *Masjed e-Shah* in

273 center A view of Isfahan includes the two minarets of the Royal Mosque and, in the background, the mosque dedicated to the Shiite theologian Sheikh Lotfollah. Though the building is small, the dome, decorated with arabesques, rivals that of the Royal Mosque for beauty.

273 bottom The only surfaces inside the Royal Mosque not to be covered by majolica tiles are the pillars in the prayer hall. The immense complex contains several Koranic schools.

the refinement of its majolica tiles and structure. On the north side of the square stands the magnificent entrance to the Qeyssarieh, the city bazaar. In order to give a fresh boost to trade, Shah Abbas I invited Armenian merchants and conceded privileges to English and Dutch representatives of the East India Company.

The two mosques, the royal palace, and the bazaar form a harmonious whole as a result of the elegant portico that encloses them on the four sides of the square, the pivot around which Shah Abbas I's power revolved. Although he won himself a position of importance in the context of Persian art, sadly he is also remembered for his cruelty. In order to introduce the Shi'a doctrine and Farsi language into Persia, he had followers of the rival Sunni doctrine massacred. And he was so afraid of plots on his life that he had his eldest son killed and two younger ones blinded so that they could not reign after him.

Consequently, he was succeeded by his granson, Shah Safi I, who also passed into history for his systematic elimination of all claimants to the throne, including his mother. He was in turn succeeded by Shah Abbas II, a child of only ten, who, a virtual prisoner of advisors and tutors, marked the decline of the Safavid Dynasty and Isfahan. At the start of the eighteenth century, the city was put to the sword by the Afghans, and in 1736 the capital of the country was moved to Mashhad.

*274 top left A detail from
a floral decoration in
polychrome faïence on a
blue background.*

*274-275 A view capturing
one of the two minarets in
the Royal Mosque and the
dome of the Sheikh
Lotfollah Mosque. The
majolica decorations of
each were produced using
the heft rangi (seven
colors) technique.*

*275 top A richly
decorated interior of Sheikh
Lotfollah Mosque. The
mosque was built between
1602 and 1619 for Shah
Abbas I and dedicated to
his brother-in-law. It was
for the exclusive use of the
royal family.*

*275 bottom Sheikh
Lotfollah Mosque. The
superb pishtaq (portal)
has a vault decorated with
geometric motifs that
imitate stalactites. This
type of decoration was
derived from Umayyad
and Abbasid architectural
styles.*

Itchan Kala
UZBEKISTAN

KHIVA, OASIS OF KHOREZM
REGISTRATION: 1990
CRITERIA: C (III) (IV) (VI)

276 top A view of the court and minarets of Aq Mosque. During the existence of the khanate, the city was one of the main cultural centers in the Islamic world, with 16 active Koranic schools.

276 bottom left A carved wooden door features lovely floral motifs.

276 bottom right In this aerial view capturing the architectural harmony of the city, it is possible to make out the huge majolica dome of the Mausoleum dedicated to the poet and philosopher Pahlavon Mahmud, the protector of Khiva, and the imposing turquoise minaret of Kalta Minor Mosque, built at the start of the nineteenth century.

When Nikolai Muraviev, the captain of the Cossack army, reached Khiva on a torrid summer's day in 1819 to negotiate the release of 3,000 Russians captured in battle, he was amazed by the size of the slave market. Apart from his compatriots, the number of prisoners awaiting a purchaser was roughly 30,000, including Persians, Kurds, Kazaks, and Turkmens. They were well-fed because a healthy man was worth as much as four camels.

The fortunes of this caravan city in the desert of Kara-Kum had been based on this infamous trafficking since the sixteenth century, when the Shaybanid Dynasty of the Uzbek people had conquered it from Timur's (Tamerlane) troops and founded an independent khanate. Until 1873, when they were forced to submit to the Russians, the Shaybanids, followed by their successors, the Kungrads, were able to accumulate riches thanks to Khiva's

strategic position on a corner of the "golden triangle" in central Asia that marked the deviations that led to the banks of the Volga and Caspian Sea along a branch of the Silk Road. Despite the continuous passage of all kinds of peoples, the khanates lived in a state of isolation, refusing every form of modernization and concerned only about the ambitions of the nearby khan of Bukhara. They governed by terror, and western travelers returned from these windswept plateaus with tales of chilling torture.

A clay-brick wall 33 feet high and one and a half miles long encloses the city-museum of ancient Khiva, known today as Itchan Kala as opposed to Dichan Kala, the twentieth century town that lies close to the walls. Although most of its monuments were built during the khanate of Alla-Kulli during the first half of the nineteenth century, its atmosphere is more like that of the tales in the *Thousand and One Nights*. The uniformity of its architecture makes it the best-preserved feudal city in central Asia.

Two main axes, running north-south and east-west, form the basis of the city's layout. The Ota Darvoza (Gate of the Father), the main entrance, lies to the west, and to its left is the Kuhna Ark, a fortress built in the twelfth century and enlarged from the seventeenth century onwards. In this huge building, the *khans* had their residence, the harem, the mint (they printed banknotes on silk), the arsenal, and lodgings for their troops. At the start of the eleventh century, they built the Summer Mosque and a court entirely covered with white and blue majolica tiles decorated with floral motifs,

with columns and doors made from finely carved wood.

The Kalta Minor minaret close by the fort dates from the nineteenth century. It is lined with Turkish tiles, 46 feet in diameter, and 82 feet tall. The original plan for the

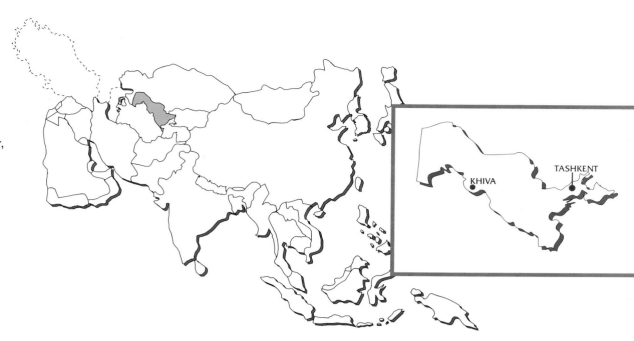

276-277 Situated next to the city's main gate, Kuhna Ark was built in the twelfth century as a defensive fort and enlarged by the khans of Khiva (now Itchan Kala) from the seventeenth century on. It was the sovereigns' residence until 1873 when the powerful central Asian khanate submitted to the Russians.

minaret, built during the reign of Alla-Kulli, called for a much taller construction, but the emissaries of Bukhara arrived in the city to warn the *khan* that if he built his minaret taller than theirs in Kalhan, the insult would be paid for in blood.

The ambitious sovereign therefore had to content himself with building a magnificent palace, the Tosh-Kohvli. Situated at the eastern end of the city, it has 150 rooms and is decorated with majolica tiles, stuccoes (*ghanch*), and carved wood.

The building's central court – overlooked by the reception room – is marked with the place where the royal *yurta* used to be erected, since the *khan* enjoyed spending his hours of relaxation as his nomadic ancestors had done.

Among the religious buildings in Itchan Kala, the Mosque of Djuma and Mausoleum of Pahlavon Mahmud stand out for the beauty of their decorations. Pahlavon Mahmud was a poet and philosopher besides being a Muslim holy man and patron saint of Khiva. The mosque was built at the end of the eighteenth century on the ruins of a tenth-century building and features a forest of 218 wooden columns. The nineteenth-century mausoleum boasts a domed room decorated with tiles hand-painted in Persian style. Lastly, there were 16 Koranic schools active inside the walls, many of which today have been turned into museums containing objects illustrating the history, art, and traditions of the city.

278 The Tosh-Khovli has the most magnificent decorations in Khiva, with a profusion of ceramic tiles, carved stones, and, as in this example, carved wood.

279 top left These geometrically patterned tiles decorate the harem in Tosh-Khovli, which was built between 1832 and 1841 for Alla-Kulli Khan as an alternative residence to the Kuhna Ark. With 150 rooms that face onto nine courts, it was supposed to rival the palaces of the khan of Bukhara.

279 top right Built in the seventeenth century over the ruins of a tenth century building, Djuma Mosque is a huge room with a coffered ceiling supported by over 200 wooden columns.

279 bottom The majolica-decorated dome of the mausoleum of Pahlavon Mahmud covers a room adorned with elegant tiles decorated with the maxims and proverbs of the great philosopher, who died in the fourteenth century.

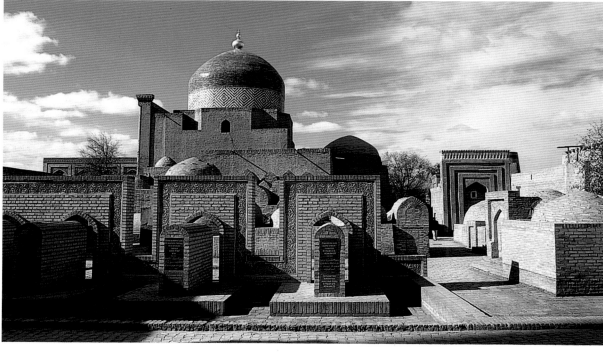

Samarkand:
a Cultural Crossroads
UZBEKISTAN

REGISTRATION: 2001
CRITERIA (I) (II) (IV)

280 top and bottom The seventeenth-century dome of the Tilla Kari (Gold-covered) Madrasah (top) and the wall onto which the gilded mihrab opens.

280-281 Ulugh Bek Madrasah was built between 1417 and 1420 to encourage mathematicians and astronomers to visit the ruler's court. Ulugh Bek's interest in astronomy is commemorated in the mosaic of the night sky in the upper part of the enormous portal.

In 1908, Vassily Viatkin, a professor with a passion for archaeology, discovered the remains of an astrolabe northeast of Samarkand, on the road to Tashkent. The curved part of the immense instrument, which had a radius of over 130 feet and an arc of 207 feet, was all that remained of the observatory of Ulugh Beg, the Timurid ruler who lived during the first half of the fifteenth century.

The son of Shah Rukh and the favorite nephew of Timur, also known as Tamerlane, Ulugh Beg had no interest in military conquests and devoted himself to astronomy. In 1420, he founded the Ulugh Beg Madrasah, the largest Islamic university of the late Middle Ages, and the school attracted renowned mathematicians and astronomers. Between 1428 and 1429, he had the astrolabe built, which he used to produce his *Catalogue of Stars*, a very accurate list detailing the positions of the sun, moon, planets, and 1,018 stars. Unknown in the West until 1648 when a copy of the book was found at Oxford's Bodleian Library, the work makes Ulugh Beg one of the great astronomers of antiquity, on a par with Tycho Brahe and Johannes Kepler. The ruler was excessive, however, on promoting debates on issues that were too ambitious for Islamic beliefs at the time. On October 29, 1449, his own son murdered him, putting an end to the period of extraordinary intellectual vivacity that had made Samarkand the cultural capital of Islam.

According to recent archaeological excavations, the settlement was founded in the third or fourth millennium B.C.,

but the city as it appears to today was built around the fifth century B.C. and was known as Afrasiab. Located at the edge of the Kizyl-Kum desert, on the banks of the Zerafshan River, Afrasiab was the capital of Sogdiana, the region located between the Oxus, Amu Darya, and Syrdarya. In 329 B.C., it was conquered by Alexander the Great following a long siege, and it quickly became a point of encounter for the Mediterranean and Chinese cultures. Already an important commercial crossroads and in the middle of the seventh century A.D., the Arabs attacked the city, but they failed to conquer it until 712. The Umayyad ruler Qutaybah ibn Muslim finally took Samarkand, and in the centuries that followed, the city continued to prosper, first under the Khorasan Samanids and then under the Seljuks and the Khwarezm shahs. In 1220, the Mongols, led by Genghis Khan, razed it, wiping out the most important crossroads of three worlds: Persia, India, and China.

During the fifteenth century, Samarkand enjoyed its greatest period of splendor, becoming the capital of Timur's kingdom, which was so powerful that it laid siege to Delhi, Baghdad, Moscow, and Constantinople. In just a few years, the city was once again the economic and commercial fulcrum of central Asia, until the sixteenth century when the Shaybanids, the Uzbek rulers, moved the capital to Bukhara. Its slow decline, compounded by a series of earthquakes, turned Samarkand into a ghost town until 1868, the year it was conquered by the Russians.

Timurid Samarkand centered on the

281 bottom left Tilla Kari Madrasah (1646-1659) was a center of learning for seventeenth-century intellectuals and the last Islamic school built in Registan Square. However, it was not limited to education and was used as the Friday mosque where thousands would assemble to pray on the Muslim sabbath.

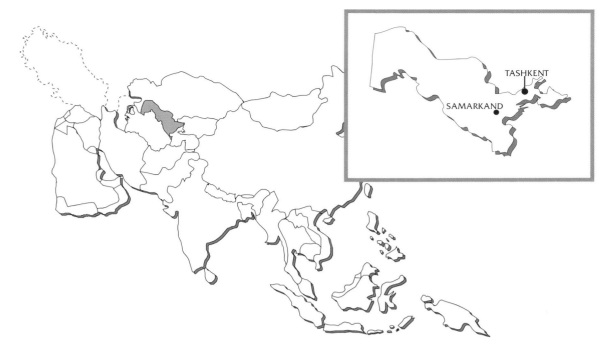

281 top right One of the tigers hunts fawns on the main entrance to the Sher Dor Madrasah, with the sun illuminating the scene. A unique example in modern Islamic art, this fresco breaks the Islamic ban on portraying animals or people.

281 bottom right Sher Dor Madrasah (right) was built between 1618 and 1635 on one side of Registan Square by the Shaybanid emir Yalangtush. Next to it stands the façade of Tilli Kari Madrasah.

Registan, the main square with the three Islamic schools. In the early seventeenth century, the Sher Dor Madrasah and then the Tilla Kari were built alongside Ulugh Beg's Madrasah, and the intellectuals of the era were schooled here. Northeast of Registan Square is one of the city's most impressive monuments, the Bibi-Khanom Mosque, named after Timur's Chinese wife who supposedly commissioned it. It was completed before the death of the great conqueror and was to be the jewel of the empire. Its main entrance was 115 feet tall and flanked by two minarets. Architects, decorators, and artists were called from the entire world of Islam, and 95 elephants were brought from India to work on a monumental project covering an area measuring 427 by 335 feet. There were two small mosques next to the main mosque. The wide colonnaded courtyard for the faithful was decorated with carved marble, and the walls of the mosque were adorned with geometric mosaics made of ceramic tiles bearing the name of Allah. All this magnificence followed the fate of the empire, however, and when Samarkand was abandoned, the Bibi-Khanom Mosque gradually fell into ruin, collapsing completely during the earthquake of 1897.

Further east is the Shahi Zinda, "the tomb of the living king," which is probably Samarkand's most fascinating monument. Its name refers to the original sanctuary that held the tomb of Qusam

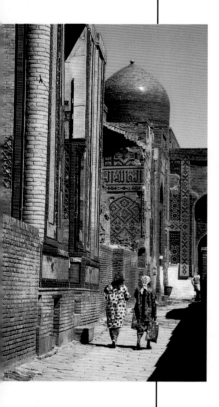

ibn Abbas. The cousin of the prophet Muhammad, Qusum traveled as far as Samarkand in 676 and brought Islam to the region. According to legend, he was robbed and decapitated by bandits while he was praying, but finished his prayer, picked up his head, and left. He is the living king to whom the funerary road of Shahi Zinda is dedicated. The road is also the site of other ancient tombs and of the mausoleums of important families from the Timurid period.

Timur and his descendants are buried in the Gur-e Amir mausoleum, "the prince's tomb," which is located in the westernmost part of the old city. It was built for Timur's grandson Muhammad Sultan and was completed in 1404. The building has light and simple lines, but it is richly decorated with colorful mosaics and culminates in a fluted turquoise cupola. The inner chamber is covered with gold, and nearly seven pounds were used when it was reconstructed in 1970.

In 1941, at the height of Soviet interest in the culture of central Asia, the famous anthropologist Mikhail Gerasimov opened the crypts and discovered that Timur was a very tall man who had apparently been wounded many times in battle. According to one story, Gerasimov found a threatening inscription on Timur's crypt, warning the profaner of his tomb of the arrival of a new despot. The next day, Hitler's troops invaded the Soviet Union.

282 left One of the narrow streets in old Samarkand lined by the brick houses built during the central Asian city's golden era. In the background there are the decorated walls and dome of Shahi Zinda.

282 top right The large funerary complex of Shahi Zinda, meaning "tomb of the living king," is where Qusam ibn-Abbas was buried. Qusam was the cousin of

the prophet Muhammad and the man who brought Islam to central Asia. To enter Shahi Zinda, one passes through a superb portal built by Ulugh Bek in 1435.

282 bottom right The mosque of Bibi-Khanym was dedicated to the wife of Timur. Built between 1399 and 1404, it was supposed to be the largest building in the world in order to celebrate the grandeur of Samarkand.

282-283 A view of the city and, in the foreground, the mausoleum of Gur-i Amir, where Timur and his successors were buried. The building was completed in 1404 on the edge of the old city.

Kathmandu Valley

NEPAL

REGISTRATION: 1979
CRITERIA: C (III) (IV) (VI)

At one end of Durbar Square in the heart of Kathmandu, there is a three-story eighteenth-century palace with elaborately carved wooden windows that has a "special" tenant. She is the Kumari Devi, the living goddess, and the incarnation of the Hindu goddess Durga. She is in fact a child, who wears precious clothes and lives in seclusion under the strict surveillance of her governesses, with the exception of the six ceremonies each year during which she can leave the palace. After a series of difficult tests, the Kumari Devi is chosen from many candidates, all belonging to the same caste. She retains her divine status until puberty when she becomes human once again and another child is selected to take her place.

The custom of venerating a young girl may seem bizarre, but Nepal is a country where daily life is very often shot through with mysticism. The valley of Kathmandu is home to a great many Hindu and Buddhist buildings that have few equals in the world, and at times the syncretism between the two religions is strong. The valley has been inhabited since time immemorial, but its development occurred during the golden period of the Malla Dynasty in the seventeenth and eighteenth centuries, when the city's current appearance was created. The Malla were Newari, a people resulting from a fusion of Mongol and Indo-Aryan blood who are still predominant among the peoples of the valley.

Until the unification of the Nepalese kingdom and the choice of Kathmandu as capital in 1768, the valley was divided into rival city-states: Kathmandu, Patan, Bhaktapur, and Kirtipur. The nucleus of each of the four was, and still is, Durbar Square in which a royal palace, the *Durbar*, is formed by a series of stone and carved wood buildings arranged around a *chowk* (court)

adorned by Hindu statues.

The palace in Kathmandu, watched over by a statue of the monkey-god Hanuman, was built at the start of the seventeenth century and inhabited until the end of the nineteenth. It has ten courts of which the most outstanding is Nasal Chowk, which is surrounded by statues of Shiva dancing. To mark the unification of the kingdom, towers were built at the sides of the palace to represent the four cities in the valley. The most impressive is Basantpur Tower, dedicated to Kathmandu, from which there is a panoramic view over the temples in the square. The temple that is most worthy of mention is Kasthamandap, dedicated to the elephant-god Ganesh. It was probably built in the twelfth century and gave the city its name.

Patan is separated from Kathmandu by the river Bagmati. Its own Durbar Square is the largest in the valley and has the most

284 bottom right A view of Nasal Chowk, the largest of the courts in Kathmandu's ancient royal palace. The current king of Nepal, lives in a more modern building, but the palace is still used for important ceremonies.

284 top right The steps in Maju Mandir, the temple dedicated to Shiva and built in Durbar Square around 1690, are the main meeting area of Kathmandu's inhabitants. The temple is in Shikhara style but was influenced by Indian architecture.

284 bottom left This is the entrance to the Kasthamandap Temple in Durbar Square in Kathmandu. Dedicated to the elephant god Ganesh, the temple was probably built in the twelfth century and gave its name to the city. Note the temple dedicated to Shiva in the background.

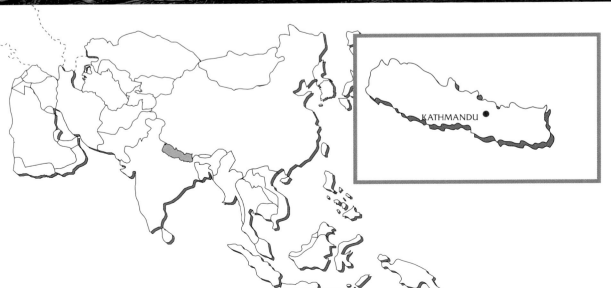

285 Nine stories high, and built of brick and wood historiated with elaborate – and erotic – decorations, Basantpur Tower and four others were raised in the second half of the eighteenth century by King Prithvi Narayan Shah to celebrate the union of the valley kingdoms. This tower represents the kingdom of Kathmandu.

287 top right Some of the oldest buildings in the ancient kingdom are to be seen on the Taumadhi Tole, Bhaktapur's widest street. Note the elaborate entrance to the Sukul Dhoka where the city's principal religious authority is based.

286 top The steps to Nyatapola Temple in Bhaktapur. Pairs of stone statues of griffins, lions, and elephants stand on each platform, which correspond to each step. Standing 98 feet tall, this is the tallest and most elegant temple in the kingdom.

286 bottom The bronze statue of King Bhupatindra Malla stands on a tall column in front of the palace in Bhaktapur. The king, who reigned from 1696 to 1722, was an arts lover and responsible for the construction of the city's most important buildings.

286-287 An overall view of Patan and its superb palace, known as the "Palace of the 55 windows." The building was begun in the fourteenth century, but its current appearance dates from the seventeenth and eighteenth centuries.

temples, some of which are five stories high. For this reason, the city is known to the Nepalese as Lalitpur (city of beauty). It is said to have been founded by Emperor Ashoka in 250 B.C. and is bounded by four stupas (semi-spherical, Buddhist sacred structures), one at each corner of the city. Its Hindu temples are especially gracious, and some of them are decorated with bas-reliefs of an erotic nature.

The temples in Durbar Square in Bhaktapur were damaged and even destroyed by an earthquake in the eighteenth century. However, its royal palace, known as the "palace of 55 windows," is a masterpiece of Newari architecture, featuring a gateway lined with gold. The fourth city, Kirtipur, is the farthest from the capital and boasts few religious buildings.

Two important places of Buddhist pilgrimage in the valley are

Swayambhunath and Bodhnath, dating from at least 2,000 years ago. Their *stupas* are some of the largest in the world in which, on top of the dome, the eyes of the Buddha are painted on a square structure. Dozens of wooden prayer-wheels stand around the *stupas*; the faithful spin the wheels as they perform their ritual clockwise walk around the temples. Around Swayambhunath and Bodhnath there are several *gompa* (monasteries) that contain precious religious objects and *tanka* (paintings on silk).

Pashupatinath is one of the most important places of Hindu pilgrimage and attracts many worshippers from India. Sacred to the god Shiva, it stands on the banks of the river Bagmati, which is a traditional place of cremation. Its many temples contain *lingam* (stone phalluses) and bas-reliefs carved between the seventh and seventeenth centuries. The crowds are most attracted to the Guhyeshwari dedicated to the goddess Kali, the most terrible of the many manifestations of Shiva. Only Hindus are allowed to enter the temple, therefore everybody else must make do with admiring this artistic gem from a distance. They are, however, able to soak up the local atmosphere formed by the many colors, smells, and mysticism.

*289 bottom right
The large temple of
Pashupatinath is crowded
with Hindus during the
Shivaratri Festival held
in February in honor of
Shiva. Standing on the
banks of the river
Bagmati, Pashupatinath
is the most important
cremation place in
Nepal.*

*289 top right A view of
Bodhnath Temple. In
Buddhist symbolism, the
mandala-shaped base
represents the earth, the
dome represents water,
the coils on the roof (on
the base of which the
Buddha's eyes are
painted) symbolize fire,
the umbrella air, and the
spire on the top the
kingdom of the gods.*

*288-289 The Buddhist
temple of Bodhnath, with
Nepal's second largest
stupa in the background, is
the center for the dynamic
community of Tibetan
refugees who came to
Nepal following China's
invasion of Tibet in 1959.*

*288 bottom Set on the
top of the eponymous
hill, Swayambunath
Temple has a typical
stupa with the painted
eyes of the Buddha
surrounded by small*

*temples that contain the
prayer wheels on which
the mantra "om mani
padme hum" is written.
The faithful walk around
the stupa, spinning the
prayer wheels as they go.*

The Shalimar Gardens and the Fort in Lahore

PAKISTAN

Punjab
Registration: 1981
Criteria: C (i) (ii) (iii)
Registration in the World Heritage
in Danger List: 2000

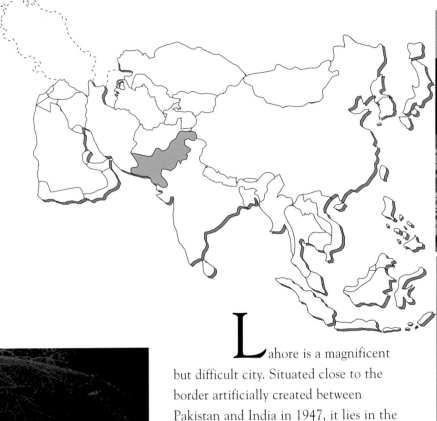

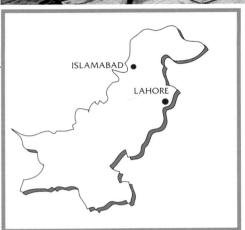

L ahore is a magnificent but difficult city. Situated close to the border artificially created between Pakistan and India in 1947, it lies in the center of the great Punjab plain, the history of which is linked to the cultures and religions of different and historically opposed peoples.

Legend says that the city was founded by Loh, the son of the general, Rama, who was the hero of the great Hindu epic poem, the *Ramayana*. The first ruler of the city was King Lalitiditya. During the eleventh century, it passed into the hands of the Muslims who instituted a strong and, later, flourishing center of Islamic studies. Lahore's greatest period of glory began with its conquest by the Mogul emperor Akbar who, in 1566, made the city his capital and began construction of the Shahi Qila (Royal Fort) on the site of the previous fort. Rectangular in form, the Shahi Qila is an extraordinary amalgam of architectural elements contributed by the Mogul emperors, the Sikhs, and the British restoration during the Raj.

Akbar's successor, Jehangir, laid out gardens and built the Khawabgarh-i-Jehangir, the pavilions that contained the royal apartments, but the real masterpieces in the Fort are the buildings constructed by Shah Jahan, the emperor who was later to build the Taj Mahal. One of these was the Shish Mahal, or Palace of Mirrors, built in 1631 for the empress and her ladies-in-waiting. Its walls are lined with tiny pieces of colored mirror and the windows are screened with carved marble so that the women could look out without being seen from the outside.

In the same year, the Diwan-i-Aam

(Audience Court) was laid out, a white marble pavilion that today houses a museum of Mogul artifacts, and the Naulakha, also made from white marble and inlaid with semi-precious stones in floral motifs. Its name comes from the words "*nove lakh,*" indicating the astronomical sum spent to build the palace. In 1644, Shah Jahan built the Moti Masjid (Mosque of the Pearls), which was restored at the start of the twentieth century by the British. The enlargement, in 1674, of the main door was the work of the ostentatious

290-291 The inner walls of the Shish Mahal are adorned with intricate stucco decorations and mirrors that reflect the candlelight to create the effect of a starry sky. The palace was built for Shah Jahan to house the empress and her ladies-in-waiting.

290 bottom left A masterpiece of Mogul architecture, the Naulakha is an elegant pavilion in white marble with windows carved to create a lacework effect. The name comes from the words "nove lakh," referring to the astronomical sum paid by Shah Jahan to build it.

290 bottom right The portico in the Moti Masjid (Mosque of the Pearls). Built in 1644 during the reign of Shah Jahan, its name is derived from the pearly luminescence of the Indian marble with which it was built.

291 top The Royal Fort boasts a pool decorated with geometrical motifs in colored marble. In the background stands the elegant Diwan-i-Khas used by the Mogul emperor, Shah Jahan, for his private audiences.

291 bottom The Kala Burj (Black Tower) is situated on the north side of the Royal Fort in Lahore. Construction was begun in 1631, the same year as that of the adjacent Shish Mahal (Palace of Mirrors).

292 top A view of the entrance façade to Lahore Fort, which faces west. Note the imposing Alamgiri gateway, built in 1674 for Aurangzeb, which was originally decorated with gold and other precious and semi-precious materials, many of which have been stolen.

292-293 Shalimar Gardens. Laid out in 1641 for Shah Jahan, they were initially much larger. Today about 47 acres remain but the buildings are rapidly deteriorating, as well as the gardens and fountains due to the recent destruction of three of the ancient water tanks.

Aurangzeb who wanted it large enough for seven elephants with their royal palanquins to pass through, and to be decorated with gold and semi-precious stones.

Another of Lahore's marvels is the Shalimar Gardens. Created for Shah Jahan on the model of the gardens in Delhi (today completely destroyed), they were divided into seven terraces to symbolize the Paradise of Allah and adorned with fountains, streams, and pavilions where the court could relax. Today only three of the seven sections remain, but they cover an area of almost 47 acres. The second of the terraces contains the Sawan Bhadon, a pool with jets of water that reproduce the relaxing patter of the rain, and niches lined with small mirrors that reflected candlelight during imperial gatherings held at night.

In 1999, due to the enlargement of the Grand Trunk Road that links Pakistan to Bangladesh via India, three of the ancient water-tanks that fed the fountains in the Shalimar Gardens were destroyed. Moreover, pollution and neglect have ensured that the condition of many of the Mogul buildings are rapidly deteriorating. In consequence, UNESCO decided to inscribe this site in the World Heritage in Danger List and to monitor the restoration project drawn up by the Pakistani government, though this remains for the moment only on paper.

293 top left and right Small pavilions and large colonnaded buildings were built throughout the Shalimar Gardens. Note the form and decoration of the pillars in the one on the right that resembles the style of a Hindu temple.

293 bottom One of the pavilions inside the Shalimar Gardens. Built for the pleasure of the Mogul court, the gardens were cooled by pools and jets of water; by night they were illuminated by hundreds of candles placed in chini khanas (small niches) in the walls.

The Qutb Minar and its Monuments in Delhi

INDIA

REGISTRATION: 1993
CRITERIA: C (IV)

In the epic Rajasthani poem *Prithvi Raj Raso*, the ruler of Delhi, Pritviraj Chauran, is described as a romantic and sentimental hero. When Muslims attacked the city for the first time in their invasion of northern India from the central Asian steppes in 1191, Chauran beat them off, but he was magnanimous with his defeated enemy and allowed their leader, Muhammad, to go free. What the poem does not recount is the story of the second attack, the following year. This time the troops of Qutb-ud-Din Aibak came out victorious from the clash, and they were

not so generous with the *rajput* sovereign. Chauran was decapitated and Lal Kot, the fort in which the Hindi royal family lived in Delhi, was looted and burned down.

This victory marked the beginning of the Muslim domination of the city and much of the sub-continent that was to last uninterrupted until 1857. To celebrate his victory, in 1193, Qutb-ud-din began the construction of the Qutb Minar within the perimeter walls of Lal Kot. The Qutb Minar is a red sandstone tower that marked the easternmost point reached at that time by the Islamic faith. Its very size and bulk was to serve as a good omen for future conquests. Besides being symbolic, the tower was a minaret from which the *muezzin* called the faithful to prayer.

The Qutb Minar stands almost 240 feet high and has five levels. The diameter at the base is 49 feet across, and it tapers as it rises to a tip only eight feet wide. The tower is entirely covered with intricate bas-reliefs of verses from the Koran. By the time of Qutb-ud-Din's death, only the first level had been completed, and another three were added by his successor Iltutmish. In 1368, the ruler Feroz Shah

Tughlaq restored the tower and replaced the fourth level with two more made from red sandstone and white marble. He completed the structure with a small dome, but this was destroyed during an earthquake in 1803.

Next to the Qutb Minar stand the attractive ruins of India's first mosque, the Quwwat-ul-Islam (power of Islam). Qutb-ud-Din built it using materials from 27 Hindu and Jain temples in Lal Kot. Enclosed in a rectangular perimeter measuring 141 by 108 feet, it comprises a colonnade-lined court and arches 52 feet high, which are the only remains of the prayer hall. The use of Hindu laborers is clearly seen in the bas-relief decorations in which Islamic calligraphic texts are mixed with images of lotus flowers, which were sacred to the Hindu religion. Iltutmish and his successors enlarged and modified the mosque with cloisters decorated with geometric motifs in pure Islamic style.

In 1311, Ala-ud-Din Khalji built the Ala-i-Darwaza, the main entrance to the mosque, in red sandstone and marble on the south side. Considered a wonder of Indian Islamic architecture, it is topped by a dome with decorations inspired by the art of the Turks and Seljuks from that period. Close by stands the Alai Minar, a tower built by Ala-ud-Din to outdo the Qutb Minar. On his death, the project remained uncompleted, and to this day the tower is nothing more than a partial construction 89 feet high.

Of the other buildings in the complex, one that merits attention is the Tomb of Iltutmish, which was built in 1235, a year before his death. It was the first funereal monument to be erected in India, as the

294 top left One of the greatest examples of Islamic architecture in India, the Ala-i-Darwaza is the principal entrance to Quwwat-ul-Islam Mosque, built in 1311.

294 bottom The tomb of Iltutmish (the son-in-law of Qutb-ud-Din Aibak) stands on a plinth – today without its dome – to the east of Quwwat-ul-Islam. The first funerary monument built in India (in 1235), the sarcophagus is carved with geometrical and calligraphic patterns.

Hindus have always practiced cremation. The starkness of the exterior walls are contrasted by the richness of Islamic and Hindu decoration inside. The dome that covered the tomb lies in pieces on an esplanade close by.

The Iron Column is in total contrast to the Islamic architecture inside the complex. Scholars are still uncertain of the origins of this artifact that stands 24 feet tall and has a diameter of 15 inches. Miraculously, it is immune to rust. It seems it was brought to what is today the state of Bihar in 1022 by the *rajput* ruler Ananpala Tomar, the founder of Lal Kot, yet the inscriptions on the surface date the column to the Gupta era in the fourth century. At one time its tip was crowned with an image of the bird-god Garuda. An ancient legend says that whoever rests his back against the column and is able to entwine the fingers of his hands on the other side will have a wish come true.

295 top left The intentions of the sultan, Alai-ud-Din Khalji, were for the Alai Minar to dwarf the Qutb Minar with its bulk, but it was never completed. Begun in 1315, all that remains is an 86-foot-tall block.

295 top right The five-story Qutb Minar seen from Quwwat-ul-Islam Mosque. Standing 240 feet tall, this red sandstone tower was built as a minaret and to mark the easternmost point reached by Islam. Construction was begun in 1193 by Sultan Qutb-ud-Din Aibak.

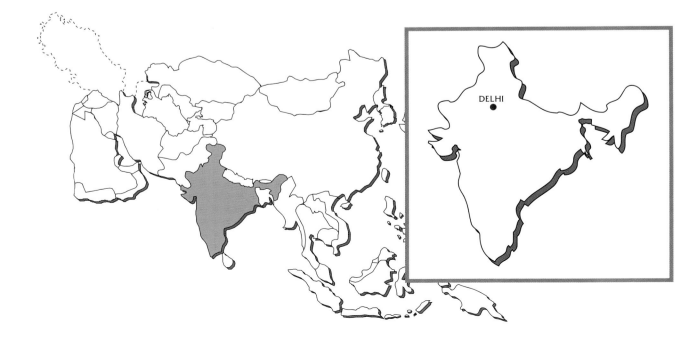

DELHI

The Taj Mahal

INDIA

AGRA, UTTAR PRADESH
REGISTRATION: 1983
CRITERIA: C (I)

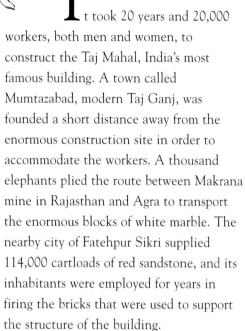

296 center Designed to represent the paradise of Allah, the gardens in the Taj Mahal combine Mogul, Persian, and Arab styles. The huge pool that runs down the center symbolizes the Kawthar, the celestial pool of abundance mentioned in the Koran.

296 bottom The Chowk-i-Jilo Khana is the building at the entrance to the site. Built from red sandstone, it is purely Islamic in style in the middle but flanked by Hindu-style temples. Calligraphic decorations on sandstone and white marble line the walls.

296-297 The traditional view of the Taj Mahal at dawn. It stands 246 feet tall on a platform 187 feet square and has a minaret at each corner that leans slightly outwards for reasons of perspective.

It took 20 years and 20,000 workers, both men and women, to construct the Taj Mahal, India's most famous building. A town called Mumtazabad, modern Taj Ganj, was founded a short distance away from the enormous construction site in order to accommodate the workers. A thousand elephants plied the route between Makrana mine in Rajasthan and Agra to transport the enormous blocks of white marble. The nearby city of Fatehpur Sikri supplied 114,000 cartloads of red sandstone, and its inhabitants were employed for years in firing the bricks that were used to support the structure of the building.

According to a Persian chronicler from the seventeenth century, the decorations in the Taj Mahal required the purchase, for outrageous sums, of lapis lazuli from Afghanistan, turquoise from Tibet, crystal from China, jasper from the Punjab, onyx from Persia, agate from the Yemen, coral from the Arabian Sea, and chalcedony from Europe. It was the task of the merchants in Jaipur to procure diamonds, both those in Gwalior magnetite and those in Baghdad cornelian.

All of this was paid for in cash by one man, the Mogul emperor Shah Jahan. He was an immensely rich man who bore the title "king of the world" and, between 1627 and 1666, ruled over a territory that stretched from Kandahar in the west to Assam in the east, and from the plateau of Pamir in the north to the plain of Deccan in the south. No Indian ruler had ever governed so vast an empire, but even for him the expense was not indifferent. Despite that, he did not tax his people even one rupee during the 20-year construction project: for him, the Taj Mahal was a "personal endeavor."

This extraordinary monument - defined by Rabindranath Tagore, the greatest Indian poet of the twentieth century, as "a teardrop on the face of eternity" - is probably the greatest and most tangible gift of love that any man has ever given to a woman. Shah Jahan had it built to hold the remains of his beloved Mumtaz Mahal so that her memory would be honored for ever.

Although Mumtaz Mahal was not his only wife (the emperor had a harem of 5,000 concubines), she was the only one he married for love rather than for reasons of state, as was the custom of the time. The daughter of a high Persian dignitary born Arjumand Bano Begum, in honor of her beauty she was nicknamed Mumtaz Mahal, meaning "chosen one of the palace," by her father-in-law Jehangir the day after her wedding on March 27, 1612. Until her death in 1631, she and Shah Jahan were inseparable. He never ceased to court her and cover her with fabulous jewels. She assisted him, with grace and intelligence, in matters of state and even accompanied him to war. They had 14 children, the last of which, born in a tent near a battlefield in the Deccan, cost her her life.

Legend has it that, with her last breath, Mumtaz Mahal made Shah Jahan promise to build the most beautiful tomb in the world for her. True or not, the emperor had no peace until the Taj Mahal was completed.

Once he returned to Agra, the emperor

purchased a plot of land on the banks of the river Yamuna that was to have two purposes. The first was to accommodate a tomb (*rauza*), the second was to become a place of pilgrimage (*urs*) during the ceremonies that marked the anniversary of the death of Mumtaz Mahal.

Over the centuries, many hypotheses have been made as to who was the architect of the building. There are those who believe that it was the work of the Venetian Pietro Veroneo who, according to documents of the period, was in the service of the emperor during the two decades of its construction. However, it seems highly improbable that an Italian, even a contemporary of Gian Lorenzo Bernini, could have conceived a monument that so perfectly weds Indian and Persian styles. Finally, experts are inclined to believe that

the design was the joint product of the best oriental minds of the time.

The complex of the Taj Mahal is entered through a red sandstone gateway 98 feet tall, historiated with verses from the Koran in elegant script. Two small temples in Hindu style stand at the sides. From here the view of the mausoleum opens. The magnificent construction stands 246 feet tall on a square platform that measures 187 feet long on each side. A minaret 154 feet tall stands at each of the four corners, built to lean slightly outwards for reasons of perspective and also so that, in the event of an earthquake, they would not collapse onto the central mausoleum. The enormous dome of the Taj Mahal is topped by a bronze pinnacle 30 feet high and was once covered entirely with gold. It was probably designed by Ismail Effendi, who was called

from Istanbul where he had built splendid buildings for the Ottoman sultans.

The Taj Mahal is a miracle of engineering. The perimetrical walls support a weight of nine tons per square foot, while the dome weighs over 13,000 tons alone. The marble-covered structure is supported by arches reinforced by bricks, wooden poles, and bands of iron driven into the platform. A system of wells protects the site from flooding by the river Yamuna, which was deviated from its natural course so that it flows past the building, providing it with a further dimension of beauty, particularly in the morning when the Taj Mahal is reflected in its waters. Apart from its technical excellence, the extraordinary art of the mosaicists, jewel cutters, and engravers who embroidered the surfaces with elegant floral decorations makes the mausoleum an unparalleled masterpiece. What strikes the observer most forcefully are the harmony and symmetry of the Taj Mahal and the complex as a whole.

The mausoleum is flanked by two identical red sandstone buildings, built in pure Mogul style and each topped by eight domes. The one on the left, which faces Mecca, is a mosque. The opposite one, called "*jawab*," meaning "the response," was designed as a welcoming area for pilgrims. In the center is the *char bagh*, the Persian style garden designed as a reflection of paradise. Filled with fountains, it too is perfectly symmetrical and characterized by the number four and its multiples. It is a square divided into four parts and originally had sixteen flowerbeds, each of which contained four hundred plants.

The only element that breaks the symmetry of the Taj Mahal is the tomb of Shah Jahan himself. Inside the mausoleum, in the huge room lined with niches and decorated with semi-precious stones, mosaics, and carvings in the marble, lie two false tombs: the one in the center is that of Mumtaz, and the one to the left that of the emperor. While he was still alive, the room was covered with carpets and adorned with candlesticks and precious objects. The asymmetrical layout is repeated in the actual tombs of the royal couple, situated in a chamber below the room. The reason for this imbalance in the mausoleum is that Shah Jahan lies here against his will. The emperor wanted another tomb to be built

for him in black marble, identical to the Taj Mahal, on the other side of the Yamuna, and for the two buildings to be connected by a solid gold bridge. However, upon Shah Jahan's death, his son Aurangzeb - who ascended the throne after having organized the assassination of half his family - did not consider the project important, and had his father placed beside his mother.

The era of Shah Jahan marked the apogee of the Mogul empire, which, from his death onwards, was pulled apart by internal struggles and went into inexorable decline. In addition, even the Taj Mahal was the target of continual plundering. The silver entrance gate was melted down and replaced by a copper one, and many of the precious stones were stolen. After their arrival in India, the British replaced the gold lining of the dome with a copper one.

The Anglo-Indian writer, Rudyard Kipling, called the Taj Mahal "the ivory gateway through which dreams pass," and many of his British compatriots considered it the eighth wonder of the world. Notwithstanding this, there were even those who proposed demolishing it and selling the parts to embellish English country houses.

With India's independence, the monument has undergone continuous restoration and has been returned to its original glory, but the toxic fumes put out by the nearly 200 foundries in Agra are seriously putting the white marble at risk.

299 top right Details of narcissi, tulips, and roses made from marble and precious and semi-precious stones. The gems were imported from all over Asia and Europe and cost enormous sums.

299 bottom right A view of the Taj Mahal from the river Jamuna. While it was being built, Shah Jahan had the river deviated so it would flow past the complex. His intention was that he would be buried in an identical building made from black marble on the other side of the river, but his successor, his son Aurangzeb, cancelled the project for economic reasons.

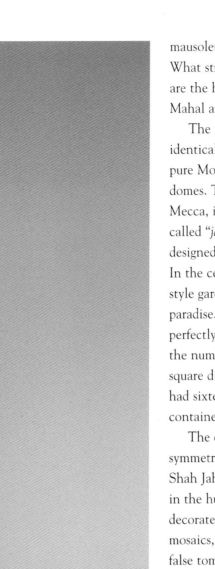

298-299 A side view of the Taj Mahal. Each side has large arched recesses called pishtaq with façades decorated with floral motifs and verses from the Koran glorifying the Muslim paradise.

299 bottom left The interior of the mausoleum with the lacework marble enclosure around the two empty tombs of the

emperor Shah Jahan and his beloved wife Mumtaz Mahal. The rulers' actual tombs lie in a crypt below the perimeter of the balustrade.

The Ancient City of Galle and its Fortifications

SRI LANKA

SOUTH PROVINCE
REGISTRATION: 1988
CRITERIA: C (V)

On the entrance to Galle Fort, the Dutch carved the letters "VOC," the abbreviation of the Dutch East India Company, supported by two rampant lions and topped by a cock. The cock was chosen to be the symbol of the city due to an etymological error: the Europeans thought that the name Galle was derived from the Latin word *gallus* (rooster), whereas it comes from *gala*, which, in Tamil, means "place sheltered by rocks."

The town of Galle had already existed

since time immemorial when the Portuguese arrived in 1505. They had been blown off course by a violent storm that quickly blew up while they were on their way to the Maldives and took shelter in the harbor in the southernmost point of the island of Ceylon. A legend identified it as the city of Tarshish, mentioned in the Old Testament, where King Solomon kept a fleet of ships. The great Hindu epic, the *Ramayana*, refers to the plant able to restore life brought from the Himalayas by the monkey Hanuman, which grew on the hills behind Galle. Leaving myths aside, a 1409 inscription in Chinese, Tamil, and

Arabic states that the merchants of the city traded in spices and precious stones with the people of the Middle and Far East.

At the start of the sixteenth century, the Portuguese established a naval base at Galle, which was a strategic stopping place between their colonies of Malacca (in West Malaysia) and Goa (western India), although they only completed the construction of a fort dedicated to Santa Cruz in 1625. This defense turned out, however, to be of no good use because, in 1640, Galle fell to the Dutch following a siege lasting just four days.

Under the new patrons, also able traders, the city prospered. At the start of the seventeenth century, under the governor Petrus Vuyst – an adventurer remembered for his cruelty – the fort was substantially enlarged. Huge blocks of granite were transported by ship and used in the construction using the labor of African slaves and former Dutch soldiers who had been court-martialed. Unfortunately, even the new defenses were insufficient, and in 1795 Galle was taken by the British who governed Ceylon until 1948 when the island became independent with the name Sri Lanka.

Galle fort, with its Dutch walls and cannon still intact and enclosing an area of 89 acres, is Sri Lanka's principal remnant of European domination. The only traces of the Portuguese presence are the Black Bastion near the Old Port and the walls of a sixteenth-century church on which, in 1899, the Hindus built the temple of Sudharmalaya.

In addition to the ramparts, lined by a walkway that has become the seaside

promenade of the town's inhabitants, the Dutch were responsible for the brick paving of the streets, the drainage system that exploited the pull of the tides, and the construction of numerous buildings, including warehouses (known as *pakhuizen*), houses, and the Groote Kerke. Built in 1755 on the foundations of a monastery of Portuguese Capuchin monks, the Groote Kerke is the oldest Protestant church on the island. Inside, there is a magnificent carved pulpit, a silver-piped organ, and the gravestones of the Dutch (and later British) governors and their wives in the floor. The

300 left The mosque in Galle Fort was built in a combination of Islamic and European styles. Today the city of Galle has spread beyond the walls, but within them a prosperous community of Muslim tradesmen still survives.

300 top right The symbol of the Dutch East India Company can be seen on the old entrance to the fort. Its abbreviation, VOC, is supported by two rampant lions and topped by a rooster.

300-301 The Anglican All Saints' Church was built in 1871 by the British on the site of the Dutch courthouse. After they took Galle in 1795, the British made extensive alterations to the appearance of the fort and built the first lighthouse in Asia.

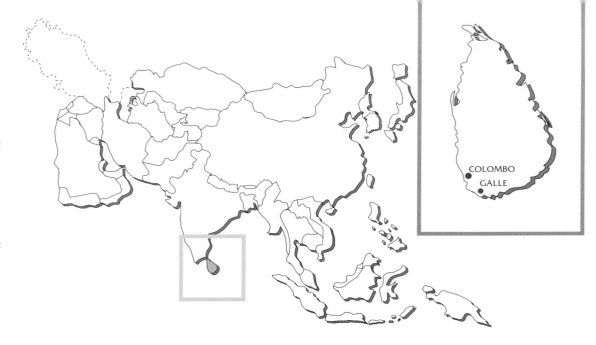

COLOMBO
GALLE

301 top right One of the tombstones of the Dutch nobles in the floor of the Groote Kerk. They were inserted in the church floor in 1853 after the closure had been ordered of all cemeteries inside Galle Fort.

301 bottom right Built in 1755 by the Dutch on the site of a Portuguese Capuchin monastery, the Groote Kerk is the oldest Protestant church in Sri Lanka. It stands in Church Street, close to the famous New Oriental Hotel built by the British.

eighteenth-century masters of Galle are remembered in the place names, for example, in the Point Utrecht Bastion and Leyn Baan Street (literally, "rope walk," because this is where the cords and ropes used to pack sea goods were made).

The British can claim the honor of having built here, in 1848, the first lighthouse in Asia, which stands on Flag Rock. At the approach of ships, cannon salvoes were fired to warn (flag) the new arrivals of submerged rocks. It is also the site of the carrier pigeon station that used to carry news to the city of Colombo. The British built many administrative and residential buildings inside the fort, as well as the famous New Oriental Hotel, one of the oldest hotels in Asia and still in operation. To provide some relaxation, they created the Esplanade to be used as a cricket pitch.

Today the town of Galle has expanded outside the walls. The Muslims built a mosque and a school there at the end of the nineteenth century and established gem-trading stations. In this way, they re-appropriated this outpost overlooking the Indian Ocean that they had seen flourish long before the arrival of the Europeans.

The Great Wall

CHINA

REGISTRATION: 1987
CRITERIA (I) (II) (III) (IV)
(VI)

In the year 1271, a Venetian merchant and his brothers set out on a long journey to the lands of the largest empire known to man. Marco Polo returned from Kublai Khan's China in 1295, after spending 25 years in the Orient. When he was captured and imprisoned three years later by Genoa, Venice's rival, he dictated his memoirs to Rustichello da Pisa, recounting that incredible journey.

Marco Polo described the customs and cities of Mongol-ruled China, and he recounted the banquets, lavish ceremonies, and endless wealth of the court of Kublai Khan. *Il Milione*, known in English as *The Travels of Marco Polo*, tells of the world, bearing witness to the cities and people along the trade routes that linked Europe and Asia. Yet even today, there are those who doubt Marco Polo's accounts, suggesting that they are tales the Venetian had heard from other travelers, without ever going to China himself. Skeptics support this theory first of all by citing an unpardonable lapse. *Il Milione* makes no mention of the most impressive work in the history of man, the Great Wall, that, at 4,150 feet long, is the only manmade structure visible from the moon.

There is no doubt that during the era of the Yuan Dynasty (the Mongols who ruled China from the year of Marco Polo's departure until 1368) the Great Wall was not yet that long. Nevertheless, the different segments that the Chinese dynasties had built to ward off the Mongol invasions, but that were unable to withstand the onslaught of Genghis Khan, spanned a total of nearly 3,100 miles.

The Xiongnu, known to the Europeans as the Huns, were nomadic tribes that lived on the steppes of Mongolia, and their incursions were the biggest threat to the cities of prosperous China. The Chinese therefore began to construct massive fortifications as early as the ninth century B.C. in order to protect themselves from these invasions. These works were done on a local scale, however, and were not part of a single project. In the third century B.C., the Qin Dynasty ousted the weak Zhou rulers. The Qin took power in 221 B.C. with Qin Shi Huangdi, who imposed his authority over the lands that would go down in history as the Middle Kingdom.

During his short reign, Qin Shi Huangdi, decided to reinforce these defense structures. For ten years, led by General Meng Tian, 300,000 soldiers, prisoners, and local laborers extended the Great Wall from Lintao in the west to Liaodong in the east. He created 3,100 miles of counterforts from which his enormous army could face an unpredictable and savage enemy. Qin Shi's Great Wall was built using materials that could be found locally, particularly stone. In areas where stone was scarce, sturdy ramparts of compacted earth were built and were then pressed between two walls. The gates were well-equipped strongholds so that even a small army could defend them.

Between the fifth and the seventh centuries A.D., the Northern Wei, Northern Qi, and Northern Zhou Dynasties helped consolidate the Great Wall. In A.D. 555, the Northern Qi Dynasty built 280 miles of ramparts uniting Nankow,

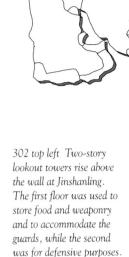

302 top left Two-story lookout towers rise above the wall at Jinshanling. The first floor was used to store food and weaponry and to accommodate the guards, while the second was for defensive purposes.

302 top right Originally built during the Northern Qi Dynasty, the wall at Simatai was completely rebuilt during the Ming period. The 17,700 feet of wall contain 35 signaling towers.

302-303 The Great Wall at Jinshanling stands about 93 miles from Beijing in the mountains of Hebei province. It was built in 1570 during the Ming Dynasty.

303 top At almost 26 feet tall and 16 to 20 feet thick, the wall at Jinshanling is a little lower and narrower than in other sections, but it has strong fortifications and parapets seven feet high fitted with arrow slits to defend the wall against the enemy.

near Beijing, and Datong, in the eastern province of Shanxi. This work, which proceeded rapidly, involved 1,800,000 people, most of whom were dragooned. However, the most substantial extension and reinforcement work did not begin until around the twelfth century, when the Jin Dynasty built over 2,480 miles of new ramparts that went from the eastern end of the empire to what is now Inner Mongolia, in the heart of the Gobi Desert.

Today, we can admire only segments of the Great Wall, from Shanhaiguan, on the Yellow Sea in the province of Hebei, to Jiayuguan, in Gansu. These sections were built mainly by the Ming Dynasty, which ruled between 1368 and 1644. During that era, the rampart, made of brick and granite, was enlarged to a thickness of 33

feet and was raised to a height of 13 to 16 feet. In addition to consolidating the Great Wall, the Ming emperors also added important structures and more sophisticated design details. Watchtowers and observation points were built along the Great Wall at intervals of few dozen miles from which the guards could send smoke or light signals, using a special code, to warn each other of enemy advances. Enormous fortresses were built near the Great Wall to house troops. For example, the Jiayuguan fortress dates from 1372. Its walls, which are 33 feet high, cover a perimeter of over 2,300 feet. There are two tall lookout towers over the two gates, and the interior housed the barracks, stables, and other buildings. The building technology used for the Wall

reached its apogee with the Ming Dynasty. At certain points, the Great Wall rises over terrains with a seventy-degree slope, snaking its way through the mountains of northern China. While its architectural value does not match that of other works, the Great Wall is deeply rooted in Chinese culture. It has become part of popular symbolism and mythology alike. One of the many stories linked to it is the legend of Meng Jiangnu. The tears she shed over her husband, who died during construction of the Ming Wall, made an entire section collapse. To commemorate her devotion, a temple was dedicated to her near the Shanhaiguan pass, and even today the Chinese continue to venerate her image there.

The Forbidden City
CHINA

BEIJING
REGISTRATION: 1987
CRITERIA: C (III) (IV)

The authorities of the People's Republic of China renamed it Gu Gong (Palace Museum), but for the rest of China the most grandiose complex of buildings – covering nearly eight million square feet and containing 9,999 rooms in the center of Beijing – in this enormous country is and always will be Zijin Cheng, the Forbidden City.

Death was the penalty for anyone who, without permission, dared to pass through the gates of the sumptuous residence that was home to the 24 emperors of the Ming and Qing dynasties. For these rulers, the Forbidden City was a gilded prison because,

owing to their status as "sons of heaven," they were not allowed to mingle with ordinary mortals. How it was possible to govern such a vast empire from that padded world is a question that does not find a ready response. Probably all the complicated ceremonies, luxuries, and vices in which the rulers spent their days provided a means for distracting their attention away from the power struggles among the army of eunuchs, emissaries, ambassadors, and ministers who governed the Middle Kingdom.

In 1407, at the start of the fifth year of his reign, Yong Le, third emperor of the Ming Dynasty, began construction of the Forbidden

City. To complete it, 14 years and one million workers were required. Of these, 100,000 were the best craftsmen in the empire. The stone used in the platforms of the pavilions and the bas-reliefs was quarried at Fangshan just outside Beijing. To aid in its transportation, wells were dug every 160 feet beside the road so that, during freezing conditions in winter, water could be flung onto the surface to form ice, thus allowing the blocks of stone to slide more easily. The much-appreciated camphor wood used in the columns came from the southern provinces of Yunnan and Sichuan. To fire the tiles of yellow majolica (the imperial color), kilns were built a short distance from the building site. The lime used to cover the perimeter walls – smooth, 28 feet thick at the base, and 22 feet thick at the top – was mixed with red pigments, sticky rice, and egg whites to make it more solid. In the pavilions, bricks were used for the flooring so that the sound of footsteps was more pleasing. With the exception of the platforms and tiles, the rest of the buildings were made from wood, and this of course has meant that many of them have been lost in fires so that a large percentage of those seen today date from the eighteenth and nineteenth centuries.

The Forbidden City is divided into two parts, one designed for the functions of government and the other residential. The complex lies north-south with the imperial buildings, bearing names associated with Confucian philosophy, all facing south along the axis. Perfectly symmetrical along the sides are the service buildings where the concubines, domestic servants, and approximately 200,000 eunuchs lived.

The main entrance to the Forbidden City, the Wumen (South Gate), is 117 feet tall. It is topped by five pavilions and has five archways. The center one was for regular use only by the emperor, by his wife on their wedding day, and by students on the day they received their diploma after passing their exams at Confucian school. The central pavilion above the gate was where the emperor dictated the laws which were then taken by emissaries to the Ministry of Rites, where a copy was made for each province in the empire.

Having crossed this monumental threshold, one enters a large court where the Golden Waters run. This is a river crossed by five bridges corresponding to the number of virtues in Confucianism. From the Taihemen (Gate of Supreme Harmony guarded by two bronze lions) one enters a court so large it can hold 100,000 people, the Taihedian (Pavilion of Supreme Harmony). This is the most impressive building in the entire city and, at 123 feet tall, was the highest in Beijing during the Ming and Qing dynasties. A symbol of imperial power, the main room, adorned with 72 columns decorated with motifs of dragons and clouds, was where state ceremonies were held and where the sovereign received homage on his birthday.

305

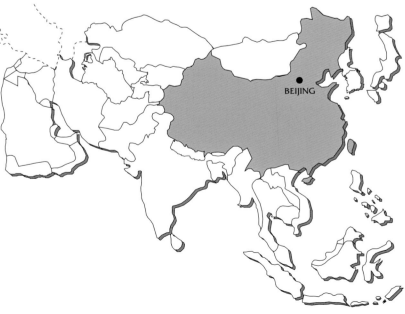

BEIJING

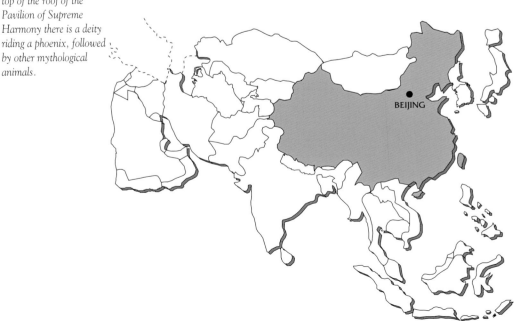

The side rooms were used for audiences and storing documents. One of these rooms, the Wenyuange (Pavilion of Literary Inspiration) was where the Sikuquanshu was held; with 36 volumes, this is oldest and largest encyclopedia in the world. In front of the Taihedian stand two enormous bronze vases, the only ones remaining from all of those that lined the perimeter of the building; they were filled with water to be used in the event of a fire. Another fire-prevention measure was represented by the bronze statues of five-taloned dragons inside, each weighing four and a half tons, which were supposed to encourage rain.

The Baohedian (Pavilion of the Conservation of Harmony) was the second most important building in the complex. Built in 1420 and rebuilt in 1625 and 1765, it combines elegant architecture with a surprisingly sophisticated hydraulic engineering system. A complicated system of drainage channels ensured that, on rainy days, water would gush from the mouth of each of the 1,412 marble dragons' heads on

the perimeter columns. The pavilion was used to hold court banquets.

Access to the residential section was marked by a horizontal marble stele 54 feet long, decorated with dragons playing with a pearl, an imperial symbol seen throughout the Forbidden City. The first residential

buildings are the Qianqinggong (Palace of Heavenly Harmony) and the Kunninggong (Palace of Terrestrial Tranquillity). In the first, built in 1420 as a private apartment for the emperor but later turned into a reception room, there are four enormous mirrors, which were very rare and precious during that period. It was in this building, in 1722 and 1785, that the emperor offered the Banquet of the Thousand Ancients to which people over 60 years of age were invited from all the provinces in the empire.

In the Kunninggong – the only example of Manchu architecture in the Forbidden City – it was customary for the emperor to spend his wedding night. The wedding chamber has walls painted red and decorated with the ideogram of double happiness. The *kang* (brick beds with a built-in heating system) are still in place. Next to the chamber is the room in which, each day, sacrifices to the gods were made.

Further on, one comes to the

306 top The entrance steps to the Baohedian (Pavilion of the Conservation of Harmony) are decorated

with a marble stela 52 feet long and ten feet wide. It weighs over 275 tons and is decorated with motifs of dragons and clouds.

306 center left Qianqingmen (the Gate of Heavenly Harmony) is the main entrance to the inner palace. During the Qing

Dynasty, the emperor, seated on a throne at the center of the gateway, would hear his advisors and render his decisions.

306 center right Qianqinggong (the Palace of Heavenly Harmony) was built in 1420 as a private apartment for the emperor but was later turned into a reception room. The imperial throne stands in the center of the room, surrounded by large mirrors and fine decorations.

306 bottom A detail of the stairway to the throne in the Palace of Heavenly Harmony. Note the superb carved balustrades and the incense burners that perfumed the emperor's rooms.

307 Two solid bronze lions guard the Gate of Heavenly Harmony, each of which has a decorated sphere under one paw to symbolize the power of the emperor and the unity of the lands he ruled.

308 bottom right and 309 right In addition to 20 or so buildings, the Imperial Garden was decorated with many lovely bronze sculptures featuring fantastic creatures or exotic animals, like the lion and elephant in this photograph.

309 left The Pavilion of Rain and Flowers in the Yuhuayuan (Imperial Garden) was built in 1417 during the Ming Dynasty. The imperial family's private garden covers an area of three acres.

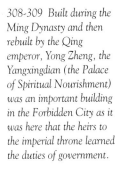

308-309 Built during the Ming Dynasty and then rebuilt by the Qing emperor, Yong Zheng, the Yangxingdian (the Palace of Spiritual Nourishment) was an important building in the Forbidden City as it was here that the heirs to the imperial throne learned the duties of government.

308 bottom left One of the entrances to the Imperial Garden where the Duixiushan (the Hill of the Collection of Beauty) was built. This was a small man-made hill from where it was possible to view the entire complex.

Yuhuayuan (Imperial Garden). It covers 129,000 square feet and is filled with attractive nooks and delicate buildings for the imperial family's leisure. Standing in front of the main pavilion is a pine tree that is thought to be 400 years old. It is a symbol of the harmony between the emperor and empress.

Of the other buildings in the residential section, the Yangxingdian (Palace of Spiritual Nourishment) stands out for its historical significance. This contained the private apartments of the emperor and it was here that on February 12,1912 Emperor Pu Yi abdicated following the coup d'état by Sun Yat Sen, but was given permission to live in the Forbidden City until 1924.

A short distance away, the Xiliugong (the Six Western Palaces) was where the concubines lived, and they are still furnished with the original items from the late Qing Dynasty. The adjacent Ningshougong (Pavilion of Tranquil Longevity) was built in 1689 as a scaled

down replica of the Forbidden City and holds a collection of 100,000 paintings. The Leshoutang (Palace of Joyful Longevity) contains a one-ton jade sculpture and an extraordinary mat measuring seven feet one inch by four feet seven inches that is woven from very thin strips of ivory. Among the many treasures on display, there are Ming jewels and furniture, Tibetan reliquaries, and silk paintings.

Many of the objects that belonged to the emperors were stolen by Sun Yat Sen's army and now form the nucleus of the National Museum of Taipei in Taiwan. In an attempt to replace them after the Maoist revolution, the administrators of the Forbidden City gathered precious objects from all over China. Above the main entrance to the complex they placed a giant picture of Mao Zedong; he smiles at the people and faces the symbol of modern Chinese power, Tiananmen Square.

The Summer Palace and Imperial Garden in Beijing

CHINA

Six miles north-west of Beijing
Registration: 1998
Criteria: C (i) (ii) (iii)

310 left Lying nine miles from Beijing, the Summer Palace covers an area of 726 acres. Although an imperial residence had been built on this site 800 years or so ago, it was the Empress Ci Xi who had the current building constructed between 1888 and 1889.

Evil, cruelty, and unbridled ambition: these were the characteristics that helped Xiao Lan, a fifth-rank concubine of Emperor Xianfeng, to become the most powerful woman in China. Little Orchid, the translation of her name, had the good fortune to give birth in 1855 to the emperor's only male child and heir. Upon the emperor's death six years later, she was given the title of widow-empress Ci Xi (Holy Mother) and began to exercise the ruthless power that she was to hold until 1908. At just

nineteen years of age, her son died, and Ci Xi, it seems, arranged for certain claimants to the throne to be poisoned and for another child to be designated heir to the title, her nephew Guangxu, whom she totally controlled for the rest of her life.

Since the revolution, Ci Xi has been viewed as a megalomaniac and a symbol of the evils and decadence of the empire. But her ambition led her to conceive the Yi He Yuan (Summer Palace), which is the most magnificent country estate in all of China. The history of this site, just north of Beijing, actually began 800 years ago when, during the Jin Dynasty, a palace was built there for the ruler. In 1750, the Qing emperor, Qian Long, had a lake excavated and a garden laid out; he called the garden the Hill of Longevity and presented it to his mother for her birthday. Destroyed in 1860 during the Opium Wars, it fell into ruin until Ci Xi decided to restore it with moneys meant for the navy and to make it her summer residence.

The Summer Palace covers an area of 726 acres, three quarters of which are covered by water. The estate was divided into three sections, and each had its own specific function: administration, accommodation, and "landscaping." The first sight the visitor sees on entering the site is a superb building crowned by a stone bas-relief of two dragons playing with a pearl, a symbol of the Qing Dynasty: it is the Renshoudian (Pavilion of Benevolence and Longevity). This was where Ci Xi performed her affairs of state while seated on a sandalwood throne. The front of the palace is lined with bronze sculptures of mythological animals. At the foot of the hill stands the Paiyundian (Pavilion of the Dispersing Clouds) built to hold the celebrations held on the empress' birthday. Two bronze lions and 12 Taihu stones in the form of animals from the Chinese zodiac stand in front of the pavilion. Halfway up the hill there is the octagonal Foxiangge (Tower of Buddhist Incense), which is the tallest building in the complex at 135 feet tall.

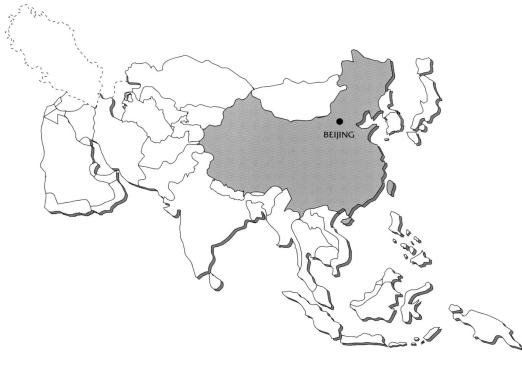

BEIJING

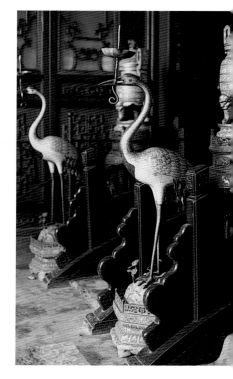

311 center right Originally called the Pavilion of Industrious Government, the Pavilion of Benevolence and Longevity is sumptuously decorated. Besides incense burners in various shapes, there are lovely calligraphic decorations, like those on the table behind the throne, and suspended sculptures, such as the phoenixes in the photograph.

311 bottom The Qing emperors performed their imperial duties in the Pavilion of Benevolence and Longevity. The large sandalwood throne is decorated with nine dragons and there are two peacock-feather fans beside it.

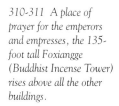

310-311 A place of prayer for the emperors and empresses, the 135-foot tall Foxiangge (Buddhist Incense Tower) rises above all the other buildings.

311 top Bronze dragons, phoenixes, and other imaginary creatures stand at the entrance to the Pavilion of Benevolence and Longevity. Originally built in 1750, the pavilion was rebuilt by Emperor Guangxu in 1890 after a fire.

312 top Built during the
reign of Qian Long, the
Bridge of Seventeen
Arches crosses the 492

feet of Lake Kunming. Five
hundred and forty-four white
marble lions decorate its
balustrades.

312 center A painting on
wood of a battle in the
Palace's long entrance
corridor. The greatness of
the Middle Kingdom was
expressed most eloquently
in the decorations in the
imperial residences.

312 bottom The Pavilion
of the Jade Sea was where
Emperor Guangxu was
held when Ci Xi had him
arrested during the early
twentieth century.

312-313 The
Qingyanfang (Marble
Boat) lies in the northwest
section of Kunming. Built
from wood painted white
and lying on a stone plinth,
it is a work with many
original touches.

The Marble Boat is anchored in the
Kunming, a man-made lake. It is made
from wood painted white and stands on a
stone platform. It is 118 feet long and
features small windows with colored glass
and a series of mirrors that reflect the
waves. It is said that Ci Xi, who liked to
admire the views from the boat, had it
made as a snub to the navy, which she
had defrauded for her personal pleasure.
The lake is crossed from east to west by
the Bridge of 17 Arches. The empress had
the Suzhoujie (Market Road) built on the
shore of the lake with shops and tea-

rooms where the court eunuchs, dressed as shopkeepers, provided the royal family with an imitation of daily life to substitute for the fact that they never went out among the ordinary people of the country.

Stretching from the hill to the lake is the longest corridor in China. Its 2,390 feet are interrupted at intervals by four octagonal pavilions, and on the walls of the corridor are hung 8,000 paintings.

In the residential section of the site lies the Xiequyuan (Garden of the Harmonious Interests) containing seven pavilions, five bridges on boats of lotus flowers, and various corridors. The Yulantang (Pavilion of the Jade Sea) became the prison where Emperor Guangxu was shut up for ten years after rebelling against Ci Xi. The Leshoutang (Pavilion of Joyful Longevity) is arranged around three courts and was Ci Xi's personal residence. The huge dining table where the empress chose her meal from the 128 dishes served to her by as many eunuchs still stands in the central court. The Leshoutang was the first place in China to have had electricity installed.

With its gardens that change color throughout the year, the Summer Palace was exclusively for the use of the imperial family until 1924 when Pu Yi, "the last emperor," was stripped of his title. Pu Yi had come to the throne following the death – on the same day – of Ci Xi and Guangxu. Since that time, the estate has been a public park.

Taishan
CHINA

PROVINCE OF SHANDONG
REGISTRATION: 1987
CRITERIA: C (I) (II) (III) (IV) (V) (VI); N (III)

314-315 Dedicated to the Taoist religion, Taishan is the most venerated sacred mountain in China. The 6,000 steps that lead to the peak are lined by 22 different groups of temples, and thousands of stones have been carved with verses by China's most famous poets.

314 bottom left Pilgrims on Heaven's Way leading to the top of Taishan. Mentioned in chronicles since the second millennium B.C., to believers, the mountain is not just the home of the gods but is itself a divinity.

An old legend says that Taishan was born from the throes of a dying dragon. His last sighs shook the land, his bones became the rocky pinnacles, his blood fed the rivers and streams, and his green scales were transformed into the trees and grass that cover the mountain. It is said that Taishan, at an altitude of 5, 069 feet, was chosen as the home of the god Tai, son of the Emperor of the Sky, hence the name: Tai + shan, meaning "mountain." From this place, the god listened to the prayers of the humans and interceded with his father on their behalf.

Taishan is the most important of the five sacred mountains in China. It lies to the east, in the province of Shandong, which is bounded by the Yellow River and the East China Sea; consequently, it is the first province in China to be blessed by the rays of the rising sun. In addition, east symbolizes spring, and therefore rebirth and fertility.

The first emperor to bestow official recognition on Taishan as a place of pilgrimage was Wu Di in the Han Dynasty (206 B.C. - A.D. 220). However, the origin of the sacredness of the mountain dates back 3,000 years to when 72 emperors of various dynasties made ceremonial and sacrificial pilgrimages here and left important architectural traces of their passing. The route - the first section of which is a paved road and the rest formed by 6,000 steps - is a sort of open air museum of the Chinese civilization and the Buddhist, Taoist, and Confucian faiths. There are 22 groups of temples, 97 archaeological ruins, 819 commemorative stelae, and roughly 1,800 texts carved in the rock. Some of these texts – grouped in the Stone Sutra Valley, at the mid-point of the route, and in Moya Bei, on the summit – are verses by the most famous Chinese poets and philosophers, such as Libai, Dufu, and above all, Confucius, who was born in 551 B.C. in Qufu, a short distance from Taishan.

At the start of the stairway that leads to the top stands the Yitian Men (the Heavenly Gate) with a stone arch that signals the exact point at which Confucius began his pilgrimage. The most important buildings that stand in the first section are the seventeenth century Temple of the Red Gate, a complex with purplish-red walls venerated by both Buddhist and Taoist faiths, and the Tower of the 10,000 Immortals, where the pilgrim emperors would receive the homage of the court. From the Zhongtianmen (the Middle Gate), one reaches the Pavilion of the Five Pines that commemorates the trees that gave shelter to emperor Qin Shi Huangdi during a violent storm in 219 B.C. In order to give thanks to the trees, the sovereign elevated them to the role of fifth-level imperial functionaries. From here, the ascent becomes more difficult. The next stopping places are the Arch of Immortality and, after 12 bends in the path, the Nantianmen, the Southern Heavenly Gate, which is framed by two attractive, almost vertical, rock formations covered with ideograms. The view can be seen from the Temple of the Blue Cloud, which was built around the year 1000 during the Song Dynasty. Venerated in particular by women wishing to bear children, the temple is a magnificent building with bronze-covered ornaments and tiles.

There are many monuments at the top, including the Temple of the Jade Emperor, which has a large bronze statue of a Taoist divinity, the Pavilion, from which one can watch the rising of the sun, and the Stela Without Words. The stela was so-named

because legend tells that the emperor Wu Di preferred not to have anything carved in the rock because he was unable to find a man wise enough to describe suitably in words the sacredness of Taishan.

Besides the deep religious and cultural importance that Taishan holds for the Chinese people, the mountain and the surrounding area is of great beauty. Its surface is marked with 112 pinnacles, 98 gullies, 18 caves, 58 unusually shaped rocks, 102 mountain torrents and valleys, 64 springs, and 56 pools and waterfalls. In addition, Taishan is home to 989 species of plant and 200 species of animal, of which 122 are birds.

Even Mao Zedong climbed Taishan during the Long March as the sun rose. It is said that he remarked, as he admired the landscape, "The East is red," a phrase that the Chinese consider prophetic. But the secularism of the People's Republic did not slow the tradition of pilgrimage that, each spring, brings millions of Chinese to the sacred mountain.

315 center right The main pavilion in the Temple of the Blue Cloud was built during the Song Dynasty. From 1754 until 1911, an imperial envoy would visit the temple on the eighteenth day of the fourth month each year with offerings from the emperor to win the favor of the gods.

315 top right Framed by two rock formations covered with ideograms, the Southern Heavenly Gate marks the start of the last section of the climb, shortly before reaching the Temple of the Blue Cloud.

BEIJING
TAISHAN

The Historic Ensemble of Potala Palace in Lhasa
CHINA

AUTONOMOUS REGION OF TIBET
REGISTRATION: 1994, 2000
(EXTENDED TO JOKHANG TEMPLE), 2001
(EXTENDED TO NORBULINGKA)
CRITERIA: C (I) (IV) (VI)

316-317 A view of Potala Palace at an altitude of 12,140 feet on the "roof of the world." Built in the seventeenth century, the immense complex is 13 stories high, contains over 1,000 rooms, and has a total of 3,900,000 square feet of floor space.

316 bottom One of the courts at the top of the Potala overlooked by the ancient lodgings of the senior Buddhist prelates. Note the yellow drapes and roofing which is the sacred color of Tibetan Lamaism.

On the night of March 16, 1959, twenty-four-year-old Tenzin Gyatso, the fourteenth Dalai Lama, fled Lhasa over the high Himalayan trails. He barely escaped capture by the Communist Chinese forces, which that very morning had begun their bloody repression of the revolt by the Tibetan population. The fighting lasted for four days and culminated with the shelling of Potala Palace, the symbol of Tibetan Buddhism.

Since then, the Dalai Lama, the spiritual leader of Tibet, has been in exile in Dharamsala, India, and along with him, 120,000 Tibetans who were forced to leave their homeland on the roof of the world. The struggle he led for the independence of Tibet, in order to preserve the historical, cultural, and religious heritage of his people, won him the Nobel Peace Prize in 1989. Today, although full sovereignty is still a dream, China has nevertheless taken important steps in acknowledging the enormous value of the culture of this population. It has recently completed the renovation of the Potala Palace. The work, which took five years to complete and cost 6.4 million dollars, was the largest investment ever made by the Beijing government for the recuperation of historical buildings.

The history of Potala began with the brotherhood between this mountain population and China. During the seventh century, King Songtsen Gampo built a palace on the peak of the Red Mountain, which dominates Lhasa from an altitude of 12,140 feet, in honor of the Chinese princess given to him in marriage by one of the emperors of the Tang Dynasty. This union also introduced Buddhism to Tibet.

The palace was named Potala after the mountain in southern India that was the home of the *bodhisattva* Avalokiteshwar, the patron saint of Tibet.

Very few rooms remain of the ancient palace, and they are incorporated in the enormous complex built by the fifth Dalai Lama, Srong-brtsan-sgam-po, starting in 1645. This impressive, maze-like building boasts 1,000 rooms, 10,000 temples and shrines, and 200,000 statues. The palace, which is divided into 13 intersecting stories, rises to a height of 384 feet, and its architecture reflects the Buddhist concept of reincarnation, the cycle of life and death that culminates in enlightenment.

Potala Palace is made of stone, clay, and wood. The load-bearing walls were injected with molten copper to protect the structure from natural disasters. It has been prophesied that one day Tibet will be

317 top right One of the portals in the Potrang Marpo (Red Palace). Unlike the adjacent White Palace, the Red Palace mostly consists of temples and rooms containing tomb stupa of the Dalai Lamas.

317 center right Each of the doors in the Potala is painted with red lacquer and decorated with richly decorated shutters and studs.

317 top left This fourteenth-century tangka (a traditional painting on silk usually commissioned by monasteries) shows a demon from the Tibetan Buddhist cosmogony.

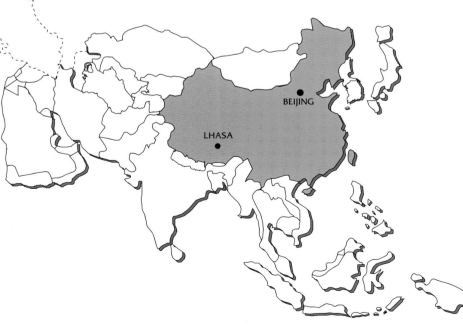

318-319 The famous golden roofs of the Red Palace were built in the eighteenth century. The largest room in this extraordinary building is the Western Audience Room with 7,800 square feet of space.

318 bottom Entirely lined with gold, this is the commemorative stupa in the mausoleum dedicated to the eleventh Dalai Lama. The Red Palace contains the remains of eight Dalai Lamas.

319 top The mausoleum of each Dalai Lama contains a stupa and a statue of him blessing the faithful. The Dalai Lama is the supreme Tibetan religious authority.

319 bottom left A corridor in the Red Palace. It took 7,000 laborers and 1,500 artists and craftsmen to build the palace between 1690 and 1694.

319 bottom right The entrance to the mausoleum of the fifth Dalai Lama, Ngawang Lozang Gyatso, who was responsible for the construction of the Potala.

struck by an apocalyptic flood but Potala Palace will float on the water, thanks to the two towers that frame it. According to another legend, in order to avoid any interruptions to the construction of the palace, when the Dalai Lama passed away his dignitaries concealed his death for 14 years, claiming that he had retired to meditate.

Potala is divided into the Red Palace and the larger White Palace. The former holds the meeting rooms, 35 temples, four meditation rooms, and seven mausoleums. The mausoleums house the embalmed remains of the fifth to the thirteenth Dalai Lamas, with the exception of the sixth, in dome-like structures known as *chorten*. The *chorten* of the fifth Dalai

Lama is 66 feet high and is covered with 8,140 pounds of gold studded with diamonds, pearls, turquoise, agates, and coral. The monastery of Namygal is located in the western part of Potala Palace, whereas the White Palace contains a library with thousands of books and prayer scrolls, storerooms, and the former printworks.

In 1751, the seventh Dalai Lama started building Norbulingka, "the Park of the Treasure," for his summer residence. Since then, other buildings have been constructed in this area covering 99 acres and surrounded by gardens. The most recent one, built in 1922, is an intriguing blend of traditional architecture and Western comfort.

320 top and center right
The faces and features of grotesque and symbolic animals decorate every corner of the Jokhang. Above, a tiger with the symbol of infinity; center right, the head of a golden crocodile.

320 center left
Construction of the Jokhang was begun in 647 by the two wives of King Songtsen Gampo. The first was Chinese and brought to Lhasa the sacred statue of Jowo Sakyamuni; the second was Nepalese and ordered construction of the temple to house the statue.

320 bottom left In order to earn merit with the Buddha, Tibetans perform the kora, a ritual sacred walk around the edge of the Jokhang.

This monumental complex that encompasses Tibetan spirituality is completed by Jokhang Temple, located in the center of ancient Lhasa. It was also built in the seventh century by King Songtsen Gampo to hold the statue of the divine Jowo Sakyamuni, and even today thousands of pilgrims continue to flock to it at all hours of the day and night. Rebuilt during the era of the fifth Dalai Lama, it is considered the most important temple in Tibet, and it safeguards many sacred relics, silk paintings (*tanka*), frescoes, and ancient musical instruments. It also holds a large vase, the *bumpa*, used by the Buddhist wise men to decide who will be the *Kundun*, the elect, or in other words, the reincarnation of the Dalai Lama.

320 bottom right The statue of the divine Jowo Sakyamuni, the oldest and most venerated Tibetan image of the Buddha. Kept on the ground floor of the Jokhang, it is three feet high, made from an alloy of gold, silver, copper, zinc, and iron, and decorated with precious stones.

320-321 The Jokhang is a majestic, three-story building of rooms and chapels. Although its origin dates from the seventh century, much of the existing structure was built in the eighteenth and nineteenth centuries. Many of its statues were produced in the late twentieth century during restoration made necessary by the Chinese invasion in 1959.

321 top The large paved area in front of the Jokhang is where the faithful gather each morning to spend the day praying, enveloped by clouds of incense.

Changgyong P'ango: the Depositories of the Tripitaka Koreana Woodblocks in Haeinsa Temple

MOUNT GAYA, PROVINCE
OF GYEONGSANG-DO
REGISTRATION: 1995
CRITERIA: C (IV) (VI)

REPUBLIC OF KOREA

The story goes that, during the Korean war, many soldiers took advantage of the hospitality of the monks and hid in Haeinsa Temple, and so the order was given to bomb the sacred buildings. However, once over the target, the pilot was so impressed by the beauty of the temples in the countryside that he refused to carry out the order. The hapless pilot was court-martialed and imprisoned, but after the war, he was rehabilitated, decorated, and treated like a national hero.

The name Haeinsa is taken from the Avatamsaka *sutra* that means "reflection on a calm sea," to which the wisdom of the Buddha was compared. The temple

over a period of 15 years, this second set consists of 81,258 wood blocks, hand-carved so they can be used for printing, held in 6,802 volumes. Each tablet is formed by 23 lines of 14 characters, thus containing a total of 52 million ideograms.

Based on the Chinese *Tripitaka* published in 983 during the Song Dynasty, this version is the oldest and most complete collection of the thoughts of the Buddha. In addition to its religious value, it is considered an immense artistic treasure, given the perfection of its calligraphy and syntactical precision; these qualities were in great part due to the efforts of the master, Sugi, who

322 top right Dragons are a central feature of mythology throughout the Far East and adorn the base of steps that lead to the temple.

322 bottom left The Changgyong P'ango (the two long buildings built to control the internal humidity levels) contain the 81,258 wooden blocks that make up the Tripitaka Koreana *(three collections) of the teachings of the Buddha.*

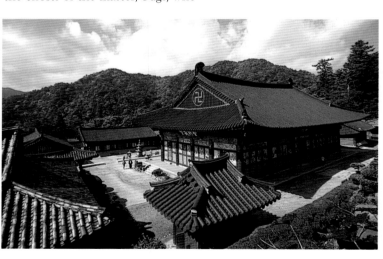

was built in 802 on the slopes of Mount Gaya by two enlightened monks, Suneung and Ijong, but its name has been associated with events that took place at a later date. In 1236, King Gojong of the Goryeo Dynasty decided to rewrite the tablets of the *Tripitaka Koreana* – the "three collections" of all the sutras that contain the teachings of the Buddha – which had been destroyed during the Mongol invasion of 1232. Completed

corrected any errors or omissions.

The excellent condition of the *Tripitaka Koreana* printing blocks is the result of the meticulous care they have received over the centuries from the monks of Haeinsa Temple, where the collection was placed in 1398. Originally, the wood blocks were placed in the temple of Jicheonsa, near the south door so that they might be sheltered from the rain. Though they had been treated for

humidity before and after carving, this was not enough to keep them in the state they exist in today. The turning point came at the end of the fifteenth century when King Sejo decided to make 50 prints from them and to renew much of Haeinsa Temple, adding a storage area where the tablets could be kept without risking damage. On Sejo's death, the project was completed by his two sisters-in-law, Insu and Inhye.

The *Tripitaka Koreana* storage area is comprised of two buildings over 197 feet long, connected by short corridors to form a rectangle. Built in the graceful Joseon style, the two buildings – called Changgyeong P'ango – stand almost 26 feet tall, and the walls have two rows of windows of different dimensions that were designed to provide ventilation. As the temple is sheltered by the mountainside, the windows facing uphill are smaller in order to hinder the formation of condensation.

Each room contains two long rows of shelving, each with five levels, on which the tablets are positioned vertically. A space on the side of each tablet allows the air to flow freely, and the earthen floor is covered by salt, coal, and lime to absorb excessive humidity during the rainy season, and to keep it at the right level during the dry season. Finally, the roofs are made from earth and tiles arranged over wooden beams to protect the interior from large changes in temperature.

What remains a mystery is why birds never perch on the roof, and why the wood has never been attacked by insects. Whatever the reasons, the tablets are still in useable condition. They were last employed between 1963 and 1968 when 13 prints were made of each, four of which were given to Japan, one to the University of California, one to Australia, and two to Great Britain. The rest are held in Korea where the magnificent legacy of the *Tripitaka Koreana* continues to be conserved.

322 bottom right A view of the temple of Haeinsa, whose origin dates from the year 802. Built on the slopes of Mount Gaya, it is one of Korea's three most important Buddhist monasteries.

322-323 The duty of the Haeinsa monks is to preserve the Tripitaka Koreana *wooden blocks. This legacy is of immense historical and religious value yet it remains inaccessible to most Koreans because it is written in traditional Chinese. Since 1992, a group of monks has worked on translating and transcribing the sacred texts on computer, but the work is slow and far from completion.*

323 bottom This is the altar of the temple dedicated to Suneung and Ijong, the monks who founded the temple on Mount Gaya.

The Historic Monuments of Ancient Kyoto

JAPAN

ISLAND OF HONSHU, PREFECTURE OF KYOTO
REGISTRATION: 1994
CRITERIA: C (II) (IV)

324 top Constructed before the capital was moved to Kyoto in A.D. 794, Kamowake-ikzuchi (Kamigamo Temple) was built to worship the guardian spirit of the powerful Kamo family.

324 bottom The large statue of the Buddha Amithaba in the Pavilion of the Phoenix in Byodoin Temple is surrounded by 52 wooden sculptures of bodhisattva playing instruments and dancing.

Around the year 1600, the powerful *shogun* family, the Tokugawa, began to transfer political power from Kyoto to Edo, though Kyoto (the name means "capital city") remained the seat of imperial power until 1868 when Emperor Meiji moved the Dajokan (Great Council of government administration) to Edo; this city then took the name of Tokyo (western capital).

The city of Kyoto, which lost its role as the political and economic center of Japan, had been founded eleven centuries earlier as a result of the subtle diplomatic shifts that took place between the great empires of the East. Piqued by the beauty of the capital city, Chang'an (present-day Xian), of his Chinese rival, the Japanese emperor, Kanmu, decided to move his court from Nagaokakyo to a new city that he decided to build in the region of Yamasiro. Thus, in A.D. 794, Heiankyo, or more simply, Kyoto, was established along three sides of the mountains in the south of the island of Honshu.

The layout of the city over nine square miles was an exact imitation of the Chinese capital, with a grid of streets that divided the city into more than 1,200 districts of identical size. Closed off by an embankment that was supposed to offer the city protection, its great southward-facing Rashomon gateway opened onto the main street, the Suzaku. The imperial palace stood at the far end of this street. The complex did not just contain the emperor's residence, but was also the seat of the government and related buildings. The original plans for Kyoto had included space for two markets, one for the craftsmen and the other for the merchants. Noble families were conceded plots of land in accordance with their rank. This first attempt at urban planning formed the basis of the city for the entire Heian period, until the end of the twelfth century, and it is still visible in the pattern of the streets, even though Kyoto suffered fires and battles that destroyed it almost completely.

The city still has elements dating from its foundation such as Shimogamo Temple, dedicated to the city's patron deities. It is said that the site of the city had been discovered by two gods, Kamo taketsu-no-mikoto and Tamayori-hime, who were worshipped in the 53 buildings that constitute the temple. Dating from even

324-325 Built as a civil building at the end of the tenth century, Byodoin Temple was transformed into a sanctuary in 1052. It centers on the Ho-oh-do (Pavilion of the Phoenix), which is a reproduction of the heavenly palace of Amithaba in the Pure Land.

earlier than the Heian era is Kamigamo Temple. This temple was built in an zone of gardens and includes an area located between the first and second *torii* (the characteristic doors in Japanese temples) where thoroughbred horses to be used in sacred ceremonies were raised.

The most important legacies of the Heian period are the Byodoin and Daigoji temples. The first was built on the west bank of the river Uji and was the residence of a noble who, in 998, donated it to the functionary Fujiwara-no-Michinaga. After the latter's death in 1052, his son wished to turn it into a place of worship in memory of his father. The beautiful Ho-oh-do (Phoenix Room) features a reproduction of the heavenly palace of Amithaba in the Pure Land; its side corridors have roofs adorned with two phoenixes whose wings are spread ready for flight. Inside, the large statue of the Buddha Amithaba is surrounded by 52 images of *bodhisattva* dancing and playing musical instruments. Partially reconstructed after the sixteenth century, Daigoji Temple boasts a five-story pagoda that was completed in 952 and is the oldest monument in Kyoto to have survived intact.

325 top right Comprising more than 100 pavilions, Daigoji Temple is dominated by a five-story pagoda built in 952 by Emperor Murakami, which is the oldest monument in the city. Most of the other buildings date from the sixteenth century.

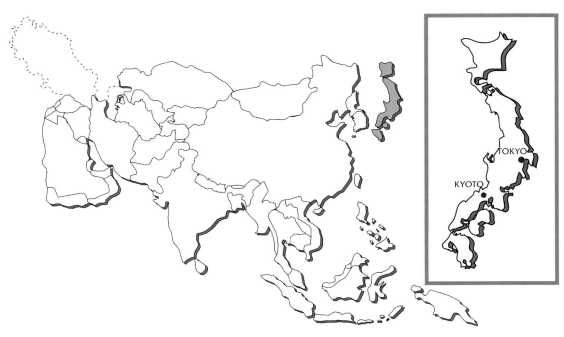

325 bottom right A detail of the elaborate carvings on the roof of the pagoda in Daigoji Temple. During the Onin War in the fifteenth century, the other buildings of the temple were destroyed in two fires.

The Toji (Temple of the East) also dates from the foundation of the city and was built in 796 to bring down divine protection on the city. Kiyomizu Temple was built two years later on the initiative of an influential general on the spot where the hermitage of the ascetic Enchin had stood. Hieizan Enryakuji Temple was founded in 788 by the Buddhist monk Saicho, who

gathered a religious community around him. Lastly, Emperor Uda ordered the construction of Ninnaji Temple, later known as Omuro Palace, in 888. The people placed in charge of the building were monks from the imperial family, and this tradition lasted until the Meiji Dynasty. However, all these buildings have suffered serious damage over the centuries, and most of them are the result of wide-ranging rebuilding.

The Heian period also saw the flourishing of extraordinary cultural centers in Kyoto that laid down the foundations for Japanese poetry, literature, and religion. In

905, the emperor ordered Ki-no-Tsurayuki to compile the *Kokin-waka-shu*, a collection of classical poems that indicated the way for works like *The Tales of Genji*, *The Happy Prince* (the first novel in history), and *The Pillow Book*. This was an intimate diary in which Shei Shonagon, a female courtier, described her amorous encounters. Two Buddhist cults, the Tendai and the Shingon, developed respectively in the Enryakuji and Toji temples.

The eras of the Kamakura (1185-1333), Muromachi (1333-1573), and Momoyana (1573-1598) dynasties were times of civil wars and cultural upheaval. The Zen, Jodo, Jodo Shin, and Nichiren schools of Buddhism made their first appearance. Kozanji Temple was built during the Kamakura period on the mountainside by the monk Myoe in a place suited to contemplation. Saihoji Temple (Temple of the Mosses) was built for the 120 species of moss that grew on its walls and roof. The temple also included Zen gardens in which rocks and sand were set out in harmonious balance. In 1339, Tenryuji Temple was built by the Zen master Muso Kokushi for Kyoto's first *shogun*, Ashikaga Takauji. The building was supposed to honor the memory of Emperor Godaigo and was founded on the site of a former imperial residence. Its garden lay behind the Hojo, one of the buildings in the complex, and was designed with pools of water surrounded by flowerbeds, integrating aristocratic traditions with Zen style, in which the forms and colors of the garden alter with the seasons.

The Muromachi period saw the

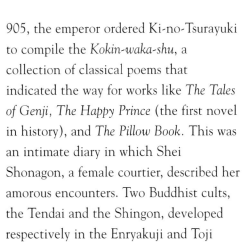

326 top left Founded in 796, the Toji (Temple of the East) was built to supplicate the gods to protect the new capital. At the end of the Heian period (twelfth century), the Buddhist Shingon cult flourished.

326 bottom left According to legend, in 778 the monk Enchin built a small chapel where, 20 years later, Kiyomizu Temple would later stand. Shogun Iemitsu Tokugawa rebuilt many of the buildings standing today during the period 1631-1633.

326 center top A recurrent motif in oriental figurative art, this dragon is part of the Todoroki Torii, one of the entrances to Kiyomizu Temple. Lined with copper, the sculpture is also a fountain and water jets from the creature's mouth.

326 top right In addition to its main pavilion and an elegant three-story pagoda, Kiyomizu Temple comprises beautiful gardens.

326-327 Completed in 1603 and renovated in 1626, Nijo Castle consists of two buildings, Honmaru and Ninomaru, the rooms of which are decorated with paintings and carved wood panels.

construction of Rokuonji Temple with a golden pagoda in 1397, the Jishoji Temple with a silver pavilion that contains the statue of the venerable Avalokiteshwar, and Ryoanji Temple with a rock garden in 1450. This was the period in which Kyoto developed arts like Noh theater, tea ceremonies, and *ikebana*, the art of flower arrangement developed by Ikenobo Senkei in 1462 to adorn the home of a noble family.

The Onin War (1467-1477) resulted in destruction for much of the city, and the following century was marked by

same brutal expedient as his predecessors: the physical elimination of all rival claimants. In the few short years of his rule, Hideyoshi began the transfer of the temples that had survived the destruction to the Teramachi District of the city. This project was continued by Iesayu, who also completed construction of the massive Nijo Castle. Completed in 1603, the castle was where most of the important events until 1867 took place, when the *shogun* Tokugawa Yoshinobu restored administrative power to the imperial family. Nijo Castle has two sections, the

to Tokyo, the Edo period (from 1600 to 1868) was marked by peace and stability, and Kyoto flourished once more as a cultural and commercial center. The *shogun* Tokugawa Iemitsu rebuilt many buildings, including Kiyomizu Temple between 1631 and 1633. In 1644, he built Japan's largest pagoda in Toji Temple; it has five stories and stands 187 feet high.

Fortunately spared from the bombing raids of World War II, Kyoto remained an island in twentieth-century Japan. To celebrate its 12 centuries of existence in 1994, large festivals in seventeenth-

internecine struggles from which the Momoyama clan emerged victorious. In 1573, Oda Nobunaga took power, followed by Toyotomi Hideyoshi and Tokugawa Ieyasu. The last of the three succeeded in restoring stability using the

Honmaru (main building) and the magnificent Ninomaru Palace. Decorated in Momoyama style, both buildings feature sophisticated architecture and superb ornamentation.

Despite the transfer of political power

century costume and events that commemorated the history of the city were organized. Entering one of the tea rooms marked by the slow rhythm of tradition, one gets the feeling that Tokyo never became the country's capital.

Himeji-jo
JAPAN

PREFECTURE OF HYOGO,
ISLAND OF HONSHU
REGISTRATION: 1993
CRITERIA: C (I) (IV)

In Japan it is known as the *Shirasagijo*, the white heron, because its walls are embellished with white stuccoes and the three towers around the central body make it resemble a bird ready to take flight. In fact, the castle of Himeji (Himeji-jo) was only built for purposes of defense, and the white stucco was used because it has remarkable fire-resistant properties. Like other Japanese buildings of the same period, Himeji-jo was mostly built from wood, and the use of stucco helped to ward off fire as well as giving the structures greater solidity.

The small city of Himeji stands on a plain 31 miles to the west of Osaka in an area that has been inhabited for over 10,000 years. A few temples from the eighth and tenth centuries indicate the presence of Buddhism, but the city's greatest development took place during Japan's feudal period. The first fortress was built in 1346 by the governor of the district of Harima, Akamatsu Sadanori, on the top of Himeyana hill to protect the city from

328-329 The white stuccoes on the walls of Himeji Castle have earned it the name Shirasagijo (White Heron). The daitenshukaku (main tower) in the center of the castle, 151 feet high, overlooks the other buildings.

329 top Squeezed by the three defensive walls, the buildings in Himeji-jo seem piled on top of one another. The maze of secret passageways, blind alleys, and corridors designed to confuse one's sense of direction reveal the military purpose of the complex.

attack by nearby warlords.

In 1580, the plain construction was altered by Hideyoshi Toyotomi and given a gentler image. He built a three-level *tenshukaku* (tower-castle) to be used as a base for military expeditions in southern Japan. The work was completed by his successor, Ikeda Terumasa. The son-in-law of a warlord who had severely tested national unity by conquering much of the south of the country at the expense of the Toyotomi, Terumasa undertook the ambitious project of rebuilding the castle on the model of the residence where Emperor Azuchi lived. Aware of the importance of a siege-proof fort, in 1601 he began a nine-year project to add an imposing five-storey *tenshukaku* to the structure, thus giving Himeji-jo its current appearance. Historians of Japanese architecture have estimated that to complete the 83 structures (the complex covers an area of 450 by 410 feet) and its protective measures, between 25 and 50 million working days were required.

Terumasa's castle is formed by a main tower, the *daitenshukaku*, 151 feet high, and three smaller side towers called *shotenshukaku*. In Japan, the *tenshukaku* had the same function as towers in contemporary European castles. In times of peace it was the residence of the *Daimyo* (feudal lord) and served to vaunt the prestige of the dynasty, while in time of war it was a lookout and a storage place for arms and foodstuffs. In addition to wood and stucco, it was constructed from tiles and metal, to reinforce the load-bearing structures. The typical features of the *fusuma* (sliding doors) and *tatami* (floor matting) were not seen in the residential section. The surrounding buildings provided accommodation for the soldiers and staff.

The most interesting aspects of Himeji-jo are its military function and the skill with which its defensive features were created: for example, the three concentric ditches built to slow the advance of the enemy and the 49-foot high walls that prevented a view of the building to those who got close. There are 84 fortified doors, numerous passages, corridors, and blind alleys meant to confuse those not familiar with the complex. Openings in the walls allow the use of *ishiotoshi* (catapults), *hazama* (slits) so that soldiers with bows or firearms could shoot unimpeded, and *musha kakushi* where defenders could hide while the enemy walked into a trap.

Himeji-jo is Japan's best-conserved medieval castle. It is not just a monument to the exceptional ability of its builders, but in a certain sense, represents the height of the Japanese concept of harmony between man and nature. The solidity and functionality of the interiors, both militarily and residentially, merge seamlessly and counterbalance the aesthetic refinement of the decorations to create an unmatched architectural symbiosis.

329 bottom A decorative detail of the roof of Himeji-jo's main tower. The complexity of the project required nine years of work by thousands of laborers.

Itsukushima Shinto Shrine

JAPAN

ISLAND OF MIYAJIMA,
PREFECTURE OF HIROSHIMA
REGISTRATION: 1996
CRITERIA: C (I) (II) (IV) (VI)

330 top Although it is missing several elements typical of Japanese temples, the Shinto sanctuary of Itsukushima is extraordinarily elegant architecturally and is a symbol of Japanese aesthetics. The covered corridors that connect the buildings have been declared a national monument.

The four vermilion columns of the Otorii, which stand in front of Itsukushima Temple in the bay of Miyajima, are famous throughout the world as a symbol of Japanese tradition. Built in 1874-1875 from camphor wood taken from the forests of Kyushu and

Shikoku, the Otorii stands 52 feet tall about 650 feet away from the main building in the waterborne religious complex.

Since antiquity, the island of Miyajima – little more than 19 square miles of land off the bay of Hiroshima – was considered a sacred place of the gods and was even worshipped as a divinity itself. The idea of a temple on the water was inspired by the mythical Rygu-jo, the "palace of the Dragon," in which the god of the sea was worshipped. Or perhaps it was suggested by the Buddhist paradise – the Gokuraku Jodo – that the dead had to reach at the end of a boat ride, a recurring image in both eastern and western tradition.

Whatever the reason, it is said that the first lake temple was built in the bay in 593 by Saeki Kuramoto, but the first mention of Itsukushima Temple, together with other important religious centers, is made in the *Nihon Koki* (Notes on Japan) from the year 881. During the time of Taira-no-Kiyomori, a famous governor of the province of Aki in 1146, the temple was frequently visited by the members of the Heike clan, a family destined to play an important role in the imperial court. In 1168, thanks to large donations by the nobility, construction began of the main temple, and a complex of 37 internal buildings and 19 external buildings that face onto the two sides of the bay that were to accommodate the devoted who came to the site to meditate. These buildings were constructed in *shinden* style and still provide an excellent example of the popular architecture during the Heian period, the same style used in the imperial palace in Kyoto.

With the fall of the Heike, the Genji clan rose to power. They were fully respectful of the religious complex built by their predecessors, and Itsukushima Temple continued to prosper despite suffering damage in two fires in 1207 and 1233. In that period, the sanctuaries were repeatedly restored, though without altering the overall design. In 1325, the temple was half destroyed by a typhoon, therefore restoration work gave it the appearance it still has today.

In the Kamakura period, Japan entered the era of its civil war. The prestige of Itsukushima Temple began to decline progressively until the famous place of worship of the emperors fell into a state of abandon. This situation lasted until 1555 when Moti Motonari won the battle of Itsukushima and decided to return the complex to its former splendor by rebuilding the main temple and secondary sanctuaries. He also built a Noh theater and new bridges and roads. Toyotomi Hideyoshi, another important general of the same period, established a library in Akokuji Temple (one of the smaller buildings) to hold Buddhist sutras.

The Henden – the main temple – was built in 1571 in *Ichiju-ryonagare* style. The building is square, roughly 79 feet long per side, but curiously, in Japanese tradition it measures eight by nine ma: a ma is a nominal unit of measurement that represents the space between two columns, and consequently, varies depending on the number of columns arranged within a certain distance. The roof is built in *shinden* style but lacks certain features usually seen in Japanese temples, for example, *chigi* (decorative projections in the shape of horns), and was built from cypress branches covered by decorative tiles.

Opposite the Henden stands the Hirabutai, the long bridge that leads to the Hitasaki, the front lantern where the gods of the temple would arrive and leave from during the musical festival of Kangensai. Each year in mid-July the colorfully decorated sacred boats cross the gigantic Otorii, while musicians and dancers on board celebrate the sacred ritual from classical antiquity.

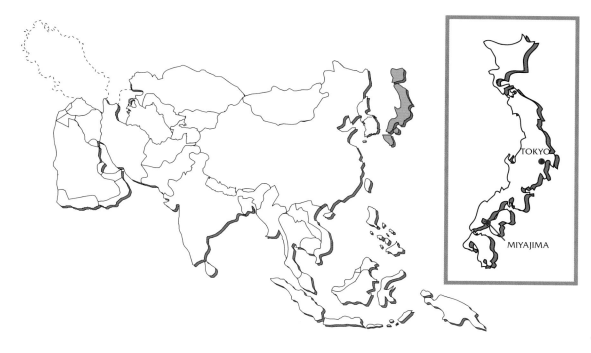

330 bottom An early
lake temple on support piles
was built in Miyajima Bay
in the sixth century, but
most of the buildings seen
today are from the twelfth
to fourteenth centuries,
except for the Henden
(main temple) from the
sixteenth.

331 top Otorii (ceremonial
doorways) are to be found
throughout Japan, but
Itsukushima's is the most
impressive and best known.
Situated in the middle of the
bay and exposed to the
current and weather, it has
had to be rebuilt several
times. The last Otorii,
made from camphor wood,
was erected in 1875.

331 bottom The temple,
built over water, was
inspired by the legendary
Rygu-jo (Palace of the
Dragon) in which the god
of the sea was glorified.
For this reason, dragons
are a recurring decorative
motif in the temple.

Luang Prabang

THE PEOPLE'S DEMOCRATIC REPUBLIC OF LAOS

REGISTRATION: 1995
CRITERIA: C (II) (IV) (V)

In the second half of the sixteenth century, the Lan Xang (Kingdom of a Million Elephants) was fighting a fierce battle against neighboring Siam when the fortunes of war turned against them. When the Siamese came close to threatening the capital, the king, Sai Setthathirath, moved his statues of the Buddha to a cave not far from the city. The tradition at the time was that anyone seen removing the statues would meet a nasty fate.

The Pak Ou is a large limestone cliff that hangs over the junction of the rivers Nam Ou and Mekong (the Mother of the Waters). The two large caves in the cliff are the location of more than 4,000 statues of the Buddha that have been placed there since Sai Setthathirath transferred his own from his palace. The assembled statues are a tribute from the faithful to the memory of the king and the salvation of the country. A few miles south, Luang Prabang can be seen on a large bend on the river.

Legend says that the original name of the city, Muang Xua, was the same as that of its first ruler who reigned there around the eighth century. In 1353, King Fa Ngum founded the first Lao kingdom and changed the name to Muang Xieng Thong (City of Gold). A few years later, Fa Ngum changed the name to Luang Prabang in honor of the Phra Bang, a gold statue of the Buddha weighing 117 pounds, originally from Ceylon, that he had received as a gift from the Khmer kings. A fervent Buddhist, Fa Ngum began the tradition of building temples with annexed schools and *wat* (monasteries) with the result that at Luang Prabang 66

temples were built, 32 of which have survived to the present day.

The spiritual center of the city is the Wat Xieng Thong because of its position on a hill overlooking the confluence of the Mekong and Nam Khan rivers. The Wat Xieng Thong was built in 1560 by King Sai Setthathirath just before he moved his capital to Vientiane. The monastery comprises many buildings that are worthy of note both archaeologically and iconographically. The nucleus of the complex is the Vihan, the temple proper, which is decorated externally by gilded frescoes on a black and red background portraying local legends. A mosaic of colored glass tiles on a red background on the rear of the temple depicts the Tree of Enlightenment and illustrates the path to nirvana. The frescoes inside tell the story of the life of Chanthaphanith, a betel trader from Vientiane to whom the foundation of the city is attributed. A 17-point decorative motif on the top of the temple is known by the Laotians as *dok so fa* (bouquet of flowers in heaven).

332 top Facing the left bank of the Mekong, Luang Prabang was the capital of the Lan Xang kingdom from 1353 to 1560. The spiritual center of the country, the city contained 66 temples, of which 32 have survived.

332-333 The residence of the highest Laotian Buddhist dignitary, the Wat Mai was completed in 1891 during the reign of Sakhalin. The huge, gilded stucco bas-relief that decorates the portico was made in 1967-1968.

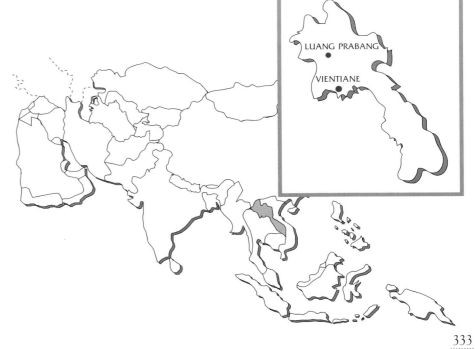

333 top Ornate wooden statues in Wat Vixun Monastery, built in 1512 by King Vixun Harath. Legend has it that the site was previously a rice paddy and that 12 wooden columns 82 feet long were required to support the monastery's weight.

333 center right The gilded wooden Buddha on the altar of Wat Vixun is recent, but between 1513 and 1560, this temple had the honor of holding the Pra Bang, the gold statue of the Buddha after which the city is named.

333 bottom right Facing onto the Mekong, the Royal Palace – also known as the Haw Kham (Gold Room) – was inaugurated in 1904 by King Sisavang Vong. Recently turned into a museum, it conserves a collection of objects that used to belong to the royal family.

The earliest of the monasteries in Luang Prabang is the Wat Vixun, built on the spot where the city's first pagoda once stood. The current building was constructed in 1512 by King Vixun Harath who, a year later, had the sacred statue of the Phra Bang transported there. Removed to Vientiane, the statue returned in the nineteenth century and remained here until 1894 when it was transferred to the nearby Wat Mai. In 1942, the Wat Vixun was turned into a museum of religious art that today houses collections of Khmer statues from the eleventh and twelfth centuries and Laotian images, in particular, the gilded-wood Buddha from the seventeenth century.

Built in the eleventh century, the Wat Mai is the residence of the Phra Sangkharath, the highest dignitary in the Laotian Buddhist Church. It is a five-story pagoda with a front portico adorned with elaborate gilded decorations. Next to it stands the Royal Palace, inaugurated in 1904 as a residence for Sisavang Vong and his family when Laos became part of the French protectorate of Indochina. From an architectural viewpoint, the building is a combination of Laotian art and French colonial style. The large entrance contains religious objects belonging to the kings. Inside, a room is dominated by a copy of the Phra Bang statue, and another room contains the throne of the Lan Xang rulers restored to its original splendor.

In the early morning mists along Thanon Phothisalath, the main street at the site lined by almost all the monasteries, lines of monks wearing their traditional orange robes process in front of the shops collecting alms. At this hour, the scene is one that has been repeated for hundreds of years, and Luang Prabang appears completely isolated from the modern world.

334 The monastery of the golden city, Wat Xieng Tong, stands on a hill overlooking the meeting point of the Mekong and Nam Khan rivers. The other façade of the building is painted with the tree of enlightenment that represents the path that leads to nirvana.

335 top left The wooden entrance to Wat Xieng Tong is decorated with figures of apsara (dancers from Hindu-derived mythology) in gold and red and images of animals, including elephants, the creatures that represent the kingdom of Laos.

335 top right The altar in the vihan (main temple) at Wat Xieng Tong bears the figure of Buddha meditating.

335 bottom Close to the city where the Nam Ou flows into the Mekong, thousands of images of Buddha were taken to the caves in Pak Ou to save them from raids by the Siamese at the end of the sixteenth century.

The Complex of Monuments in Hué

VIETNAM

PREFECTURE OF THUA THIEN
REGISTRATION: 1993
CRITERIA: C (IV)

"Non-cooperative elements" is the term the North Vietnamese used when referring to the aristocratic inhabitants of Hué, all related to the Buddhist religion, and after occupying the city in 1968, they began a systematic plan for the inhabitants' liquidation.

Hué was a symbolic place for Vietnam and thus became the setting for the bloodiest battle in the Tet Offensive unleashed by the South Vietnamese and American forces that same year, 1968. Ten days were required to retake the city, during which time 10,000 people lost their lives. In addition to this high price, the imperial city was devastated by the rain of bombs dropped by American planes, but thanks to a huge restoration project undertaken by UNESCO,

as Hué by its inhabitants, so this became its official name about 200 years ago. The Citadel on the north bank was built in 1804 by Gia Long, the first emperor of the dynasty. Designed using principles of geomancy, the city took 10,000 men 30 years to complete.

Its architecture is inspired by the Forbidden City in Beijing. It has a ring of walls about six miles long surrounded by a dike. The walls have ten entrances, each of which is crowned by a two-story tower. The main one is the Ngo Mon (Gate of Midday) which was built by Emperor Minh Mang in 1833 and is one of Hué's most spectacular structures. Also used as a platform for court ceremonies, the gate is supported by 100 columns and divided into

1805, it is watched over by nine dragons and supported by 80 columns engraved with motifs of dragons and clouds. Access to the palace was allowed to the emperor, his family, and the court mandarins, and it was used for ceremonies and government meetings.

In the center of the citadel stands the Tu Cam Thanh (Prohibited Purple City), which was where the emperor and his concubines lived; eunuchs, working as servants, were also allowed access. Only the building that houses the library has been partially rebuilt, but the apartments that remain in ruins are made attractive by the sprawling vegetation that covers them.

The oldest and most symbolic building in Hué stands on a hill outside of the walls. It is

which has defined Hué as "a masterpiece of urban poetry," much of the city has now been returned to the splendor of the period between 1802 and 1945 when it was the capital of the country under the Nguyen Dynasty.

Built in 1687 on the banks of the Song Huong (Perfume River) with the name Than Hoa – the word *hoa* means "harmony" – the city was always referred to

two parts, the base and the Pavilion of the Five Phoenixes, both U-shaped to symbolize open arms welcoming a guest. The central roof is covered with gilded baked clay.

Ngo Mon leads to a second enclosure wall, this time four miles long. It encloses the Dien Thai Hoa (Palace of Supreme Harmony), which contains the thrones of the 13 emperors of the dynasty. Begun in

336 top right One of the imperial temples inside the Citadel. Lovely furniture painted red and gold and many Buddhist devotional objects from the nineteenth century can be seen in the wide colonnaded room, made entirely from teak.

336 bottom left The Ngo Mon (Midday Gate) is the main entrance to the Royal Enclosure. The building is U-shaped to symbolize open arms and a welcome to guests.

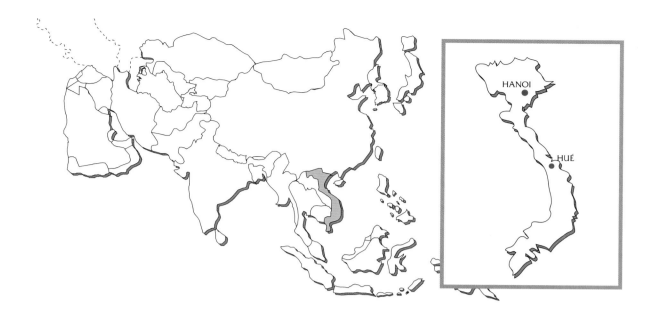

336 bottom right The interior of the beautiful teak building was built in 1845 as an assembly room, and since 1923 it has been the home of the Imperial Museum. Though

many of its most valuable items were stolen during the war with the United States, there are still clothes and furniture that once belonged to the Nguyen Dynasty.

337 The entrance on the east side of the Citadel. Enclosed by six miles of walls, construction of the Citadel was begun in 1804 by Emperor Gia Long on a "propitious" site chosen by geomancers.

338-339 The main court in the Tomb of Khai Dinh. Built between 1920 and 1931 in a strongly French-influenced eclectic style, the complex is an architectural metaphor of the loss of Nguyen power to the country's colonial rulers.

338 bottom left One of the entrances to the Tomb of Minh Mang. Blending harmoniously into the landscape, this the most impressive of the royal tombs in Hué, built between 1820 and 1840.

338 bottom right The seemingly opulent funerary monument of Emperor Khai Dinh. In fact, the decorations on the sarcophagus, the false drapes over it, and the walls of the room were made using cheap materials like porcelain, bits of broken glass, and mirrors held together with stucco.

339 top A view of the Pagoda of Thien Mu overlooking the River of Pearls. Octagonal in shape, the 69-foot tall building is divided into seven floors, each representing a stage in the life of the Buddha, and is the most symbolic religious building in Hué.

339 bottom Adorned with the statues of warriors, this is the square of the Dinh Vuong (Pavilion of the Stelae) in the Tomb of Minh Mang complex.

the seven-story Thien Mu Pagoda, 69 feet high, and built at the start of the seventeenth century on the site where, it is said, a divine figure appeared who ordered the people to build a pagoda there in order to propitiate peace in the country. The pagoda became the main place of worship in central Vietnam. A pavilion stands on either side of the pagoda, one containing a stela that stands on a marble tortoise, a symbol of longevity, and the other a bronze bell weighing two tons.

The masterpieces of Nguyen architecture, however, lie about six miles containing about 30 buildings in Chinese style. The tomb of Khai Dinh (1885-1925) is clearly influenced by French architecture, as his kingdom was, by that time, little more than a puppet of the French protectorate and his personal sphere of influence did not extend far beyond the walls of Hué. His son, Bao Dai, proclaimed his abdication from the Gate of Midday on August 25, 1945 in favor of the National Liberation Committee under Ho Chi Minh. That same year, Ho declared the independence of the Republic of Vietnam.

from the city in a setting of great beauty. These are the seven Royal Tombs built by the emperors. In addition to being burial places, they were also designed for public relaxation, and their architecture fully reflects the personality of each ruler. The complexes are surrounded by walls that imitate the citadel and contain pavilions, temples, and gardens. The stateliest tomb is that of Minh Mang, who reigned from 1820 to 1840. The tomb of Tu Duc, who was born in 1829 and died in 1883 after a 35-year reign, is an architectural representation of his love for philosophy and poetry,

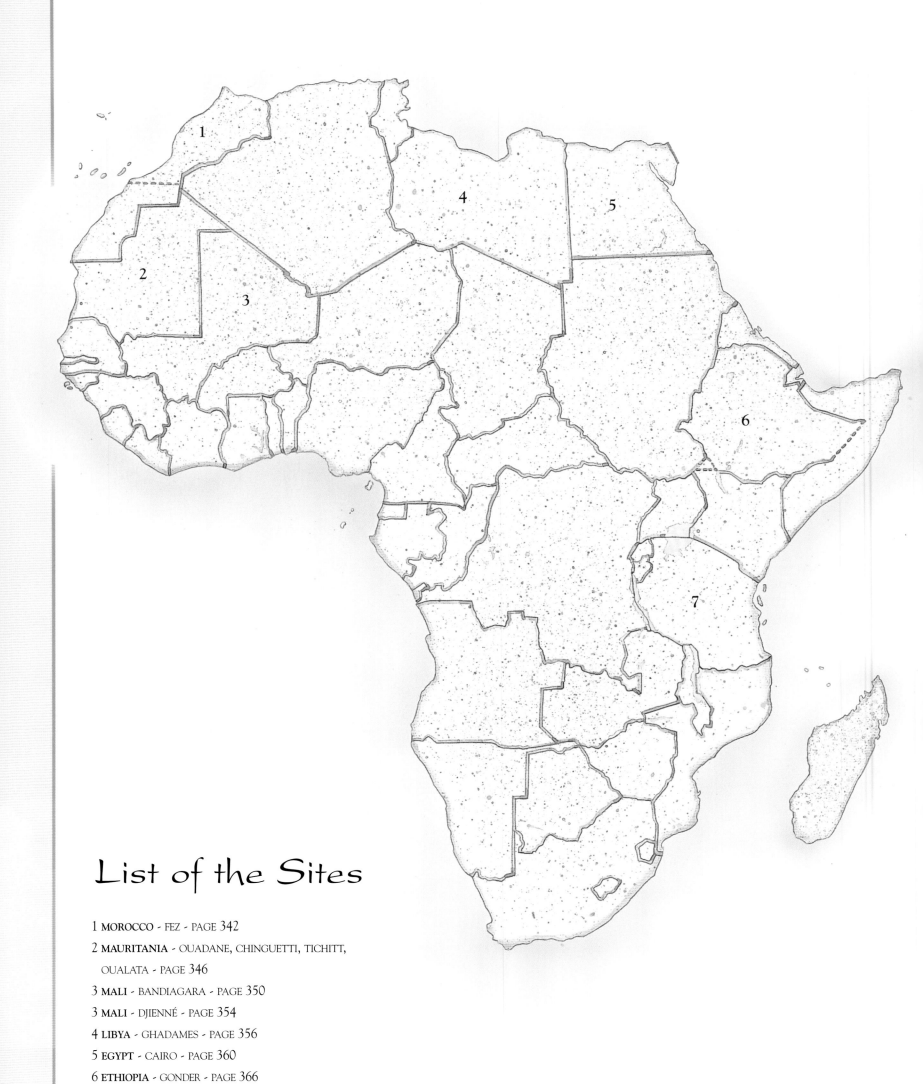

List of the Sites

Africa

After Oceania, Africa is the least densely populated continent on Earth. The harsh climates, the enormous desert areas such as the Sahara and Kalahari, and vast regions of impenetrable rainforest have often made human settlement too demanding. Although anthropology teaches us that the cradle of humanity is to be found in the Rift Valley – the long fault-line that passes through both Kenya and Ethiopia – our ancestors left the continent in prehistoric times and the last few thousand years of African history have encompassed varying phases.

There should be no surprise, therefore, if Africa offers few sites that form part of the world's architectural heritage, and those that do exist are mostly linked to Islamic art. Of the 31 sites in the World Heritage List, roughly half lie in Mediterranean Africa or on the southern edge of the Sahara. They are medieval *medinas* with decorated mosques and minarets such as Fez and Marrakech, *ksour* (fortified citadels) along the caravan routes that joined the Mediterranean to black Africa, or legendary desert cities like Djenné and Timbuktu.

Further south, Africa's architectural legacy is the result of the colonial era. In Gorée and St. Louis in Senegal there are the remains of the dark centuries of the slave trade, while the presence of the British is attested to in Zanzibar, on the east coast, and Robben Island, in South Africa, and the Portuguese in Ile de Mozambique.

Although the architecture of the great tribal civilizations is few in number and relatively recent, it is of extraordinary originality and exceptional anthropological interest. This is the case, in western Africa, of the royal palaces in Abomey in Benin, of the Ashanti buildings in Ghana, and of Bandiagara cliff of the Dogon tribe in Mali. In addition there are the tombs of the Buganda kings in Kasubi in Uganda, the royal hill in Ambohimanga in Madagascar, and the capital of the Ethiopian empire, Fasil Ghebbi.

Unfortunately, much of this modest legacy is exposed to numerous threats. Many African countries, including those mentioned, are periodically racked by bloody tribal conflicts that also put their cultural heritage at risk. Moreover, the low level of development of almost the entire continent means that the individual states are unable to safeguard their monuments without the help of international organizations. But it is perhaps the mirage of modernity that poses the most serious threat, especially to traditional cultures, which risk being sacrificed in the name of indiscriminate progress from which few will derive any benefit.

The Medina in Fez
MOROCCO

FEZ
REGISTRATION: 1981
CRITERIA: C (II) (V)

In 1921, the French General Lyautey issued a circular that prohibited non-Muslims entry to mosques or places of Islamic study in Morocco. The document summarized directives that had been part of the institutional treaty of the French protectorate, signed on March 30, 1912. Although visitors are not allowed to enter sacred buildings to admire the beauty of their decorations, they may at least enjoy the appeal of the Medina in Fez, with its intricate labyrinth of roughly 1,000 alleys, where the colors, smell, and sounds remind one of the age in which the city was the capital of the Moroccan empire.

At the eastern end of the fertile Saïss plain, ringed to the south by the foothills of the Atlas mountains, Fez was founded in 789 by Moulay Idris I, a sultan who was able to boast direct lineage from the Prophet Mohammed. The name of the city comes from the word *fas*, the Arabic word for the gold and silver hoe given to him to mark the place where the city would stand. It was his son, Idris II, who made Fez the capital of the Idrisid dynasty in 809. A decade or so later, the sultan accepted 8,000 Muslim families into the city that had fled from the Umayyad sultanate in Cordoba; they settled on the right bank of the Oued Fez, the seasonal river that crosses the valley. In 825, Jews and Berbers arriving from Kairouan in modern Tunisia took their turn and occupied the left bank of the river.

At the time, the two settlements, each enclosed by high walls, led separate lives. The Cordovans built the Mosque of Al-Andalus on their bank, in the Hispanic Islamic architectural style, while the foundation of the Mosque of Al-Qarawiyin

on the other bank was, surprisingly, inspired by a woman, Fatima, the daughter of a trader from Kairouan. A *madrasa* (Koranic school) – today considered to have been the first university in the West – was soon annexed to the mosque of Al-Qarawiyin. Over the following one hundred years, both communities prospered and other mosques, public baths, markets, and *fonduk* (caravanserai) were built.

In 1055, Fez fell under the rule of the Almoravids who moved the capital to Marrakech, but they were overthrown a century later by the Almohads. In trying to win the goodwill of the people, the Almohad sultans demolished the walls of the two separate communities to build a new one, fortified by *birj* (defensive towers), around both of them.

The advent of the Almohads marked the start of the commercial success of the city and its development as a religious and cultural center. They enlarged Al-Qarawiyin Mosque so that it could hold 20,000 worshippers and built a huge court surrounded by columns similar to the Alhambra in Granada. They also decorated the mosque by covering it with white and blue *zellij* (majolica tiles). Under the leadership of Sultan Youssef Ben Tachfine, the city was also provided with an elaborate water system so that, by

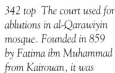

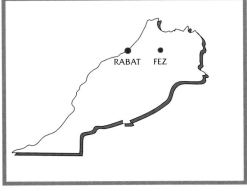

342-343 Fez el Bali, the original nucleus of the city, was founded in 789 by Sultan Moulay Idris I at the eastern end of Saïss plain. Seen from above, Fez medina is striking for its uniform and compact layout.

342 top The court used for ablutions in al-Qarawiyin mosque. Founded in 859 by Fatima ibn Muhammad from Kairouan, it was enlarged in 956 and again in 1135. It is the country's largest mosque and is still an important centre of Islamic studies.

RABAT FEZ

342 bottom The roofs of al-Qarawiyin covered with green majolica tiles. This enormous religious complex includes a library that contains over 30,000 ancient volumes.

343 top The birj (defensive towers) of Fez' walls date from the twelfth century. They were built by the Almohad sultans to replace the ninth-century fortifications. Originally the city was divided in two settlements, one inhabited by the Jews who fled from Cordoba, and the other by the Berbers from Kairouan.

343 center right One of the large entrances to the Medina that indicate the importance of the city throughout the centuries and the skill of the Moslem architects during the late Middle Ages.

343 bottom left The entrance to al-Andalus mosque, built in the ninth century. The architecture and decorations are typical of the Moorish style in Spain.

the end of the twelfth century, the mosques, *madrasa*, and most of the houses had running water.

In 1250, the Marinid dynasty took power and moved the capital back to Fez, but the walls were by then too restricting to accommodate the civilians and troops that arrived with the new rulers. This led to the construction of Fez el Jedid, "New Fez," which in turn led the original city (what is now the Medina) to be known as Fez el Bali, "Old Fez."

With the rise to power of a new dynasty at the start of the sixteenth century, the Sa'adi, Fez's continuing development

suffered a pause until 1666 when it entered a second period of prosperity under Sultan Moulay Abdullah. The traders in the Medina formed corporations controlled by a *mohtasseb*, and the *fonduk* and the markets were divided into sections based on the goods they sold, a system that is still in use in what has become the largest market in North Africa, Medina del Maghreb.

Bab Bou Jeloud is the gate decorated with majolica tiles – green ones in tribute to Islam and blue ones that celebrate the color of the city – that leads into Fez el Bali and signals the start of the Talaa Kebira (the Great Street), lined by Almohad

buildings. The alleys that head off from this street lead to the various souks, where shops of potters, fabric sellers, cobblers, spice sellers, and most typical of all, the tanneries and leather dyers can be found.

Although the arrival of the French in Morocco brought the definitive transfer of the capital to Rabat, they insisted on preserving the historical importance of Fez as a spiritual and intellectual center. They forbade the construction of new buildings in the Medina and began a program of restoration still active today in which the crafts and trading traditions for which the city is famous are safeguarded.

344 The elegant stone and wood decorations in a palace built during the Merinid era in the heart of the Medina in Fez el Bali.

345 top left The Fonduk en-Nejjarin ('Palace of the Carpenters') built during the Merinid dynasty. It was one of the caravanerais where traveling merchants stayed.

345 top right One of the souks in the alleys next to Talaa Kebira, the main street in the largest medina in the Maghreb. In 1666, the merchants in the Medina formed regulated guilds.

345 bottom left A detail of the Bab Bou Jeloud. Decorated with green (the color of Islam) and blue (the color of the city) majolica tiles, it leads into the madrasa *of the same name and Talaa Kebira.*

345 bottom right Fez is famous throughout the world for its tanneries. The coloring vats usually stand on the terraced roofs of the hide-treatment workshops.

The Ancient Ksour of Ouadane, Chinguetti, Tichitt, and Oualata

MAURITANIA

346-347 The houses in Oualata are renowned for being the most decorated in the Arab world. The women of the city create the attractive wall designs using plaster and clay but, unfortunately, many inhabitants in the old village are abandoning the traditional houses.

346 bottom Tichitt is the most inaccessible of the oases in the Mauritanian desert. Founded in the twelfth century by Moslems at the foot of Dhar cliff, it quickly became one of the most famous cities in West Africa.

OUADANE AND CHINGUETTI, ADRAR REGION; TICHITT, TAGANT REGION; OUALATA, HODH ECHCHARGUT REGION
REGISTRATION: 1996
CRITERIA: C (III) (IV) (V)

In February 1352, the most famous historian and traveler in the medieval Arab world, Ibn Battuta, left the oases of Morocco to cross the Sahara towards Timbuktu. On his arrival in Oualata, he was welcomed with great honor, so he decided to stay there for 50 days as a result of which he wrote a controversial description of the place. The oasis of date palms was extremely hot, but the people were welcoming and wore fine clothes of Egyptian manufacture. The inhabitants of the desert were fervent Muslims, but their women did not cover their heads and the people of Oualata enjoyed an ambiguous promiscuity that vexed their famous guest.

About 190 miles west of Timbuktu, Oualata was one of the main trading centers on the routes between sub-Saharan Africa and the Maghreb. Situated on the edge of the Sudanese empire, they traded gold, ivory, and amber from the Sahel for salt, metals, and glass from Morocco. Founded between the eleventh and twelfth centuries beside a clay cliff that stands over the Wadi Oualata, at the time of Ibn Battuta it was also inhabited by a large community of scholars and *ulema* (religious dignitaries from the world of Islam). The city achieved its maximum prosperity in the fifteenth and sixteenth centuries after the cultural and mercantile elites from Timbuktu had sought refuge there from the raids of the Tuareg in 1446. From that period, a Koranic school was established in Oualata that is still operative.

Difficult to reach along the desert tracks, the city's medieval appearance has remained unchanged due to the characteristic decoration of its houses. This embellishment is the work of the women who have perpetuated the tradition of ornamenting the houses of Oualata with patterns made from chalk and red earth, which, including the historiated wooden doors, make their houses the most decorated in the Islamic world. Many of the dwellings have since been abandoned by the local population, which has preferred to move to the capital Nouakchott.

Further north there are three other caravan cities that played a role in communications across the Sahara. At the foot of Dhar Cliff in the heart of the desert stands Tichitt, the most inaccessible of all. Founded by the wise man Abdel Moumin in the twelfth century, it was one of the most famous medieval cities in northwest Africa. The other two *ksour* (an Arabic term derived from the Latin *castrum* meaning "fortified city") of Ouadane and Chinguetti lie further north in the more accessible region of Adrar. Built at the end of the tenth century, Ouadane was the largest caravan town in the region and its fame in scientific trade spread as far as Europe. Portugal became so interested that it sent a party to conquer it in 1487 in order to profit from the busy commercial activities that took place there. Reflecting

347 *top Reading the Koran in Oualata madrasa. An important religious center in the late Middle Ages, the city's Koranic school still very active.*

347 *bottom Oualata touched its maximum prosperity in the fifteenth and sixteenth centuries when merchants from Timbuktu took refuge there from Tuareg raids.*

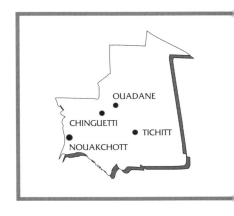

its ancient prosperity, Ouadane still boasts a superb minaret and the characteristic stone houses that climb up the face of the cliff.

The town of Chinguetti is a place where Muslim philosophy found its maximum expression. Considered the seventh city of Islam and founded in 776, it stands where Dhar Cliff meets the erg of Arouane, but the first settlement was supplanted in 1262 by the current town that was built close by. The cultural capital of west Africa, Chinguetti welcomed hundreds of scholars who left a heritage of manuscripts that is proving a headache for the modern world to conserve. The plain stone construction of the minaret betrays its defensive function. The Prefecture is one of the best-known examples of the local architectural style. The mud-lined façade, with its merlons and windows decorated with white lime, is evidence of the challenge presented by living in as extreme an environment as the Sahara.

Impoverished by emigration and exposed to harsh climatic conditions, the *ksour* of Mauritania are in serious danger. In consequence, they were placed under the protection of the Fondation Nationale pour la Sauvegarde des Villes Anciennes in 1993 which works together with UNESCO to safeguard them. Nonetheless, only 400 of the 3,000 decorated houses remain in Ouadane, many of the rest having been buried by the sandstorms of the desert.

348 top left The mosque and plain thirteenth-century minaret in Chinguetti, Islam's seventh holy city. Square in plan and made from stone, it resembles a tower in a medieval European castle.

348 bottom left Chinguetti was founded in 776 but, like in other desert cities, houses here are being abandoned and the sand is getting the upper hand over these marvelous buildings.

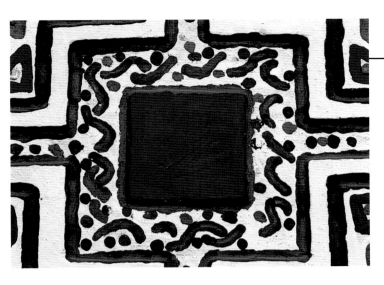

348 right The symmetrical patterns in a wall decoration on a house in Chinguetti. Abstract figurative art from Africa had a large influence on avant-garde Western artists in the early twentieth century.

348-349 The Chanaguita – as the small handful of inhabitants of Chinguetti are called – were expert merchants. It was they who provided the contacts between the Maghreb and the Gulf of Guinea in the Middle Ages and played a decisive role in spreading Islam.

349 top The entrance to a house in Chinguetti. The buildings in the desert city also boast original architectural features designed to ventilate the buildings from the baking Saharan temperatures.

Bandiagara Cliff

MALI

REGISTRATION: 1989
CRITERIA: N (III), C (V)

Every 60 years (the next occasion will be in 2030) the Dogon play music and dance to celebrate the Sigui, a colorful purification festival that marks the end of one life cycle and the start of another. The Sigui coincides with the passage of a tiny star they call Po Tolo that has always been used to decide the period of the festival. Surprisingly, Western astronomers only identified the star (Sirius B) during the 1960s and the fact that it was already known to the Dogon is unexplainable. Many theories have been offered, both serious and less so, but whatever the reason, the Dogon who live along Bandiagara Cliff are the subject of study for flocks of anthropologists.

Roughly 300,000 Dogon live in the shelter of the spectacular reddish rock wall that stretches for 125 miles along the border between the dry Sahel and the Niger plain. The main villages, Bandiagara and Sanga, on the top of the cliff are the only ones reachable by a road worthy of the name. Consequently, these are the ones in which the traditional culture is being invaded by a rudimentary form of modernity.

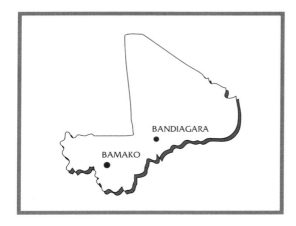

350 top right On the highest point of every village, in the lee of the cliff wall, stand the houses of the hogon, the village elder who acts as the spiritual head of the Dogon community.

350-351 The village of Ireli. The inhabited centers along the cliff can only be reached on foot or by donkey, and this relative isolation has meant that the Dogon people have been able to preserve their culture.

To reach the other villages, it is necessary to walk or take a donkey down the steep, narrow paths that lead to the bottom of the cliff. Built from *banco*, a mixture of clay, straw, and dung, when seen from afar these villages are almost indistinguishable from the rock, and the houses seem to be almost placed at random. Each village is "laid out" in the form of a human body. The head is formed by the house of the *hogon* (often the oldest

between the floor and the roof is no more than a few feet in height to prevent anyone from getting up quickly if an argument should break out.

The hands of the village are formed by the houses to which the women withdraw during menstruation, who, considered impure, are not allowed to prepare food or work in the fields. Finally, the *ginna*, the houses of extended families, represent the arteries and veins. The houses themselves

man in the community), who lives alone with the task of looking after the altar of the *Lebé*, the mythical ancestor brought back to life in the form of a snake. The *hogon* is thought to be an oracle and is consulted to settle disputes and give advice on sacrificial ceremonies to be undertaken if drought or sickness strike.

The heart of the body is the *togu-na* (house of words), which is a shelter formed by eight carved wooden posts – representing the gods of the Dogon cosmogony – topped by a thick roof made from strips of millet. This is where the men gather to relax and chat. The space

350 bottom left Graffiti on the rock wall near the village of Sanga. These are symbols of the Dogon cosmogony and the ritual masks used during the sacred ceremony of the Sigui.

351 top Each Dogon house is built to accommodate an extended family. The ginna (granaries) can be recognized by their conical straw roofs and are the property of the women. Each granary normally contains the yearly needs of a nuclear family.

351 bottom The village of Teli at the foot of Bandiagara Cliff. It is estimated that the zone is home to about 300,000 Dogon.

352 top left The small mosque in the village of Nando. The religion of the Dogon is a syncretism of traditional animist beliefs and Islam, brought to Mali along the caravan routes of the Sahara.

352 top right The Dogon are famous as wood carvers. Their carvings are eagerly sought after by collectors of African art. The photograph shows carved doors and a typical stairway formed from a single tree trunk.

are built in the shape of a human body, with a rectangular court (the bust), a round kitchen (the head), various square rooms with flat roofs, round grain stores (the limbs), and an entrance (the genitals).

The entire cliff is studded with caves that can only be reached by means of a complicated system of baobab fiber ropes. The Dogon do not permit strangers to enter because the caves are used as tombs and are thus considered sacred. The popular legend recounts that a tribe of giants lived here who today, having become pure spirits, are the custodians of the dead. However, anthropological studies contradict the Dogon tradition and

claim that the caves were used as tombs by the Tellem, a people of semi-nomadic hunters who settled in the zone about 2,000 years ago. The caves have been found to contain roughly 3,000 skeletons and a number of headrests which are the oldest wooden manufactured items found in West Africa.

The Dogon probably originated in what is today Burkina Faso and settled below the Bandiagara Cliff in the sixteenth century to escape the Arabs who were raiding the area for the slave market. Since that time the Dogon have practiced agriculture on small plots of land at the base of the cliff. They grow the onions and millet which almost exclusively form their

diet. They use the millet to prepare *kondjo*, a fermented and slightly alcoholic drink that they consume in great quantities on market day.

Often hit hard by drought, and consequently by malnutrition and sickness, the Dogon are at risk of extinction.

With inscription in UNESCO's list of World Heritage Sites, international aid has helped the villages to construct wells of drinking water. During famines before these wells were dug, mothers were forced to throw their children from the top of the cliff because – the Dogon say – it was a better fate than to die of hunger and thirst.

352 bottom left The mosque in Kani-Kombolé is larger and more complex than that of other villages. Together with Bandiagara and

Sanga, this village stands on the top of the cliff and can be reached by road, which has exposed it to outside influences more than other settlements.

352 bottom right A house in Banani, a village at the foot of the Bandiagara Cliff, is decorated with zoomorphic motifs, and,

like all Dogon buildings, is made using banco, a material made from a mixture of clay, straw, and dung.

353 Detail of a carved door with images of the daily life of Dogon men and women.

The Old Town of Djenné

MALI

ONE MILE FROM THE SHORES OF THE RIVER BANI,
INLAND DELTA OF THE NIGER
REGISTRATION: 1988
CRITERIA: C (III) (IV)

Every Monday in the vast square in front of Djenné Mosque, there is a busy market where Songhai, Peul, and Bozo people mingle to sell dry fish, cola nuts, live chickens, goats, colorful cotton, pottery, and basic furnishings. These are humble goods that have little to do with modernity and which therefore confer on the town an atmosphere that seems to have remain unchanged for centuries.

Djenné is the oldest town in sub-Saharan Africa. It was founded around 250 B.C. near the banks of the river Bani about two miles from the modern town. It used to be called Djenné-Jeno, and this is the name used by archaeologists to refer to the civilization that flourished independent of North African influence and that produced a complex urban layout of over 82 acres

using a peculiar style of architecture based on sun-baked bricks. The people of Djenné-Jeno also produced handmade items of extraordinary manufacture – in particular terracotta statuettes of animist divinities – which are widely sought after by museums and collectors all over the world.

The existing version of the town was founded in the ninth century and grew as

Djenné-Jeno gradually lost importance. It developed into the meeting place for merchants coming from the Sudanese desert and others from the tropical forests of Guinea. Around 1240, the sultan, Koi Kunboro, the ruler of Djenné, converted to Islam and turned his palace into a mosque. The town became a place of pilgrimage for Muslims and gradually acquired importance as an academic center for the peoples of the Niger delta until it had 100 Koranic schools. In 1498, Djenné was incorporated into the Songhai empire, but in 1591 was subjugated by the rulers of Morocco who made it a trading center for gold and salt from North and Central Africa thanks to its favorable location on the river and its proximity to the caravan center of Timbuktu.

The town revolves around the Great Mosque, which was built by the master mason Ismaila Traoré in 1906 on the site of a mosque one century older. That earlier mosque, in turn, replaced the thirteenth-century building that had been demolished by Sheik Amadou for being impious due to its sumptuous nature. The Great Mosque stands on a large rectangular platform of sun-baked bricks. It has brick walls covered with *banco*, which is a mixture of river mud and rice gleanings. Supported by 90 columns made from palm trunks covered with mud bricks, it is distributed around various courts used as prayer halls, and features many minarets are topped by an ostrich egg, which is a symbol of fertility and purity. The walls include 18 bastions that contribute to the vertical impact of the building. To support the structure and insulate the interior from the intense

354 top The city of Djenné was a trading center between the Sahara and the Sahel plain. It was founded on a branch of the Niger's inland delta around 250 B.C. and is the oldest city in sub-Saharan Africa.

354 bottom Like the rest of the building, the main entrance to the Great Mosque is strengthened by palm trunks.

summer temperatures, the walls of the mosque vary in thickness, from 24 inches at the bottom to 16 inches at the top. Parts of the building are topped with roofs in the form of a ceramic hat which are removed at night to allow for the ventilation of the building.

Dirt roads fan out from around the Great Mosque. They are lined by old, two-story houses also made from sun-baked brick and covered with *banco* that are arranged around a central court. There are about 2,000 of them in all, of which 198 are part of a conservation project in

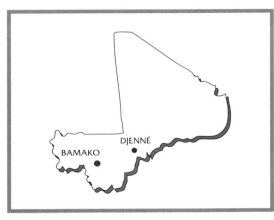

354-355 The current building of the Great Mosque dates from 1906. It was built from sun-baked bricks covered with banco (a mixture of river mud and rice gleanings). Its several courts are used as prayer rooms, and it has unusual conical-pointed minarets. Some of these are crowned by ostrich eggs, which are a symbol of fertility.

collaboration with UNESCO.

During the rainy season, the outer sections of the Great Mosque and houses in Djenné are "melted" by the torrential rains, and each spring the inhabitants restore them to their original form. It is an occasion for celebration; it is the women's responsibility to prepare and transport the water to mix the *banco*. Patterns are not used in the restoration of those washed away: the cultural heritage and collective memory of the people of Djenné allow them able to reproduce the ancient buildings –a combination of early-Islamic and primeval Djenné-Jeno styles – exactly as they were. Modeling the mud with their bare hands, they produce surprisingly smooth walls without sharp edges.

Unfortunately, after the "incident" a few years ago in which a group of fashion photographers shot a display in the Great Mosque, thereby profaning the sacredness of the place, the building has been placed off-limits to non-Muslims. In recompense, the friendly people of Djenné are always happy to offer a cup of tea to visitors in the cool of their houses.

The Ancient City of Ghadames
LIBYA

AL-HAMADAH AL-HAMRA
REGISTRATION: 1986
CRITERIA: C (V)

A Tuareg legend says that the name Ghadames comes from Arabic and that it refers to the misadventure that occurred when a caravan accidentally left some of its food supplies behind. When it was time to prepare the meal the next day, someone remembered back to earliest civilizations. The first settlements in the area were formed roughly 10,000 years ago as the Paleolithic age gave way to the Neolithic, when the Sahara was still a fertile plain. The Ain al-Faras spring was the source of a large oasis that measured about 185 acres and which became a stopping-place on the caravan route that linked the Sudan with the Mediterranean. Its importance grew from 19 B.C. on when the Romans founded the city of Cidamus there, which remained under their control for several centuries. A fairly large garrison was stationed in the oasis during the third century, and, in the fourth and fifth, during the Byzantine empire, a bishopric was founded.

The Arab conquest led by Sidi Uqba in 667 during their sweep across North Africa marked the beginning of Ghadames' greatest period. Just a few decades later, Ghadames became a major link in the Arab world, which soon extended as far as the Atlantic. An important trading town from the eighth century on, Ghadames was laid out around a central square and the large Jami' al-Atiq and Yunus mosques, two of the oldest in Libya. Both are transversal

356 left The narrow streets in Ghadames oasis. The urban center is built around a majlis (square) where the ancient Jami al-Atiq and Yunus mosques stand.

having left the provisions in the place where "yesterday's lunch" (*ghada ams* in Arabic) had been eaten.

In fact, the history of the magnificent oasis in the highlands of al-Hamadah al-Hamra – where the borders of Libya, Algeria, and Tunisia meet – dates right

356 right Many of the buildings in Ghadames are whitened with lime and have external walls with sharp triangular points. The significance of these architectural details is still unknown.

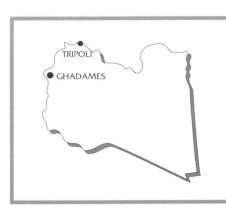

in plan, with, respectively, two and three aisles parallel to the *qibla*.

The most notable aspect of Ghadames, known as the Pearl of the Desert, is its layout and the original, harmonious architecture of the city. Its isolation at the northern edge of the great desert encouraged unique city-planning solutions; to protect the city from the torrid summer heat and winter cold, the narrow, winding streets of the oasis were covered with buildings, thereby transforming the city into a single tangle of private buildings and common areas.

356-357 A view of Ghadames. The ancient artesian spring known as Ain al-Faras ('Spring of the Mare') makes the existence of the 75 hectare oasis and its roughly 25,000 palms possible.

357 top The ajard (entrance) to a typical house in the oasis. Next to it on the ground floor is the tali ni ajard (storeroom) and another service room.

Built from mud, clay, and palm trunks, the houses in Ghadames had three floors, each with its own function: near the entrance on the ground floor, there were two service rooms; the *tamanat* on the first floor, illuminated by a large skylight, was house's main living space, and this was surrounded by other rooms connected to it by various flights of steps; the upper floor, reached from the *tamanat*, consisted of terraces that were used for the kitchen and the women's area.

The traditional houses in Ghadames have survived until the modern era though the oasis has suffered various tribulations over the past century and a half. In 1860, once the prosperity of the trans-Sahara trade routes came to an end, Ghadames passed under the dominion of Tripoli. Later, during Italy's rule over Libya, it offered fierce resistance to the Europeans, but fell in 1924, ten years after it had first been besieged. In 1940, it came under French control and experienced its

most difficult years. Heavily damaged during World War II, it was contested until 1951 when Tunisia accepted its cession to Libya.

During the 1950s, it was provided with electricity but its fate was already decided by the fact that there was no longer enough water to go around. Women carried water from the wells to the mosque and were obliged to remove used water. Ghadames' final abandonment by its inhabitants began in 1982.

358 The entrance to a house. All the buildings in the oasis are built from raw earth but the horizontal load-bearing structures are made from palm trunks.

359 top The streets in Ghadames closely connect with the houses. Together the two elements form a unique (internal) urban fabric that has developed over the centuries to improve living conditions in the Saharan climate.

359 center left The streets in the oasis are between 8 and 10 feet in width and run beneath decorative arches or living spaces.

359 center right The main living area in Ghadames' houses is the tamanat. It is 13-16 feet high, fairly cubic in shape, and is surrounded by rooms on different levels connected by stairways.

359 bottom Ajurer (kitchens) in Ghadames are on the top floor of the house, the one reserved for women. They face onto a terrace that give access to the nearby houses.

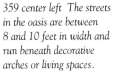

Islamic Cairo

EGYPT

CAIRO GOVERNORATE
REGISTRATION: 1979
CRITERIA: C (I) (V) (IV)

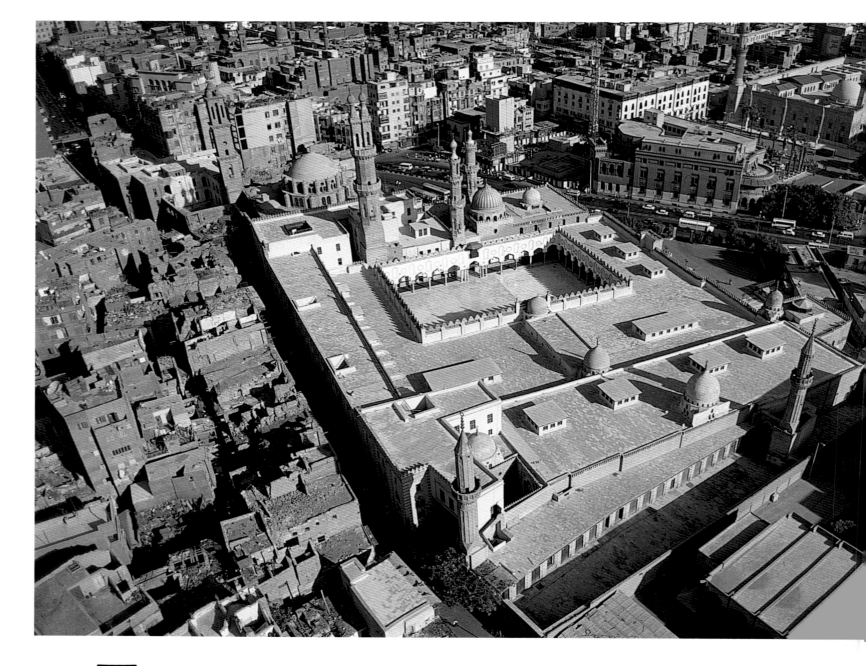

The people of Cairo claim that Khan al-Khalili, the city's largest bazaar, built in 1392, played a pivotal role in the discovery of America. They say that Christopher Columbus' caravels set sail to open a new trade route in order to break the monopoly that Cairo, then governed by the Mameluks, held on the spice markets throughout the known world.

This may be an exaggeration, but ever since it was founded, the city's importance has reached beyond the boundaries of Egypt and even of the African continent. Today, with its immense urban area and a population of 15 million, al-Qahirah, the city's name in Arabic, meaning "victorious," is Africa's largest metropolis. It is so important that the Egyptians themselves refer to it simply as *Masr*, or "Egypt."

Contrary to what one might think, given that the Egyptian civilization dates from the dawn of known history, Cairo is a relatively young city, officially founded in only A.D. 969. Before then, three towns stood on the site of al-Qahirah along the banks of the Nile. Clustered in an area of four square miles, they are now part of the Islamic heart of Cairo. The first, al-Fustat, was little more than a military encampment established in 641 by Amr, the first Arab to govern Egypt.

The little city flourished under the Umayyad caliphs until 750 when it was conquered by the Abbasids, who founded al-Qatai on the other bank of the Nile. In 870, the Abbasid caliph ibn Tulun rebelled against Baghdad's power and proclaimed himself the king of Egypt, founding the Tulunid dynasty and, with it, the new city of al-Qata'i. In 879, he ordered a mosque built in his honor, which is the largest and oldest building of its kind in Egypt. It has a simple plan, with a fountain for ablutions that forms the heart of the entire complex. It has survived to the modern day virtually unaltered, despite the addition of a splendid *mihrab* decorated with mosaics from the Mameluk era, and the restoration work done by the Ottomans. The prayer room covers five naves along the side facing Mecca, and there are two naves on the opposite side. It has sycamore panels carved with writings from the Koran.

A little more than thirty years later, the Abbasids avenged the insurrection of ibn

Tulun by destroying the royal palace and the legendary gardens of al-Qata'i and re-establishing al-Fustat as the seat of power. Nevertheless, Abbasid Egypt was in chaos by this time, while a new dynasty, the Fatimids, had risen to power in what is now Tunisia. Legitimated by the fact that they were the direct descendents of Fatima, the daughter of the Prophet Muhammad, the Fatimids headed east to conquer the Arab world and spread the true doctrine, the Shi'a. The Fatimids appointed Gawhar, a former slave from Sicily who had become their most courageous general, to lead the expedition to conquer al-Fustat.
The first monument built by Gawhar honored the Shi'ite doctrine. The mosque of al-Azhar, dedicated to Muhammad's daughter Fatima Az-Zahra', was inaugurated in 972. An Islamic school was annexed to it shortly after, and the first lesson was held in 975, making al-Azhar one of the oldest universities in the world. At approximately the same time, following the decline of Baghdad and the Spanish *reconquista* of Cordoba, the universities in both these

360 top Decorative tiles on the outer walls of Ahmed ibn-Tulun Mosque, built in 789 by the Abbasid caliph of the same name.

360-361 Al-Azhar Mosque. Dedicated to Fatima, the daughter of the Prophet, it was built in 972 by the Shi'ite sovereign, Gawhar, and soon included a Koranic school that was to become one of the most important universities in the Islamic world.

361 top right The porticoed court of ibn-Tulun mosque with, in the center, a large building for devotees to perform their ablutions. It is the oldest building of its kind in Egypt.

361 top center The portico in Taybesir madrasa. Situated in the university complex of al-Azhar Mosque, it was built in 1309 and is surrounded by the library building.

361 bottom center The interior of al-Azhar Mosque. The architectural features of the complex have been repeatedly altered over the centuries and thus reflect the influence of all the dynasties that governed Cairo.

CAIRO

362

362 top left The domes of Mohammad Ali Mosque, designed by Yousef Bushnaq and built between 1830 and 1857 in Ottoman style by Mohammad Ali Pasha, the governor of Egypt.

362 top right The interior of Mohammad Ali Mosque, commonly called the 'alabaster mosque' because of its extensive use of the material, excavated in Beni Suef, in the prayer hall.

362-363 The Citadel is the superb fortified complex built by Saladin between 1176 and 1183 to protect the city from the Crusaders. Since then, the fort has never been without a military garrison. The walls are 32 feet high and 9 feet thick.

363 top Built by Caliph el-Aziz and his son, el-Hakim, between 990 and 1013, el-Hakim Mosque is the second largest Fatimid mosque in Cairo. It has been used as a confinement for Crusader prisoners, as stores for Napoleonic troops and as a school during the presidency of Gamal Nasser.

cities were closed, and as a result men of learning from the entire Muslim world flocked to Cairo. By the end of the eleventh century, 10,000 students had attended al-Azhar, and since then it has never lost its role as a beacon of Islamic culture. Over the centuries, it has also become the driving force behind all of Egypt's political and social changes.

From an architectural standpoint, the modern-day al-Azhar, located in the heart of Islamic Cairo, is a superb palimpsest of all the cultural styles and influences that have passed through Egypt. Five minarets dotted with small balconies and elegant bas-reliefs tower over it, and it has six entrances. The main one, Bab el-Muzayini, or Barber's Gate (because the students had to shaved here before they could attend the university), dates from the eighteenth century. From here, a small courtyard leads to the Aqbaughawiya Madrasah, built in 1340 and now used as a library. Bab el-Qaitbay, on the other hand, leads to the largest courtyard, which is lined with patios dating from various periods. The patios reflect the names and decorations of the areas in the Islamic world from which the students and teachers came.

The Mosque of al-Hakim, built between 990 and 1013, also dates from the Fatimid era. Despite renovation work done during the Mameluk period, it still has its original marble walls and exquisite stuccowork. It is also of great historic significance because it was commissioned by the founder of the Druse sect. The mosque of al-Aqmar (the Grey Mosque) is an elegant stone building whose entryways feature stalactite decorations. This mosque as well as some of the loveliest gates to the city, such as Bab

el-Nasr and Bab Zuwaylah, were built at the end of the eleventh century.

Nevertheless, Fatimid domination was waning by this time. At the beginning of the twelfth century, Egypt had become the battleground for the conflict between the Crusaders and the Seljuks, the new Islamic power that had come down from the steppes of Central Asia. Led by Nureddin, in 1168 the Seljuks conquered Cairo. The new ruler died the next year and the leadership of the city was taken over by a young commanders, who was destined to become one of the most important figures in medieval history: Salah-ad-Din, better known as the cruel Saladin.

Despite the reputation attributed to him by the Christians, as a ruler Saladin promoted coexistence between the peoples of Cairo, and he embellished the city with new architecture. His Citadel, whose only "flaw" is that part of it was built with stone blocks taken from the pyramids, is one of Cairo's treasures. Its walls are 33 feet high and ten feet thick, and the buildings inside demonstrate Saladin's military genius. They include a cistern that is 285 feet deep and could guarantee an almost unlimited reserve of water in case of siege. The complex was subsequently expanded to add a royal palace and stables, which could house 4,800 horses.

In 1182, Saladin left to defend Palestine and Syria, but he never returned to Cairo. Most of the members of his army and his court dignitaries were former slaves or prisoners of war who had converted to Islam. As a result, they won the trust of the Seljuks and became very influential in the government. They were referred to as Mameluks and, following the death of Saladin's successor, they inherited the rule of Cairo in 1249. They ruled as absolute

363 bottom left Bab Zuwayla marks the southern boundary of Fatimid Cairo. The city did not have proper fortifications until 1087 when Badr ad-Din el Gamali decided to build a defensive wall with three large gates. It design was commissioned from Syrian architects.

363 bottom right One of the five minarets in al-Azhar Mosque seen against the background of the city. Today Cairo has fifteen million inhabitants and is the largest city in Africa.

364 top right Some of the tombs of the Mameluke rulers. The Mamelukes were the freed slaves that took power on the death of Saladin's grandson.

364 bottom left Stylistically, Sultan Hassan Mosque and its madrasa is considered the most unitary and harmonious monument in the city. Built in 1256 for Sultan Hassan bin Mohammad bin Qala'un, it was designed so that each of the four Sunnite sects had its own school, though sharing the building with the other three.

monarchs until the end of the fifteenth century, further embellishing Cairo with mosques, public and residential buildings, *hammam* (public baths), theological schools, caravanserais, markets, and fountains. The complex that best epitomizes typical Mameluk architecture is the Qala'un Mosque complex, which includes a mosque, a madrasah (Koranic school), a mausoleum, and a *mauristan* (hospital), which remained open until 1920. Noteworthy mosques include the fourteenth-century Aqsunqur, better

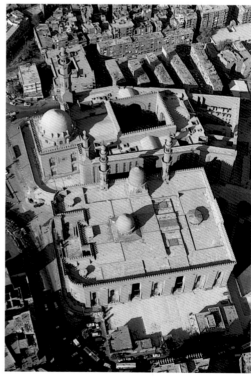

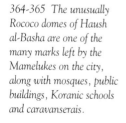

known as the Blue Mosque because of its blue and turquoise ceramic tiles from Iznik, and the fifteenth-century al-Mu'ayyad, or Red Mosque, which has elegant marble decorations set with ivory and mother-of-pearl.

Cairo reached its apogee during the

Mameluk era, becoming the crossroads for trade between East and West. The opening of the trade route via the Cape of Good Hope in 1488 marked the end of Egypt's monopoly, and it also coincided with the defeat of the Mameluks by the Ottomans, who ruled Egypt until the

364-365 The unusually Rococo domes of Haush al-Basha are one of the many marks left by the Mamelukes on the city, along with mosques, public buildings, Koranic schools and caravanserais.

365 top The city's southern cemetery is where the Mameluke tombs lie, in Haush al-Basha. The Mamelukes governed the city from the mid-thirteenth century to the end of the fifteenth.

early nineteenth century.

The city's tradition of trade continues to thrive, as demonstrated by its numerous markets, particularly Khan al-Khalili. The excellent craftsmanship of Cairo's residents, who are highly skilled at jewelry-making, glassblowing, wood carving, and embroidery, can be seen behind the walls of El-Ghuri Wakala, one of the city's most intriguing buildings, built as a hotel for merchants from Asia, Africa, and Europe.

365 bottom right This is el-Mu'ayyad (the Red Mosque) situated near Bab Zuwayla and built between 1415 and 1420 by Sultan Mu'ayyad. Inside, the walls are completely lined with geometric patterns made from polychrome marble.

365 center right The Mameluke ruler el-Mansur built the Sultan Qala'un complex along Sharia el-Muizz, a street *in Fatimid Cairo, in 1284. It was the first example of the Syrian architectural style that was to typify the Mameluke era.*

Fasil Ghebbi, Gonder Region
ETHIOPIA

GONDER REGION, LAKE TANA
REGISTRATION: 1979
CRITERIA: C (II) (III)

The legend goes that during the sixteenth century an angel appeared to the Ethiopian emperor Lebna Dangal in a dream and told him to seek a place whose name began with the letter "G," where he was to establish the capital of his kingdom. Until then, the Ethiopian kings had been nomads, frequently moving their royal encampment. For another century, perhaps in their quest for the "G" mentioned in the dream, they built palaces in different cities. The first imperial palace was built in Guzara on the east coast of Lake Tana, and King Susenyos installed his court a little further north, in Gorgora.

Nevertheless, the fateful "G" was to be Gonder, located further north in a valley protected by mountains. In 1636, King Fasilides, Susenyos' son, established his headquarters in the Gonder basin. Susenyos, who had converted to Catholicism, was forced to relinquish his throne to his son following the rebellion of the powerful Coptic church. It is not known when the king decided to build his first castle, but the monumental fortified complex had undoubtedly already been completed by 1648, the year a Yemenite dignitary described it with awe and admiration. In the two centuries that followed, Gonder apparently became the capital of the turbulent kingdom of Ethiopia, and what is now known as Fasil Ghebbi was supposedly transformed into a fortified complex enclosing about twenty royal palaces and approximately thirty churches.

Fasilides, who also built other palaces, died

366-367 *Construction of the imperial enclosure in Fasil Ghebbi, the capital of the Ethiopian kings for almost two centuries, was begun in 1636 by King Fasillidàs. The complex contains 20 or so royal palaces and about 30 churches.*

in 1667 and was succeeded by his son Yohannes I, who added the library and the chancellery to the imperial complex. He also imposed strict observance of the Coptic faith, expelling all Catholics who refused to convert and segregating Muslims and Falasha Jews. Yohannes was succeeded by Iyasu I, Fasilides' grandson. Under this king, at the end of the seventeenth century Gonder was transformed into an extraordinary trading center that attracted travelers from Europe, the Middle East, and the Arabian peninsula. Iyasu I built the church of Debre Berhan Selassie and other important buildings in Fasil Ghebbi, but his reign ended in 1715 when his son, Tekle Haimanot, had him murdered. Tekle himself reigned for only two years before he, in turn, was killed during an ambush.

Bakaffa, a despot, came to power in 1721 and for a short period managed to control the empire, which was being devastated by bloody fighting that led to complicated intrigues at the royal court. He turned the throne over to his son Iyasu II, who surrounded himself with artists and men of letters. Iyasu helped trade flourish once again in Gonder, and a large Muslim community settled there. This was the city's swan song, however, and the empire soon fell apart. It was reunited much later by King Tewodros, but the king did not like Gonder, and in 1855 he moved the capital to Debre Tabor and then to Magdela.

The walls around the Makababya, the imperial enclosure that was probably built under Iyasu I, are 3,000 feet long, and the architectural layout of the interior reflects many different influences. There are sections resembling medieval fortresses and others that look like Oriental palaces, and Arab, Indian, and Baroque influences appear in sections built during the second period. The

castle built by Fasilides is the most impressive building, with dark basalt merlons and staircases, four round towers, and stone domes that complement the arches of the doors and windows. However, there is no longer any trace of the riches that must have welcomed dignitaries and merchants from around the world, and the damask carpets and gold and silver decorations are gone.

The other buildings, now in ruins, suffered an even worse fate, such as the two-story library decorated with red tuff crucifixes, and the chancellery, once adorned with ivory friezes. Next to Fasilides' castle is the castle of Iyasu I, a castle-hall with a square plan surrounded by three towers. It is commonly referred to as the "Palace of the Saddle" because of the unusual shape of its roof. Other buildings include the Music House, the Wedding House, the Turkish baths, and the churches, including Debre Berhan Selassie, whose walls and ceiling are covered with frescoes. The church is located in a park surrounded by a merloned wall.

During the twentieth century, the imperial palaces of Gonder were abandoned to their fate, but today the government of Addis Ababa has launched a campaign to restore them. A great city that fell into disgrace, Gonder is an extraordinary legacy to its history, an imperial capital that is eternally veiled with nostalgia.

367 top left *Fasillidàs residence is the most impressive and best conserved of the buildings in Fasil Ghebbi. Its design merges several architectural influences, including European elements like the crenellated walls and Arab features such as the four round towers and domed roof.*

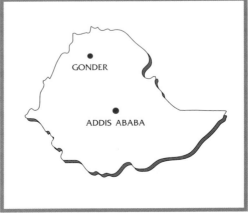

367 center *The palace of King Iyasu II, who returned Fasil Ghebbi to its original splendor in the mid-eighteenth century after a period of bitter internal fighting. An understanding and cultured man, the king surrounded himself with artists, men of letters, and merchants.*

367 bottom *A Copt priest inside the splendid church of Debre Birhan Selassié, built in the early eighteenth century by King Iyasu I. Its walls and ceiling are entirely covered in frescoes.*

Stone Town, Zanzibar

TANZANIA

WESTERN COAST OF THE ISLAND OF UNGUJA OR ZANZIBAR

REGISTRATION: 2000

CRITERIA (II) (III) (VI)

368 top left The old pier in Stone Town. Note the Bait el-Ajaib (House of Marvels) clock tower in the background. Erected in 1883 by Sultan Bargash, it was the first building on the island to have electricity.

368 center left Recent restoration has returned the Old Dispensary building to its former glory. It was built in colonial style by a rich Indian merchant who wished to celebrate the silver jubilee of Queen Victoria.

368 bottom right The Anglican cathedral was built between 1873 and 1880 by the British on the site of the old slave market. Today 97 percent of the population of Zanzibar is Muslim and the rest either Christian, Hindu, or Sikh.

Zanzibar was founded as the result of a nightmare. In 675, Abi Ben Sultan Hassan, heir to the throne of Shiraz, dreamed that mice had devoured his palace. A superstitious man, he interpreted this is as a grim omen and decided to abandon Persia. After a long voyage over land and sea, a storm forced him to go ashore on an island in the Indian Ocean.

The sultan and his crew must have liked the spot. Their descendants, who intermarried with the Africans, created a community with its own language that, over the centuries, spread to the coastal areas of Eastern Africa: Swahili. The name is derived from the Arabic *sawahili*, meaning "of the coast." More than a thousand years later, the Shirazi have maintained a strong identity. Despite the fact that the island was a hub for commerce in antiquity – the Assyrians, Egyptians, and Phoenicians landed here, followed by the Portuguese, Chinese, Indians, and English – the Shirazi had a decisive influence on the culture of Zanzibar. Today, 97 percent of the population is Islamic and the remainder is divided between Christians, Hindus, and Sikhs.

In the seventeenth century, the island became the leading center for the slave trade of the Indian Ocean. The Shirazi are proud of the fact that they never participated in this base traffic, which was exclusively run by other Arab populations from Oman. From Zanzibar, these populations controlled about 620 miles of the African coast, from Mozambique to Somalia.

In 1832, the ruler of Oman, Seyyid Sa'id, transferred his sultanate from Muscat to Zanzibar, built a fortress over the ruins of a Portuguese settlement, and established the Busaidi Dynasty, which ruled for 130 years. In addition to the sale of slaves and ivory, the spice trade soon prospered. At the beginning of the nineteenth century, Indian merchants introduced the cultivation of cloves, and because of its favorable climate, within just fifty years Zanzibar became the world's leading producer of this spice. In the wake of this success, cinnamon, cumin, ginger, pepper, and cardamom were also planted.

Stone Town, the island's main settlement, is located on a triangular peninsula. Many buildings, mainly the homes of the Arab merchants, date from this period. The architecture of these two- and three-story homes, made of coral stone and set around a courtyard, reflects an Arab layout combined with Indian and European stylistic elements. The Indian influence can be seen in the decorated window jambs and the carved wooden doors with metal studs, used on the sub-continent to ward off elephants, which do not exist on Zanzibar. The Europeans introduced the custom of embellishing houses

368-369 Stone Town seen from the air. From the seventeenth century on, this port was the main slave-trading center in the Indian Ocean. With the abolition of slavery in the nineteenth century, it became known as the "spice port."

with balconies, loggias, and verandas. Instead, the *barazas*, stone benches set along the walls, are typical of the island, and even today they are still the "meeting place" preferred by the local population.

The *hamman*, the Balnara Mosque, the Sultan's Palace, and Bait el-Ajaib (House of Wonders) were built in the nineteenth century. Bait el-Ajaib is the largest building in the city and was commissioned by ibn Sa'id Barghash in 1870 for ceremonial purposes. In order to save it from being damaged by cannon fire, in 1873 the sultan surrendered to the English who had declared war on him for failing to observe the anti-slavery treaty. After the first shots were fired, Barghash waved the white flag just 38 minutes after the hostilities had started. To celebrate their victory, the English built an Anglican cathedral over the site of the slave market. The building has a curious neo-Gothic style with an Arabian air and was completed in 1879 when the clock, a gift from the sultan, was placed on the bell tower. The Catholic church funded by the French was built at the same time. One of the most noteworthy "European" buildings is the Old Dispensary, built by a wealthy Indian merchant in honor of Queen Victoria's silver jubilee.

The English arrived in Zanzibar before the slave trade was abolished. The most famous British visitor was Dr. David Livingstone, who stayed there in 1871 before he set out on his last expedition to Black Africa. After discovering Victoria Falls, he continued toward the mouth of the Zambezi. He died on the journey and his body, which was embalmed by the locals, was brought back to Zanzibar, where it was kept for some time before being taken to Westminster Abbey for burial. Some of his valuable notes and his doctor's chest are on exhibit at the Peace Memorial Museum.

369

369 center right Wood carvings typical of a port city. The style of the doorframes is typical of the Indian sub-continent, as are the elaborate metal studs that in some areas of India were used to keep elephants at bay.

369 bottom right Built over an earlier Portuguese fort between 1698 and 1701 by the Busaids from Oman, the Arab Fort was later occupied by the British.

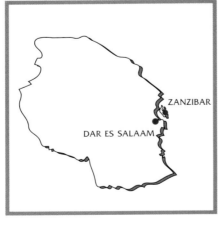

ZANZIBAR

DAR ES SALAAM

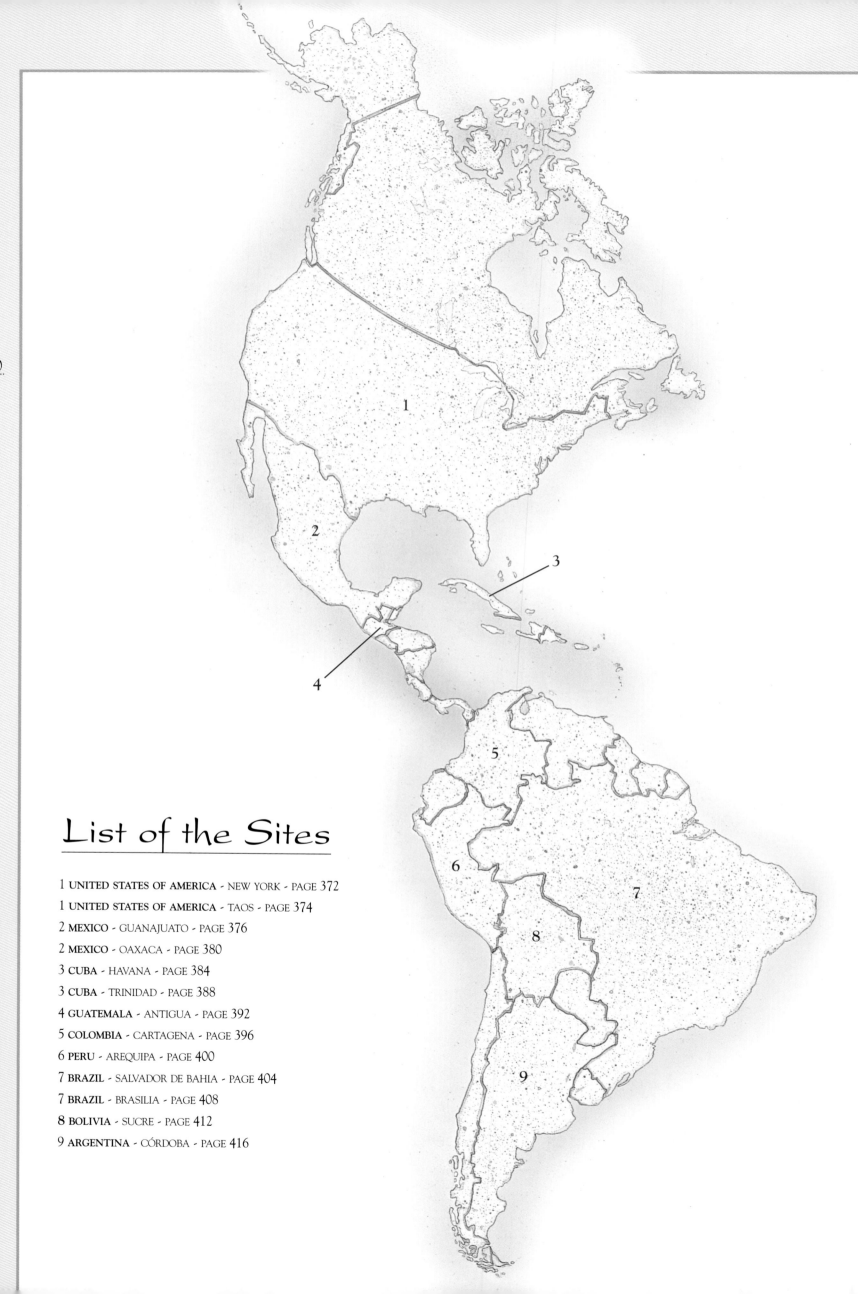

List of the Sites

The Americas

On October 12, 1492 the caravels of Christopher Columbus landed on the island of Hispaniola, marking the start of a profound change in the history of humanity, but above all in the destiny of the peoples that inhabited the American continent. Despite occurring in different phases and in different ways, the arrival of European colonizers caused the progressive loss of identity of the indigenous populations and the destruction and abandonment of villages and cities in North and Latin America.

In consequence, of the more than 50 sites inscribed in the World Heritage List in the American continent, only one represents the surviving heredity of the American civilizations, Pueblo de Taos in the United States, which is still inhabited by Pueblo Indians. The few other sites in North America are mostly linked to the history of colonization by the English and French or are symbols of independence like Independence Hall and Statue of Liberty. Nor has the extraordinary artistic vitality of the United States during the twentieth century earned it a place, at least for the moment, in UNESCO's World Heritage classification.

Similarly, most of the cultural legacy in Latin America is explicitly linked to the centuries of Spanish domination. From Mexico to Argentina, the traces of great civilizations like those of the Maya and Inca are still impressed in the cultural memory of the Amerindian peoples, but their ceremonial centers have been uninhabited for centuries. The continent's Spanish cities were built over previously inhabited centers, either erasing all vestiges of the earlier civilization or resulting in a mixture of the new and indigenous architectural styles.

Latin America's architectural legacy therefore coincides with the era of the Spanish Conquest and follows the footsteps of Pizarro and the *conquistadors* from the Gulf of Mexico to the Pacific Ocean. Latin America's inheritance is composed of the cities and defensive walls built by the Spanish and the missions built by the Jesuits who came to the New World to spread Christianity.

The continent's architectural styles originated in seventeenth-century Europe. The Baroque triumphed in South America even if often the use of local labor resulted in a unique blend of forms, original decorations, and an art in which human figures bear the semblances of Indian populations.

Having regained their independence at different times, the countries of Latin America have re-established their origins, but a devastating colonial legacy has slowed their economic development and influenced their cultural evolution. Thus, since the nineteenth century, architecture has also felt the influence of the difficult political and economic conditions suffered by the entire continent. The only exception is Brasilia, the masterpiece by town-planner Lucio Costa and architect Oscar Niemeyer, an entire city designed and built with the express purpose of functioning as a capital.

The Statue of Liberty
UNITED STATES OF AMERICA

NEW YORK
REGISTRATION: 1984
CRITERIA: C (I) (VI)

372 left Donated to the United States to celebrate the centenary of its independence in 1776, the Statue of Liberty was not in fact inaugurated until October 28, 1886.

On the night of July 3, 1986, thousands of people were present in the New York harbor to watch a fireworks display that cost two million dollars. It was a large sum, but negligible compared to the 87 million that had been spent on restoring the Statue of Liberty to celebrate its centenary. Nonetheless, the return to the original splendor of what has been the symbol of America for nearly one hundred and twenty years was well worth the expense.

The idea to create a work of sculpture that symbolized the brotherhood of France and the United States in their battle for liberty began to torment Frédéric-Auguste Bartholdi in spring 1865, when the Confederate troops surrendered at the end of the Civil War. In 1871, the artist crossed the Atlantic to present his project to the President, Ulysses Grant. In the end it was decided that, to celebrate the centenary of American independence, the work would be unveiled on July 4, 1876, and the American government would further contribute with the creation of the pedestal.

Alas, the forecasts were optimistic. The economies of the two countries were not in good shape, and for several years the finances stagnated, until Joseph Pulitzer (after whom the journalistic prize is named) launched a campaign to collect funds through the columns of his newspaper, *The World*, with a series of blistering editorials that invited all Americans to participate in the venture. In 1884, the Statue was finally completed, and a year later, when the base had been prepared, the 350 pieces of copper of which it was composed were sent across the Atlantic on the French frigate Isère.

On October 28, 1886, on Bedloe Island, right in front of the port of New York, "Freedom enlightening the world" was

inaugurated by President Grover Cleveland, more than ten years later than had been planned. It stands 151 feet high (305 feet and weighs nearly 30,000 tons if the cement pedestal is included), and is formed by a central steel pylon designed by Alexandre Gustave Eiffel that provides the load-bearing structure. The copper skin, weighing 34 tons but only 2.37 millimetres – under one-tenth of an inch – thick, is hung on this central support system and has a tormented history. In order to create the largest metal statue ever built, Bartholdi made models on ever larger scales, some of which are preserved in the Statue Museum inside the base. In order to forge the face of Liberty, the French sculptor chose his mother as his model, but the pose tired her too quickly during production of the work, so Bartholdi went out into the streets of Paris in search of a young woman whose facial features resembled those of his mother. He met Jeanne-Emilie Baheux de Puysieux who, after finishing her task as model, became the sculptor's wife.

Starting from the base of the Statue of

Liberty, it is necessary to climb 354 steps to reach the crown, the highest point open to the public, from where one has a superb view of the bay of New York. The crown is one of the most symbolic sections: its seven points represent (or so it is interpreted) the seven seas (the Arctic, Antarctic, North Atlantic, South Atlantic, North Pacific, South Pacific, and Indian oceans), or perhaps, the seven continents (North and South America, Europe, Asia, Africa, Australia, and Antarctica). The windows in the crown are supposed to represent the 25 natural minerals of the Earth. The torch (rebuilt in 1986 and lined with 24 carat gold) that the woman holds in her right hand represents the light that Freedom brings, and the tablet she carries in her left hand bears the date of American independence, July 4, 1776, in Roman numerals. The figure's toga commemorates the Roman republic, the first democratic "experiment" in history, and the broken chain at her feet symbolizes the victory over slavery.

Built within the walls of Fort Wood, which stood on Bedloe Island to protect New York port, the Statue of Liberty was first administered by the United States Lighthouse Board, then responsibility was passed to the Department of War, and finally in 1933, to the National Park Service. In 1956, the island was renamed Liberty Island.

A strange fact is that no one ever saw the statue with her original copper color; rapid oxidation of the material meant that when she reached New York she had already turned a very dark brown, almost black. Twenty years later, she turned her characteristic green, the color that signified the hope of a new life for entire generations of immigrants who went to America in search of fortune.

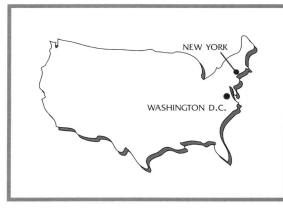

372 right Standing in the court of Fort Wood on Bedloe Island, at the mouth of the Port of New York, the statue is placed on an eight-point star that contains the Immigration Museum.

The torch, covered with 24-carat gold, represents the light that accompanies Freedom, and the toga she wears commemorates the Roman Republic, the first national experiment in democracy.

373 left Many elements of "Freedom Enlightening the World" (the official name of the monument) are symbolic.

373 top right The tablet that Liberty holds in her left hand bears the date July 4, 1776, Independence Day in the United States.

NEW YORK

WASHINGTON D.C.

Pueblo de Taos

UNITED STATES OF AMERICA

TAOS VALLEY, NEW MEXICO
REGISTRATION: 1992
CRITERIA: C (IV)

374

374 top Taos Valley, through which flows a tributary of the Rio Grande of the North, is still a wild region today. The Pueblos Indians built several villages in this area starting in the early thirteenth century, and the Pueblo de Taos that exists today dates from 1350.

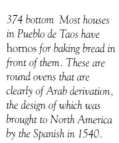

374 bottom Most houses in Pueblo de Taos have hornos for baking bread in front of them. These are round ovens that are clearly of Arab derivation, the design of which was brought to North America by the Spanish in 1540.

Each year at the end of August, the Pueblo de Taos initiation ceremony is held at the Blue Lake. It is a required rite if one is to be admitted to the religious life and political positions of the community. For the Pueblo Indians of Taos Valley, through which a small tributary of the Rio Grande runs to the north, the lake was the origin of the native population living in the New Mexico and Arizona region. In a 1970 decision that represented a turning point in the reconciliation between the United States and the remaining indigenous population, the Federal government returned to the Pueblo tribe the sacred lake, high up on the mountain, that dominates the valley in which they live.

Indications have been found of primitive human settlements in the valley from 5,000 years ago, but the first occupants of whom there exists solid evidence are the Anasazi Indians – the "Ancients" – who lived in the region around the ninth century A.D. Little is known of their civilization, but it is certain that they lived in shelters dug in the ground before the era in which the Pueblo buildings were built. The village of Pueblo de Taos, a few miles north of the modern city of Taos, was built in the mid-fourteenth century.

The first Europeans to set foot in Pueblo de Taos were, in 1540, the *conquistadors* led by Hernán Alvarado, who was later followed by Franciscan missionaries. Thanks to the goodwill of the Spanish king, Philip II, the Pueblo Indians were allowed a certain degree of autonomy, and the communities lived in relative peace until the end of the century. During this period, the baked brick constructions of the Pueblos felt the Spanish influence and, indirectly, that of the Arab architecture that dominated the south of the Iberian peninsula. The Pueblos had known the technique of baking bricks for centuries, but it was only then that they began to use wooden moulds to give their bricks a regular shape and to build circular ovens for baking bread that were clearly Arab in nature.

In the seventeenth century, the Spaniards made their presence felt more strongly, and in 1680 the Pueblos rebelled but were put down in 1692. The following century brought a large number of agricultural settlers to New Mexico and saw the founding of self-sufficient farms near the local villages. The closure of Spanish settlements gave the Pueblos a certain degree of isolation that allowed them to continue their traditions and the spirit of independence that they still embrace. When Mexico won its independence from Spain in 1821, friction soon sprang up between the new country and the fur traders who traveled the long distance from the East Coast. These "mountain men" – symbolized in the collective unconscious by Daniel Boone and the backwoods image of the politician Davy Crockett – lived side by side with the Indians, learning their hunting techniques and adopting their customs. They also fought beside them when defending the villages of the sedentary Pueblos against the attacks of the

374-375 All the buildings in the village are made from adobe – a mixture of mud and straw – which is formed into bricks and lined with mud. Though it requires maintenance after every rainy season, the material holds warmth during winter and cool during summer.

nomadic tribes of the plains such as the Navajo and the Apache. The expansion of the United States westwards culminated in the 1846 war after which the province joined the United States' Territory of New Mexico, which included Arizona. These were the years that Kit Carson fought in the Civil War, defending the flag of the Union that flew over Pueblo de Taos.

The arrival of the "intruders" did not end there, and in the 1870's the Gold Rush occurred, which brought new inhabitants in search of fortune into the valley. Then, at the start of the twentieth century, it was the turn of the artists; Ernest Blumenschein and Bert Phillips were the first of a "colony" joined by intellectuals like painter Georgia O'Keeffe, photographer Ansel Adams, psychoanalyst Carl Jung, and writer D.H. Lawrence.

Notwithstanding the many outside influences, the architecture and culture of the Pueblo de Taos community have survived, and today the village is one of the oldest settlements on American soil. The Pueblos maintain their sovereignty over the land through the Governor of the Tribe and the Tribal Council. Their economic independence is ensured by flourishing craft and tourist industries.

375

375 bottom The church of San Francisco de Asis is one of the most interesting constructions in Pueblo de Taos. Since the end of the nineteenth century, artists and avant-garde intellectuals have been interested in the primitive architecture of the village.

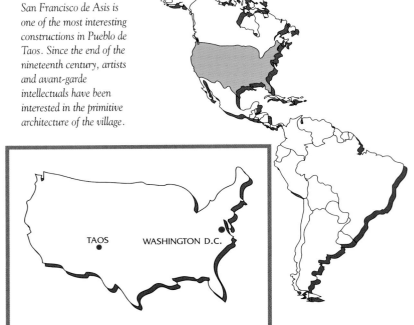

TAOS   WASHINGTON D.C.

The Historic Town of Guanajuato and its Silver Mines

MEXICO

STATE OF GUANAJUATO
REGISTRATION: 1988
CRITERIA: C (I) (II) (IV) (VI)

376-377 The city was built in a valley that was considered inaccessible until the arrival of the Spanish. In the center of the photograph, the Basílica de Nuestra Señora de Guanajuato dominates the Plaza de la Paz.

376 bottom left A cloister in the Hospicio de la Santísima Trinidad, the ancient seat of Guanajuato University founded by the Jesuits in 1732. Behind we see the dome of the Templo de la Compañía de Jesús.

376 bottom right Painted in bright colors, a colonial house in one of the alleys that wind around Guanajuato Hill.

W hen in 1541 the Viceroy, Antonio de Mendoza, gave a plot of land on the Barranca de Cuanax Huata to Don Rodrigo de Vázquez as a gift, Rodrigo did not feel especially honored. The steep hillsides that marked the edge of the ravine were inaccessible even to the Indios who lived in the area. As only amphibians and reptiles were able to draw comfort from the place, the natives called it Cuanax Huata (hill of frogs), a name that the Spaniards' mispronunciation turned into Guanajuato.

Nonetheless, even though it took him seven years to discover it, Don Rodrigo was a lucky man because, in 1548, a mule-driver in his service discovered specks of silver in the ashes of the fire he had lit to warm himself during a chilly night on the top of the ravine. Whether the story is fact or fiction, this episode represented the discovery of the mine of San Barnabé, the first of the silver and gold deposits that, in less than a century, were to turn a rough frontier village into Santa Fe y Real de Minas de Guanajuato, the third largest city in the Spanish empire after Mexico City and Havana.

Midway through the seventeenth century, Guanajuato was a "split" city. Gangs of slaves mined a third of the world's production of silver in the mines underground while, above their heads, nobles and adventurers became rich within the space of a generation. They built splendid residences from pink stone, mixing the cement (or so it is said) with silver dust.

Guanajuato was the first city in the New World to build ramparts, but surprisingly, they were not for defensive purposes; rather, they were used to bank up the land to prevent landslides during the frequent heavy rains. For this reason a large underground passage was dug that allowed the water to drain away below the residential area. Today this area is a warren of squares, flights of steps, and alleyways, some of which were so narrow (like the Callejon del Beso) that two lovers could kiss leaning from their windows on either side of the street.

Religious sentiment was stronger in Guajuanato than elsewhere in New Spain. Those who had made their fortune through the inhumane treatment of

thousands of Indios felt obliged to pay some penalty to ensure their entrance to Heaven. Consequently, they built magnificent churches and monasteries like the Templo de la Compañía de Jesus and the Basílica Menor de Nuestra Señora de Guanajuato. This church, in Plaza de la Paz, features an intricate Baroque façade painted yellow and, inside, an eighth-century wooden statue of the Virgin donated to the city by King Philip II in 1557 in a demonstration of thanks for the discovery that filled the coffers of Spain.

The most extraordinary religious building in the city – if not all Mexico – is the Iglesia de San Cayetano, known as La Valenciana. The interior has three

377 top The façade of Casa Rul y Valenciana, built at the end of the eighteenth century in a style that blends Colonial and Neo-Classical. Its original owner, Don Antonio de Obregón y Alcocer, Conde de la Valenciana, was one of the city's silver barons.

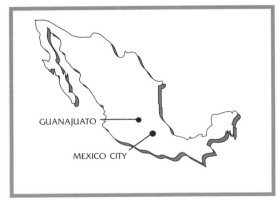

377 bottom The entrance to one of the mines still in operation. Silver was the reason for Guanajuato's phenomenal development, becoming Latin America's third largest city after Mexico City and Havana in the mid-seventeenth century.

378 top left The Churrigueresque façade of the Iglesia de San Cayetano, known as La Valenciana. It was built in the second half of the eighteenth century under the direction of architects Andrés de la Riva and Jorge Archundia.

378 top right A detail of the exuberant Baroque decoration in wood and gilded stucco that characterizes the three altars in the Valenciana.

378 bottom This painted wooden sculptural group stands on the top of the Valenciana's high altar. It depicts the Virgin and Child surrounded by angels.

378-379 A view of the three altars and octagonal dome in the Valenciana. The altars respectively celebrate St. Cayetano, the Virgin Mary, and the triumph of the Roman Catholic Church.

379 bottom left The pink stone façade of the Templo de San Diego de Alcántara, built in 1784 on the site of the Convento de San Pedro de Alcántara after the latter had been seriously damaged by a flood.

379 bottom right The Templo de la Compañía de Jesús, one of the most original constructions in Churrigueresque style, dates from the mid-eighteenth century. It was built using the donations of a group of distinguished citizens who wished to thank God for the wealth they had accumulated.

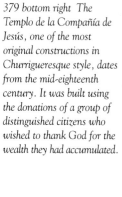

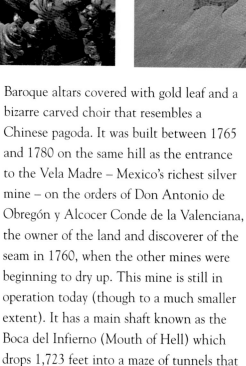

Baroque altars covered with gold leaf and a bizarre carved choir that resembles a Chinese pagoda. It was built between 1765 and 1780 on the same hill as the entrance to the Vela Madre – Mexico's richest silver mine – on the orders of Don Antonio de Obregón y Alcocer Conde de la Valenciana, the owner of the land and discoverer of the seam in 1760, when the other mines were beginning to dry up. This mine is still in operation today (though to a much smaller extent). It has a main shaft known as the Boca del Infierno (Mouth of Hell) which drops 1,723 feet into a maze of tunnels that overall total 25 miles in length.

The end of the eighteenth century was also the period of construction of the Alhóndiga de Granaditas, the largest civil building in the city. It was built as a granary,

then used as a prison, and today is the home of the Regional Museum. In 1810, the Alhóndiga was the setting for the fiercest battles of the War of Independence. The Spanish had barricaded themselves in to defend themselves from the rebel army led by Miguel Hidalgo, but they were flushed out by an *indio* called El Pípila, who attacked the gate and set fire to it, losing his life in the process.

In 1886, Mexico's most famous artist was born in a small red house on the steep Calle Pocitos in the heart of the city. The murals of Diego Rivera are filled with color and passion and are perhaps the best representation of the spirit of Guanajuato, a city where fortune and good cheer have always gone hand in hand with physical toil and death.

The Historic Center of Oaxaca

MEXICO

STATE OF OAXACA
REGISTRATION: 1987
CRITERIA: C (I) (II) (III) (IV)

380

380 top The porticoes in the zócalo, where the inhabitants of Oaxaca meet. Behind, note the Plateresque-style façade of the Iglesia de la Compañía de Jesús, built by the Jesuits in 1579.

380-381 Evening in the Alameida di Plaza de la Constitución, or zócalo, overlooked by the cathedral. Oaxaca's most important religious building is not the most impressive architecturally. Built in 1574, it underwent substantial alterations over the next four centuries, thereby losing its stylistic unity.

A colonial house in Calle García Vigil in Oaxaca is home to a museum in honor of Benito Juárez, the city's favorite son. Elected President of Mexico in 1858, Juárez – a Zapotec *indio* of humble origin who was educated by Franciscans in his own home – has passed into history for his resistance against social prejudice, the overwhelming power of the Catholic Church, and from 1862 on, against the invasion of the French. His motto, "*El respecto al derecho ajeno es la paz*" (peace is respect for the rights of

others), soon became a symbolic expression for all liberals who fought for the democratization of the country.

Since its beginning, Oaxaca was a city to which Olmec, Zapotec, and Mixtec Indios migrated and then mixed peacefully with the Spanish *conquistadors*. In the area today, there are still 16 different ethnic groups that speak roughly 150 dialects. Every July, the Guelaguetza is celebrated, a colorful festival in which the indigenous groups dance and exchange gifts as a sign of mutual respect.

In 1521, after the conquest of Tenochtitlán, Hernán Cortéz sent troops under his lieutenant, Francisco Orozco, towards Huaxyacac, as the city was then known. It was the most important town in the valley situated at an altitude of 5,250 feet and surrounded by hills. Although Orozco had sent Cortéz a letter stating he was against the occupation of the area (it had no precious metals and was inhabited by highly combative Indios), Cortéz wanted the situation checked in person. Orozco fell in love with the natural beauties of the place and succeeded in reaching an agreement with the natives. On April 25, 1532, the king of Spain approved the founding of the city and conferred the title of Marqués del Valle

de Oaxaca on Cortéz.

The layout of the city was designed by Alonso García Bravo, the architect of the Escorial who had also planned the structures of Mexico City and Veracruz. At either ends of the *zócalo* (one of Mexico's loveliest squares), construction began on the headquarters of Spanish power and on the cathedral (on the site of a Zapotec temple in honor of the dead).

The city's main streets fanned out from the square, and according to the planner, portrayed the balance between sacred and profane. What is unusual is that it was never necessary to build a city wall, and, in fact, Oaxaca was left relatively free to get on with its own business. Crops grown in the surrounding area were maize, wheat, coffee, and sugarcane, the latter used to provide the court in Spain with sweet delicacies. This was also where it was discovered that a red tint could be extracted from cochineal, a wheat parasite, which could be used to dye fabrics.

Shortly after the founding of the city, the Dominican monks arrived who began to construct religious buildings. The Spanish

381 left The city's main pedestrian street, Calle Macedonio Alcalá, is lined with the old houses of the Spanish notables. Some of these have been turned into museums and art galleries.

381 right The brilliant colors and elaborate wrought iron railings distinguish the façades of typical colonial-style houses in Oaxaca's historical center.

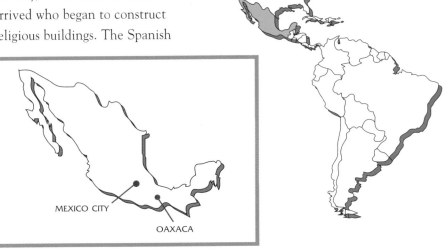

MEXICO CITY

OAXACA

Baroque is harmoniously combined in Oaxaca with indigenous traditions and the city's churches and elaborate decorations represent the best of Mestizo architecture in Mexico. Construction of the cathedral dragged on until 1733, but more magnificent and extravagant is the Iglesia de Santo Domingo. The late sixteenth-century façade is made from finely sculpted stone and is flanked on either side by a bell tower. The interior is lined with hundreds of pounds of gold. The high altar and the decorations on the walls and ceiling illustrating biblical scenes are all extraordinary. On the choir's lower wall, a gilded stucco bas-relief illustrates the genealogical order of the Dominican Order in the form of a vine. Attached to the church is a large monastery that today holds the Regional Museum. One of its displays contains a collection of Mixtec gold objects found in a tomb during excavation of the nearby archaeological site of Monte Albán.

Other fine examples of Baroque architecture are the Basilica della Nuestra Señora della Soledad and the Iglesia de San Felipe Neri. The latter was used as a barracks during the Mexican Revolution and was restored in 1920. It was redecorated with the addition of Art Nouveau elements, a touch that is also to be seen in the elegant Teatro Macedonio Alcalá, near the city square. The porticoes of the zócalo are the heart of the busy life of the city.

Many writers and artists have illustrated the beauties of Oaxaca. Friedrich Nietzche wanted to retire there, and Aldous Huxley and Italo Calvino both stayed in the city. Its atmosphere today resembles that of the novels of the father of magical realism, Gabriel García Márquez.

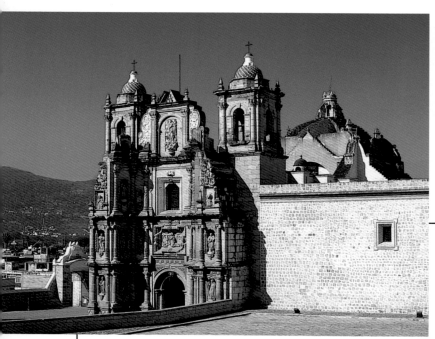

382 top left Consecrated in 1697 to the Virgen de la Soledad, Oaxaca's patron saint, the Basilica is one of the city's most resplendent examples of Baroque architecture. Inside, the image of the Virgin is venerated for its miraculous powers.

382 top right The imposing façade of the Iglesia de Santo Domingo has a central section 85 feet tall and two towers 115 feet high. The domes are covered with azulejos. The plainness of the exterior is in stark contrast to the exuberant Baroque decorations inside.

382 bottom The main entrance to the Teatro Macedonio Alcalá. Officially opened on September 15, 1909, it also functioned as a casino for its first 50 years. The interior is decorated in grand Empire style.

383 top The interior of the Iglesia de Santo Domingo is one of the best examples of Mexican Baroque and covered with hundreds of pounds of gold. Like the vault, the high altar is extraordinary, decorated with medallions depicting biblical scenes and Dominican martyrs.

383 bottom The façade of the Iglesia de Santo Domingo has a bas-relief of St. Dominic and St. Hippolyte supporting the church, onto which the image of the Holy Spirit is descending.

Old Havana and its Fortifications

CUBA

HAVANA
REGISTRATION: 1982
CRITERIA: C (IV) (V)

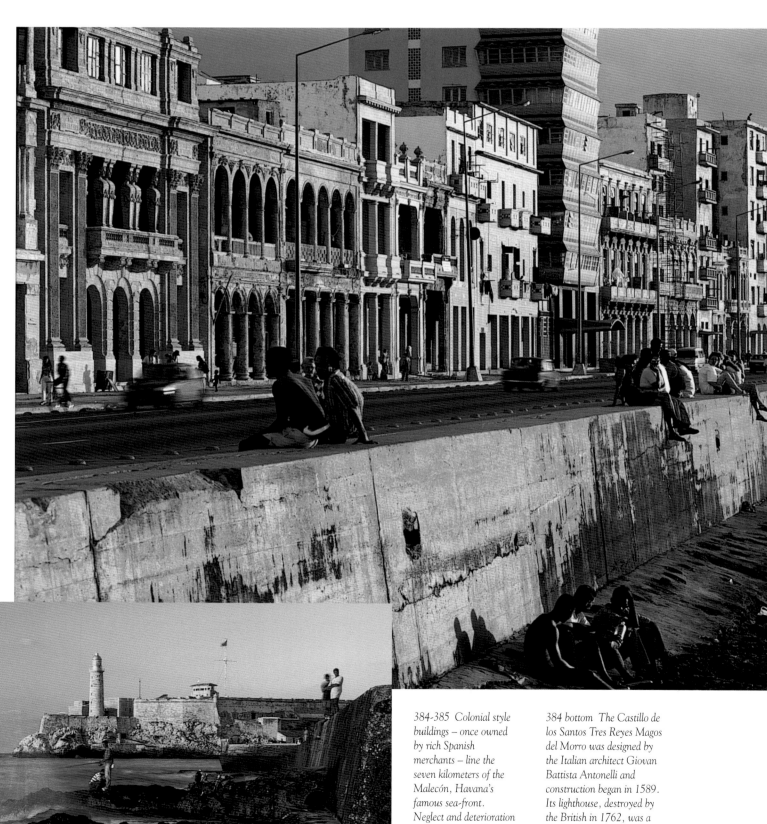

384-385 *Colonial style buildings – once owned by rich Spanish merchants – line the seven kilometers of the Malecón, Havana's famous sea-front. Neglect and deterioration present these buildings with a serious threat.*

384 bottom *The Castillo de los Santos Tres Reyes Magos del Morro was designed by the Italian architect Giovan Battista Antonelli and construction began in 1589. Its lighthouse, destroyed by the British in 1762, was a landmark for Spanish galleons but it was rebuilt in 1845.*

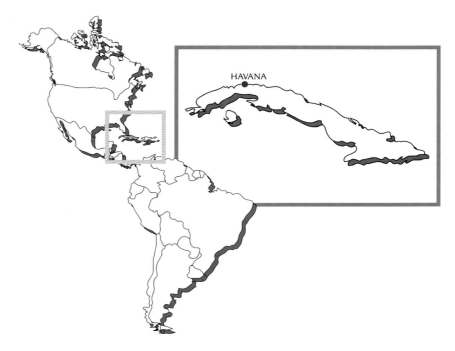

A precisely nine o'clock each evening, a salvo of cannon fire from the walls of the Fortaleza della Cabaña signals the closure of the port and the city of Havana. It seems peculiar that the revolutionary Cuba of Fidel Castro has maintained this ancient tradition, and the sight of soldiers in old-fashioned uniform moving around the ramparts of Latin America's mightiest fort bring to mind images of the age of colonialism and pirates.

About two weeks after the first, fateful

landing in the Americas, Columbus' crew disembarked on the most beautiful island ever seen by a human being, as the captain noted in his diary. He wished to call it Juana, in honor of the daughter of Queen Isabella of Spain, his patroness.

In Cuba, as the natives called it, the city of San Cristóbal de la Habana was founded by Diego Velázquez in 1519. Protected by a broad inlet, the city was soon to become an important port, and in 1550 the Spanish made it the headquarters of the Governor of the island. But the splendor of the city was soon learned of by the pirates who plied the waters of the Gulf of Mexico. Five years later, the Frenchman Jacques de Sores sacked the city, breaking the way for the raids by the famous Francis Drake.

A fortress was needed to protect the city. The symbol of the city, la Giraldilla, can still be seen on the tower of the 1577 Castillo de la Real Fuerza. It is a weathercock that bears the image of Inés de Bobadilla, wife of the governor Hernán de Soto. Despite the omens, the construction was inadequate, and the Spaniards began to build two more massive forts in 1589.

Situated on the shore opposite the mouth of the Bahia de la Habana, the

Castillo de lo Tres Santos Reyes Magos del Morro and the Castillo de San Salvador de la Punta were joined by a strong chain that prevented pirate ships from entering. However, it was not enough to thwart the English fleet in raiding Havana throughout the seventeenth century and, in 1762, from taking the city. Only a year later, it was returned to Spain in return for Florida, and

the Spanish king, Charles III, began construction of the large Fortaleza de la Cabaña, which was terminated in 1777. In the same year, the cathedral begun thirty years before by the Jesuits was finally inaugurated. Its Baroque façade made from coralline limestone dominates the portico-lined square in the old city onto which government buildings face. The cathedral, with its nave and two aisles, is plain and rather dark and is composed of a curious mix of styles as a result of the many restorations that have been carried out over a period of two centuries. Apart from the high altar, magnificently decorated in gold, silver, and onyx, there are paintings by Jean-Baptiste Vermay and many sculptures. This is where the remains of Christopher Columbus were laid until 1898 when they

385 top left The lookout towers of the Castillo de la Punta at the mouth of Havana port face the Castillo del Morro directly. The two forts were completed around 1630 but were not enough to withstand the assault of the British.

385 bottom right Plaza San Francisco de Asís was named after the monastery of the same name built in 1628. The Fuente de los Leones stands at its center. It was built in 1836 by Giuseppe Gaggini using Carrara marble.

were transferred to Seville as Spain withdrew from its last colony.

Havana's first cathedral was destroyed in the eighteenth century but used to stand in the Plaza de Armas, Parque Céspedes, which is Havana's oldest square and has been the heart of political and military life since the sixteenth century. It is overlooked by some of the city's finest buildings such as the Palacio de los Capitanos Generales (home to the Civic Museum), the Palacio del Conde de Santovenia, and the Castillo de la Real Fuerza. The Palacio del Segundo Cabo, on the other hand, is one of the best examples of Cuban Baroque architecture. Built in 1772 on a marvelous colonnade to house the post office, it faces onto an Andalusian-style courtyard and became the residence of the Vice-Governor in 1853. The square is the starting point for the calles of the colonial capital (like the Calle Obispo, which connects the Plaza de Armas and the Paseo de Martí, named after the hero of independence) onto which colonial and Art Nouveau style residences face with their large patios.

Havana's most attractive street is probably the Malecón, the road which runs for four miles along the sea from the Castillo de la Punta to the mouth of the river Almendares. Its first stretch is lined with the colonnades of Spanish colonial houses that were probably used to negotiate business deals, given their proximity to the port. Today, despite attempts by the Cuban government to counter the trend, many of these buildings are becoming increasingly rundown.

386

386 top left This typical colonial porticoed house in the city center is painted in bright colors. International interest has prompted a number of old buildings to be restored.

386 top right Several buildings in the Paseo del Prado, today called the Paseo de Martí after the hero of Cuban independence. In the late nineteenth and early twentieth centuries, this was the city's most renowned street.

386 center The Plaza Vieja is lined by magnificent eighteenth-century palaces that were used as a model to create the city's particular architectural style.

386 bottom left A detail from the Neo-Classical facade of the Gran Teatro in Havana, officially opened in 1838 with the name Gran Teatro de Tacón. Since 1950 it has been the home of the National Ballet of Cuba.

387 The Baroque façade of Havana Cathedral is made from coral limestone. Its construction was begun by the Jesuits in 1748 but was interrupted for twenty years when the religious order was expelled from the island by a government decree.

Trinidad and the Valle de los Ingenios

CUBA

PROVINCE OF SANCTI SPÍRITUS
REGISTRATION: 1988
CRITERIA: C (IV) (V)

HAVANA

VALLE DE LOS INGENIOS

TRINIDAD

Sitting in the shade of the patios in the old colonial houses painted blue, yellow, and pink, the old people of Trinidad like to tell the story handed down through the generations of the city's happiest day. It took place in 1850 when a ship loaded with French furniture berthed in the nearby port. The cargo had been ordered by Conde de Brunet to furnish his newly-constructed home in Plaza Mayor. All the mule-owners in Trinidad were hired to carry the precious load along the path that connected the port to the town. In the evening, everyone gathered in the square to celebrate the arrival of mirrors with

Trinidad that, four years later, Cortéz sailed to conquer Mexico. Yet Trinidad remained a hideout for smugglers until the end of the eighteenth century, when a number of landowners emigrated there from Haiti following the uprising of the slaves and the burning of the sugarcane plantations.

In the eyes of the new arrivals, the Valle de San Luis near Trinidad – dominated by the Escambray massif and made fertile by the Río Agabama – was a perfect place to grow sugarcane. The idea was particularly attractive as the price of sugar had risen sharply with the closure of the Haitian refineries. Thus, the initiative of the French, copied soon after by the Spanish, led to the establishment of 50 or so Ingenios (plantations with sugar mills) within 20 years across the 107 square miles of the Valle de San Luis. It is estimated that 2,800 macheteros slaves worked there cutting the 4,400 tons of cane necessary to produce 770 tons of sugar-loaves, 1,000

388 bottom This splendid patio is part of Casa Brunet, which was owned by a rich family of sugarcane barons. In 1974, the building was turned into the Romantic Museum.

389 top The large number of perfectly conserved colonial houses makes Trinidad one of the loveliest places in the Caribbean.

389 bottom left A room in the Romantic Museum, opened in 1974 in a lovely two-storey house built for the Conde de Brunet around 1840.

magnificent gilded frames, four-poster beds, and Limoges porcelain.

Today these treasures and other objects from Trinidad's aristocratic mansions are displayed in the Museo Romantico in the former Casa Brunet, and they perfectly represent the era in which this small town in central Cuba was the flourishing territory of the sugarcane barons.

In fact, the history of Trinidad began in the early days of the Spanish colony when, in 1514, Captain Diego Velázquez founded a base there for the expeditions to be made throughout the New World. It was from

barrels of *aguardiente* (firewater), and 1,000 barrels of molasses each year.

Made rich by the profitable trade, the landowners of Trinidad competed to build magnificent mansions embellished with flower-filled patios and decorations made from carved wood, wrought iron, and stucco. In 1817, construction of Cuba's largest cathedral began, the Iglesia Parroquial de la Santísima Trinidad, which, thanks to its splendid architectural features and altar, greatly overshadowed the Iglesia del Convento de San Francisco de Asís, built a century earlier.

389 bottom right A symbol of the Valle de los Ingenios, the Manacas-Iznaga tower was built at the start of the nineteenth century. It was used to monitor the work of the macheteros in the sugarcane fields. It stands 43.5 meters tall and has 184 steps.

388-389 A street in the center of Trinidad, flanked by brightly-painted houses from the colonial era. In the background, the bell-tower of the Iglesia de San Francisco de Asís.

390-391 Facing onto Plaza Mayor, the Iglesia de la Santísima Trinidad is Cuba's largest church. It was built in 1892 in Neo-Classical style on the site of a sixteenth-century church. Its wooden altar substituted the traditional marble version.

391 top left Some of Trinidad's old houses have been turned into museums. The Architecture Museum can be seen in the 1738 house that belonged to the Sánchez Iznaga family of landowners.

391 top right Another street in the colonial center of the city. In the eighteenth century, an entire district in Trinidad was inhabited by pirates. Their houses can be seen in what is now Calle Ciro Redondo.

The sugar production industry flourished until the start of the twentieth century when the land began to become less fertile and the importance of Trinidad started to diminish with the construction of the port in nearby Camagüey.

The richest period of Trinidad's history is marked by the city's buildings that were either assigned to the common people – probably descendants of the slaves who had performed the backbreaking work in the plantations – after the Cuban revolution or turned into museums. Those buildings that stand in what is referred to by all as the Valle de los Ingenios represent what was the most important agricultural complex in all of the Caribbean. The structures number 77, of which eleven were the homes of the plantation owners, three are the ruins of sugar mills, and the rest are warehouses, machine rooms, and bohíos, the huts where the macheteros lived.

The best preserved buildings are those on the plantation called Ingenio Manacas-Iznaga, which was the largest and most productive until 1857. Here, the tren jamaiquin still works, so named because the railway was brought to Cuba from Jamaica, which was a British colony at the time. For a while the train was used to transport the cane juice to the mills for refining. This plantation is also the location of the Torre de Manacas-Iznaga which was built at the start of the nineteenth century to allow the plantation owner to watch his slaves at work. This was the first building in the valley to be declared a national monument, and it has since become the symbol of the valley.

390 top A view of Trinidad city center. The first Spanish settlement in San Luis valley dates from 1514 when Captain Diego Velázquez founded a base there to explore the New World.

390 center and bottom Two of the fourteen rooms in the Romantic Museum that contains nineteenth-century furnishings and decorations that belonged to the rich landowners of the city.

Antigua
GUATEMALA

DEPARTMENT OF SACATEPÉQUEZ
REGISTRATION: 1979
CRITERIA: C (I) (II) (IV)

392

Having left for the Americas with Hernán Cortéz, Don Pedro de Alvarado enjoyed a long series of conquests along the coast of the Gulf of Mexico. He pushed further east where, in 1523, he explored lands covered with luxuriant vegetation and punctuated by a series of volcanoes. On July 25, 1524, he founded the city of Santiago de los Caballeros on the site of the native village of Iximiché in Guatemala. However, just three years later, due to the continuous attacks of the rebellious Cakiquel Indios, Don Pedro abandoned the city to found another in a safer place, and a new Santiago was built at the foot of the Volcano del Agua.

The first monks arrived from Spain, and as soon as a worthy house was built, so did Don Pedro's wife, Doña Beatriz de la Cueva. The natives were subjugated and all seemed to be going for the best when, following his *conquistador* nature, Don Pedro headed to Mexico to support the Spanish troops in Michoacán.

Although the mission cost him his life, he did not have to live to see the

earthquake that completely destroyed his city and also killed Doña Beatriz.

His brother, Don Jorge, who succeeded him as governor, decided to found a third Santiago in the Valle de Panchoy, not far from the earlier two cities. On March 16, 1543, the new city was given the title of *Muy Noble y Muy Leal Ciudad de San Juan de los Caballeros del Guatemala* by King Philip II and became the capital of a

392 top left A detail from the exquisite sculptures and low reliefs that adorn Antigua cathedral.

392 bottom left The colonnaded portico added to the Renaissance-style Palacio de los Capitanes Generales in the eighteenth century. The palace was originally built in 1558 in Plaza de Armas as the seat of Spanish power.

392-393 A view of the city with the cathedral built in 1680. The Catedral de Santiago (its full name) was repeatedly damaged by earthquakes and it almost completely collapsed in 1773. It was partially rebuilt between 1780 and 1820 but its wonderful Baroque interior was lost forever.

territory that included Chiapas, Belize, El Salvador, Honduras, Nicaragua, and Costa Rica, as well as Guatemala.

Designed by Italian architect Battista Antonelli, it was the first city in the New World to be based on an urban plan. For two centuries it grew until it had 53 superb churches, monasteries, oratories, and chapels, five hospitals, San Carlos University, a series of town houses belonging to the nobility, solid administrative buildings, parks, and a municipal water system. The splendor of its architecture was only rivaled by Mexico City and Lima. Its sculptors were

known throughout the continent and were invited to decorate churches in Mexico and Quito. Unfortunately, it all came to an end on July 29, 1773, St. Martha's Day, when the earth trembled once again and much of the town was destroyed. It was decided not to rebuild it but to found a new Guatemala City. The abandoned city, from that time on, was named La Antigua Guatemala (Old Guatemala).

Today, Antigua is a town of 66,000 inhabitants, roughly the population it had during the eighteenth century. It also represents an extraordinary paradox; thanks to its "death," it is a place in which the

Spanish colonial epoch has truly remained alive. Many of the buildings destroyed by the earthquake have not been restored, but the ruins, covered with bougainvillea, make the town even more lovely.

The Palacio de los Capitanes Generales stands in the Plaza de Armas. The seat of Spanish power, it was built in Renaissance style in 1558 and renovated with the addition of a Baroque portico in the eighteenth century. On the other side of the square stands the façade of the cathedral, built in 1680, where Don Pedro de Alvarado was buried after his remains were transported from Michoacán to lie beside those of his wife. The church once boasted the most magnificent decorations in Central America, but sadly they have been destroyed. In 1840 a more modest parish church was built in the lee of the façade. In the center of the square stands the Fountain of the Sirens, a Baroque

393 left Today Antigua Guatemala – once the capital of a vast Spanish colony in Central America – has about 66,000 inhabitants. This is roughly the same figure as in 1773 when a violent earthquake razed much of it to the ground.

393 right A court in the building of the Universidad de San Carlos de Borromeo, founded in 1673, which today houses the Museum of Colonial Art.

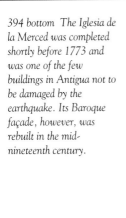

394 top left Part of a column elegantly decorated with stucco. Antigua's golden era lasted from the mid-sixteenth century to the 1773 earthquake when the city was filled with sculptures that were famous throughout the capitals of Latin America.

394 top right The monastery next to the Iglesia de la Merced was never rebuilt. In the center of this heavily damaged cloister stands the solid Fuente de Pescados (Fountain of Fish) which is where the friars carried out their famous pioneering experiments in aquiculture.

394-395 *Little remains of the colonial Iglesia de San Francisco, built in the mid-sixteenth century. The rest of it has been altered and rebuilt several times, once using reinforced concrete in 1961 which, though it does not match the colonial architecture, saved it from collapse in 1976.*

395 top *The cloister of the Convento de las Capuchinas, completed in 1736 for a group of nuns under the direction of architect Diego de Porres. Currently the building contains a museum of the religious life of that period.*

masterpiece by the architect Miguel de Porres.

The nearby Convento de las Capuchinas, arranged around an unusual circular patio, was completed in 1736 by Diego de Porres, the most famous of the local architects. Other important buildings in Antigua are the Convento de Santa Clara, the Monasterio de San Francisco (which contains a collection of *retablos*), and the Convento de la Merced. Its eccentrically Baroque church was completed just a few years before the earthquake and remained intact. From here, every Good Friday, a procession leaves to make its way through the streets strewn with a carpet of pine needles and flowers.

Hundreds of worshippers commemorate the Passion of Christ as they carry a heavy statue of Jesus for approximately eight hours. This is the most important Holy Week celebration in Central America, and it is fitting that it should be Antigua to remember the sacrifice that culminated in a resurrection.

The Port, Fortresses, and Monumental Group of Cartagena
COLOMBIA

CARTAGENA
REGISTRATION: 1984
CRITERIA: C (IV) (VI)

Thirty-one tons of gold is the amount the Spanish crown spent to build the fortifications that were supposed to protect Cartagena de Indias and its trade in precious goods and slaves from pirate attacks. It is said that, when the cost of these works was made known to King Philip II, he went out onto the balcony exclaiming, "At that price, we should be able to see them from Spain!"

However, the enormous expense justified itself years later, in 1741, when Cartagena heroically withstood the assault of the British fleet led by Admiral Edward Vernon. After months of siege, while commemorative medals of the triumph were already being minted in England, the English ships returned meekly home, worn out by the battle and illness. The hero of the resistance was Don Blas de Lezo,

the brave Basque commander who had already lost an eye, an arm, and a leg in battle. On his death, a statue was raised in his honor in the Castillo de San Felipe de Barajas, the largest fort in the city, which was built to defend the hill of San Lazaro.

Colombia had been discovered by Rodrigo de Bastidas in 1502, and the inlet on the coast of the Caribbean had been given the name Bahía de Cartagena because of its resemblance to its Spanish counterpart. The attempt by the Spanish to settle the land met with hostility on the part of the local populations. It was only on June 1, 1533 that Pedro de Heredia from Madrid succeeded in founding the city of Cartagena on the spot where the native village of Curamari stood. The first colonial port in South America, Cartagena became the point of reference for Spanish galleons loading riches brought from Santa Fé, Antioquia, Popayán, and even Quito, the capital of Ecuador.

Viceroys on their way to and from Peru would stop there, and with them high dignitaries on their way to Lima, Santiago, and Buenos Aires. At the end of the sixteenth century, the Cartagena fleet numbered between 80 and 90 galleons, and the city had achieved the dubious fame of being the top-ranking port for the slave trade. Consequently, it became a favorite target of pirates, and this led to the construction of the city's massive fortifications.

In 1811, Cartagena was the first Colombian city to declare independence from Spain, but in spite of the unshakable faith of Simón Bolívar in the invincibility of his defenses, he was forced to surrender to colonial troops in 1815. The longed-for freedom was achieved just six years later, but that first insurrection had already earned the city the title of *Ciudad Heroica* (heroic city).

The original nucleus of the city lies inside the fortified triangle, the Ciudad Amarullada, which is formed by 27 ramparts. The design of the fortifications was commissioned from the Italian engineer, Battista Antonelli, and the Spanish architect, Juan de Tejada. Begun in 1634, construction lasted over a century. In 1657, the Castillo di San Felipe de Barajas was built, and in 1697 under the direction of Alonso de Solís, the Castillo de San Fernando de Bocachica. Inside the walls, the city was

397 top A view of the Castillo de San Felipe de Barajas, the largest of the fortifications built by the Spanish to protect Cartagena.

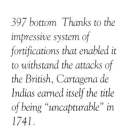

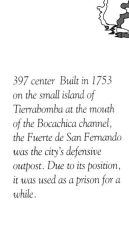

396-397 The dome of the Iglesia de San Pedro Claver. Baroque in style, it is considered the most beautiful religious building in Cartagena. It was built by the Jesuits in 1764 in honor of the priest canonized posthumously in 1654 who struggled to improve the living conditions of the slaves who arrived at the port.

397 center Built in 1753 on the small island of Tierrabomba at the mouth of the Bocachica channel, the Fuerte de San Fernando was the city's defensive outpost. Due to its position, it was used as a prison for a while.

397 bottom Thanks to the impressive system of fortifications that enabled it to withstand the attacks of the British, Cartagena de Indias earned itself the title of being "uncapturable" in 1741.

398 top left A view of the Iglesia de San Pedro Claver and its monastic annex. Founded by the Company of Jesus in 1604, the monastery is the oldest section of the complex. The following year, the first school for New World novices opened there.

398 bottom left The elegant bell tower of the cathedral is also known as the Basílica Menor. It was built between 1575 and 1612 in a simple style that varies little from that of the majority of the city's buildings, which had a military function.

398-399 The Palacio de la Inquisición is one of the most important buildings in eighteenth-century Cartagena. Its lovely Baroque architecture contrasts with its purpose at the time: until 1811, it was the seat of the Holy Office with jurisdiction over the New Kingdom of Granada and Venezuela, and also over Nicaragua.

399 top The attractive colonial houses in the city center were built with repisas, traditional projecting balconies made with finely historiated wood, known in local slang as panzas (bellies).

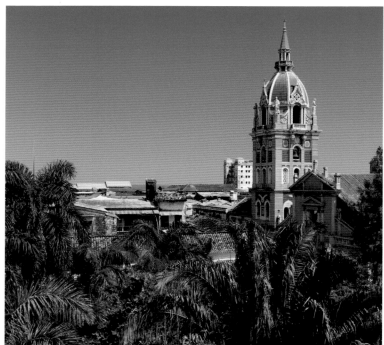

divided into three districts: San Pedro, San Diego, and Getsemaní. The district of San Diego was the section in which the bourgeois merchants lived, Getsemaní the popular quarter, and San Pedro the location of the cathedral, built between 1575 and 1612, and fine Andalusian-style townhouses in which the Spanish governors and functionaries lived. The Dominican bishop, Dionisio de Santis, decided on the construction of Cartagena's most important religious building; it was a plain and massive basilica that did not vary much from the military style of the city's fortifications.

Interesting examples of Cartagena's religious architecture remain, for instance, the 1603 Iglesia de San Pedro Claver, the Iglesia y Convento de Santo Domingo, the oldest in the city, built between 1559 and 1570, and the Palacio del Inquisición, a magnificent example of colonial architecture that was completed in 1770. But the beauty of the city is most of all to be seen in the civil buildings dating from the seventeenth century. Calle Factoría, Calle Santo Domingo, and Calle de las Damas are lined with superb colonial style houses with windows and balconies adorned with finely historiated wood. The streets are overlooked by *repisas*, the characteristic projecting balconies that are known in local slang as *panzas* (bellies). Splendid examples of the style of the woodcarvers of Cartagena, it is said that they performed an important social function: in a city dominated by the strict rule of the Jesuits, the young women rarely went out, and on the occasions that they did, they were always accompanied; consequently, these balconies were the setting for encounters in which the daughters of good families were able to find themselves a husband without leaving their home.

400 top This painting of
the Marriage of Santa
Rosa de Lima dates from
the seventeenth century
and hangs in the
Monasterio de Santa
Catalina.

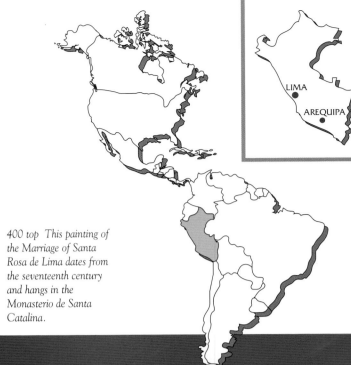

400-401 The fountain
inside the residential
section of the Monasterio
de Santa Catalina. The
complex covers roughly
215,000 square feet and is
characterized by its red
walls and the contrasting
blue areas dedicated to
cloistered life.

401 top The facade of
Casa Ricketts in the Calle
de San Francisco. It is one
of the more elegant
residences in Arequipa and
was originally used as the
San Jeronimo Seminary.

401 center One of the silent
porticoes in the Monasterio
de Santa Catalina onto
which the confession room
faces. A rich Spanish
widow, María de Guzmán,
founded the convent in 1580.

The Historic Center of Arequipa

PERU

PROVINCE OF AREQUIPA
REGISTRATION: 2000
CRITERIA: C (I) (IV)

On June 23, 2001 at about three P.M., a violent earthquake with its epicenter in Noroeste de Ocoña rocked southern Peru, leaving numerous victims in its wake and causing extensive damage. In Arequipa, the main city in the region, the vault of the cathedral fell in and one of two bell towers flanking the façade collapsed. The circumstances are tragic, but earthquakes are a feature of the history of this city and have repeatedly damaged its architecture.

Villa Hermosa de Arequipa was officially founded on August 15, 1540 by Don Garcia Manuel de Carbajal on the orders of governor Francisco Pizarro. There had previously been an Inca settlement known as *Ary Quippay*, which means "place beyond the peak" in Aymara. The summit in question must have been Misti, the nearest of the volcanoes circling the fertile basin where the city was located.

Misti, Chachani, and Pichupichu, three giants with an altitude of more than 16,000 feet, are more than a scenic backdrop for the city: the volcanoes are also the source of *sillar*, the white rock used for all the buildings in the colonial town. This rock came from an enormous eruption of Mount Chachani over two million years ago, when the mountain spewed an immense amount of magma over 30 miles from the crater.

Four years after the arrival of the Spanish, a church was built on the esplanade that, upon the request of Emperor Charles V, was named Plaza de Armas. The church underwent extensive reconstruction, not only because of earthquake damage, but also to expand it, and over the centuries, the original church was transformed into an impressive cathedral. Its current appearance dates from the mid-nineteenth century when much of the building had to be reconstructed following a fire. Its façade is the only one in Peru to cover the entire side of a square, and the cathedral of Arequipa is one of only 100 churches around the world that is allowed to fly the Vatican flag. Its architecture is neo-Renaissance, but the interior of the church does not match the majesty of its façade.

On the opposite side of Plaza de Armas, a square surrounded by tall porticoes and elegant buildings from the colonial and republican periods, stands the Iglesia de la Compañia, completed in 1698, nearly a century after construction began. The two-story façade features spiral columns and bas-reliefs with motifs reflecting the Andean flora, in a style that reinterprets the Spanish Baroque. Inside, there is an immense and finely carved cedar altar finished in gold leaf. The Chapel of St. Ignatius, with its multicolored cupola, is located to the left of the altar.

The colonial architecture of the "Ciudad

401 bottom A "private" cloister in the Monasterio de Santa Catalina. This institution was reserved exclusively to nuns from "good families." Of the roughly 450 inhabitants in the convent, only a third were nuns, the rest were servants.

Blanca" (white city) triumphs in the streets behind the cathedral. This is the area of the *casonas*, the homes of the city notables, which cover a single floor with rooms that open onto patios bedecked with flowers. The most sumptuous ones such as Casa del Moral (at 318 Calle Moral) and Casa Ricketts (in Calle de San Francisco) have been purchased by private foundations and are now open to visitors. They still contain their original furnishings as well as seventeenth- and eighteenth-century paintings.

The gem of Arequipa is the Monasterio de Santa Catalina, with approximately 215,000 square feet of chapels, cloisters, cells, and refectories that cover an entire city block surrounded by high walls. Just forty years after Arequipa was founded, María de Guzmán, a wealthy Spanish widow, established the convent, in accordance with the tradition by which the second-oldest daughters of well-to-do families gave up their worldly possessions to live in communion with God. In reality, for three centuries only one-third of the 450 guests at Santa Catalina were actually nuns. The rest were the servants of these noblewomen who, although cloistered, organized concerts and continued to live in luxury. In 1871, the nuns' shameless behavior attracted the attention of Pius IX, who sent a Dominican nun from Europe to restore order.

For the next 100 years, the nuns observed the strictest rules of cloistered life, but by 1970 there were only twenty left, too few to handle the proper upkeep of the large complex. That year, the convent was opened to the public, and after four centuries the people of Arequipa finally had a chance to discover the treasures hidden behind the walls.

402 top left The side wall of the Sacrestia, also known as the Capilla de San Ignacio, named for the founder of the Jesuit Order, in the Iglesia de la Compañía. The historiated wooden decorations are one of the most important works of art in Peru.

402 top center A view of the multicolored wall decorations in the Capilla de San Ignacio. The religious art imported from Europe underwent substantial modifications during the seventeenth century due to the influence of the traditions of local artists.

402 top right Two eighteenth-century cloisters connected to the Iglesia de la Compañía feature ornamentation that harmonizes with that of the original building. Today the cloisters are occupied by shops selling crafts and souvenirs.

402 bottom The Plaza de Armas di Arequipa is surrounded on three sides by two orders of porticoes and is one of the loveliest squares in Peru. In the center there is a bronze fountain decorated with an angel.

403 top The mestizo facade of the Iglesia de la Compañía is famous for its extraordinary decorations and bears the date "Año 1698." This indicates the completion of the construction, which was begun over a century earlier.

403 bottom The cathedral (or Basilica Menor) as it was before the 2001 earthquake that caused the collapse of the left bell tower and damaged the right one and the interior of the building. The imposing building was built in the second half of the nineteenth century.

404 Situated in the
Pelourinho district, the
Igreja do Rosário dos
Pretos was built by slaves
in Baroque style in the
eighteenth century. They
mostly worked at nighttime
and used smuggled
materials.

SALVADOR DE BAIA

BRASILIA

The Historic Center of Salvador de Bahia

BRAZIL

BAHIA STATE
REGISTRATION: 1985
CRITERIA: C (IV) (VI)

405 top left The colonial houses in Praça da Sé in the heart of the city. The square is named after the Sé da Bahia, one of Latin America's most magnificent churches, which was built in 1533 and demolished four centuries later.

On the evening of December 31 each year, the image of Senhor bom Jesus dos Navegantes is carried to the Igreja Nossa Senhora da Conceição. To celebrate the arrival of the new year, the next morning it is accompanied from there by dozens of boats in a sea procession to the Igreja Nossa Senhora da Boa Viagem, packed to the rafters, where it is kept until the following year. Although this rite was inherited from a Portuguese tradition, it should not be surprising that Salvador de Bahia begins the new year with a ceremony that is both religious and marine in nature because these are the two elements that have always determined the lifestyle of the city.

Salvador is the capital of the state of Bahia in northeast Brazil. It stands on the Baía de Todos os Santos, the huge and peaceful bay named by the crew of Amerigo Vespucci on their arrival there on November 1, 1501. A few years later, a ship under the command of Diogo Álvares was wrecked there, and he was given shelter by the Tupinambá tribe who lived on the coast. He married the daughter of Chief Taparica and ended up by playing a decisive role when the king of Portugal, João III, gave orders that a city should be built in the bay.

In 1549, a fleet carrying more than 1,000 colonists left European shores under the command of captain Tomé de Souza. When they arrived on the shores of the Baía de Todos os Santos, they were welcomed with all honor by Álvares and the local populations. This was the beginning of Salvador de Bahia, the capital of the new colony, and Tomé de Souza was bestowed with the title Governor of Brazil.

After half a century the city had 1,600 inhabitants and traded sugarcane, tobacco, and cotton. A little later, the profitable trade in slaves began, which through the mixing of South American natives, Portuguese colonists, and African slaves made Bahia a multiethnic city. Such sudden prosperity naturally attracted the attention of foreigners who prepared expeditions to conquer Bahia.

405 center right The Baroque altar of the Igreja do Convento do Carmo. Founded in the seventeenth century, the complex unites great architecture with important events linked to Brazilian independence.

405 bottom left The majestic main façade of the Municipio, the former residence of the governors, is crowned by a dome.

Bahia was the capital of Portuguese America until 1763 when the monarch decided to move the capital to Rio de Janeiro.

405 bottom right Bahia Port. On the left is the Elevator Lacerda, the massive elevator installed in 1868 to facilitate access to the upper part of the city.

406 top The cloister of the Convento de São Francisco decorated with blue and white azulejos. The Franciscans arrived in Bahia in 1587 but had to wait a century before they were provided with land to build a monastery.

406 bottom A view of Pelourinho shows its colonial houses dominated by the twin bell towers of the Igreja Nossa Senhora de Conceição. The name of the district means "whipping place" because the slaves were bought and sold there.

First came the Dutch of the East India Company, who ruled the city in 1624-1625. Once peace returned, Bahia became a repository for the new treasures coming from the gold and diamond mines in the interior. The rich Portuguese dignitaries began to build themselves magnificent houses and Baroque churches. By 1763, the city had grown enormously, numbering 60,000 inhabitants of every caste and nationality, but then the Portuguese monarch decided to move the capital south to the equally prosperous city of Rio de Janeiro. This marked the start of a slow decline for Salvador de Bahia which did

not halt even with independence from Portugal in 1822.

The city is famous for the beauty of its colonial architecture. The greatest evidence of its European past in the lower part of the city can be seen in the remains of the fortifications built to protect the important port and the Mercado Modelo where goods arrived. On the top of the hill, on the other hand, there is the large Igreja do Nosso Senhor do Bomfim, dedicated to the patron saint of the city. Daily life in Bahia for the most part takes place in the upper section, which is linked to the port by an elevator

originally built in 1610 by Jesuits to lighten the work done by slaves. Today no trace remains of the first apparatus but the Elevator Lacerda, a massive steam-driven, iron piece of equipment installed in 1868, can still be seen. The upper section of Bahia contains not only the houses of the nobility and merchants but most of the city's churches. Legend has it that there were 365 at one time, one for each day of the year, bearing witness to the strength of religion in a city where Catholicism was often united with the animist beliefs of the African slaves to form the syncretistic cult of Candomblé.

The loveliest church is undoubtedly the Igreja de São Francisco, the walls and altar of which are completely covered with gold leaf.

Nearby lies the ancient quarter of Pelourinho, an impressive cluster of seventeenth and eighteenth-century buildings. The name Pelourinho means "place of the whips" because it the slaves were bought and sold here. Today the old slave market, in Largo do Pelourinho, is the site of the Fundação Casa de Jorge Amado, in honor of the great Brazilian writer who lived in a nearby hotel during his university years.

407 top left Situated in the square of the same name, the Igreja de São Francisco was built between 1708 and 1723 in exuberant Baroque. It is considered the loveliest church in Brazil.

407 top right The Igreja do Nosso Senhor do Bonfim is dedicated to the patron saint of the city and is the best-loved church in Bahia. Located in the Cidade Baixa, it was completed in 1722 and has a Rococo façade decorated with Portuguese azulejos.

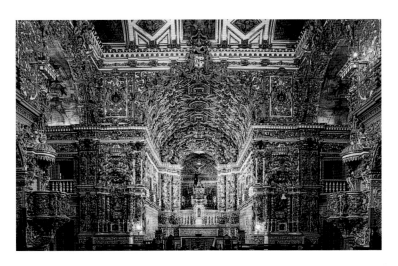

407 bottom The best example of Portuguese Baroque in the world, the interior of the Igreja de São Francisco is a celebration of jacaranda wood decoration entirely covered with gold leaf.

Brasilia
BRAZIL

FEDERAL DISTRICT
REGISTRATION: 1987
CRITERIA: C (I) (IV)

At the start of the 1950s, Brazil was a land of inexhaustible natural resources and violent social contrasts. It was also a country badly in need of direction. In the euphoria of the postwar era, when the developed countries were experiencing frantic activity, it found three different sources of leadership: the first was Juscelino Kubitscheck, an ambitious politician of long-standing who became President in 1956; the second was Lucio Costa, a brilliant town-planner who had grown up in Europe and returned to Brazil to collect the rewards of

408 left The pool in front of the Ministry of Foreign Affairs reflects the other public buildings that face onto the Esplanada dos Ministerios at the southern end of the Avenida Eixo Monumental, the widest road in the world.

his apprenticeship; and the third was the best known, the architect Oscar Niemeyer, a pupil of Costa and Le Corbusier.

The partnership of the two designers in 1956 led to the plan for Brasilia, the country's new capital, which was to be built in the center of the country on a semi-arid plateau 3,600 feet high. The site had been chosen theoretically following long reconnaissance flights. The various governments of Brazil had thought about moving the capital from overcrowded Rio de Janeiro to an internal

site for almost 200 years, with the purpose of speeding up development in areas traditionally depressed. Once the geographical co-ordinates had been agreed, Kubitscheck announced a competition for the design of what was to be a model city and an image of the fast progress of the country.

It was won by Costa and Niemeyer. Costa concerned himself with the layout of the city while Niemeyer's was responsible for the design of the most important public buildings. Because of the era's obsession with the automobile, both as status symbol and means of transport, Costa gave the city exceptionally wide roads – the Avenida Eixo Monumental is still the widest in the world – to the benefit, naturally, of car owners and not pedestrians. The symbol of urban progress, Brasilia was laid out along two perpendicular axes: the east-west axis was lined with the government buildings, and the north-south axis with residential districts. With the exception of the Rua da Ingrejinha, the streets were not given names but designated with letters and numbers. These superquadras (major blocks) were connected by roads allocated to commerce, and service and relaxation areas. The dominant feature of the city, the parks, contrasts with the aridity of the region and makes Brasilia the city with most green areas per capita in the world. The largest buildings are surrounded by pools of water for aesthetic reasons and because evaporation increases the humidity of the air and thus alleviates the dry climate of the plateau.

The epitome of the power of this country as large as a continent is the twin towers where the two arms of the Parliament are housed. At 28 floors tall, they are joined by a

408-409 A spectacular aerial view of Brasilia. Inaugurated on April 21, 1960, the modern Brazilian capital was the result of the association of President Juscelino Kubitschek, town planner Lucio Costa, and the architect Oscar Niemeyer, who created the design for the city in 1956.

409 top The Palacio do Itamaratí, also known as the Palacio dos Arcos owing to the large reinforced concrete arches surrounding it, is the seat of the Foreign Ministry.

409 center right " La Meteora," by Italian sculptor Bruno Giorni, symbolizes the five continents. It stands in a pool in front of the Foreign Ministry.

409 bottom The Palacio do Congreso Nacional stands in the triangular Praça dos Três Poderes where the offices of the executive and judicial branches of the government are based. Their arrangement represents the independence and equality of each of the three powers.

410 top The sculpture "Os Candangos" – also known as "Os Guerreiros" – is also situated in the Praça dos

Três Poderes. In the background, there is the "Tancredo Neves" Pantheon of Freedom and the Pyre of the Nation.

410 bottom left The circular nave of the cathedral can seat 4,000 and lies below the concrete dome with windows by

Maienne Perreti. Niemeyer built the nave on a lower level than the road so that only the dome would rise above the ground.

footbridge to form the letter H, which represents the words *Homem, Honra, Honestidade*: man, honor, honesty. A hemisphere on one side of the buildings faces up and an identical one on the other side faces down to represent universal balance. At the corners of the triangular plaza of the Três Poderes (Three Powers) stand the executive, legislative, and judiciary branches of the Brazilian government, in a relationship that symbolizes the independence and equality of the three. The Parliament building itself, the J.K. Memorial Museum (which also contains Kubitscheck's mausoleum since his death in a car accident in 1976), and the bus terminal are all aligned on the same axis.

Niemeyer really let his creativity loose in the cathedral by creating soft and wavy lines using the proverbially rigid material of reinforced concrete. Preferring to favor beauty over functionality, the architect created a structure that combines rationalism and traditional Brazilian Baroque. He

personally worked with and oversaw artists and sculptors on the decoration of the building. The enormous windows are the work of Maienne Perreti, and the massive bronze sculptures of the four Evangelists in front of the entrance by Alfredo Ceschiatti. Another Italian was responsible for the Meteora, the impressive symbol of the five continents placed in a pool of water in front of the Ministry of Foreign Affairs.

Inaugurated on April 21, 1960, Brasilia has been the country's capital for just over 40 years, but it is already showing signs of the times. The original plan was made to accommodate half a million inhabitants, but today the city has a population of two million and the new suburbs do not respect the planning criteria imagined by the city's creators. Consequently, many people wonder just how successful the project has been. In 1997, just a few months before his death, Lucio Costa replied to his critics that, "the truth is that my dream turned out to be smaller than reality."

410 bottom right Outside the cathedral designed by Oscar Niemeyer stand the gigantic bronze sculptures by Alfredo Ceschiatti representing the Evangelists.

410-411 A sculpture of President Juscelino Kubitschek in the Praça dos Três Poderes. In the background stands the Palacio da Justiça.

411 bottom A futuristic arched building in one of the residential districts. Costa and Niemeyer kept the residential and administrative areas of the city strictly separate to create a unique urban setting.

The Historic Center of Sucre

BOLIVIA

REGISTRATION: 1991
CRITERIA: C (IV)

412 bottom The Baroque facade of the Universidad de San Francisco Javier. The university was the fourth to be built in Latin America and was founded by the brothers of the Company of Jesus in 1624.

412-413 The University cloister – originally the residence of the Jesuit missionaries – overlooked by the tower of the Iglesia de San Miguel. The church was built in Andalusian style in 1621.

413 top right The great hall in the Casa de la Libertad. The portrait in the center portrays the national hero Simón Bolívar. Bolivia proclaimed its independence in this room in 1825.

On August 6, 1825, in the rooms of the Universidad de San Francisco Xavier, the Republic of Charcas was proclaimed, which, from that moment on, was known as Bolivia in tribute to the architect of the country's liberation and the hero of all Latin America, Simón Bolívar. Five days later, in the same rooms, the capital of the new country was renamed Sucre. The Casa de la Libertad (the modern name of the University building) is a lovely edifice built before 1700 by the Society of Jesus around a broad cloister to be the residence of the missionaries. However, from the date of the country's independence until 1898, the building became the seat of the Congreso Boliviano, the legislative arm of the country.

Sucre is also famous as being the "city of four names." In addition to the current one, it was also called Ciudad Blanca, because of the whiteness of its buildings, Charcas, from the name of the indigenous people that inhabited the region, and La Plata, the name that was given to it on November 30, 1538 (the date of its foundation) by Pedro de Anzures, the Marquis of Campo Redondo and guide to the armies of Gonzalo Pizarro. The town – built on the site of the indigenous village of Choke-Chaca – was founded on the orders of Pizarro to exploit the mining deposits in Potosí. Tt was also to become the departure point for exploration of the lands to the west of the Andes.

By 1552, it had been appointed a bishopric, and seven years later, Philip II of Spain ordered the institution of the Audiencia de Charcas to govern over the vast area that included Paraguay, southern Peru, northern Chile, Argentina, and Bolivia. In 1609, the city was elevated to the rank of archbishopric.

The chronicles of the sixteenth century already spoke of a population of several thousand, including farmers, miners, soldiers, missionaries, and traders. On May 27, 1624, the Jesuit Juan de Frías Herrán founded the Universidad de San Francisco Xavier, which was moved into the Jesuits' monastery in 1767 when the order was expelled from all of the Americas. In its new building, the university played a decisive role in the education of the intellectual avant-garde that supported independence, as founded on St. Thomas Aquinas' idea of popular sovereignty.

In the seventeenth century, La Plata was the most important political, religious, and cultural center in western Latin America. Today its historic center represents a perfect example of Spanish colonialism, in particular the religious art from the sixteenth century. The city's most important

413 bottom left The lovely colonial style building from the late seventeenth century is known as the Casa de la Libertad because it was the center of the events that led to the independence of the country. It is located in Plaza 25 de Mayo.

413 bottom right The historical center of Sucre boasts a succession of lovely colonial houses. This city of 150,000 inhabitants was the capital of Bolivia until 1898 before the honor passed to La Paz.

buildings stand around the Plaza de Armas: the Iglesia Mayor, the Archbishop's palace, the capitol, the Real Audiencia, and the prison. However, the oldest building in Sucre is the Iglesia de San Lázaro, construction of which was begun in 1544. Built not far from the site where the indigenous divinity Tanga-Tanga was worshipped, the church is surrounded by arches and has a side chapel were the local Indios were indoctrinated.

In 1559, work began on the cathedral, whose long and controversial construction made it a compendium of the architectural

414-415 A masterpiece of Renaissance art, the Iglesia de San Francisco is one of Bolivia's oldest buildings. It was designed by Juan de Vallejo and completed in 1581.

415 bottom The splendid Baroque portal of the cathedral. Begun in 1559, the building was not completed until the early eighteenth century and exhibits a blend of styles that ranges from Renaissance to Neo-Classical.

414 bottom left The wide and luminous nave in the cathedral. The fine white and gold stucco decorations were executed in a refined Neo-Classical style.

414 bottom right The elaborate Baroque retablo made from wood and covered with gold leaf in the Iglesia de San Miguel. The architecture of the building was strongly influenced by Andalusian mudéjar style.

415 top A view of the cathedral domes. Originally, Sucre's mother church had no aisles and was covered by a cross vault. Later, to reinforce the structure, four side chapels were added.

styles diffused through Latin America from the sixteenth to eighteenth centuries: it has Renaissance decorations, Neo-Classical naves and splendid Baroque entrances to the Capilla de la Virgen de Guadalupe.

Sucre's religious architecture harbors other surprises, like the Gothic transverse aisles in the Iglesia de Santo Domingo, and the Andalusian ornamentation in the Iglesia de San Miguel (1621) and Iglesia de San Francisco (1581). The latter is a masterpiece of Renaissance art, heavily influenced by the elegant *mudéjar* style,

derived from Moorish architecture, that spread across Spain starting in the thirteenth century. In contrast, the Iglesia de San Francisco provides an admirable fusion of Hispanic and local decorative traditions using the *mudéjar* ornamentation, comprising octagons, points, and stars in red, blue, and gold to be seen in the nave, the two chapels, and the presbytery.

In 1898, the capital of Bolivia was moved to La Paz, and Sucre, today with 150,000 inhabitants, became a quiet provincial city.

The Jesuit Block and the Estancias in Córdoba

ARGENTINA

PROVINCE OF CÓRDOBA
REGISTRATION: 2000
CRITERIA: C (II) (IV)

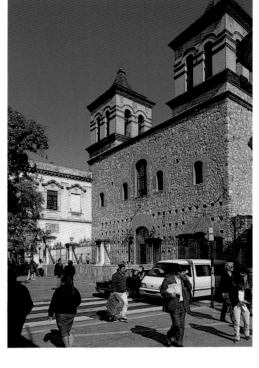

416 bottom left Dating from the late seventeenth century, the Colegio Convictorio de Nuestra Señora de Monserrat was built to accommodate the university students. The current building was rebuilt in 1782 and later modified, but the cloisters are identical to the original ones.

416 bottom right The church of the Estancia de Santa Catalina is one of the most outstanding examples of Argentine Baroque. The property was purchased by the Jesuits in 1622 and was the most productive of all the order's agricultural properties.

417 top An external view of the Iglesia de la Compañía designed by the Flemish Jesuit Philippe Lemaire. Its construction was begun in 1645 but the church was not completed until 1671.

Following a year of consideration and changes of mind, between March 31 and April 2, 1767 King Charles III of Spain signed the decree expelling the Society of Jesus from Spanish possessions in the Americas. The result was as expected: by wiping the slate clean, one of the most successful socio-economic experiences in Spanish colonialism in Latin America was erased, and in suppressing the Order, the farming, educational, and religious system inspired by the Jesuits was weakened.

In 1599, about twenty years after the founding of the city, the Society had established itself in Córdoba in the area bounded by Avenida Vélez Sársfield and the Calle Obispo Trejos, Caseros, and Duarte Quirós. Within only ten years the small building the Society occupied was too small to accommodate the friars, students, and faithful. Therefore, in 1610 work began on building the Colegio Máximo, and three years later the Seminario Convictorio de San Javier, which, in 1622, was promoted to the rank of University. In a few years, the Jesuits welcomed into their schools and colleges a large number of natives, who began to learn trades like carpentry, building, and blacksmithing, but who also had the possibility of studying to be jewelers, artists, or men of letters. The Jesuits had no lack in their ranks of historians, paleontologists, geographers, or naturalists, and it is to these men that many of the early scientific observations made in Argentina were due.

Before the mid-seventeenth century, the activities of the Manzana Jesuitica – the Jesuit quarter – were so famous and profitable that the Order decided to build the Iglesia de la Compañía. The Flemish friar, Philippe Lemaire, was in charge of the works, which began in 1645 and lasted until 1671. The style of the building is an unusual Latin American Baroque,

416-417 In Córdoba in 1613, Brother Fernando de Trejo y Sanabria started the construction of the Seminario Convictorio de San Javier (a cloister is shown in the photo). It was elevated to the rank of university in 1622 and later became the Universidad Nacional 'Fernando de Trejo y Sanabria'.

with a bell tower on either side of the façade. Below the vaults inside there is an altar that is considered one of the continent's greatest works of art of the seventeenth century. During the same period, the Jesuits also built the Capilla Doméstica, smaller in size but equally interesting, which contains another splendid altar and outstanding ornamental frescoes.

Towards the end of the century, the Noviziato was also built, and the Colegio Convictorio de Nuestra Señora de Monserrat to house the university students. The latter is an admirable

building with silent cloisters and vaulted corridors. In the Salón de Grados, at the time of the Capilla de Españoles, there used to be a valuable collection of books belonging to the Jesuit library that included not only religious works but scientific essays and literary writings from the sixteenth to eighteenth centuries.

The Jesuit quarter also formed the hub of substantial trading linked to the farming activities of the estancias (the farms that the Society of Jesus had created around the city). The first of the estates belonging to the Order was, in 1616, the Estancia de Caroya, ceded in 1661 to the friar Ignacio Duarte Quirós, the

417 bottom The nave of the Iglesia de la Compañía. Its wooden altar decorated with gold leaf, seen at the far end, is considered one of the finest in South America.

founder of the Colegio Convictorio de Monserrat. The estate was formed by a residence built around a central cloister, a chapel, and various farm buildings.

The largest of the five was the Estancia de Santa Catalina, which was a proper agricultural company founded in 1622, 43 miles to the north of Córdoba in the middle of a large and fertile plain. Its church is a marvel of Argentinean colonial Baroque architecture and the modernity of the farm buildings is surprising. There were enclosures and stalls that could hold thousands of cattle, sheep, and mules, large vegetable gardens, orchards, and fields for cultivating maize and corn. Naturally

there were silos to store the cereals, a *tamajar* (water tank), a flour mill, and water mills to feed the irrigation canals. Even in the *estancias* – the other three were those of Jesús María, Alta Gracia, and Candelaria y San Ignacio – the Jesuits did not cease to support intellectual activities, thereby contributing to the education of the children of the *campesinos*.

With the expulsion of the Jesuits, some of the buildings in the Jesuit quarter were made available to the Franciscans, while their properties were sold to private entrepreneurs. The Estancia de Santa Catalina was bought at auction by Francisco Antonio Diaz and still belongs to his heirs.

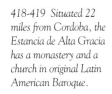

List of the Sites

ALGERIA
1982 M'Zab Valley
1992 Kasbah of Algiers

ARGENTINA
2000 Jesuit Block and Estancias of Córdoba

ARGENTINA and BRAZIL
1984 Jesuit Missions of the Guaranis: San Ignacio Miní, Santa Ana, Nuestra Señora de Loreto and Santa María la Mayor (Argentina); Ruins of São Miguel das Missões (Brazil)

ARMENIA
1996 Monasteries of Haghpat and Sanahin
2000 Monastery of Geghard and Upper Azat Valley
2000 Cathedral and Churches of Echmiatsin and the Archaeological Site of Zvartnots

AUSTRIA
1996 Historic Centre of the City of Salzburg
1996 Palace and Gardens of Schönbrunn
1997 Hallstatt-Dachstein / Salzkammergut Cultural Landscape
1998 Semmering Railway
1999 City of Graz - Historic Centre
2000 Wachau Cultural Landscape
2001 Historic Centre of Vienna

AUSTRIA and HUNGARY
2001 Cultural Landscape of Fertö/Neusiedlersee

AZERBAIJAN
2000 Walled City of Baku with the Shirvanshah's Palace and Maiden Tower

BANGLADESH
1985 Historic Mosque City of Bagerhat

BELARUS
2000 Mir Castle Complex

BELGIUM
1998 La Grand-Place, Brussels
1998 Flemish Béguinages
1998 The Four Lifts on the Canal du Centre and their Environs, La Louvière and Le Roeulx (Hainault)
1999 The Belfries of Flanders and Wallonia
2000 Historic Centre of Brugge
2000 Major Town Houses of the architect Victor Horta
2000 Notre-Dame Cathedral in Tournai

BENIN
1985 Royal Palaces of Abomey

BOLIVIA
1987 City of Potosí
1990 Jesuit Missions of the Chiquitos
1991 Historic City of Sucre

BRAZIL
1980 Historic Town of Ouro Preto
1982 Historic Centre of Olinda
1985 Historic Centre of Salvador de Bahia
1985 Sanctuary of Bom Jesus do Congonhas
1987 Brasilia
1997 Historic Centre of São Luis
1999 Historic Centre of the Town of Diamantina
2001 Historic Centre of the Town of Goiás

BULGARIA
1979 Boyana Church
1979 Rock-hewn Churches of Ivanovo
1983 Rila Monastery

CANADA
1985 Historic District of Québec
1995 Old Town Lunenburg

CHILE
2000 Churches of Chiloé

CHINA
1987 The Great Wall
1987 Mount Taishan
1987 Imperial Palace of the Ming and Qing Dynasties
1994 Mountain Resort and its Outlying Temples, Chengde
1994 Temple and Cemetery of Confucius and the Kong Family Mansion in Qufu
1994 Ancient Building Complex in the Wudang Mountains
1994, 2000, 2001 Historic Ensemble of the Potala Palace, Lhasa
1997 Old Town of Lijiang
1997 Ancient City of Ping Yao
1997, 2000 Classical Gardens of Suzhou

1998 Summer Palace, an Imperial Garden in Beijing
1998 Temple of Heaven: an Imperial Sacrificial Altar in Beijing
2000 Ancient Villages in Southern Anhui - Xidi and Hongcun
2000 Imperial Tombs of the Ming and Qing Dynasties

COLOMBIA
1984 Port, Fortresses and Group of Monuments, Cartagena
1995 Historic Centre of Santa Cruz de Mompox

CROATIA
1979 Old City of Dubrovnik
1979 Historical Complex of Split with the Palace of Diocletian
1997 Episcopal Complex of the Euphrasian Basilica in the Historic Centre of Porec
1997 Historic City of Trogir
2000 Cathedral of St James in S(ibenik

CUBA
1982 Old Havana and its Fortifications
1988 Trinidad and the Valley de los Ingenios
1997 San Pedro de la Roca Castle, Santiago de Cuba
1999 Viñales Valley

CYPRUS
2001 Painted Churches in the Troodos Region

CZECH REPUBLIC
1992 Historic Centre of Prague
1992 Historic Centre of Cesky Krumlov
1992 Historic Centre of Telc
1994 Pilgrimage Church of St John of Nepomuk at Zelena Hora
1995 Kutná Hora : the Historical Town Centre with the Church of St Barbara and the Cathedral of Our Lady at Sedlec
1996 Lednice-Valtice Cultural Landscape
1998 Holasovice Historical Village Reservation
1998 Gardens and Castle at Kromeríz
1999 Litomysl Castle
2000 Holy Trinity Column in Olomouc
2001 Tugendhat Villa in Brno

DENMARK
1995 Roskilde Cathedral
2000 Kronborg Castle

DOMINICAN REPUBLIC
1990 Colonial City of Santo Domingo

ECUADOR
1978 City of Quito
1999 Historic Centre of Santa Ana de los Ríos de Cuenca

EGYPT
1979 Islamic Cairo

ESTONIA
1997 Historic Centre (Old Town) of Tallinn

ETHIOPIA
1978 Rock-Hewn Churches, Lalibela
1979 Fasil Ghebbi, Gondar Region

FINLAND
1991 Old Rauma
1991 Fortress of Suomenlinna
1994 Petäjävesi Old Church
1996 Verla Groundwood and Board Mill

FRANCE
1979 Mont Saint-Michel and its Bay
1979 Chartres Cathedral
1979 Palace and Park of Versailles
1979 Vézelay, Church and Hill
1981 Palace and Park of Fontainebleau
1981 Amiens Cathedral
1981 Cistercian Abbey of Fontenay
1982 Royal Saltworks of Arc-et- Senans
1983 Place Stanislas, Place de la Carrière and Place d'Alliance in Nancy
1983 Church of Saint-Savin sur Gartempe
1988 Strasbourg - Grande Ile
1991 Paris, Banks of the Seine
1991 Cathedral of Notre- Dame, Former Abbey of Saint-Remi and Palace of Tau, Reims
1992 Bourges Cathedral
1995 Historic Centre of Avignon
1996 Le Canal du Midi
1997 Historic Fortified City of Carcassonne
1998 Routes of Santiago de Compostela in France
1998 Historic Site of Lyons

1999 Jurisdiction of Saint-Emilion
2000 Loire Valley between Sully- sur-Loire and Chalonnes
2001 Provins, Town of Medieval Fairs

FRANCE and SPAIN
1997 Pyrénées - Mont Perdu

GEORGIA
1994 City- Museum Reserve of Mtskheta
1994 Bagrati Cathedral and Gelati Monastery
1996 Upper Svaneti

GERMANY
1978 Aachen Cathedral
1981 Speyer Cathedral
1981 Würzburg Residence with the Court Gardens and Residence Square Pilgrimage
1983 Church of Wies
1984 Castles of Augustusburg and Falkenlust at Brühl
1985 St Mary's Cathedral and St Michael's Church at Hildesheim
1986 Roman Monuments, Cathedral of St Peter and Church Our Lady in Trier
1987 Hanseatic City of Lübeck with the Nordic countries.
1990 Palaces and Parks of Potsdam and Berlin
1991 Abbey and Altenmünster of Lorsch
1992 Mines of Rammelsberg and Historic Town of Goslar
1993 Town of Bamberg
1993 Maulbronn Monastery Complex
1994 Collegiate Church, Castle and Old Town of Quedlinburg
1994 Völklingen Ironworks
1996 Cologne Cathedral
1996 Bauhaus and its Sites in Weimar and Dessau
1996 Luther Memorials in Eisleben and Wittenberg
1998 Classical Weimar
1999 Museumsinsel (Museum Island), Berlin
1999 Wartburg Castle
2000 Garden Kingdom of Dessau- Wörlitz
2000 Monastic Island of Reichenau
2001 The Zollverein Coal Mine Industrial Complex in Essen

GHANA
1979 Forts and Castles,Volta Greater Accra, Central and Western Regions
1980 Ashanti Traditional Buildings

GREECE
1988 Mount Athos
1988 Meteora
1988 Palaeochristian and Byzantine Monuments of Thessalonika
1989 Mystras
1990 Monasteries of Daphni, Hosios Luckas, and Nea Moni of Chios

GUATEMALA
1979 Antigua Guatemala

HAITI
1982 National Historic Park - Citadel, Sans Souci, Ramiers

HUNGARY
1987 Budapest, the Banks of the Danube and the Buda Castle Quarter
1987 Hollokö
1996 Millenary Benedictine Monastery of Pannonhalma and its Natural Environment
1999 Hortobágy National Park

INDIA
1983 Agra Fort
1983 Taj Mahal
1984 Sun Temple, Konarak
1986 Churches and Convents of Goa
1986 Fatehpur Sikri
1987 Brihadisvara Temple, Thanjavur
1993 Humayun's Tomb, Delhi
1993 Qutb Minar and its Monuments, Delhi.
1999 The Darjeeling Himalayan Railway

IRAN, Islamic Republic of
1979 Meidan Emam, Esfahan

ITALY
1980 Church and Dominican Convent of Santa Maria delle Grazie with 'The Last Supper' by Leonardo da Vinci
1982 Historic Centre of Florence
1987 Venice and its Lagoon
1987 Piazza del Duomo, Pisa
1990 Historic Centre of San Gimignano
1993 I Sassi di Matera
1994 City of Vicenza and the Palladian Villas of the Veneto
1995 Historic Centre of Siena

1995 Historic Centre of Naples
1995 Crespi d'Adda
1995 Ferrara, City of the Renaissance and its Po Delta
1996 Castel del Monte
1996 Trulli of Alberobello
1996 Early Christian Monuments of Ravenna
1996 Historic Centre of the City of Pienza
1997 18th-Century Royal Palace at Caserta with the Park, the Aqueduct of Vanvitelli, and the San Leucio Complex
1997 Residences of the Royal House of Savoy
1997 Botanical Garden (Orto Botanico), Padua
1997 Portovenere, Cinque Terre, and the Islands (Palmaria, Tino and Tinetto)
1997 Cathedral, Torre Civica and Piazza Grande, Modena
1997 Costiera Amalfitana
1998 Historic Centre of Urbino
2000 Assisi, the Basilica of San Francesco and Other Franciscan Sites
2000 City of Verona
2001 Villa d'Este, Tivoli

ITALY and the HOLY SEE (each according to its jurisdiction)
1980 1990 Historic Centre of Rome, the Properties of the Holy See in that City Enjoying Extraterritorial Rights and San Paolo Fuori le Mura

JAPAN
1993 Buddhist Monuments in the Horyu-ji Area
1993 Himeji-jo
1994 Historic Monuments of Ancient Kyoto (Kyoto, Uji and Otsu Cities)
1995 Historic Villages of Shirakawa-go and Gokayama
1996 Hiroshima Peace Memorial (Genbaku Dome)
1996 Itsukushima Shinto Shrine
1998 Historic Monuments of Ancient Nara
1999 Shrines and Temples of Nikko
2000 Gusuku Sites and Related Properties of the Kingdom of Ryukyu

JERUSALEM (proposed for inscription by Jordan)
1981 Old City of Jerusalem and its Walls

KENYA
2001 Lamu Old Town

LAO PEOPLE'S DEMOCRATIC REPUBLIC
1995 Town of Luang Prabang

LATVIA
1997 Historic Centre of Riga

LIBYAN ARAB JAMAHIRIYA
1986 Old Town of Ghadamès

LITHUANIA
1994 Vilnius Historic Centre

LITHUANIA and RUSSIAN FEDERATION
2000 Curonian Spit

LUXEMBOURG
1994 City of Luxembourg : its Old Quarters and Fortifications

MACEDONIA, Former Yugoslav Republic of
1979 Ohrid Region with its Cultural and Historical Aspect and its Natural Environment

MADAGASCAR
2001 Royal Hill of Ambohimanga

MALI
1988 Towns of Djenné
1988 Timbuktu
1989 Cliff of Bandiagara (Land of the Dogons)

MALTA
1980 City of Valletta

MAURITANIA
1996 Ancient Ksour of Ouadane, Chinguetti, Tichitt and Oualata

MEXICO
1987 Historic Centre of Mexico City and Xochimilco
1987 Historic Centre of Puebla
1987 **Historic Centre of Oaxaca** and Archaeological Site of Monte Albán
1988 Historic Town of Guanajuato and Adjacent Mines
1991 Historic Centre of Morelia
1993 Historic Centre of Zacatecas
1994 Earliest 16th-Century Monasteries on the Slopes of Popocatepetl
1996 Historic Monuments Zone of Querétaro
1997 Hospicio Cabañas, Guadalajara
1998 Historic Monuments Zone of Tlacotalpan
1999 Historic Fortified Town of Campeche

MOROCCO
1981 Medina of Fez

1985 Medina of Marrakesh
1987 Ksar of Ait-Ben-Haddou
1996 Historic City of Meknes
1997 Medina of Tétouan
2001 Medina of Essaouira

MOZAMBIQUE
1991 Island of Mozambique

NEPAL
1979 Kathmandu Valley

NETHERLANDS
1995 Schokland and Surroundings
1996 Defence Line of Amsterdam
1997 Mill Network at Kinderdijk- Elshout
1997 Historic Area of Willemstad, Inner City, and Harbour, Netherlands Antilles
1998 Ir.D.F. Woudagemaal (D.F. Wouda Steam Pumping Station)
1999 Droogmakerij de Beemster (Beemster Polder)
2000 Rietveld Schröderhuis (Rietveld Schröder House)

NIGERIA
1999 Sukur Cultural Landscape

NORWAY
1979 Urnes Stave Church
1979 Bergen
1980 Røros

PAKISTAN
1981 Historical Monuments of Thatta
1981 Fort and Shalamar Gardens in Lahore
1997 Rohtas Fort

PANAMA
1980 Fortifications on the Caribbean Side of Panama: Portobelo - San Lorenzo forts on the Caribbean coast form part of the defence system built by the Spanish Crown to protect transatlantic trade.
1997 Historic District of Panamá, with the Salón Bolívar

PARAGUAY
1993 Jesuit Missions of La Santísima Trinidad de Paraná and Jesús de Tavarangue

PERU
1983 City of Cuzco
1991 Historic Centre of Lima
2000 Historical Centre of the City of Arequipa

PHILIPPINES
1993 Baroque Churches of the Philippines
1995 Rice Terraces of the Philippine Cordilleras
1999 Historic Town of Vigan

POLAND
1978 Cracow's Historic Centre
1978 Wieliczka Salt Mine
1979 Auschwitz Concentration Camp
1980 Historic Centre of Warsaw
1992 Old City of Zamosc
1997 Medieval Town of Torun
1997 Castle of the Teutonic Order in Malbork
1999 Kalwaria Zebrzydowska: the Mannerist Architectural and Park Landscape Complex and Pilgrimage Park
2001 Churches of Peace in Jawor and Swidnica

PORTUGAL
1983 Central Zone of the Town of Angra do Heroismo in the Azores
1983 Monastery of the Hieronymites and Tower of Belém in Lisbon
1983 Monastery of Batalha
1983 Convent of Christ in Tomar
1986 Historic Centre of Évora
1989 Monastery of Alcobaça
1995 Cultural Landscape of Sintra
1996 Historic Centre of Oporto
2001 Alto Douro Wine Region
2001 Historic Centre of Guimarães

REPUBLIC OF KOREA
1995 Seokguram Grotto and Bulguksa Temple
1995 Haeinsa Temple Janggyeong Panjeon, the Depositories for the Tripitaka Koreana Woodblocks
1995 Jongmyo Shrine
1997 Changdeokgung Palace Complex
1997 Hwaseong Fortress
2000 Gyeongju Historic Areas

ROMANIA
1993 Villages with Fortified Churches in Transylvania
1993 Monastery of Horezu
1993 Churches of Moldavia
1999 Historic Centre of Sighisoara
1999 Wooden Churches of Maramures

RUSSIAN FEDERATION
1990 Historic Centre of Saint Petersburg and Related Groups of Monuments

1990 Kizhi Pogost
1990 Kremlin and Red Square, Moscow
1992 Historic Monuments of Novgorod and Surroundings
1992 Cultural and Historic Ensemble of the Solovetsky Islands
1992 White Monuments of Vladimir and Suzdal
1993 Architectural Ensemble of the Trinity Sergius Lavra in Sergiev Posad
1994 Church of the Ascension, Kolomenskoye
2000 Ensemble of the Ferapontov Monastery
2000 Historic and Architectural Complex of the Kazan Kremlin

SAINT KITTS AND NEVIS
1999 Brimstone Hill Fortress National Park

SENEGAL
1978 Island of Gorée
2000 Island of Saint-Louis

SLOVAKIA
1993 Vlkolínec
1993 Banska Stiavnica
1993 Spissky Hrad and its Associated Cultural Monuments
2000 Bardejov Town Conservation Reserve

SOUTH AFRICA
1999 Robben Island

SPAIN
1984 Historic Centre of Cordoba
1984 Alhambra, Generalife and Albayzín, Granada
1984 Burgos Cathedral
1984 Monastery and Site of the Escurial, Madrid
1984 Parque Güell, Palacio Güell and Casa Mila in Barcelona
1985 Altamira Cave
1985 Old Town of Segovia and its Aqueduct
1985 Monuments of Oviedo and the Kingdom of the Asturias
1985 Santiago de Compostela (Old Town)
1985 Old Town of Ávila with its Extra-Muros Churches
1986 Mudejar Architecture of Aragon
1986 Historic City of Toledo
1986 Old Town of Cáceres
1987 Cathedral, Alcázar and Archivo de Indias, in Seville
1988 Old City of Salamanca
1991 Poblet Monastery
1993 Royal Monastery of Santa María de Guadalupe
1993 Route of Santiago de Compostela
1996 Historic Walled Town of Cuenca
1996 La Lonja de la Seda de Valencia
1997 The Palau de la Música Catalana and the Hospital de Sant Pau, Barcelona
1997 San Millán Yuso and Suso Monasteries
1998 University and Historic Precinct of Alcalá de Henares
1999 Ibiza, Biodiversity and Culture
1999 San Cristóbal de La Laguna
2000 Catalan Romanesque Churches of the Vall de Boí
2001 Aranjuez Cultural Landscape

SRI LANKA
1988 Sacred City of Kandy
1988 Old Town of Galle and its Fortifications
1991 Golden Temple of Dambulla

SWEDEN
1991 Royal Domain of Drottningholm
1993 Engelsberg Ironworks
1994 Skogskyrkogården
1995 Hanseatic Town of Visby
1996 Church Village of Gammelstad, Luleå
1996 Laponian Area
2000 Agricultural Landscape of Southern Öland
2001 The Mining Area of the Great Copper Mountain in Falun

SWITZERLAND
1983 Convent of St Gall
1983 Benedictine Convent of St John at Müstair
1983 Old City of Berne
2000 Three Castles, Defensive Wall and Ramparts of the Market Town of Bellinzone

SYRIAN ARAB REPUBLIC
1979 Ancient City of Damascus.
1986 Ancient City of Aleppo

TUNISIA
1979 Medina of Tunis
1988 Medina of Sousse
1988 Kairouan

TURKEY
1985 Historic Areas of Istanbul
1985 Great Mosque and Hospital of Divrigi
1994 City of Safranbolu

TURKMENISTAN
1999 State Historical and Cultural Park 'Ancient Merv'

UGANDA
2001 Tombs of Buganda Kings at Kasubi

UKRAINE
1990 Kiev: Saint-Sophia Cathedral and Related Monastic Buildings, Kiev-Pechersk Lavra
1998 L'viv - the Ensemble of the Historic Centre

UNITED KINGDOM
1986 Durham Castle and Cathedral
1986 Ironbridge Gorge
1986 Studley Royal Park including the Ruins of Fountains Abbey
1987 Blenheim Palace
1986 Castles and Town Walls of King Edward in Gwynedd
1987 City of Bath
1987 Westminster Palace, Westminster Abbey and Saint Margaret's Church
1988 Tower of London
1988 Canterbury Cathedral, St Augustine's Abbey and St Martin's Church
1995 Old and New Towns of Edinburgh
1997 Maritime Greenwich
2000 Blaenavon Industrial Landscape

2000 Historic Town of St George and Related Fortifications, Bermuda
2001 Derwent Valley Mills
2001 New Lanark
2001 Saltaire

UNITED REPUBLIC OF TANZANIA
2000 Stone Town of Zanzibar

UNITED STATES OF AMERICA
1979 Independence Hall
1983 La Fortaleza and San Juan Historic Site in Puerto Rico
1984 Statue of Liberty
1987 Monticello and the University of Virginia in Charlottesville
1992 Pueblo de Taos

URUGUAY
1995 Historic Quarter of the City of Colonia del Sacramento

UZBEKISTAN
1990 Itchan Kala

1993 Historic Centre of Bukhara
2000 Historic Centre of Shakhrisyabz
2001 Samarkand - Crossroads of Cultures

VATICAN CITY (also see *Italy and the Holy See*)

VENEZUELA
1993 Coro and its Port
2000 Ciudad Universitaria de Caracas

VIETNAM
1993 Complex of Hué Monuments
1999 Hoi An Ancient Town

YEMEN
1982 Old Walled City of Shibam
1986 Old City of Sana'a
1993 Historic Town of Zabid

YUGOSLAVIA
1979 Stari Ras and Sopocani
1979 Natural and Culturo-Historical Region of Kotor
1986 Studenica Monastery

The 1972 Convention

Convention Concerning the Protection of the World Cultural and Natural Heritage

THE GENERAL CONFERENCE of the United Nations Educational, Scientific and Cultural Organization meeting in Paris from 17 October to 21 November 1972, at its seventeenth session,

Noting that the cultural heritage and the natural heritage are increasingly threatened with destruction not only by the traditional causes of decay, but also by changing social and economic conditions which aggravate the situation with even more formidable phenomena of damage or destruction,

Considering that deterioration or disappearance of any item of the cultural or natural heritage constitutes a harmful impoverishment of the heritage of all the nations of the world,

Considering that protection of this heritage at the national level often remains incomplete because of the scale of the resources which it requires and of the insufficient economic, scientific, and technological resources of the country where the property to be protected is situated,

Recalling that the Constitution of the Organization provides that it will maintain, increase, and diffuse knowledge, by assuring the conservation and protection of the world's heritage, and recommending to the nations concerned the necessary international conventions,

Considering that the existing international conventions, recommendations and resolutions concerning cultural and natural property demonstrate the importance, for all the peoples of the world, of safeguarding this unique and irreplaceable property, to whatever people it may belong,

Considering that parts of the cultural or natural heritage are of outstanding interest and therefore need to be preserved as part of the world heritage of mankind as a whole,

Considering that, in view of the magnitude and gravity of the new dangers threatening them, it is incumbent on the international community as a whole to participate in the protection of the cultural and natural heritage of outstanding universal value, by the granting of collective assistance which, although not taking the place of action by the State concerned, will serve as an efficient complement thereto,

Considering that it is essential for this purpose to adopt new provisions in the form of a convention establishing an effective system of collective protection of the cultural and natural heritage of outstanding universal value, organized on a permanent basis and in accordance with modern scientific methods,

Having decided, at its sixteenth session, that this question should be made the subject of an international convention,

Adopts this sixteenth day of November 1972 this Convention.

I. DEFINITION OF THE CULTURAL AND NATURAL HERITAGE
Article 1
For the purposes of this Convention, the following shall be considered as "cultural heritage":

- monuments: architectural works, works of monumental sculpture and painting, elements or structures of an archaeological nature, inscriptions, cave dwellings and combinations of features, which are of outstanding universal value from the point of view of history, art or science;
- groups of buildings: groups of separate or connected buildings which, because of their architecture, their homogeneity or their place in the landscape, are of outstanding universal value from the point of view of history, art or science;
- sites: works of man or the combined works of nature and man, and areas including archaeological sites which are of outstanding universal value from the historical, aesthetic, ethnological or anthropological point of view.

Article 2
For the purposes of this Convention, the following shall be considered as "natural heritage":
- natural features consisting of physical and biological formations or groups of such formations, which are of outstanding universal value from the aesthetic or scientific point of view;
- geological and physiographical formations and precisely delineated areas which constitute the habitat of threatened species of animals and plants of outstanding universal value from the point of view of science or conservation;
- natural sites or precisely delineated natural areas of outstanding universal value from the point of view of science, conservation or natural beauty.

Article 3
It is for each State Party to this Convention to identify and delineate the different properties situated on its territory mentioned in Articles 1 and 2 above.

II. NATIONAL PROTECTION AND INTERNATIONAL PROTECTION OF THE CULTURAL AND NATURAL HERITAGE
Article 4
Each State Party to this Convention recognizes that the duty of ensuring the identification, protection, conservation, presentation and transmission to future generations of the cultural and natural heritage referred to in Articles 1 and 2 and situated on its territory, belongs primarily to that State. It will do all it can to this end, to the utmost of its own resources and, where appropriate, with any international assistance and co-operation, in particular, financial, artistic, scientific and technical, which it may be able to obtain.

Article 5
To ensure that effective and active measures are taken for the protection, conservation and presentation of the cultural and natural heritage situated on its territory, each State Party to this Convention shall endeavor, in so far as possible, and as appropriate for each country:
1. to adopt a general policy which aims to give the cultural and natural heritage a function in the life of the community and to integrate the protection of that heritage into comprehensive planning programmes;
2. to set up within its territories, where such services do not exist, one or more services for the protection, conservation and presentation of the cultural and natural heritage with an appropriate staff and possessing the means to discharge their functions;
3. to develop scientific and technical studies and research and to work out such operating methods as will make the State capable of counteracting the dangers that threaten its cultural or natural heritage;

4. to take the appropriate legal, scientific, technical, administrative and financial measures necessary for the identification, protection, conservation, presentation and rehabilitation of this heritage; and
5. to foster the establishment or development of national or regional centres for training in the protection, conservation and presentation of the cultural and natural heritage and to encourage scientific research in this field.

Article 6
1. Whilst fully respecting the sovereignty of the States on whose territory the cultural and natural heritage mentioned in Articles 1 and 2 is situated, and without prejudice to property right provided by national legislation, the States Parties to this Convention recognize that such heritage constitutes a world heritage for whose protection it is the duty of the international community as a whole to co-operate.
2. The States Parties undertake, in accordance with the provisions of this Convention, to give their help in the identification, protection, conservation and presentation of the cultural and natural heritage referred to in paragraphs 2 and 4 of Article 11 if the States on whose territory it is situated so request.
3. Each State Party to this Convention undertakes not to take any deliberate measures which might damage directly or indirectly the cultural and natural heritage referred to in Articles 1 and 2 situated on the territory of other States Parties to this Convention.

Article 7
For the purpose of this Convention, international protection of the world cultural and natural heritage shall be understood to mean the establishment of a system of international co-operation and assistance designed to support States Parties to the Convention in their efforts to conserve and identify that heritage.

III. INTERGOVERNMENTAL COMMITTEE FOR THE PROTECTION OF THE WORLD CULTURAL AND NATURAL HERITAGE
Article 8
1. An Intergovernmental Committee for the Protection of the Cultural and Natural Heritage of Outstanding Universal Value, called "the World Heritage Committee", is hereby established within the United Nations Educational, Scientific and Cultural Organization. It shall be composed of 15 States Parties to the Convention, elected by States Parties to the Convention meeting in general assembly during the ordinary session of the General Conference of the United Nations Educational, Scientific and Cultural Organization. The number of States members of the Committee shall be increased to 21 as from the date of the ordinary session of the General Conference following the entry into force of this Convention for at least 40 States.
2. Election of members of the Committee shall ensure an equitable representation of the different regions and cultures of the world.
3. A representative of the International Centre for the Study of the Preservation and Restoration of Cultural Property (Rome Centre), a representative of the International Council of Monuments and Sites (ICOMOS) and a representative of the International Union for Conservation of Nature and Natural Resources (IUCN), to whom may be added, at the request of States Parties to the Convention meeting in general assembly during the ordinary sessions of the General Conference of the United Nations Educational, Scientific and Cultural Organization,

representatives of other intergovernmental or non-governmental organizations, with similar objectives, may attend the meetings of the Committee in an advisory capacity.

Article 9
1. The term of office of States members of the World Heritage Committee shall extend from the end of the ordinary session of the General Conference during which they are elected until the end of its third subsequent ordinary session.
2. The term of office of one-third of the members designated at the time of the first election shall, however, cease at the end of the first ordinary session of the General Conference following that at which they were elected; and the term of office of a further third of the members designated at the same time shall cease at the end of the second ordinary session of the General Conference following that at which they were elected. The names of these members shall be chosen by lot by the President of the General Conference of the United Nations Educational, Scientific and Cultural Organization after the first election.
3. States members of the Committee shall choose as their representatives persons qualified in the field of the cultural or natural heritage.

Article 10
1. The World Heritage Committee shall adopt its Rules of Procedure.
2. The Committee may at any time invite public or private organizations or individuals to participate in its meetings for consultation on particular problems.
3. The Committee may create such consultative bodies as it deems necessary for the performance of its functions.

Article 11
1. Every State Party to this Convention shall, in so far as possible, submit to the World Heritage Committee an inventory of property forming part of the cultural and natural heritage, situated in its territory and suitable for inclusion in the list provided for in paragraph 2 of this Article. This inventory, which shall not be considered exhaustive, shall include documentation about the location of the property in question and its significance.
2. On the basis of the inventories submitted by States in accordance with paragraph 1, the Committee shall establish, keep up to date and publish, under the title of "World Heritage List," a list of properties forming part of the cultural heritage and natural heritage, as defined in Articles 1 and 2 of this Convention, which it considers as having outstanding universal value in terms of such criteria as it shall have established. An updated list shall be distributed at least every two years.
3. The inclusion of a property in the World Heritage List requires the consent of the State concerned. The inclusion of a property situated in a territory, sovereignty or jurisdiction over which is claimed by more than one State shall in no way prejudice the rights of the parties to the dispute.
4. The Committee shall establish, keep up to date and publish, whenever circumstances shall so require, under the title of "List of World Heritage in Danger", a list of the property appearing in the World Heritage List for the conservation of which major operations are necessary and for which assistance has been requested under this Convention. This list shall contain an estimate of the cost of such operations. The list may include only such property forming part of the cultural and natural heritage as is threatened by serious and specific dangers, such as the threat of disappearance caused by accelerated deterioration, large- scale public or private projects or rapid urban or tourist development projects; destruction caused by changes in the use or ownership of the land; major alterations due to unknown causes; abandonment for any reason whatsoever; the outbreak or the threat of an armed conflict; calamities and cataclysms; serious fires, earthquakes, landslides; volcanic eruptions; changes in water level, floods and tidal waves. The Committee may at any time, in case of urgent need, make a new entry in the List of World Heritage in Danger and publicize such entry immediately.
5. The Committee shall define the criteria on the basis of which a property belonging to the cultural or natural heritage may be included in either of the lists mentioned in paragraphs 2 and 4 of this article.
6. Before refusing a request for inclusion in one of the two lists mentioned in paragraphs 2 and 4 of this article, the Committee shall consult the State Party in whose territory the cultural or natural property in question is situated.
7. The Committee shall, with the agreement of the States concerned, co-ordinate and encourage the studies and research needed for the drawing up of the lists referred to in paragraphs 2 and 4 of this article.

Article 12
The fact that a property belonging to the cultural or natural heritage has not been included in either of the two lists mentioned in paragraphs 2 and 4 of Article 11 shall in no way be construed to mean that it does not have an outstanding universal value for purposes other than those resulting from inclusion in these lists.

Article 13
1. The World Heritage Committee shall receive and study requests for international assistance formulated by States Parties to this Convention with respect to property forming part of the cultural or natural heritage, situated in their territories, and included or potentially suitable for inclusion in the lists mentioned referred to in paragraphs 2 and 4 of Article 11. The purpose of such requests may be to secure the protection, conservation, presentation or rehabilitation of such property.
2. Requests for international assistance under paragraph 1 of this article may also be concerned with identification of cultural or natural property defined in Articles 1 and 2, when preliminary investigations have shown that further inquiries would be justified.
3. The Committee shall decide on the action to be taken with regard to these requests, determine where appropriate, the nature and extent of its assistance, and authorize the conclusion, on its behalf, of the necessary arrangements with the government concerned.
4. The Committee shall determine an order of priorities for its operations. It shall in so doing bear in mind the respective importance for the world cultural and natural heritage of the property requiring protection, the need to give international assistance to the property most representative of a natural environment or of the genius and the history of the peoples of the world, the urgency of the work to be done, the resources available to the States on whose territory the threatened property is situated and in particular the extent to which they are able to safeguard such property by their own means.
5. The Committee shall draw up, keep up to date and publicize a list of property for which international assistance has been granted.
6. The Committee shall decide on the use of the resources of the Fund established under Article 15 of this Convention. It shall seek ways of increasing these resources and shall take all useful steps to this end.
7. The Committee shall co-operate with international and national governmental and non-governmental organizations having objectives similar to those of this Convention. For the implementation of its programmes and projects, the Committee may call on such organizations, particularly the International Centre for the Study of the Preservation and Restoration of cultural Property (the Rome Centre), the International Council of Monuments and Sites (ICOMOS) and the International Union for Conservation of Nature and Natural Resources (IUCN), as well as on public and private bodies and individuals.
8. Decisions of the Committee shall be taken by a majority of two-thirds of its members present and voting. A majority of the members of the Committee shall constitute a quorum.

Article 14
1. The World Heritage Committee shall be assisted by a Secretariat appointed by the Director-General of the United Nations Educational, Scientific and Cultural Organization.
2. The Director-General of the United Nations Educational, Scientific and Cultural Organization, utilizing to the fullest extent possible the services of the International Centre for the Study of the Preservation and the Restoration of Cultural Property (the Rome Centre), the International Council of Monuments and Sites (ICOMOS) and the International Union for Conservation of Nature and Natural Resources (IUCN) in their respective areas of competence and capability, shall prepare the Committee's documentation and the agenda of its meetings and shall have the responsibility for the implementation of its decisions.

IV. FUND FOR THE PROTECTION OF THE WORLD CULTURAL AND NATURAL HERITAGE
Article 15
1. A Fund for the Protection of the World Cultural and Natural Heritage of Outstanding Universal Value, called "the World Heritage Fund", is hereby established.
2. The Fund shall constitute a trust fund, in conformity with the provisions of the Financial Regulations of the United Nations Educational, Scientific and Cultural Organization.
3. The resources of the Fund shall consist of:
  1. compulsory and voluntary contributions made by States Parties to this Convention,
  2. Contributions, gifts or bequests which may be made by:
    1. other States;
    2. the United Nations Educational, Scientific and Cultural Organization, other organizations of the United Nations system, particularly the United Nations Development Programme or other intergovernmental organizations;
    3. public or private bodies or individuals;
  3. any interest due on the resources of the Fund;
  4. funds raised by collections and receipts from events organized for the benefit of the fund; and
  5. all other resources authorized by the Fund's regulations, as drawn up by the World Heritage Committee.
4. Contributions to the Fund and other forms of assistance made available to the Committee may be used only for such purposes as the Committee shall define. The Committee may accept contributions to be used only for a certain programme or project, provided that the Committee shall have decided on the implementation of such programme or project. No political conditions may be attached to contributions made to the Fund.

Article 16
1. Without prejudice to any supplementary voluntary contribution, the States Parties to this Convention undertake to pay regularly, every two years, to the World Heritage Fund, contributions, the amount of which, in the form of a uniform percentage applicable to all States, shall be determined by the General Assembly of States Parties to the Convention, meeting during the sessions of the General Conference of the United Nations Educational, Scientific and Cultural Organization. This decision of the General Assembly requires the majority of the States Parties present and voting, which have not made the declaration referred to in paragraph 2 of this Article. In no case shall the compulsory contribution of States Parties to the Convention exceed 1% of the contribution to the regular budget of the United Nations Educational, Scientific and Cultural Organization.
2. However, each State referred to in Article 31 or in Article 32 of this Convention may declare, at the time of the deposit of its instrument of ratification, acceptance or accession, that it shall not be bound by the provisions of paragraph 1 of this Article.
3. A State Party to the Convention which has made the declaration referred to in paragraph 2 of this Article may at any time withdraw the said declaration by notifying the Director-General of the United Nations Educational, Scientific and Cultural Organization. However, the withdrawal of the declaration shall not take effect in regard to the compulsory contribution due by the State until the date of the subsequent General Assembly of States parties to the Convention.
4. In order that the Committee may be able to plan its operations effectively, the contributions of States Parties to this Convention which have made the declaration referred to in paragraph 2 of this Article, shall be paid on a regular basis, at least every two years, and should not be less than the contributions which they should have paid if they had been bound by the provisions of paragraph 1 of this Article.
5. Any State Party to the Convention which is in arrears with the payment of its compulsory or voluntary contribution for the current year and the calendar year immediately preceding it shall not be eligible as a Member of the World Heritage Committee, although this provision shall not apply to the first election.

The terms of office of any such State which is already a member of the Committee shall terminate at the time of the elections provided for in Article 8, paragraph 1 of this Convention.

Article 17
The States Parties to this Convention shall consider or encourage the establishment of national public and private foundations or associations whose purpose is to invite donations for the protection of the cultural and natural heritage as defined in Articles 1 and 2 of this Convention.

Article 18
The States Parties to this Convention shall give their assistance to international fund-raising campaigns organized for the World Heritage Fund under the auspices of the United Nations Educational, Scientific and Cultural Organization. They shall facilitate collections made by the bodies mentioned in paragraph 3 of Article 15 for this purpose.

V. CONDITIONS AND ARRANGEMENTS FOR INTERNATIONAL ASSISTANCE
Article 19
Any State Party to this Convention may request international assistance for property forming part of the cultural or natural heritage of outstanding universal value situated within its territory. It shall submit with its request such information and documentation provided for in Article 21 as it has in its possession and as will enable the Committee to come to a decision.

Article 20
Subject to the provisions of paragraph 2 of Article 13, sub-paragraph (c) of Article 22 and Article 23, international assistance provided for by this Convention may be granted only to property forming part of the cultural and natural heritage which the World Heritage Committee has decided, or may decide, to enter in one of the lists mentioned in paragraphs 2 and 4 of Article 11.

Article 21
1. The World Heritage Committee shall define the procedure by which requests to it for international assistance shall be considered and shall specify the content of the request, which should define the operation contemplated, the work that is necessary, the expected cost thereof, the degree of urgency and the reasons why the resources of the State requesting assistance do not allow it to meet all the expenses. Such requests must be supported by experts' reports whenever possible.
2. Requests based upon disasters or natural calamities should, by reasons of the urgent work which they may involve, be given immediate, priority consideration by the Committee, which should have a reserve fund at its disposal against such contingencies.
3. Before coming to a decision, the Committee shall carry out such studies and consultations as it deems necessary.

Article 22

Assistance granted by the World Heritage Committee may take the following forms:

1. studies concerning the artistic, scientific and technical problems raised by the protection, conservation, presentation and rehabilitation of the cultural and natural heritage, as defined in paragraphs 2 and 4 of Article 11 of this Convention;
2. provisions of experts, technicians and skilled labour to ensure that the approved work is correctly carried out;
3. training of staff and specialists at all levels in the field of identification, protection, conservation, presentation and rehabilitation of the cultural and natural heritage;
4. supply of equipment which the State concerned does not possess or is not in a position to acquire;
5. low-interest or interest-free loans which might be repayable on a long-term basis;
6. the granting, in exceptional cases and for special reasons, of non-repayable subsidies.

Article 23

The World Heritage Committee may also provide international assistance to national or regional centres for the training of staff and specialists at all levels in the field of identification, protection, conservation, presentation and rehabilitation of the cultural and natural heritage.

Article 24

International assistance on a large scale shall be preceded by detailed scientific, economic and technical studies. These studies shall draw upon the most advanced techniques for the protection, conservation, presentation and rehabilitation of the natural and cultural heritage and shall be consistent with the objectives of this Convention. The studies shall also seek means of making rational use of the resources available in the State concerned.

Article 25

As a general rule, only part of the cost of work necessary shall be borne by the international community. The contribution of the State benefiting from international assistance shall constitute a substantial share of the resources devoted to each programme or project, unless its resources do not permit this.

Article 26

The World Heritage Committee and the recipient State shall define in the agreement they conclude the conditions in which a programme or project for which international assistance under the terms of this Convention is provided, shall be carried out. It shall be the responsibility of the State receiving such international assistance to continue to protect, conserve and present the property so safeguarded, in observance of the conditions laid down by the agreement.

VI. EDUCATIONAL PROGRAMMES
Article 27

1. The States Parties to this Convention shall endeavor by all appropriate means, and in particular by educational and information programmes, to strengthen appreciation and respect by their peoples of the cultural and natural heritage defined in Articles 1 and 2 of the Convention.
2. They shall undertake to keep the public broadly informed of the dangers threatening this heritage and of the activities carried on in pursuance of this Convention.

Article 28

States Parties to this Convention which receive international assistance under the Convention shall take appropriate measures to make known the importance of the property for which assistance has been received and the role played by such assistance.

VII. REPORTS
Article 29

1. The States Parties to this Convention shall, in the reports which they submit to the General Conference of the United Nations Educational, Scientific and Cultural Organization on dates and in a manner to be determined by it, give information on the legislative and administrative provisions which they have adopted and other action which they have taken for the application of this Convention, together with details of the experience acquired in this field.
2. These reports shall be brought to the attention of the World Heritage Committee.
3. The Committee shall submit a report on its activities at each of the ordinary sessions of the General Conference of the United Nations Educational, Scientific and Cultural Organization.

VIII. FINAL CLAUSES
Article 30

This Convention is drawn up in Arabic, English, French, Russian and Spanish, the five texts being equally authoritative.

Article 31

1. This Convention shall be subject to ratification or acceptance by States members of the United Nations Educational, Scientific and Cultural Organization in accordance with their respective constitutional procedures.
2. The instruments of ratification or acceptance shall be deposited with the Director-General of the United Nations Educational, Scientific and Cultural Organization.

Article 32

1. This Convention shall be open to accession by all States not members of the United Nations Educational, Scientific and Cultural Organization which are invited by the General Conference of the Organization to accede to it.
2. Accession shall be effected by the deposit of an instrument of accession with the Director-General of the United Nations Educational, Scientific and Cultural Organization.

Article 33

This Convention shall enter into force three months after the date of the deposit of the twentieth instrument of ratification, acceptance or accession, but only with respect to those States which have deposited their respective instruments of ratification, acceptance or accession on or before that date. It shall enter into force with respect to any other State three months after the deposit of its instrument of ratification, acceptance or accession.

Article 34

The following provisions shall apply to those States Parties to this Convention which have a federal or non-unitary constitutional system:

1. with regard to the provisions of this Convention, the implementation of which comes under the legal jurisdiction of the federal or central legislative power, the obligations of the federal or central government shall be the same as for those States parties which are not federal States;
2. with regard to the provisions of this Convention, the implementation of which comes under the legal jurisdiction of individual constituent States, countries, provinces or cantons that are not obliged by the constitutional system of the federation to take legislative measures, the federal government shall inform the competent authorities of such States, countries, provinces or cantons of the said provisions, with its recommendation for their adoption.

Article 35

1. Each State Party to this Convention may denounce the Convention.
2. The denunciation shall be notified by an instrument in writing, deposited with the Director-General of the United Nations Educational, Scientific and Cultural Organization.
3. The denunciation shall take effect twelve months after the receipt of the instrument of denunciation. It shall not affect the financial obligations of the denouncing State until the date on which the withdrawal takes effect.

Article 36

The Director-General of the United Nations Educational, Scientific and Cultural Organization shall inform the States members of the Organization, the States not members of the Organization which are referred to in Article 32, as well as the United Nations, of the deposit of all the instruments of ratification, acceptance, or accession provided for in Articles 31 and 32, and of the denunciations provided for in Article 35.

Article 37

1. This Convention may be revised by the General Conference of the United Nations Educational, Scientific and Cultural Organization. Any such revision shall, however, bind only the States which shall become Parties to the revising convention.
2. If the General Conference should adopt a new convention revising this Convention in whole or in part, then, unless the new convention otherwise provides, this Convention shall cease to be open to ratification, acceptance or accession, as from the date on which the new revising convention enters into force.

Article 38

In conformity with Article 102 of the Charter of the United Nations, this Convention shall be registered with the Secretariat of the United Nations at the request of the Director-General of the United Nations Educational, Scientific and Cultural Organization.

Done in Paris, this twenty-third day of November 1972, in two authentic copies bearing the signature of the President of the seventeenth session of the General Conference and of the Director-General of the United Nations Educational, Scientific and Cultural Organization, which shall be deposited in the archives of the United Nations Educational, Scientific and Cultural Organization, and certified true copies of which shall be delivered to all the States referred to in Articles 31 and 32 as well as to the United Nations.

Bibliography

UNESCO publications

On 18 April 1996, UNESCO began publication of the World Heritage Review, a quarterly, 80 page, color magazine that focuses on the *World Heritage sites*. The magazine is published simultaneously in English, French and Spanish.

The list of publications below includes those produced by UNESCO or in partnership with other publishing companies. All are available from the UNESCO offices in Paris. All enquiries should be sent to: The World Heritage Centre, UNESCO, 7 Place de Fontenoy, 75352 Paris, France.

Les villes du patrimoine mondial, CD-ROM, UNESCO Publishing/Cyberion, Paris.

The World Heritage Series for Children (recommended for children aged 8-15, available in English, French and Spanish), UNESCO Publishing/Childrens Press, Paris.

Patrimonio de la Humanidad (12 volume encyclopedia), Planeta/UNESCO Publishing, Madrid, 1995.

World Heritage Encyclopedia (in German), in 12 volumes, Verlagshaus Stuttgart/Plaza y Janes/UNESCO Publishing, Stuttgart, 1996/1997.

Schätze der Menschheit, Frederking & Thaler/UNESCO Publishing, Munich, 1996/1997.

The World Heritage Encyclopedia (in Japanese), in 12 volumes, Kodansha/UNESCO Publishing, Tokyo, 1996/1997.

Masterworks of Man and Nature, Harper-MacRae Publishing, Sydney, 1994.

Paradise on Earth, Harper-MacRae Publishing, Sydney, 1995.

World Heritage Twenty Years Later, by Jim Thorsell, IUCN, Switzerland and Great Britain, 1992.

World Cultural and Natural Property (available in Japanese), for children, Gakken, Tokyo, 1994.

Cultural Landscapes of Universal Value, by B. von Droste, H. Plachter, M. Rössler, Fischer Verlag, Jena, 1995.

Index

425

426

428

Photographic Credits

ASIA

Syrian Arab Republic
Page 256 top M. Gratton/Vision
Page 256 bottom Christopher Wood/LPI
Page 257 center left Charles Lenars
Pages 256-257 and pages 257 center right AISA
Page 258 left and right Andrew Humphreys/LPI
Page 259 top AISA
Page 259 bottom center SIE
Page 259 bottom right Elio Ciol

Israel
Pages 260-261 Itamar Grinberg
Page 260 bottom left, page 261 center right, bottom right and page 262 top left, top right and bottom Marcello Bertinetti/Archivio White Star
Page 262 top center Antonio Attini/Archivio White Star
Page 263 Stefano Amantini/Atlantide
Page 264 top left, top right and bottom, pages 264-265 and page 265 top Marcello Bertinetti/Archivio White Star
Page 266 Antonio Attini/Archivio White Star
Page 266 bottom, page 267 top left Marcello Bertinetti/Archivio White Star
Page 267 top center, top right, bottom left and bottom right Antonio Attini/Archivio White Star

Yemen
Pages 268-269 AISA
Page 269 top left Index
Page 269 center right Alfio Garozzo/Archivio White Star
Page 269 bottom Harry Gruyaert/Magnum/Contrasto
Page 270 bottom Index
Page 270 top, page 271 top left, top right and bottom Alfio Garozzo/Archivio White Star

Iran
Page 272 top AISA
Pages 272-273, page 273 top right, center and bottom Henri Stierlin
Pages 274-275 and page 275 top AISA
Page 274 top left and page 275 bottom Wojtek Buss

Uzbekistan
Pag 276 bottom left Henri Stierlin
Page 276 top, bottom right, pages 276-277 and page 278 Martin Moos/LPI
Page 279 top left, top right and bottom, page 280 top and bottom, pages 280-281, page 281 top right, bottom left and bottom right Henri Stierlin
Page 282 left Charles Lenars
Page 282 right top and right bottom Martin Moos/LPI
Pages 282-283 Keren Su/China Span

Nepal
Page 284 top right, bottom left and bottom right, page 285, page 286 top and bottom, pages 286-287, p. 287 top left Wojtek Buss
Page 287 top right Christophe Boisvieux
Page 288 bottom and page 289 top right Wojtek Buss
Pages 288-289 and page 289 bottom right AISA

Pakistan
Page 290 bottom left and bottom right and page 291 bottom Christophe Boisvieux
Pages 290-291 and page 291 top Tibor Bognar
Page 292 top Michel Gotin
Pages 292-293 Tibor Bognar
Page 293 top left Christophe Bosvieux
Page 293 top right Mit Collection/Corbis/Grazia Neri
Page 293 bottom Ric Ergenbright/Corbis/Grazia Neri

India
Page 294 top Henri Stierlin
Page 294 bottom Massimo Borchi/Archivio White Star
Page 295 top left Thomas Dix
Page 295 top right, page 296 center left and bottom left Massimo Borchi/Archivio White Star
Pages 296-297 Thomas Dix
Pages 298-299 and page 299 top right and bottom right Massimo Borchi/Archivio White Star
Page 299 bottom left Henri Stierlin

Sri Lanka
Page 300 left Damm/Zefa
Page 300 top right, page 301 top right and bottom right Christophe Boisvieux

China
Page 302 top right Jen Rey Chine/Ag.ANA
Page 302 top left, pages 302-303 and page 303 top Keren Su/China Span
Pages 304-305 AISA
Page 304 top left, page 305 center left, center right and bottom right, page 306 top, center left, center right and bottom right Marcello Bertinetti/Archivio White Star
Page 307 Wojtek Buss
Page 308 bottom left and bottom right, pages 308-309, page 309 top and bottom right Marcello Bertinetti/Archivio White Star
Page 310 left Michael S. Yamashita/Corbis/Grazia Neri
Pages 310-311 AISA
Page 311 top, center right and bottom and page 312 center Marcello Bertinetti/Archivio White Star
Page 312 bottom Dean Conger/Corbis/Grazia Neri
Page 312 top and pages 312-313 James Davis/Corbis/Grazia Neri
Pages 314-315 Craig J. Brown
Page 314 bottom left Georgia Lowell/Corbis/Grazia Neri
Page 315 top right E. Mucchiati/Double's

Page 315 center Craig J. Brown
Pages 316-317, page 316 bottom, page 317 top left, top right and center right and pages 318-319 Marcello Bertinetti/Archivio White Star
Page 318 bottom Summerfield/Index
Page 319 top, bottom left and bottom right, page 320 top, center left, center right and bottom left Marcello Bertinetti/Archivio White Star
Page 320 bottom right and pages 320-321 Christophe Boisvieux
Page 321 top Marcello Bertinetti/Archivio White Star

Repubic of Korea
Page 322 top right and bottom right Massimo Borchi/Atlantide
Page 322 bottom left and pages 322-323 Christophe Boisvieux
Page 323 bottom Suzanne Held

Japan
Page 324 top and bottom and pages 324-325 AISA
Page 325 top right and bottom right Henri Stierlin
Page 326 top left AISA
Page 326 bottom left Benjamin Rondel/The Stock Market/Contrasto
Page 326 top center Stefano Cellai
Page 326 top right Stefano Amantini/Atlantide
Pages 326-327 AISA
Pages 328-329 and page 329 bottom Marcello Bertinetti/Archivio White Star
Page 329 top Luca Tettoni
Page 330 top and bottom left and page 331 bottom Henri Stierlin
Page 331 top PowerStock/Zefa

Repubblica Democratica Popolare del Laos
Page 332 top, pages 332-333, page 333 top, center right and bottom right and page 334 Christophe Boisvieux
Page 335 top left, top right and bottom Luca Tettoni

Vietnam
Page 336 top right and bottom left Luca Tettoni
Page 336 bottom right Antonio Attini/Archivio White Star
Page 337 and pages 338-339 Luca Tettoni
Page 338 bottom left and bottom right Suzanne Held
Page 339 top and bottom Luca Tettoni

AFRICA

Morocco
Page 342 top AISA
Pages 342-343 Giovanni Simeone/Simephoto
Page 342 bottom left Alfio Garozzo/Archivio White Star
Page 342 bottom right AISA
Page 343 top Tiziana and Gianni Baldizzone
Page 343 center Giovanni Simeone/Simephoto
Page 344 and page 345 top left AISA
Page 345 top right Sandro Vannini/Franca Speranza
Page 345 bottom left and bottom right Alfio Garozzo/Archivio White Star

Mauritania
Page 346 bottom, pages 346-347, page 347 top and center right Tiziana and Gianni Baldizzone
Page 348 top Alfio Garozzo/Archivio White Star
Page 348 bottom left and page 349 top Paolo Novaresio
Page 348 bottom right and page 349 bottom Tiziana and Gianni Baldizzone

Mali
Page 350 top right and pages 350-351 AISA
Page 350 bottom left Giusy Giublena
Page 351 Charles Lenars
Page 351 bottom AISA
Page 352 top left Anne Conway
Page 352 top right Boisseaux-Chical/Contrasto
Page 352 bottom left AISA
Page 352 bottom right and page 353 Giusy Giublena
Page 354 top and bottom and pages 354-355 AISA

Libyan Arab Jamahiriya
Page 356 top and bottom, page 357 top, pages 356-357, page 358 and page 359 bottom Anne Conway
Page 359 top, center left and center right Tiziana and Gianni Baldizzone

Egypt
Pages 360-361 Marcello Bertinetti/Archivio White Star
Page 360 top, page 361 top right and top center Antonio Attini/Archivio White Star
Page 361 bottom center K.M. Westrmenn/Corbis/Grazia Neri
Page 362 top left, pages 362-363 and page 363 top Marcello Bertinetti/Archivio White Star
Page 362 top right, page 363 bottom left and bottom right, page 364 top, pages 364-365 and page 365 bottom Antonio Attini/Archivio White Star
Page 364 bottom left and page 365 top Marcello Bertinetti/Archivio White Star
Page 365 center Anzenberger

Ethiopia
Pages 366-367 and page 367 top right David Else/LPI
Page 367 top left Frances Linzee Gordon/LPI
Page 367 bottom right Guenay Ulutuncok Laip/Contrasto

United Republic of Tanzania
Page 368 center Steve Davey/LPI
Page 368 top, bottom and pages 368-369 Angelo Tondini/Focus Team
Page 369 top Marcello Bertinetti/Archivio White Star
Page 369 bottom David Else/LPI

THE AMERICANS

United States of America
Page 372 top left Antonio Attini/Archivio White Star
Page 372 center and page 373 top right AISA
Page 373 Giulio Andreini
Page 374 top and bottom and page 375 bottom Massimo Borchi/Archivio White Star
Pages 374-375 AISA

Mexico
Pages 376-37 and page 376 bottom left AISA
Page 376 bottom right Chris Sharp/South American Pictures
Page 377 top AISA
Page 377 bottom Damm/Zefa
Page 378 top left Chris Sharp/South American Pictures
Page 378 top right Anne Stierlin
Page 378 bottom Henri Stierlin
Pages 378-379 Henri and Anne Stierlin
Page 379 bottom left AISA
Page 379 bottom right Henri Stierlin
Page 380 top and pages 380-381 Massimo Borchi/Archivio White Star
Page 381 top and center AISA
Page 382 top left, top right and bottom Massimo Borchi/Archivio White Star
Page 383 AISA

Cuba
Pages 384-385 Andrea Pistoleri
Page 384 bottom left Antonio Attinio/Archivio White Star
Page 385 top left Livio Bourbon/Archivio White Star
Page 385 center Massimo Ripani/Simephoto
Page 386 top left and bottom left Antonio Attini/Archivio White Star
Page 386 top right Giovanni Rinaldi/Il Dagherrotipo
Page 386 center right and page 387 Livio Bourbon/Archivio White Star
Pages 388-389 Giovanni Rinaldi/Il Dagherrotipo
Page 388 bottom left Antonio Attini/Archivio White Star
Page 389 top and bottom left Livio Bourbon/Archivio White Star
Page 389 bottom right and page 390 top Antonio Attini/Archivio White Star
Page 390 center and bottom Martino Fagiuoli/CV Export
Page 391 top left and top right and pages 390-391 Livio Bourbon/Archivio White Star

Guatemala
Page 392 top left Tony Wheeler/LPI
Pages 392-393 KCharles Lenars/Corbis/Grazia Neri
Page 392 bottom left Paola Ragazzini/Corbis/Grazia Neri
Page 393 left and right, page 394 bottom and pages 394-395 AISA
Page 394 top left and top right and page 395 top Laura Accomazzo/archivio Archivio White Star

Colombia
Pages 396-397 and page 397 top Sergio Pitamitz/Sie
Page 397 center Susanne Held
Page 397 bottom AISA
Page 398 top left Krzysztof Dydynski/LPI
Page 398 bottom left and pages 398-399 AISA
Page 399 top Jean-Baptiste Rabquan/Hemispheres

Peru
Page 400 top AISA
Page 401 top Scala Group
Page 401 center and bottom and pages 400-401 Andrea Pistolesi
Page 402 top left AISA
Page 402 top center Matteo Bazzi/Il Dagherrotipo
Page 402 top right Charles Lenars
Page 402 bottom Sepp Puchinger/Anzenberger
Page 403 top AISA
Page 403 bottom Charles Lenars

Brazil
Page 404, page 405 top left, top right, bottom left, bottom right, page 406 top and bottom and page 407 top left AISA
Page 407 top right and bottom Giulio Andreini
Page 408 bottom, page 409 top and pages 408-409 Jean Charles Pinheira
Page 409 center right and bottom AISA
Page 410 top Jean Charles Pinheira
Page 410 bottom left and bottom right and pages 410-411 AISA
Page 411 bottom Jean Charles Pinheira

Bolivia
Pages 412-413 Massimo Borchi/Atlantide
Page 412 bottom, page 413 right and bottom left AISA
Page 413 bottom right Christophe Boisvieux
Pages 414-415 Scala Group
Page 414 bottom left, bottom right and page 415 top AISA
Page 415 center Massimo Borchi/Atlantide

Argentina
Pages 416-417, page 416 bottom left and bottom right and page 417 bottom Fotoscopio
Page 417 top, page 418 top left and top a detra, pages 418-419, page 419 top and bottom Alfio Garozzo/Archivio White Star

The maps are by Elisabetta Ferrero/Archivio White Star

432